# The Century of Total War

BEACON CONTEMPORARY AFFAIRS SERIES

*General Editor,* Sol Stein

Raymond Aron, long the chief news analyst for the Paris newspaper *Le Figaro,* is a professor at the Institut d'Etudes Politiques. During World War II he joined General Charles de Gaulle in London and edited the Free French newspaper *La France Libre.*

# THE
# CENTURY
## OF
# TOTAL WAR

*Raymond Aron*

THE BEACON PRESS · BOSTON

*First Beacon Paperback edition published 1955*
*Reprinted by arrangement with Doubleday and Co.*

*First printing, April 1955*
*Second printing, March 1956*
*Third printing, March 1959*

# Contents

## PART I

## FROM SARAJEVO TO HIROSHIMA

## PART II

## CROSSROADS OF HISTORY

# PART III
## LIMITED WAR

# PART IV
## A HELPLESS EUROPE?

# CONCLUSION
## THE STAKE

# PART ONE

*From Sarajevo to Hiroshima*

*Chapter I*

## THE TECHNICAL SURPRISE

FREDERICK THE GREAT left to his legal apologists the justification of his conquests after they had taken place. Public opinion played hardly any part in the limited warfare of the eighteenth century; the professional soldiers, recruited from the lower classes of society, felt no need to know why they were fighting. In the twentieth century, the soldier and citizen have become interchangeable; and the general public, believing itself peacefully disposed, demands an accounting from its leaders. To prove the enemy responsible for a war has become each government's duty. On each side, historians and intellectuals strive not so much to maintain the morale of the fighting forces alone as to clear the conscience of the whole nation.

The analysis of the origins of the First World War, originally based upon the need for propaganda between 1914 and 1918, was carried on, even after the Allied victory, by a sort of revolt against what had happened. Middle-class Europe, proud of its civilization and sure of its progressiveness, regarded war as a monstrosity out of another age. The authors of the Treaty of Versailles demanded reparations, invoking not the defeat in arms, which the vanquished Germans (well aware of what they themselves would have done had they been victorious) would have accepted without demur, but the fact of aggression. The study of the causes of the war was inspired not as much by historical curiosity as by that spirit of moral righteousness. Who were the criminals who had plunged Europe into the abyss of violence? What fortuitous elements had revived the horrors of the past?

Historical research yielded inconclusive results. It did not make an end of uncertainties. Inevitably it disappointed both the pacifists and those who sat in judgment.

The historian, concerned to show the causes of an event, puts two questions, both legitimate, but which must be carefully distinguished. First of all, why did war come at that particular time; and, given the stiuation, who were the men, or what were the circumstances, that precipitated war? Secondly, how was the situation which led to war created? The first question refers to what are generally called the immediate causes, the second to what are called the remote origins. Historians attribute to the former more or less importance according to their philosophy and also to the results of their inquiry. If they come to the conclusion that the situation led inevitably to war, the immediate causes obviously lost importance.

In their study of the First World War, historians were deeply interested in the immediate causes. The actual events marshaled themselves in a highly orderly fashion. Before the assassination of the Archduke Francis Ferdinand, Europe was living in a state of preparedness, but no one expected an outbreak from one day to the next. Following the assassination, and especially after the Austrian ultimatum to Serbia, chancelleries and populations alike felt the dread of approaching disaster.

A multitude of books and commentaries have attempted to explain the week that passed between July 23, when Austria dispatched her ultimatum to Serbia, and the thirtieth, the day on which Russian mobilization was decreed. Archives have been exhausted, responsible leaders have published their memoirs, and historians have reconstituted the conversations, negotiations, and interviews that had taken place in Vienna, Berlin, St. Petersburg, and Paris. The very accumulation of documents seemed to result in confusion.

More apparent than real, the confusion is based upon three interrelated questions: What were the actions that rendered war not only possible, but probable, and finally inevitable? Up to what point were those actions morally or politically legitimate? What were the intentions of those responsible for them?

No one denies today, as no one doubted then, that the Austrian ultimatum introduced the possibility not only of war, but of general war. The statesmen at Vienna were aware of that risk, just as the German statesmen had recognized it at the discussions in Berlin at the beginning of July. Russia, who regarded herself as protectress of the European Slavs in the Balkans, would not allow Serbia to be crushed or permit her to be transformed from an independent kingdom into a sort of protectorate of the Dual Monarchy. The ultimatum was a challenge to Russia. All Europe realized that the initiative, heavy with menace, had come from Vienna, and that it would not have been taken without the promise of support given in Berlin.

The Serbian reply was moderate in its terms, though it rejected the proposal that Austrian officials participate in an inquiry. If we add to the ultimatum the refusal to accept Serbia's reply, and then the severance of diplomatic relations and the bombardment of Belgrade, we have a succession of acts for which Austrian diplomacy (and indirectly German diplomacy) may be held responsible. This, then, was the European situation in 1914, which made likely the advent of a general war.

Controversy has centered mainly on the legitimacy of the Austrian policy. To what extent did the conduct of the Serbian Government justify what were exorbitant demands under international law? Whatever particular Serbian officials or private politicians might have had to do with the preparation of the Archduke's assassination, the facts known at the time gave no ground for holding the Belgrade Government responsible, and consequently gave the Vienna Government no authority to make demands incompatible with Serbian sovereignty. For the rest, there is little doubt that the Austrian diplomats neither desired nor expected a simple acceptance of their ultimatum. They wanted to "teach a lesson" to the little country that was disturbing its powerful neighbor by supporting or tolerating the "liberation" propaganda of the European Slavs. The men who had determined at Vienna to "teach the lesson" resolutely accepted the possible consequences, including general war.

Thus the real issue is whether we may consider these consequences to have been possible, probable, or inevitable. There is little likelihood of a unanimous conclusion. The historian may ponder the influence of one event on another but his conclusions can never be final. In the present case, one must at least say that the

Central Powers had created conditions which rendered war probable. Would its avoidance have required a miracle, or merely more diplomatic patience and imagination in the opposite camp? Speculations on what *might* have happened are endless.

The same sort of controversy was carried on over the Russian general mobilization, the first in date (though, before it became known, the Austrian mobilization had been decided on). Was not that mobilization politically legitimate as a reply to the first operations against Serbia? The German military leaders themselves regarded the Russian mobilization as different in nature from all the other ones because of the time that it required. When that mobilization took place, had not the die been cast, and were not the general staffs in the different capitals impatient to set going a mechanism which left diplomacy no further room for action?

As long as we consider only the two questions of causality and legitimacy, careful inquiry compels us to qualify, but without fundamentally modifying, the Allied contention. It was the Vienna Cabinet that took the initiatives which all Europe has held to be bellicose. It was that Cabinet which threw down the glove to Serbia, and therefore to Russia; it was that Cabinet which wanted a *succès de prestige,* even at the risk of general war. Germany, in giving Vienna a free hand, shared the responsibility, whatever may have been the secret thoughts of her rulers. Even though it were shown that the Entente, and Russia in particular, was too prompt in taking up the challenge, the burden of guilt in the diplomatic sequence of actions and rejoinders would remain with the "initiators."

But such guilt, positive and limited—diplomatic, so to speak—is incommensurable with that imagined by popular passion. Search was made, not for this or that Minister bent on extirpating the Irredentist propaganda of the European Slavs, but for the men who had knowingly embarked on aggression. They were not discovered or, in any case, they were not discovered in the simple guise of storybook villains.

The search for motives or incentives leads to unending controversies. It is possible on the basis of certain testimony to represent German policy as inspired by the desire to launch as soon as possible a war considered to be inevitable. The proposals of Wilhelm II to the King of the Belgians may be adduced, for example. In certain military quarters it was obviously thought that the reorganization of the Russian Army would not be completed until 1917, and that the French forces were short of machine guns and heavy artillery. Such considerations, reinforcing the confidence of the general staff, must have influenced the generals in the discussions at the beginning of July. But the study of archives has revealed a German policy less sure of itself and less definite in its aim. Berlin accepted general war, but it could not be said that the responsible statesmen deliberately set out to provoke it over the Austro-Serbian dispute. That idea certainly crossed the minds of some persons at some moments, but it did not constantly determine the action of the Chancellor, the Emperor, or the Ambassadors.

In other words, when we search for motives the simple picture of aggressors and victims does not stand up to rigorous analysis.

The French statesmen certainly desired war even less. The Tsar and a good many (but not all) of the Russian leaders were afraid of war, perhaps more out of concern for the regime than for the war itself. But the Allies were determined not to tolerate the Austrians' resorting to force in the Balkans, while Viennese diplomacy was no less determined to use force if necessary to gain a *succès de prestige* at the expense of Serbia. On both sides the will to peace was conditional, not absolute. The European situation in 1914 made the localization of the conflict extremely improbable, but both Berlin and Vienna would have been satisfied to attain the immediate objective without starting a general war.

The European scene was not occupied by "sheep and wolf" states, but by sovereign states equally determined to maintain their power and prestige. In Britain and France there was no equivalent of the Pan-Germans or the romantic theorists of violence. Both countries were inclined to be conservative and to renounce dreams of conquest. The Germany of Wilhelm II, actively expansionist, was more inclined to the call of arms than the middle-class democracies. For all that, the explosion in 1914 was the result of diplomatic failure.

For a century Europe had enjoyed relative stability. Neither the Crimean War nor the Franco-Prussian War became general. With greater effort the Balkan Wars were brought to an end without irreparable injury to the European equilibrium. The "war monster" that had shaken the Continent from 1792 to 1815 had been chained up. It broke loose again in August 1914.

As soon as we leave the narrow limits of our inquiry into the assassination of the Archduke and the Austrian declaration of war, going back before the crisis of June and July 1914, there is no longer any date that can be regarded as marking the origin of the historical situation that produced the First World War. The Franco-German hostility leads us back at least to the Treaty of Frankfurt, the Russo-German hostility at least to the abandonment of the Reinsurance Treaty by the young Emperor Wilhelm II. But rather than retrace a half century of European diplomatic history, our critical inquiry must restrict itself to the formulation of definite questions.

Any student of the crisis was bound to be struck by the rapidity with which an incident involving an individual prince set all Europe ablaze. Why had the situation become so explosive? Why did so many statesmen and common men alike vaguely sense the rising storm?

The replies of the historians, although differing in detail, are on the whole irresistibly simple, disconcerting to those who want to penetrate beyond the superficial facts and root out the deep-seated forces of which the very participants themselves had no knowledge.

In accordance with an unwritten law of European diplomacy, the very fact of Germany's growth in power provoked a grouping of nations to make a stand against her. The course of the war proved abundantly that the Triple Entente had no surplus of strength over the German-Austrian alliance. But the fact that the Entente was necessary for equilibrium does not explain why it was formed. It had not yet been formed at the end of the last century, though the same considerations had already made it necessary. We must therefore remember simply that the grouping of the great European nations into more or less close alliances was something neither novel nor monstrous that required a special explanation or implied the existence of a culprit.

France, once she had surmounted the consequences of defeat, would normally, in accordance with an old tradition, seek support in the East. It may be that the Franco-Russian rapprochement was facilitated or accelerated by the mistakes of the Wilhelmstrasse. But it would have been difficult, in the long run, for Germany to remain very friendly with both Russia and Austria-Hungary. In preferring the latter she inevitably brought about a rapprochement between Paris and St. Petersburg. As for Great Britain, she was bound to fear a German victory that would eliminate France as a major power and give the conqueror almost unlimited hegemony over the Continent. British diplomacy would perhaps not have heeded the peril to its own profound interests had not the Second Reich, by building a military fleet, delivered a challenge which the British Empire could not refuse.

For the rest, from the beginning of the century there was a lack of definition in the diplomatic "fronts." Contacts between the courts of Berlin and St. Petersburg were frequent until the eve of the rupture. Wilhelm II tried several times to take advantage of his personal ascendancy over Nicholas II for purposes of high diplomacy. The treaty signed by the two Emperors at Björkö in July 1905, although subsequently rejected by the Tsar's Ministers, must not be forgotten. Until the eve of the catastrophe the relations between London and Berlin, quite apart from dynastic ties, were not those of irreconcilable enemies. As late as 1914 British Ministers had the idea of appeasing German ambitions by negotiating a partition of the Portuguese colonies. In spite of the efforts of French diplomacy, no British Government had entered into any formal engagement: discussions between the general staffs did not interfere with the freedom of decision of the London Cabinet.

The division of the principal nations of Europe into two camps did not necessarily make for war. It only made it inevitable that any conflict involving two great powers would bring general war. From the moment when there was formed in the center of Europe a German empire, industrially foremost in Europe, with a population exceeding that of France by more than fifty per cent, and allied to the Dual Monarchy, a war on the small scale of that of 1870 had become impossible. Neither Russia nor Great Britain would have tolerated a new German victory which would have made of the Reich no longer merely the dominant European state, but a claimant to empire over the Continent.

The two camps were not condemned to mortal combat by any mysterious fatality. The relations between the coalitions had simply deteriorated until clear-sighted observers foresaw the inescapable outcome of armed peace. Who was to blame? The issue has been passionately argued. One side denounced the intolerable manners of Teutonic diplomacy, the demand for Delcassé's dismissal, the spectacular visit to Tangier, the dispatch of a gunboat to Agadir, the annexation of Bosnia-Herzegovina; on the other side it was pointed out that in the course of the half century during which she had been the foremost power on the Continent, Germany had added less to her overseas possessions and profited less by arms or negotiation than weakened France. Germany had made herself intolerable by her brutality, by her arrogance, and by the ambitions of which she was suspected. But under the rules of diplomacy she was not wrong in demanding compensation when France established her protectorate over Morocco. She could not fail to notice that the international conferences were not turning out to her advantage.

The growing tension centered about three principal difficulties: the rivalry between Austria and Russia in the Balkans, the Franco-German conflict over Morocco, and the arms race—on sea between Britain and Germany, and on land between all the powers. The two last causes had produced the situation, the first one kindled the spark.

There are doubtless those who contend that the immediate cause matters little, and that war might have broken out just as easily in 1911 as in 1914. The contention readily suggests itself and is not easily disproven. The fact remains that the Balkan quarrels brought about the actual rupture, just as they had helped to dissolve the pact of conservation which, despite divergent alliances, still united the sovereigns of Russia and Germany. For one thing, the clash between Russia and Austria-Hungary had a diplomatic cause. Repulsed in Asia after her defeat by Japan in 1905, Russia conformed to tradition and redirected her attention and her ambitions to Europe. But, apart from diplomacy, the clash had a deeper cause in the movement of ideas and passions. For two supranational empires still existed in an age of nationalism. The Ottoman Empire had not yet been liquidated, and already diplomats were anxiously anticipating the time when they would have to face the problem of the succession to Austria-Hungary.

Henceforth Viennese diplomacy is more understandable. It was no longer so much a question of avenging the assassination of an Archduke who had favored trialism and whose disappearance pleased many persons in high places. It was a matter of ending once and for all the nationalist propaganda that challenged the existence of Austria-Hungary. Obviously, Russia could not allow the Vienna Government a free hand.

The quarrel between chancelleries interested also the general public in each country. Diplomacy had succeeded in integrating into the Europe which followed the Congress of Vienna a united Germany and a united Italy without a general war. It was unable to perform such a feat again in the twentieth century. The national conflicts in Eastern Europe unleashed general war.

The inquiry into political responsibility carries with it no authority to banish as criminals either men or nations. But inquiry does clarify the significance and the origins of the war. The immediate occasion and the deeper cause largely coincide; for, as we have seen, the reasons for hostility among the various nations of Europe were manifold. The relative strengths and the relationships of alliance excluded partial conflicts. The rise of Germany, whose hegemony France dreaded and whose Navy menaced England, had created an opposition that claimed to be defensive but was denounced by German propaganda as an attempt at encirclement. The two camps alarmed each other, and each tried to soothe its own fears by piling up defensive armaments. The atmosphere grew heavy with multiplied incidents, which spread the conviction of approaching disaster. The explosion finally came in the East, where Russia and Austria were advancing contradictory claims, and where the principle of national sovereignty had ruined the Ottoman Empire and was beginning to undermine the still imposing edifice of the Austro-Hungarian Empire.

Wars are essentially unpredictable. But the wars of the twentieth century have been much more so than were those of the past. The very situations that bring about a modern war are destroyed in its wake. It is the battle in and for itself, and not the origin of the conflict or the peace treaty, that constitutes the major fact and produces the most far-reaching consequences.

It is impossible to recall without a smile the plans drawn up by the French general staff in the period before hostilities began in 1914. They anticipated a daily supply of 13,600 rounds for 75 mm. guns, 465 for 155 mm. guns, and 2,470,000 cartridges for the infantry; a daily production of 24 tons of B powder; 50,000 workers to be employed in 30 factories. The estimated production was to be attained on the eighty-first day after general mobilization. On September 19, instead of 13,600 rounds the general staff asked the Ministry of Armament for 50,000. It obtained that quantity in March 1915, but meanwhile, in January, it had demanded 80,000. This last figure was reached in September 1915, but by then the general staff was demanding 150,000—more than ten times the prewar estimate. This increasing demand for artillery ammunition had its parallel in all other military supplies.

Both in France and in Germany it was expected that the decisive battles would be fought and won within a few weeks. Peacetime reserves of equipment and munitions would suffice, it was thought, for the operational needs requisite to victory. The result, in France, of this remarkable optimism was that on September 15, after thirty days of operations, stocks were half depleted, and the arsenals held no more than 120,000 rounds for 75 mm. guns. If in October the peacetime reserves had not been exhausted virtually at the same moment on both sides, lack of ammunition might have brought to one or the other the decision vainly sought in the field. During the first two years, guns of one caliber were kept supplied only at the expense of guns of other calibers. Not until 1917 did production more or less fulfill the constantly increasing requirements of the battlefield. Instead of 50,000 employees, 1,600,000 were engaged in defense plants, and to these workers should be added those in the United States employed directly or indirectly in the Allied war effort. Ministers and their military advisers thought they were undertaking a war "like any other," expecting its issue to be determined by a few battles of annihilation. Instead, they had committed the people of their countries to a long trial by attrition. Between the aspiration and its fulfillment there intervened what I propose to call the "technical surprise."

In the last century the American Civil War had offered a fairly good preview of what we call total war, with regard particularly to the relentless mobilization of national resources and the competition over new inventions.[1] The period of European peace between 1871 and the Balkan Wars had been marked by rapid progress in armaments. The underwater mine, the torpedo, and the submarine revolutionized naval tactics. On land, the universal use of the semi-automatic rifle and of the carbine, the perfecting of the machine gun, and the adoption of rapid-fire artillery gave unprecedented firepower to armies of greatly increased manpower.

Finally "technical surprise" came as the climactic element of an evolution in which the wars of the French Revolution and Empire represent an important stage, if not actually the beginning. National wars are fought by the people as a whole, and no longer by professional armies; the stakes are no longer dynastic interests or the fate of a province, but the future of the collective society or its ideals. In the epoch of democracy (that is to say, of compulsory military service) and of industry (i.e., of mass production and destruction), national wars naturally tend to expand into total wars. What needs to be explained is not how the war of 1914 spread across the Continent and became "hyperbolic,"[2] but the fact that the nineteenth century was able to escape a similar outcome to the French Revolution and the industrial revolution.

Europe had been spared in the nineteenth century by a streak of good fortune. Diplomacy was able to localize the conflicts because none of them definitely threatened the general balance of power. Neither the victory of Great Britain and France over Russia, nor

[1] "In the Civil War in America the rifled gun came more and more to the fore. Yet, from the armament point of view, the main characteristic of this war was the extraordinary inventiveness displayed throughout it. During it the magazine-loading rifle and a machine gun were invented. Torpedoes, land mines, submarine mines, the field telegraph, lamp and flag signalling, wire entanglements, wooden wire-bound mortars, hand-grenades, winged grenades, rockets and many forms of booby traps were tried out. Armoured trains were used; balloons were employed on both sides. Explosive bullets are mentioned, searchlights for 'stinkshells' to cause 'suffocating effects' were asked for. The use of flame-projectors was proposed and the U.S.S. Housatonic was sunk on February 17, 1864, by a small man-propelled Confederate submarine." J. F. C. Fuller, *Armament and History* (New York: Scribner, 1945), pp. 118–19.

[2] The term "hyperbolic" war was first used by Pareto.

that of France over Austria, nor that of Germany over Austria and, subsequently, over France, appeared to endanger seriously the onlooking powers. These events modified the balance established at Vienna, but did not destroy it. And none of them threatened the economic or social regime of any of the warring countries. The wars were limited both in regard to the resources employed and to the issue at stake, and they did not arouse ungovernable popular passion. They were fought mainly by professional armies (except for the second phase of the Franco-Prussian War). The general staffs, wedded to their habitual methods, were slow in making use of new weapons. The superiority of infantry weapons contributed largely to the Prussian victory in 1866, as did the superiority of artillery (breech-loading instead of muzzle-loading guns) to that of 1870. The brutality of the initial successes in 1866 and in 1870, due to the disparity of military organization, armament, and fighting strength, prevented any resort to a strategy of attrition and the progressive mobilization that is its normal result. But such good fortune could not be repeated indefinitely.

After 1815 the principal European powers, whether out of wisdom, fear of the "monster," or obedience to tradition, had returned to the professional army. Only Prussia had maintained conscription, and she had won the foremost place in Europe. No one could fail to learn the lesson. All the nations, beginning with France, bitter in her defeat, conformed to the logic of democracy and re-established compulsory military service. The general staffs remained, on the whole, conservative. Obliged to modernize rifles and machine guns and field artillery, they made mistakes, especially the French staff, as to the strategic and tactical implications of the new weapons. They failed to grasp certain lessons of the Russo-Japanese War and the Balkan Wars, underestimated the machine gun, and almost entirely ignored the air arm and the role of the internal combustion engine. But in spite of all of this, in 1914 the nations rose in arms supplied by modern industry and went out to do battle. Hyperbolic war could have been averted only by a lightning victory of one side or the other. That possibility was removed by the Battle of the Marne, and the die was cast.

It is often contended that decisive results are impossible because of the democratic and industrial structure of modern armies. Nothing can be more mistaken, as we now know, than to imagine armies of millions of men to be essentially incapable of dealing a mortal blow, to be doomed to clash and wear each other away where they stand. The events of June 1940 dissipated that illusion. If the German Army had had the tactical and organizational superiority over the French in August 1914 that it had in June 1940, it would have gained the day as quickly; and for some years or decades the potentialities of total war would have remained unknown in Europe. Greater numerical strength, which the German general staff could have obtained by further drafts from the Eastern front, might very well have been sufficient. In short, the conditions for total war were present: all that was needed for its development was an opportunity, which in this case was offered by the approximately equal strength of the opposing forces.

Through an accidental and transient condition of warfare, which affected the West especially, total war, for four years, limited itself to the trenches. Defensive techniques were superior to offensive, so that by accumulating formidable firing power, it became possible to pulverize the enemy's front lines without too much difficulty; but the terrain won was so broken up that it became in itself an obstacle. Enemy defenses, improvised by hastily assembled reinforcements, halted the attack, which could not be supported by an artillery paralyzed by its lack of mobility and the effects of its own fire.

Until 1917 the intensification of warfare was mainly quantitative. The cry "More guns, more shells!" had a meaning that went beyond propaganda. Month after month, in offensive after offensive, more and more guns were massed and more and more rounds were fired. When there were not enough guns at the front, the artillery preparation went on for several days—giving the enemy time to prepare his resistance. Later the duration was reduced and the intensity increased. In the Somme offensive in 1916, there were 900 heavy guns and 1,100 light guns massed along 10 miles of front.[3] Neither side was able to win a decisive battle. Every breach in the line was more or less quickly filled. After initial successes, the offensive petered out. Even during the latter months of 1918, when the

[3] At Stalingrad, in January 1943, the Russians massed 4,000 guns along 4 kilometers of front, i.e., 1 gun per meter of front.

Allies were considerably superior in men and matériel, they were able to strike heavy blows against the German Army, but there was no victory of annihilation.

Quantitative extention of warfare obviously does not prevent what might be called qualitative extention, recourse to new arms and new tactics. The French Army possessed about one hundred airplanes in August 1914, and several thousand by 1918. The use of motor vehicles for transport, of wireless communication, of armored tanks, gradually transformed the methods of operation, especially after 1917. But whatever share in the successes of the Allies may be attributed to tanks, essentially the war was brought to an end by means of the same arms with which it began. Machine guns and artillery, partly in improved models but mostly in larger numbers, completed the task they had begun. The new arms—aircraft and tanks—were not yet dominant, but they had shown that they would be in the next war.

Total war, as it took place in 1914–18, with problems of supply, strategy of attrition, stable fronts, and field fortifications, left the public with a horrifying memory of tens of thousands of soldiers sacrificed to conquer a few square miles, the inhuman life of the trenches, the crushing and startling technical superiority of arms, organization, and production over personal qualities—all of which helped dissipate the traditional romanticism of warfare and nourish revolt. Or rather, revolt against war, as old as humanity, was to be reinforced by revolt against war machines, a revolt comparable with the first revolt of craftsmen against industrial machines. But as long as the struggle continued, that latent revolt had to be repressed and enthusiasm maintained.

Thus the "technical surprise" is among the main causes of the geographical extension of war and the growth of wartime passions.

The extension of the war in Europe took a classical form. In the event of a conflict between great powers, said Machiavelli, the small ones generally have no chance to remain neutral, and nothing to gain by doing so, for their attitude arouses the enmity of the conqueror, whoever he may be; whereas if they take sides they may get into the good graces of the distributors of booty. The successive interventions of Turkey, Italy, Bulgaria, and Rumania were preceded by negotiations in conformity with tradition. Each of the major opponents exerted itself to secure a fresh ally by offering gains which ordinarily neither owned. The result of these competitive promises was usually determined in advance. Italy's aspirations could only be satisfied at Austria's expense. Great Britain and France had no difficulty in parading a generosity that Germany could match only by sacrificing her comrade in arms. On the other side, the Central Powers rallied Bulgaria, who coveted Serbian territory, whereas it was in Serbia's defense that the Allies had drawn their sword. Needless to say everyone's choice was determined by other considerations as well—a gamble on the result of the fighting, moral affinities, popular feeling, and so on.

In any case, none of these European interventions greatly increased the initial scale of hostilities or decisively modified the balance of power. Japan seized the opportunity to appropriate some strategic positions held by the Germans. Only the American intervention represents an unprecedented fact and marks a historic date, whose retrospective significance is very clear. That intervention was essentially due to the technical amplification of the war. The provocation was, of course, the German Government's declaration of unrestricted submarine warfare in violation of an agreement made several months earlier in Washington. The new technique of naval warfare, contrary to international law as understood at the time[4] (as was the British long-range blockade), precipitated the decision of the United States and thereby assured the defeat of the Second Reich.

There has subsequently been an attempt to minimize the validity of the provocation. During the isolationist period there was criticism of the bankers and industrialists who had supplied the Allies with credit, equipment, or raw material and who were now afraid, it was alleged, of losing their money or their customers. But such an interpretation, implying capitalist machinations, would, even if true, refer us back to the same reality. Even the Anglo-French alliance lacked the means to bring the total war to an end. The United States had been involved economically in the struggle

---

[4]When the United States entered the Second World War, the naval staff ordered unrestricted submarine warfare. The war technique that had aroused indignation twenty-five years earlier was now accepted as normal.

before becoming militarily involved, because the joint resources of the British and French empires were insufficient to maintain the monstrous lethal machine.

Still other commentators claim that the submarine warfare was merely a pretext, and that the American leaders simply recognized at the time of that menace that British control of the seas was indispensable to the United States. American security would be endangered if Great Britain were defeated; a virtually hostile power would rule the Old World and be free to extend its domination, or at least its enterprises, across the oceans. But one may very well ask if the Americans would have recognized their solidarity with Great Britain had submarine warfare not shaken the ascendancy of the Home Fleet, revealed the German naval potential, and produced a general apprehension of a peace dictated on the scale of the war itself, that is to say, a Carthaginian peace.

At the same time we must not overlook the part played by sentiment or ideology. In critical moments the kinship of Britons and Americans dissipates mutual misunderstandings, resentments, and irritations. By inscribing on its banners the sacred words Democracy and Freedom, the Entente aroused general sympathy in America. Since it was universally inspired, the language used by the Allied representatives was understood in every continent. A crusade to make the world "safe for democracy" was, so it seemed, of world-wide concern. What meaning had the defense of German *Kultur* outside of Germany itself?

It was ideology that won over American opinion to participation in the war, arousing and maintaining the enthusiasm of a young nation. The fundamental consideration, nevertheless, was primarily materialistic. The Allies had sought American aid to help support the burden of the hyperbolic war. Economic participation became military partnership when the submarines tried to break the bond already existing between the European and American democracies, and so threatened to leave a navy regarded as hostile ruling the oceans and separating ancient Europe from the New World.

There has been incessant inquiry into the origin of the First World War, but no one has ever asked why it became hyperbolic. Did the people of different countries fight to the death because they detested each other, or did they detest each other because they fought so furiously? Did the belligerents set themselves unlimited objectives from the outset, or did they acquire those objectives in proportion to the increase in violence? Was it passion that produced the technical excess, or techncial excess that fomented passion? Not unreservedly or without qualification, and fully recognizing the interaction of the two phenomena, I would maintain that the motive force of the evolution at that time was technical. Technique it was that imposed the organization of enthusiasm, condemned to failure the efforts at conciliation, drove out the old diplomatic wisdom, and contributed to the spread of the crusading spirit, finally producing a peace that created the situation from which the second war started.

The start of the first war was marked in all countries by an explosion of national fervor. Patriotism overrode social resentments and revolutionary aspirations. In a few days, sometimes in a few hours, the socialists, who had been pitiless critics of the diplomacy of both the Wilhelmstrasse and the Quai d'Orsay, were carried away by the collective enthusiasm and embraced the popular sentiment. National unity was established at once in France against German aggression, and in Germany against the Russian peril.

The German victories during the first weeks redoubled the fighting spirit of the Germans and steeled the resolution of the French. German terrorism and atrocities (which Allied propaganda exaggerated but did not invent), far from depressing the morale of the French, aroused a sort of fury, nourished by both military tradition and the "pacifist" revolt against the horrors of war.

As the sterile process of slaughter continued with no sign of an early end, enthusiasm waned and social claims, repressed by the sudden surge of ancestral passions, disrupted this national unity. Though neither side would give way, resolution was succeeded by resigned persistence, fervor gave place to reluctant acceptance. Propaganda and ideology usurped the place of genuine feeling.

At first both were adapted mainly to the needs of the country behind the lines. As a rule the combatants were killing one another without contempt or hatred. At times they felt bound together by a mystical communion of fate. Even when they hated, they hated a being of flesh and blood, the enemy whom it was necessary to kill so as not to be killed. The abstract hatreds that are ravaging our century are the work of urban masses, not of soldiers at the front. What Elie Halévy called "organized enthusiasm" forms a chapter in the history of civil mobilization. The need was desperately obvious: it was essential to maintain the nation's unity and will to fight. Defeat must be made to appear catastrophic, victory an unmixed blessing. In other words, the stake at issue escaped definition by the rules and regulations of diplomacy. It was no longer a question of shifting frontier posts a few miles. Only sublime—and vague—principles, such as the right of peoples to self-determination or "the war to end war," seemed commensurate with such violence, sacrifice, and heroism. It was technical excess that gradually introduced ideologies in place of war aims. Both sides claimed to know what they were fighting *about,* but neither said what it was fighting *for*.

Once general war had started, its provocation was bound to be forgotten, and the stake no longer had anything in common with the cause. All past relations between the European powers were reviewed and challenged. The chancelleries discovered forgotten grievances and ambitions in their files, the people in the memories.

Secret diplomacy was given free play. The British Ministers accepted Russia's claim to Constantinople, the French secured recognition of their claims in Alsace-Lorraine. The great powers signed with Italy, Rumania, and Serbia secret agreements that were not all indefensible but promised a sharing of booty rather than a peace in conformity with principles. It was easier to proclaim that the war was being fought in defense of freedom than to publish the results of such negotiations, which were interconnected and sometimes contradictory.

The same is true of the other side. At the time of its first victories, the German Government had not made known the conditions it would impose on the vanquished. But influential private associations, from the industrial groups to the Pan-German League, broadcast the most grandiose projects. Should they annex Belgium or merely require guarantees? Should they appropriate only France's colonial empire or part of her continental territory as well? The leaders of the Central Powers were also hoping for total victory; they, too, refused to bind themselves in advance by any formal announcement of their war aims. They, too, left it to the intellectuals to define the "ideas of 1914" in whose name Germany was carrying on the war for the defense and glory of her unique *Kultur*.

After two years of war, it may be that some of the German leaders, and even those of Austria-Hungary, would have been glad to return from "war ideologies" to "war aims," to silence the tumult of propaganda and allow the diplomats to speak again. But it was too late. A vague note was dispatched on December 1916 to which the Entente replied on January 10, 1917, with a note that was not precise on every point but which, by suggesting the liberation of the Czechs, seemed to imply the disintegration of Austria-Hungary. In July 1917, the German Parliament adopted a motion in favor of a peace without annexations or indemnities, but the Entente was not prepared to accept. The secret negotiations with the Emperor Charles of Austria for a separate peace collapsed, and everyone turned again to await the outcome of the battle.

From 1914 to 1918 there were special obstacles to a compromise peace. The strategic situation was temporarily favorable to the side that had the lesser chance of final victory. A war can be cut short when the side whose superiority is established on the battlefields shows moderation and renounces some of the gains that might come from victory, in order to save itself the trouble of bringing the enemy to his knees. Germany had won the first successes, and the fighting had taken place outside her territory. For all that, as the fighting went on she became the probable loser, so greatly did the resources of the Entente, which was mistress of the seas, come to exceed those of the Reich, suffocated by the blockade. In other words, according to the actual battle maps, Germany had the advantage; but according to the soundest predictions, the Entente would win in the end. In such a case, neither side could afford to make any important concessions.

Yet, quite apart from what might be called this element of chance, it was peculiarly difficult to end by negotiation in the traditional way a war that had become a war of peoples and of ideas. Nobody had started a crusade in 1914, nobody then was out to liberate oppressed nationalities, to make an end of secret diplomacy, or to spread democracy. To win sympathy in the world, and to maintain the morale of their suffering nations, governments resorted to ideology, and that element played an important part in the Allied conduct of the war from the time of the American intervention and the Russian Revolution. The war had not been started in order to bring about the triumph of particular views of life and society; but as the cost of operations mounted these views were felt to be essential to inflate the prospective profits of victory. It was declared that the peace would be durable only if it were dictated unconditionally after crushing the enemy. The demand for total victory was not so much the expression of a political philosophy as a reflex reaction to total war.

The Treaty of Versailles was far more the logical consequence of the war than its critics have admitted, both in view of the war's origins and of the ideological meaning which it progressively acquired in the course of the fighting. The Austro-Serbian diplomatic dispute had symbolized the quarrels of nationalities in Southeastern Europe. It had assumed exceptional gravity in proportion as it compromised the existence of Austria-Hungary. From 1917 onward, by proclaiming the principle of the liberation of nationalities (which often had no desire for liberation), the statesmen of the Entente gave to their enterprise a revolutionary character. They did so without calculating the consequences, and without strong convictions, so far were they carried away by the force of events. Austria-Hungary was not destroyed by the negotiations at Versailles. The recognition of the Masaryk Committee dealt the Dual Monarchy a first blow. The rejection of Emperor Charles' peace offers struck the deathblow, and all that had to be done at Versailles was to sign the death certificate. In essence, it was the acceptance of a *de facto* situation which was not so much the result of human activities or intentions as of the war itself and its irresistible dynamism.

Some of the Ministers at Vienna had believed that a sharp lesson for Serbia was indispensable to the survival of the Dual Monarchy: very likely they were wrong. Federalism, as conceived by the assassinated Archduke, offered the best method of reinforcing the old Hapsburg edifice, which the war showed to be rather solid. For two years desertions were rare; most of the South Slavs and even many of the Czechs fought to the end. Masaryk had as much difficulty in persuading his compatriots as in persuading Allied Ministers. In the end Austria-Hungary succumbed to the ideology that had been provoked by the length of the war. The effect rejoined the cause: the Europe of nationalities emerged from a war that had been kindled by a quarrel of nationalities.

But the logic of ideas did not accord with the logic of forces. It had been demonstrated that national states no longer possessed the resources needed for total war. Even Britain and France had sustained their effort only with the aid of the New World. If there was to be some sort of balance between the size of military and political units, the technique of twentieth-century warfare clearly demanded larger political units. The "Balkanization" of Europe, though probably in harmony with European passions and ideas, ran counter to the economic and military tendency toward giantism.

Nor is that all. As soon as the guns began to thunder, there appeared the critical problem of counterbalancing Germany's power. The treaty would solve nothing if it did not solve the "German problem." Would the Weimar Reich be integrated in a peaceful Europe more easily and more permanently than that of Wilhelm II?

Everything depended on Germany's acceptance of or conversion to a conservative attitude. That sort of acceptance would require, at least during a first phase of two or three decades, a mixture of contentment and impotence. The Treaty of Versailles created a maximum of discontent and an impotence that was only transitory. Whichever way she turned her eyes, toward Poland or Czechoslovakia or Austria, Germany saw grievances which she could only consider legitimate. The disarmament clauses, the demilitarization of the Rhineland, and the Little Entente made her temporarily helpless; but they did not weaken her for good and all. Having saved her unity and her industry, she had thereby kept intact the means of recovery. As Jacques Bainville put it in a famous phrase, "The treaty was too harsh for its softer elements, and too soft for the harsher ones."

The small and medium-sized states that surrounded the Reich

feared her above all else. But each of them had interests, grievances, and ambitions of its own. Poland and Czechoslovakia, for example, never settled their difference over Teschen.

So long as Germany was disarmed, the French system held together with apparent solidity. As soon as the Reich recovered its sovereignty and began once more to brandish its arms, each nation sought its own safety, until all were dragged into common disaster.

That evolution had not been inescapable. France should have regrouped her allies, putting a stop to the Hitlerian enterprise at the outset. But the very consequences of the preceding war made that attitude unlikely on her part.

As soon as Russia was eliminated from the European concert by her revolution and the United States had withdrawn into isolationism, the once victorious group was potentially weaker than the vanquished. The sacrifice of a million and a half Frenchmen weighed more heavily in the balance of history than that of two million Germans. By a vital reflex France, apprehensive of the future and satisfied with her own "place in the sun," was bound to be more pacifist than the powerful but shackled Germany.

Clear-sighted calculation would have shown that the best way for France to maintain both peace and her position would have been for her to force Germany to respect the disarmament clauses, or at least the demilitarization of the Rhineland. Concern for peace should have encouraged France to resist German rearmament. Instead, by a psychological contradiction, it inspired her to appease the formidable neighbor. Unluckily that undeliberated effort was entered into with a Germany that could be appeased by nothing short of slavery.

The First World War had shown that the alliance of the Western democracies with Russia was the only means of creating a force that could hold its own against Germany. Without the Russian front, without the shifting of two German army corps to East Prussia, the Battle of the Marne would probably not have been won. The Third Reich, rearmed and adventurous, could be deterred only by enrolling Russia in the conservative camp. But Communist Russia, on its emergence from the world war, was no more interested than Germany in maintaining the status quo and the peace.

Whether we consider the international balance of power or the internal structure of each country, to say nothing of its economic organization, the Europe of Versailles was less stable than that of 1914. Territorial partition had not put an end to international quarrels, it had replaced the old quarrels by new ones. The nationalism of the new states encouraged trade barriers and became a cause of impoverishment for all. Germany was more bitter, virtually more revolutionary, and in the long run not without means of action.

It is clearly impossible to say what would have happened had a compromise peace been concluded late in 1916 or early in 1917. Speculation on what might have been the outcome of a different policy would be a waste of time. Yet the principal causes of the Second World War resulted from prolongation of the first war and, above all, of the Russian Revolution and the Fascist reactions to it in Italy and Germany.

The war destroyed those traditional institutions that might have checked the tendency in Western societies toward social leveling and other forms of collectivism. The monarchies that had crumbled in defeat would not have prevented the "democratization" of the regimes of Central Europe, but they would have reduced the risk of mass passions, secular religions, and totalitarian parties. Parliaments are soundly established only insofar as they are self-imposed by the majority, and not by violence.

Everything happened as if at a certain point violence became self-supporting. In war, as with fissionable materials, there is a critical mass. Since 1914, Europe has been shaken by wars in "chain reaction."

*Chapter II*

# DYNAMISM OF TOTAL WAR

L IKE THE FIRST, the second war of the twentieth century originated and centered in Germany. Like the first, it grew out of all proportion, extending from its European origins until in the end it covered the planet, unleashing monstrous cruelties and passions until the atomic bomb finally brought the technique of destruction to a ghastly perfection that was, and still is, scarcely imaginable. The second war, like the first, was lost by the aggressor; but this time again after the ordeal, the world remains unconverted to the values for which the West has fought. European democracy and freedom and civilization are the victims, even more than Germany, of a victory won in their name.

Leaving aside these fundamental analogies, the second war was nearly a replica of the first. Everything happened differently but the final outcome is much the same. No one disagrees over the immediate causes of the Second World War, for Hitler signed his own works. This time there was not the approximate balance of power, as in 1914, but German superiority that brought into play the "law of amplification." The stake was still the principle of the formation of political units, but one camp at least proclaimed that the era of national sovereignty was ended. Twenty years after its triumph, the idea of nationalism belonged already to the past: the age of empires had begun. The material consequences of the war created the threat of a new conflict, not because the defeated power, powerful still and embittered, was dreaming of retaliation, but because in Europe and Asia, vanquished and victors, alike overwhelmed, were now caught between two peripheral superstates.

Public opinion and the chancelleries had learned from the much discussed events of July 1914 certain lessons which Anglo-French diplomacy did its best to apply. The statesmen made the same mistake as the French general staff. The latter, regretting the follies of the all-out offensive, placed blind faith in firepower and in the continuous front line; so that, in trying to avoid the preceding war, they precipitated the Hitlerian adventure.

British statesmen were convinced that there might have been no war if, on July 25, 1914, Downing Street had taken a definite stand and made it known to Berlin. Hence the touchingly ineffectual energy of Mr. Neville Chamberlain during the crises of 1938–39 when he made it unmistakably clear to the world and to the Führer that this time the British Empire would not remain neutral if France had again to face the Reich.

His word was not doubted in Berlin, but the times had changed. In 1939 the equivalent of the British warning of 1914 could only have come from Washington.[1] Roosevelt and most clear-sighted Americans were convinced in advance that the United States would be drawn into the war, but the backwardness of public opinion and the bonds of democracy condemned them to pass a bill, not for rearmament, which might have impressed Hitler, but for neutrality, which seemed to prohibit supplies to the belligerents on either side. Roosevelt was reduced to the prediction of a catastrophe which he might have been able to prevent.

Even apart from the American defection, the British warning would have carried more weight if it had been accompanied by additional military preparations. Hitler did not expect the British to remain neutral either in 1938 or 1939, but he was equally unconvinced that the Empire would engage in a life-and-death struggle. It was no longer enough to sever diplomatic relations (which Berlin anticipated calmly); practical proof should have been given of unshakable resolve. The Labour Party was opposed to appeasement, but also opposed to compulsory military service.

The British and French were still obsessed by the horrors of war. Even the leaders sincerely believed that no one, and certainly not a

---

[1] The statesmen are making the same mistake today. An undertaking by Washington in 1939 might have prevented the last war. But will it suffice to prevent the next one?

former soldier, could take the initiative in cold blood. Hence they developed a series of theories attempting to explain how wars broke out, without either side wanting them, by an enigmatical chain of circumstances. The admission that war is inevitable helps, it was said, to make it so. The widespread diplomatic opinion in 1914, that war was bound to come sooner or later, may indeed have paralyzed the efforts towards a peaceful settlement of the Austro-Serbian crisis. But faced with such a regime as that of the Nazis, with their almost unlimited ambitions, such considerations were anachronistic. Was it possible to satisfy Hitler? Could he not be stopped except by force? These were the only questions. The Western democracies tried first to satisfy Hitler, and then in 1939 to stop him, when the superior strength, in the short run at least, was no longer theirs.

Other observers had been impressed by the German accusations of encirclement. Seen from Berlin, had not the alliances seemed before 1914 to threaten the security of the Reich? Had they not given the impression beyond the Rhine of a conspiracy against an actively expansionist power? Hence the British concern to declare at every moment that the London Government had no thought of encirclement, whereas, in fact, the so-called encirclement had been no more than an alliance to counterbalance Germanic force. To renounce that alliance would have increased the risk of war: the weaker the victims, the stronger the aggressor's temptation.

Finally, other observers recalled that, as of a certain day in 1914, perhaps July 29, and in any case the thirtieth, the automatism of the mobilizations had tied the hands of the diplomats. The generals had assumed control and the civil leaders had abdicated. In September 1938 and in August 1939, quite comic efforts were made to escape from that supposed automatism. It was declared again and again that mobilization was not war: true, but an essential fact was forgotten. In July 1914 the Central Powers may have wanted only a diplomatic success established by local operations at Serbia's expense, so that the peace might have been saved by allowing them that satisfaction. But there was no such situation in 1938 or 1939. In 1938 the aggressor intended to annex the Sudetenland, which amounted to the destruction of Czechoslovakia. Then, after the seizure of Prague, Poland's existence was at stake. It was reasonable to hesitate over the decision to be adopted, but not to be guided by a completely irrelevant precedent.

In retrospect the essential aspects of the situation seem remarkably simple. The arrival of the Nazis in power heralded a new diplomatic initiative. The new regime would rearm and seek a revision of the territorial clauses in the Treaty of Versailles. What would be the extent of its ambitions? Would it pursue objectives obtainable by peaceful means, or did it intend to go so far that the other nations must either resist or concede? Although some discussion was possible in 1933, one thing was certain: Hitler should never have been allowed advantages which prevented his being stopped without general war.

So long as the Rhineland remained demilitarized, France was able, even alone, to impose her will. After March 1936, not even Britain and France together could intervene locally to prevent Hitler in his enterprise. The decisive capitulation, dividing the period 1933–39, was agreed to not at Munich in 1938, but at London and Paris in March 1936. From that date, war was not inevitable (what, indeed, is the meaning of inevitability, applied to a chain of historical events?), but it had become probable. To avoid it, it would have been necessary for the conservative coalition to possess at every moment forces superior to those of the revolutionary coalition. But that superiority would have demanded the steady cooperation of one or the other of the two great powers whose intervention did in the end bring victory, the United States or Soviet Russia. Roosevelt, however, while encouraging the Western democracies to resist, permitted the Congress to take precautions against the chain of events that had brought about intervention in 1917. (The New World, too, was moving into the future with its eyes on the past.) As for the Soviet Union, it was more afraid of being exposed alone to German aggression than of a possible world war, which could assist its subversive plans.

Western diplomacy might have rallied Soviet Russia to its side had it not hesitated so much, thereby giving the master of the Kremlin the impression that there would be no objection to German expansion eastward. (So I thought at the time; I no longer think so today, and will refrain from speculating as to what might have happened.) It was Stalin who, in March 1939, took the initiative towards an agreement with Hitler. In 1938, in the absence of a common frontier, he would not have had to enter a total war, at least in its first phase. After the elimination of Czechoslovakia as a bastion, the perspectives changed and Stalin maneuvered subtly to redirect the mounting war to the West. Britain and France, moreover, had already promised, for nothing in return from Poland and Rumania, to intervene in case of German aggression in the East—a promise for which Stalin would have eventually paid dearly. From then on, he had everything to gain (or so, at least, he thought, for his calculations were upset by the quick French defeat) from securing, through a pact with Hitler, a respite while the others would be fighting and he would be reserving his strength for the final decision.

Apart from an alliance between the Western democracies and the Soviet Union, which would have been almost impossible in view of mutual suspicion and divergence of interests, was there no chance of peace after 1936? There are those who still claim that Hitler could have been appeased; but such a hypothesis is unlikely. Germany, after establishing her protectorate over Bohemia and after destroying or bringing Poland to heel, would have so enlarged her territory and increased her resources that a less ambitious leader than Hitler could hardly have resisted temptation. There was no longer any equilibrium possible in Europe. By what miracle could a regime dedicated to unlimited dynamism stop halfway?

The truth is that in 1939 there was only one card left to play, that of "national" opposition within the Third Reich. Hitler's opponents were amazed by his successes, and wondered desperately what would come next. It is known that on the eve of Munich certain generals had decided to overthrow the Führer rather than precipitate general war. What would have happened had the democracies stood firm? What were really the chances of General Halder and the other conspirators? We shall never know. The truth is that only the replacement of the Nazis by a nationalist but not revolutionary regime would still have offered a chance of peace after 1936. A traditionalist Germany, either authoritarian or democratic, might have been appeased, but not Hitler's Germany.

It is easy to understand that the immediate causes of the second war should have provoked fewer and less passionate controversies. The first war had arisen from a "diplomatic failure." There is room for unending argument as to the likelihood of an ultimate explosion if the Sarajevo crisis had been peacefully overcome. The second war arose from Hitler's schemes of conquest. It might have broken out a year earlier if the democracies had decided to fight for Czechoslovakia; it might have been delayed had the democracies not come to the aid of Poland. But it is impossible to see how Hitler could have stopped of his own accord, or how Great Britain and France could have saved themselves without stopping him, that is to say, without fighting. Thus, what really matter are the remote origins. What were the sources of Hitler's rise to power and Germany's imperial desires? Why did the conservative states give the Teuton Caesar time to accumulate enough arms, not for victory, but for his own burial beneath the ruins of a civilization?

Western thinkers had concluded from the tragic events of 1914–18 that modern war could not pay. It would no longer leave the victors and the vanquished, but death and ruin everywhere. The spoils of victory could no longer be commensurate with the cost of battle. The only road to victory would be the avoidance of war. An irreproachable conclusion: from the point of view of England and France, the only victory would indeed have consisted in avoiding war. But it was a sterile conclusion, for if other nations have not the same opinion, how can that peaceful victory be secured?

Certain English theorists had pictured another conclusion. They thought that what was absurd was not war in itself, but total war. The 185 men who died at Trafalgar had won more for their country than the 800,000 who died in 1914–18. Wisdom would counsel that, instead of madly throwing men and wealth into the furnace, some limit should be set. War, yes, if necessary but, as Captain Liddell Hart put it, "with limited liability."

The Germans drew quite another lesson from their earlier experience. Hyperbolic war would not develop inevitably from industrial societies; it was due to a combination of chance circumstances: the approximate balance between the warning coalitions, the temporary superiority of the defensive over the offensive, and the difficulty of demolishing field fortifications. By isolating its adversaries on the principle of plucking the artichoke of its leaves, one by one, German diplomacy would provide the *Wehrmacht* with campaigns that could be brought quickly and economically to an end. The weapons tested in the last stages of the preceding war, tanks and aircraft, would restore to the offensive its chances of success. In Spengler's famous phrase, mechanical power had reopened the era of great invasions that had ended with the supremacy of the Mongol cavalry. Finally, the cost of the fighting, even if high, would not be excessive if the yield of victory were lasting. The irrationality of the war of 1914–18 had lain in the impossibility of reconciling a life-and-death struggle with the maintenance of sovereign states. A system of independent states is compatible with limited war, but not with total war. This last consideration must inevitably herald the peace of the empires.

In 1939–40 the German calculations seemed at first to be confirmed. The campaigns in Poland and France gave a relation between output and yield that reversed the experience of 1914–18, fulfilling the most optimistic forecasts. Germany lost fewer than 40,000 dead between May 10 and June 25, 1940, and no more than 66,000 in the West up to June 6, 1944. The total casualties (killed, wounded, and prisoners) in the campaign in France were less than 100,000; and the victor added, on paper, some 30 to 40 per cent to his industrial potential, and still more if we include the gains in Czechoslovakia, Poland, and France.

Aware that the stalemate in the mud in Flanders and Lorraine had prolonged the fighting and increased its violence, Hitler—master of Europe from the Vistula to the Atlantic, but the prisoner of his conquests—was driven to extend his field of operations immeasurably, and to rush headlong from victory to victory on his way to ultimate disaster. The democracies were loath to negotiate between 1914 and 1918, though thousands of men were falling every day—but how could Great Britain have negotiated with a Caesar more powerful than Napoleon?

In his eastward drive in June 1941, Hitler was trying to secure a permanent hold on his continental empire. Henceforth, events conspired to forge the coalition which he had exerted himself to prevent. Japan, whose enterprise in the Far East was parallel to his own, but quite different in origin and significance, challenged the American giant. At once the war became no longer merely European like the first war, with extra-European prolongations, but truly global. The conflagration steadily spread. The extent and intensity of the fighting increased without limit. The successive stages of that amplification illustrate the irrepressible dynamism of modern war with its strategic bombing, guerrilla warfare, deportation of civilians, and death camps.

The theorists had conceived in advance the idea of reducing a nation by systematically bombing its towns. The Italian General, Douhet, had been the promoter of the doctrine, and its test was anticipated in a conflict between the great powers. It was, however, uncertain how much destruction could be wreaked from the air and what effect bombing would have on popular resistance. The German Air Force had been established and trained with a view to coordinated action with the Army; it did not include the equivalent of the British heavy bombers, and it had not expected important night attacks. In the course of the campaign in the West it attacked lines of communication, headquarters, strategic points in the front lines, and as far as thirty miles to the rear. It did, however, undertake "terror raids" in Holland (an entire section of Rotterdam was destroyed) and in France; these raids over inhabited districts aimed at reducing the enemy morale. The German general staff seemed to believe in the material efficacy of bombing in support of the Army and in the psychological efficacy of certain forms of bombing in full daylight, where it had the mastery of the air against a weak enemy, as in Holland, or a discouraged one, as in France.

The effect of this strategy in 1940 was to tempt the British, and then the Americans, to resort to strategic bombing on a scale unknown till then. Besieged in their island, with no likelihood of an early landing in Europe, the British had only the choice between inaction and air attacks. Daylight bombings were possible only with fighter escort. Technical resources were scarcely sufficient to enable a distinction to be made between zone bombing and the bombing of targets. Accordingly British and Germans engaged in a rivalry in more or less "indiscriminate" night bombings. Blind destruction entered into the habits of combat.

Already in the preceding war the distinction between combatants and noncombatants had been narrowed if not destroyed by firepower. In this respect the Germans had largely taken the initiative, from poison gas to the heavy artillery that shelled Paris. Bombing had added to the risks run by civilians; open cities, which in principle were spared, had become difficult to define, so greatly had the number of military objectives increased in the epoch of industrial warfare; and badly aimed bombs made it impossible for populations to distinguish between an attack on a railway station and an attack on a town. With the enormous increase in the number, tonnage, and flying range of bombers, what in 1914–18 had been a spectacular but relatively harmless episode assumed between 1939 and 1945 the dimensions of a major operation, whose military efficacy is still doubtful but whose destructive effects remain to this day.

Ten thousand tons of bombs were dropped over Germany in 1940; 30,000 in 1941; 40,000 in 1942; 120,000 in 1943; 600,000 in 1944; and 500,000 during the five first months of 1945. According to the figures of a British economist, the annual loss of production in the Reich was estimated at 2.5 per cent in 1942, 9 per cent in 1943, 17 per cent in 1944. No doubt these figures are only approximate. The losses indirectly attributable to the Allied air offensive must have been considerable. Four and a half million people were employed in clearing away ruins and in air-raid precautions, including the production of anti-aircraft weapons. But, above all, 61 cities of more than 100,000 inhabitants, on which some 500,-000 tons of bombs were dropped, had 70 per cent of their dwellings (3,600,000) destroyed. Strategic bombing seems to have played a smaller part in the victory than in the postwar difficulties.

The Germans had given their enemies the right to resort to this horrible process. But two questions might have been asked: What was its military usefulness, and what would be its long-term consequences? When strategic bombing was concentrated on certain works (synthetic fuels, ball bearings), or on transportation, the military results were incomparably greater. The generals apparently miscalculated, even from their own point of view. The civilian war leaders in the democracies might have measured their responsibility toward the common civilization they claimed to be defending, but they seem to be as incapable of thinking about peace once war has started as of preparing for war before the first shot has been fired.

The strategic bombing followed a British tradition—to use as few men as possible with costly equipment in a situation where with limited losses a decision can be forced. Each nation has its cherished military memories. The French like to recall pitched battles or cavalry charges, even vain ones. The British idolize the "stalwart few" of Trafalgar or of the Battle of Britain. Millions of workers in the factories, hundreds of thousands of underlings (squires, as it were, to the modern knights), and a few thousands or tens of thousands of airmen—were not these the rejoinder to the sterile butcheries of Flanders? Apart from that, will the side with superiority in any one means of destruction ever have the wisdom to restrict the employment of that superiority when the national existence is at stake? And is anything more unlikely than a complete equilibrium in all forms of weapons?

By another departure from tradition, Hitler's conquests helped to confuse the distinction between combatants and noncombatants and to universalize violence. Wars with limited stakes, between nations whose frontiers, but not their structures, will be modified can be fought entirely by soldiers in uniform. An imperial war, whose outcome would be the installation of a higher sovereignty (*de facto,* if not *de jure*) over those of the belligerent states, almost inevitably becomes a war between whole populations. A country that passively accepted the yoke of the occupying state might be acting reasonably (in military terms, the cost of resistance might exceed the "yield"), but would it not have renounced nationhood? The enemy presence reanimates that national feeling. Total mobilization by the occupying power incites revolt; the recruitment of factory workers strengthens the underground resistance.

One of the most frequent consequences of imperialism is the conqueror's reinforcement through his conquests. The army with which Alexander set out for the East was half composed of Greeks who had fought against Philip. Less than half the army with which Napoleon crossed the Russian frontiers on June 21, 1812, was composed of Frenchmen. Hitler, too, had added to the *Wehrmacht* Finnish, Italian, Hungarian, and Rumanian divisions, to say nothing of the Spanish contingents or the League of French Volunteers.

In our time the contribution of combatants is the most spectacular but the most superficial form of mobilization of the vanquished. The German factories needed manpower: whence should it be drawn if not from occupied Europe? In 1945 the prisoners of war and foreign workers in Germany numbered between 5 and 10 mil-

lions. Applied over a wide region, the technique of total mobilization carried civilized Europe back to the time of the great migra-
tions, whose rigors, however, were softened by administrative
experience.

Centuries earlier, when armies lived on the invaded countries for
lack of organized supply, their pillage provoked guerrilla fighting as
soon as normal poverty became widespread, unbearable destitution,
as in Spain and Russia during the Napoleonic invasions. In our age,
guerrilla warfare on a grand scale was provoked, at least in the
West, by incidental consequences of total war—food requisitions
that merely exasperated the populations by reducing the ration below the habitual, if not the physiological, minimum; and transfers of
workers, inciting tens of thousands of young men to flee conscription and swell the ranks of the Resistance.

In the East, guerrilla warfare was organized either by the government or by a revolutionary party. National resistance arose in Yugoslavia immediately following the disaster. But General Mikhailo-
vitch, who had witnessed the atrocities committed by Croats against
Serbs, had been struck by the disproportionate losses inflicted on
populations by active guerrilla warfare so long as liberating armies
were unable to intervene, and wanted to spare his forces. Tito did
not hesitate to carry on partisan warfare for years, but his aim was
as much to secure power after Germany's defeat as to hasten that
defeat.

In Russia, group leaders were parachuted behind the enemy lines
with precise instructions. Filling the enemy rear with a sense of insecurity was conceived as a military task, among others, that the
general staff had to carry out by arousing and exploiting popular
passion. In fact, the ferocity of the occupying forces contributed
quite as much to the spread of revolt as the patriotism of the population and the threats of reprisals published by the Soviet authorities.
In 1941 the Ukrainians had no thought of rising against the invaders—what really happened has been carefully dissimulated. The
atmosphere of a national war was largely created by the very
methods of biological warfare, conceived by certain German theorists, and applied by the S.S., under the orders of some Gauleiters.
On the pretext that Russia was not a signatory of the Geneva Convention, hundreds of thousands of Russian prisoners of war were

allowed to starve to death during the winter of 1941–42. In the West, the German armies had behaved "correctly" to the populations and refrained from deliberately increasing the burden of occupation; but in the East, the Government General of Poland had subjected that unhappy country to a pitiless regime, and the occupied territories in Russia soon suffered a reign of terror. Among the follies committed by Hitler's representatives, none had more disastrous repercussions for the criminals themselves. The Germans finally became victims of the fury they had aroused.

Strategic bombing, deportations of workers, guerrilla warfare, terrorism, the police state—this multiplication of violence proceeds logically from an imperialist war conducted with the aid of modern industry. But there was nothing yet to imply the extermination, deliberated in cold blood and scientifically organized, of 6 million Jews; nothing to imply the concentration camps, or at least their sadistic methods of degradation and slow murder. We cannot deny Hitler's henchmen the unhappy merit of having foreseen and exceeded the requirements of total war. They have precipitated those zoological wars to which Renan, in 1871, predicted that racial passions would lead humanity.

Hitler's venture considered as a whole in 1940 gave the impression of a plan elaborated in advance and methodically carried out. In a first phase, Germany rearmed, perhaps more ostentatiously than effectively, in order to deter France from any military rejoinder. Even before the *Wehrmacht* had attained fighting strength, contingents were sent into the Rhineland, a tactic based upon the accurate foresight of British blindness, French pacifism, and the diplomatic imbroglio of the sanctions against Italy. From that moment the Western democracies had repeatedly no other choice than to capitulate or to risk general war. In February 1938 the Nazi regime proceeded, in perfect safety, to annex Austria, Czechoslovakia, encircled and isolated, fell in September 1938 after a simulacrum of resistance from Great Britain and France. The Siegfried line was hastily set up to discourage any French inclination to an offensive; then Germany turned against Poland, which the day before had been its accomplice in the partition of Czechoslovakia and now suffered in its turn. At the last moment the Western democracies made a serious effort to form a common front with Soviet Russia. But Hitler had more to offer: Stalin could have half of Poland; a second world war was a virtual certainty, and he would be able to remain neutral during its first phase. What advantages for an empire, still insecure, but always hoping to extend its revolution! In the spring of 1940 France, herself isolated, succumbed in a few weeks. Hitler's empire, extending from the Vistula to the Atlantic, had been created.

The imperialistic theories that fill German literature seemed to have been miraculously confirmed. *Militarily,* the internal combustion engine, supplying power to tanks and aircraft, seemed to have recreated the superiority of force needed for a break-through and its exploitations; railways and trucks seemed to have given land armies a mobility comparable with that of the naval powers. *Economically,* the wide territory of the new empire would restore the unrestricted trade that had been lost in Europe in the first third of the twentieth century. *Politically,* national states would belong to the past because they would no longer possess either the resources needed for total war on the dimensions needed for economic rationalization. Popular feeling, though it had not kept up with events, seemed already to be influenced by that irresistible evolution. The external threat no longer sufficed to unite the French or to steel their national spirit. The country that had given to Europe the perfect example of the national state revealed the irremediable decline of that political unit.

The fifth column is a typical element of the age of empires. It is recruited mainly among three sorts of men: pacifists, revolted by the material and moral cost of total war who, at the bottom of their hearts, prefer the triumph of an empire to the independent sovereignty of bellicose states; defeatists, who despair of their own country; and idealogues, who set their political faith above their patriotism and submit to the Caesar whose regime and ideology they admire. The elements of the German fifth column, though much less influential and numerous than has been alleged, were recruited mainly from the two first categories. Quisling in Norway, Mussert in Holland, probably belonged to the third category. In Britain and France there were scarcely any convinced Nazis who paved the way for Germany's victory because they adhered to the credo of National Socialism. Certain reactionaries saw compensation for defeat in the chance that it offered for a national revolution. Others, with Fascistic tendencies, bowed, not without satisfaction perhaps, before a military decision which they thought would be final. Obviously there could not be many genuine Nazis outside Germany.

As an imperialist ideology, in fact, Hitlerism was a challenge to common sense. Any empire that is imposed upon old nations proud of their civilization can be stabilized only by inducing the vanquished to accept their lot. The Roman Empire could not have existed if Italians, Gauls, and Africans had not been able to become Roman citizens. Once the Jews had been exterminated (a few more months would have sufficed), racialism would have lost its only international appeal. Of what use would have been the slogan "Anti-Semites of the world, unite!" when there were no longer any Jews for the gas chambers? Racialism had either to disappear or remain for the Germans to profit by. Subject peoples are not to be won over by proclaiming the superiority of the master race.

Europe in 1940 offered an approximate picture of what the empire of the immediate future might have been. Carefully plotted gradations of popular subjection were making their appearance. Poland was ruled by Germans, the Czech territory protected; non-occupied France had the right to diplomatic representation abroad. Warsaw would have received a Governor, Prague a Protector, Paris a Nazi Ambassador. The degree of autonomy and the methods of rule were to vary. In the occupied half of France, for example, the Germans had already shown how they would "legally" control the French economy. Political assimilation would be guaranteed by the military impotence of the French. For the rest, the visible forms of independence would be respected.

The real difficulties remained. It is easy to start an imperial enterprise, but difficult to end it. Hitler, with the unsolicited, unwanted collaboration of Japan, provoked the alliance of the three greatest powers in the world: the British Commonwealth, the Soviet Union, and the United States. With this alliance, Hitler's calculated plan of conquest dissolved. We no longer witness the realization of a plan but the improvisations of an adventurer.

Even the opening phase of the enterprise, which at first glance seemed the result of imperialistic theory and technique, was really marked by constant good fortune rather than by any close attention to strategy. Hitler was deliberately following the old rule of warfare by disposing of his adversaries one by one. He tried, and almost succeeded, to make sure of being ahead with the mobilization of his troops and even of his factories. Confident of the efficacy of modern offensive weapons, he calculated that his more rapid mobilization would enable him to win a decisive victory over adversaries who had not had time to assemble their forces. This conception, based as usual on past experience, seemed to assure his success in an operation almost identical with that which had so nearly succeeded in September 1914. Thus the master of the Third Reich, to the stupefaction of his generals, eliminated Austria and Czechoslovakia without firing a shot, and liquidated at small cost Poland, Holland, Belgium, and France.[2] But the secret of these triumphs was not as much military or political as psychological. When, in 1935, Hitler proclaimed that he no longer recognized the military clauses of the Treaty of Versailles, Germany was defenseless. Hitler's superiority over his generals lay in his intuitive understanding of crowds and of peoples. He was convinced that France would not move, and he was right. The *Wehrmacht* contingents that occupied the de-militarized zone in March 1936 had orders to retire if the French Army crossed the frontiers of the Reich. The Führer was obliged to make that concession to G.H.Q., but he had accurately gauged the French state of mind. In 1938, General Beck resigned when Hitler revealed his projects in regard to Austria and Czechoslovakia. Such projects, declared the old-style generals, would inevitably lead to a world war. They were nationalists, but they were also Christians, and feared for Germany especially, but also for European civilization.

At Munich in 1938, Hitler judged correctly and achieved a peaceful success for the last time. Events had belied the fears of his professional advisers and had justified the amateur's optimism. The Führer believed more than ever in his mission and his manifest destiny. He went on to make his fatal mistake. The generals' objections seemed to be contradicted by the facts in September 1938,

[2]In the West the superiority of the German armies, except in aircraft, was not so much quantitative as qualitative. Even in tanks the French were outclassed more because of inferior tactics and organization than numbers.

again in March 1939, and even in September 1939 and June 1940. The military victories of 1939 and 1940 exceeded the always cautious anticipations of the experts. But their pessimism as to the ultimate outcome was well founded. Peaceful triumphs and lightning victories made inevitable a war to the uttermost, in a chain of events which Hitler had refused to foresee and refused almost up to the end to recognize.

When he ordered his troops to cross the Polish frontier, he had no doubt that the result would be an Anglo-French declaration of war. But he did not think that their symbolic gesture implied fierce determination to fight to the bitter end and destroy the Third Reich. After the Polish campaign and during the campaign in France, Hitler seems still to have been unconvinced that the British would prove irreconcilable. It may be that he spared the British army at Dunkirk by holding up his armored divisions for forty-eight hours so as not to offend the *amour-propre* of the British and to leave open the opportunity of negotiating with them.

From that point onward, one searches in vain for any trace in Hitler's successive decisions of a plan elaborated in advance. For several months, without any strong conviction, he played with the idea of a landing in England; but the defeat of his aircraft led him to renounce the attempt, for which the general staffs were unenthusiastic, and in which he himself had been unable to put faith. He thought of attacking Gibraltar, and of sending his armored divisions to Alexandria and Suez. Finally, in the autumn of 1940, after the interview with Molotov, he decided on Operation Barbarossa—the invasion of Russia.

There is no lack of historical precedent to suggest that this decision followed inevitably in the wake of conquests in the West and the Battle of Britain. Hitler, like Napoleon, was pursuing the elusive Albion into the snows of Russia. For how could he strike a mortal blow at the British Commonwealth so long as the Russian Army and Air Force were intact, compelling him to keep part of the *Luftwaffe* and the *Wehrmacht* in the East, or at least in reserve? If the war of attrition continued in the West for years, would not the Soviet Union inevitably become the arbiter of the situation? Such arguments are easily mustered—as are those to the contrary. The Soviet Union was carrying out the clauses of the Russo-German

Pact with scrupulous loyalty; it delivered all the promised supplies, and offered still more. There had been nothing to suggest that it would have, in the near future, to turn against the Third Reich. Thus, in concentrating its forces against the British Commonwealth in 1941, had not Germany a chance of weakening England to the point of inducing her not to capitulate, but to negotiate? During the first months of 1941, Great Britain was losing 500,000 tons of merchant shipping every month. If the submarine war had been accompanied by the bombing of ports, and if the German Army had utilized some of its "unemployed" divisions against Gibraltar and Suez, it is questionable whether Roosevelt would have been able to bring about American intervention before Great Britain had been overcome by discouragement.[3]

There is little need to answer these questions. Our purpose is not to speculate on what might have happened, but to arrive at a simple statement of fact. The master of the Third Reich wanted to be an empire builder, and probably would never have reached the limit of his ambitions. But his own mind was not made up as to the order of the various operations. The pact with Stalin seemed to him at the time to be a masterpiece of diplomacy. He then hesitated before the prospect of a life-and-death struggle with the British Commonwealth, either because from a racialist point of view he deplored the reciprocal extermination of the higher peoples, or because he had not abandoned hope of a reconciliation.

The industrial mobilization of the Reich bears the marks of this indecision. In 1940, after the collapse of France, the general output was reduced. Similarly, in October 1941, when it was firmly believed that the Russian Army had been destroyed (as the communiqués from the Führer's headquarters declared), production was again slowed down. Not until Stalingrad and the first Eastern defeats did the Third Reich seem at last to be filled with a sense of urgency. At that point total mobilization ceased to be a subject for declamations. Even then, subsequent study has shown that

[3]It is true that such a compromise peace in 1941 or 1942 would have been only a truce, and would have settled nothing. So long as Great Britain subsisted on one side, supported by the United States and the Soviet Union on the other side, Hitler's empire, regarded as an enemy by both, would remain in a precarious situation.

industrial mobilization was less complete in Nazi Germany than in democratic Britain.

Improvisation and amateurishness mark the last phase of Hitler's adventure. His fundamental mistake was the counterpart of the accurate intuitions of the first phase. He refused to admit that, in spite of his theories, he had repeated the Kaiser's error in launching a war on two fronts, against the Russians and the Anglo-Saxons. When he could no longer deny the facts, he clung to an argument that seemed to him unanswerable: How could the capitalist democracies and the Soviet empire co-operate to the extent of jointly crushing Germany? Would it not be the height of folly for the British and Americans to lend a hand in the destruction of the only barrier that could protect Europe from the Communist flood? It may have been folly, but it was a folly that he himself had led the Anglo-Saxons to commit.

The Allies of 1914–18 were united against Germany. It was to be expected that on the day of victory the normal difficulties of victorious coalitions—divergencies of interest and competition for shares in the spoil—would show themselves. But after the elimination of Russia from the alliance, Great Britain, France, Italy, and the United States belonged to one world. They had similar national policies; none of them nurtured unlimited ambitions, and none of them regarded its Allies as possible future enemies.

Between 1939 and 1945 the United Nations, whose common hostility to Germany formed the only bond that held them together, were divided into two groups—the Soviet Union on one side and the bourgeois democracies on the other—which were bound to oppose each other when the Third Reich foundered. Rarely can hostility have been so predictable. The Germans never ceased to proclaim the fact, and Goebbels was unable to understand that the more he insisted the more he forced the Americans to camouflage it. Not for a moment, of course, did the Russian authorities forget, but the Anglo-Saxons, and particularly the Americans, often acted as if they did not regard the hostility as fundamental.

On the very day when the German armies invaded Russia Churchill delivered a speech that automatically created an Anglo-

Russian alliance. The British war leader passed over the German-Soviet pact, ignored the fact that the U.S.S.R. had been guilty of aggression against Poland, and laid down the principle that the enemies of our enemies were our friends. It was a normal decision, ratified by the President of the United States and public opinion in both countries. It had been decided to destroy the Third Reich: the Soviet Union brought to the struggle its hundreds of divisions and was destined to offer millions of lives in the common cause.

The material aid sent by Great Britain and then by the United States to Russia, who had suffered heavily from the first blows of the *Wehrmacht,* was no less logical. Because there were fears in London and Washington that the Red Army might collapse, it was sent unconditionally all available equipment. But in 1943, after Stalingrad, the strategic situation changed radically: the balance of power had become favorable to the Allies, and German defeat had become only a question of time. Postwar problems appeared on the horizon. What were the ambitions of Soviet Russia? Was the army that was about to liberate Eastern Europe still a revolutionary army? Would it spread Communism, or respect the independence of sovereign nations and the rules of bourgeois democracy? The fate of the Continent depended on the reply to those questions. If the liberating army brought Soviets with it, one tyranny would have been replaced by another. The Anglo-Saxon leaders may have foreseen the danger, but they did nothing to forestall it.

As long as the war lasted, pressure could be applied by means of lend-lease. But, as General Deane has told in his book *The Strange Alliance,* Washington refused to take advantage of its position. Until 1945 the Russians' demands were met without qualification and without demanding anything in return, even when they requested material that could only be of service after the war. The Lublin Committee, composed almost exclusively of Communists, was accepted as the provisional Polish government and the only precaution taken was to send a few representatives of the British Government, who found themselves impotent hostages. The principle of distinct zones of occupation in Germany was accepted, and the Soviet zone, about a third of the Reich, was pushed forward into the heart of Western Europe. The Curzon line was recognized as the Russo-Polish frontier, and, at least provisionally, the Oder-Neisse line as the Polish-German frontier. At once the transfer was begun of 5 to 6 millions of Germans, who were expelled from the territories annexed by Poland and went to swell the population of the Reich, 70 millions crowded in a territory smaller than that of France. To induce the Russians to participate in the war against Japan, they were granted the Kurile Islands, the southern half of Sakhalin, Port Arthur, and the restoration of special rights in Manchuria (i.e., the port of Darien, and joint administration of the railway sold to Japan). Everything happened as if the Soviet Union, which had been ravaged by invasion, were the stronger party, and as if the Anglo-Saxon powers, in spite of their inexhaustible resources, had to give in to the stiff demands of their partner.

The British and American leaders seem to have been obsessed by the fear of a new Russo-German pact. Stalin had once lent a hand to Hitler: why should he not do so again if he found it to his interest? Roosevelt and Churchill, determined to crush Hitler at the least possible expense, felt themselves to be in a weaker position than Stalin,[4] whose armies were bearing the main burden of the war, and whose defection would have imposed on the Anglo-Saxons either a negotiated peace or a considerably greater sacrifice of lives.

Some of the German leaders (Goebbels, for example), if not Hitler himself, were inclined to come to terms with Stalin; but their proposals never materialized. Early in 1942 Hitler would not have offered terms acceptable to Stalin, and after Stalingrad, the Kremlin would have demanded still more. The Allies' fears were probably excessive. It was not easy, even for a despot, to forget the bloodshed, the atrocities, and the mutual invectives. Stalin was also credited with the intention of halting his troops at the frontiers and leaving it to the Anglo-Saxons to finish the job; but here again the profits that Stalin was expecting from victory were grossly underestimated.

It is striking, in any case, that Western statesmen never were aware that they had the means of countering Soviet pressure with

[4]At the time of the Yalta Conference, the Anglo-American armies were hard pressed by the last offensive of the *Wehrmacht,* the so-called Ardennes offensive.

pressure of their own. After all, if there had been a race for a separate peace, they were in the better position. (Or, rather, they would have been if such a proceeding were permissible for democracies: probably it is not.)

Modern war cannot be carried on without propaganda. This propaganda, apart from its more directly military aspects (convincing the enemy of his inevitable defeat, and maintaining civilian and military morale at home), tends more and more to assume a political character. By importing Nazism into the occupied countries, the Germans compelled the democracies to broadcast to Europe an ideology of liberation. In the sense given to the term during and after the war, the Soviet regime was no less totalitarian than that of Hitler. Was it possible to exalt the valor and the sacrifices of the Russian people and at the same time dissociate them from the Soviet regime? What seemed the easiest solution was chosen: a theoretical democracy was invented whose two related expressions were the parliamentary regime and Sovietism—a theory which brought the foreign policy of the Allies into precise agreement with Communist propaganda of the popular-front period.

Were the Western statesmen themselves prisoners of this propaganda? Did they really think that the directory of the Big Three was going to assure world peace? Roosevelt and some of his entourage, some State Department officials and New Dealers in sympathy with the Communists, seemed to have been genuinely convinced that Stalin was no longer the prophet of world revolution but the head of a national state. They believed that Stalin's war aims were not in opposition to the permanent interests of the United States and of democratic Europe. In any case, Roosevelt considered that the best means of realizing these optimistic views was to deal frankly with the master of the Kremlin: to show him constant good will, agree to everything that he could legitimately request, and treat him as a friend in order to make him one. It may be, as William C. Bullitt claims, that Roosevelt hoped to win over Stalin as he had won over so many others. Let us not forget, too, that at Yalta Mr. Roosevelt was a dying man. He was sustaining at all costs the coalition that was to crush Hitler and the Third Reich, and he had scarcely begun to think about the conflicts to follow.

There was no need of Soviet aid in defeating Japan: by 1944

probably, and in any case by early 1945, the Mikado was ready to negotiate for peace. But in order to secure capitulation without having to land on the Japanese islands, a promise of Russian intervention in the Far East was asked for and secured at Yalta. Even in Europe, the Anglo-Saxons were afraid that Stalin might leave them to complete alone the destruction of the German armies. They felt weak in Stalin's presence because they envisaged an objective difficult to attain without him. But why had they fixed on that objective?

The Westerners were interested in weakening Germany, but not in destroying her. They wanted to re-establish conservative regimes, and they could not want the Reich to resist to the death. Yet they did nothing to detach and encourage those elements in Germany that opposed the Nazis, nothing to allow the generals or the men in the ranks to anticipate anything but unconditional surrender. They acted as if their purpose were to drive the National Socialists and the nation to defend a common cause; in other words, their actions were completely unreasonable.

Even apart from the rivalry to be expected between the great powers, their attitude toward Germany was hardly justifiable. If the victors really intended to suppress Germany as an independent state and to incorporate her in an empire or a federation, the crushing of the vanquished might have passed as necessary. But nothing of the sort was envisaged. There was no question of re-establishing a federation, as in the time of the American Civil War. There was no national state in Europe that could have kept Germany permanently in subjection. The truth was that the nonrevolutionary powers, even if a new imperial enterprise had not been outlined on the horizon, should for their own sake have spared an enemy that was an indispensable member of the European community. The fact that the Westerners actually encouraged the Germans to continue a hopeless struggle can only be explained by the apparently irresistible momentum of total war. So that it should be the "war to end wars," it was carried to its limit. Because it was carried to its limit, it gave rise to a successor.

It is not known what influence the formula of "unconditional surrender" actually had on the course of events. No one can show that by a different policy the Allies would have avoided the nine last months of war, which have so heavily burdened the peace. It is possible that the conspiracy of July 20 would have failed as it did regardless of the threat of "unconditional surrender." It is possible that, whatever happened, Hitler would have remained faithful to his insistent determination never to surrender. But at least it should have been possible to foment internal opposition in Germany, instead of discouraging it.

It is suggested today that no other policy would have made any difference. Certain promises had been obtained from Stalin in regard to the liberated countries: he did not keep them. In return for lend-lease, it might have been possible to accumulate some additional promises; but how would they have protected Poland or Rumania from Sovietization? Similarly it is conceded that the high American military commanders were mistaken as to the prospects of the campaign against Japan. They feared fierce resistance from an army which was virtually intact, and they estimated losses among invading troops at some hundreds of thousands. They had not taken account of the atomic bomb, which at the time of Yalta was no more than a project, nor of the Emperor, who, faced by his cities in ruins, his Navy almost annihilated, and his islands cut off from all maritime communication, had the power to impose unconditional capitulation even on those who wanted to fight to the bitter end. But, it is added, admitting that miscalculation, what difference could it have made? At the first sign of Japanese surrender, would not the Russian Army still have invaded Manchuria, transferred the Chinese factories to Russia, and handed over the Japanese arms to the local Communists?

It is quite clear that, with or without the assent of the West, the masters of the Kremlin would have attempted to play the game they did play. But they would not have been able to play it in the Far East if Japan had conceded her defeat before the hostilities had ended in Europe. In any case, would not their game have been more difficult if they had not been allowed to camouflage it behind the unity of the Big Three? Would not the diplomatic and moral position of the Western powers have been much stronger if the Sovietization of Poland and Rumania had made its appearance from the beginning as the violation of an agreement and as a proof of imperialism? Finally, if the peril had been realized, why should there not have been an attempt to prevent the arrival of Soviet troops in Eastern Europe by planning an invasion through the Balkans?

The only justification of the Western statesmen is that their conduct of the war was characteristic of democracies in our age: they submitted passively to the dynamism of hyperbolic war. They propagated the simplest and most convincing of myths: the United Nations were the harbingers of Justice, the enemy was the incarnation of Evil. Incapable of thinking about peace, which comes after war and is its real purpose, until the end of the destruction, they made no effort to alienate the German people from the Hitler clique and took no precautions against their ally, whose ambitions were hardly more of a mystery than those of Hitler. By the time the illusions of propaganda were dissipated and the governments in London and Washington had the support of public opinion in their will to resist, the rewards of victory had been lost: Eastern Europe was Sovietized, Germany divided, and the Chinese Communists armed by courtesy of the Russian Army. The Second World War had laid the foundations for the third.

Here as earlier, it could not be said that the outcome did not logically follow the causes. In 1914 the quarrels of nationalism had set fire to Europe: out of the furnace came the Europe of nationalities. In 1939, the German will to empire had plunged Europe anew into a war between irreconcilable opponents. Patriotism was reawakened in resistance to occupation, and the victors re-established the sovereignty of the national states. That restoration was more apparent than real. In the East, the liberated states were subjected to the law of the Soviet Union and its agents, the Communist parties. In the West, they are paying for isolation by impotence and are groping their way towards a supranational organization that will not infringe on their national pride.

Europe today, divided internally and caught between two hostile empires, haunted by the memories of past grandeurs and by resentments—can it live?

Since, under a July sun, bourgeois Europe entered into the century of total war, men have lost control of their history and have been dragged along by the contradictory promptings of techniques and passions. Out of national war came a first imperial war. How far will we be dragged by the chain reactions of violence?

## Chapter III

# THE LENINIST MYTH OF IMPERIALISM

THE CONTRAST between industrial and military societies seemed an obvious fact to many sociologists of the last century. From Saint-Simon to Spencer it was accepted that societies based on peaceful labor and exchange represented a type in marked contrast with societies dominated by the military caste and motivated by ambition for conquest. Europe knows today that industry, far from preventing war, gives it a limitless scope. Consciously or not, contemporary philosophers of history have made this fact central in their thought.

In 1914 the reading of Thucydides and then of Spengler suggested to Professor Arnold Toynbee a comparative theory of cultures. The success of his book, *A Study of History,* is largely due to the fact that this monumental work gives an interpretation of the present "troubled age." But Toynbee's interpretation has a weakness insofar as the masses are concerned. It suggests no remedy. On the contrary he advises us to expect peace through the very exhaustion of violence, and the emergence of universal empire that will subject the belligerent states to its law. Only Marxism gives a rule of action as well as an explanation. The industrial societies, we are told, would be peaceful if they were not capitalist. The internal contradictions of a regime bound up with private ownership and with a free market condemn nations to imperialism and—when the partition of the planet has been completed—to sanguinary conflicts.

The Marxist theory of imperialism appears, in various forms, in the works of Rosa Luxemburg, Bukharin, Lenin, and others. But the ideas common to all of them may be reduced to a few propositions. First, capitalist economy cannot, because of its very structure, absorb its own production,[1] and is therefore compelled to expand; the individual is not even aware of the mechanism that is carrying him away. Second, the race among the European nations to win overseas territories for colonial exploitation is a fatal consequence of competition. In Africa, in Asia, in Oceania, Europeans seek raw materials, markets, places to invest their surplus capital. The period of colonial expansion marks a stage of capitalist development characterized by the dominance of financial capital and the power of monopolies. Third, the European wars are the fatal result of imperialism: their real stake is the division of the planet, even though they may be set off by some European dispute. They are accelerated by the growing disparity between the mother countries and the colonial empires—by the advent of the era of the closed world. Having reached the limits of the planet, the will to power that has driven the capitalists to the remotest corners of the world now must turn upon itself.

This theory enjoys tremendous prestige even in non-Marxist circles. It is intellectually satisfying because it accounts for a variety of circumstances. The interest in the Near East manifested by Britain, and more recently by the United States, is measured in terms of the oil resources of this region. The Boer War is linked with the South African gold mines, and with the propaganda carried on in London by agents of large development companies. In the course of the last twenty years of the nineteenth century the European nations carved out empires in Africa for themselves, and simultaneously the foremost of these nations (with the exception of England) returned to protectionism. The great German coal and steel trusts financed a press campaign for an ambitious program of naval construction before 1914, just as they financed National Socialism before 1933; similarly, certain American trusts torpedoed the disarmament conferences. The First World War ended in a partition of the German colonies among the victors, and if the Germans had won, they would have done the same thing—an

---

[1]This was the concept particularly of Rosa Luxemburg, which Lenin refused to accept in such a simplified form.

assumption for which their notorious plan for an "African belt" is sufficient proof.

But the objections to these summary and superficial interpretations are as strong as the arguments adduced in their favor are plausible. There is no relation between the purely economic need for expansion, such as should have obtained according to theory, and the actual facts of colonial expansion. French capitalism was one of the least dynamic in Europe yet the African empire that France acquired at the end of the nineteenth century is second in importance only to that of Great Britain. Russia, which at that time was only entering upon its capitalistic career and whose immense territory was still undeveloped, was nevertheless diplomatically active both in Europe and in Asia. The Russian interest in Manchuria and in the Slavic peoples of Europe was not dictated by economic considerations, nor was it the result of capitalist machinations.

Neither the First nor the Second World War originated directly in a conflict over colonies. Morocco was provocation for several international crises, yet all were settled by diplomatic negotiations —it was as though none of the great powers regarded these remote rivalries as sufficient justification for resorting to arms. The twenty years preceding the first war were probably among the most prosperous in the history of capitalism. The discovery of the Transvaal gold mines had resulted in a steady advance in prices, which was not accompanied—as it had been during the preceding advance in prices—by a slowing down of mechanization and technological progress: it was rather linked with an acceleration of these processes, owing to a number of new discoveries. The prevailing protective tariffs remained moderate, the national income of Germany doubled in twenty years, international trade continued to grow. Therefore, the image of a Europe constrained by its economic contradictions to destroy itself is a myth.

It will not be denied that capitalism tends to incorporate undeveloped territories into its system. Nor is it to be denied that colonial conquest may be regarded as a function of economic expansion. But whatever the plausibility of such a view, two questions remain to be answered: Were the African colonial empires founded in accordance with this pattern? Were the European

wars a consequence of these quarrels for the division of the planet?
The facts, if invoked without bias, answer these two questions
negatively.

During the period between 1870 and 1914, there were instances
in which the diplomatic services of nations were mobilized on
behalf of capitalists, and in which they vigorously defended certain
private investments (as in Venezuela and Persia). Not that Foreign
Ministers were manipulated by capitalists, but they felt there were
valid reasons for defending certain economic positions. The fact
is that under the system of private ownership, the ambitions of
certain corporations are genuinely identical with national interests.
But (except for the Boer War, which was largely the result of
intrigues by a large development company)[2] none of the colonial
undertakings that caused important diplomatic conflicts in Europe
was motivated by the quest for capitalist profits; they all originated
in political ambitions that the chancelleries camouflaged by invoking "realistic" motives. In other words, the actual relationship is
most often the reverse of that accepted by the current theory of
imperialism: the economic interests are only a pretext or a rationalization, whereas the profounder cause lies in the nations' will to
power.

The timber concessions on the Yalu River that gave rise to the
Russo-Japanese War were not the result of a business deal in the
current sense of this term.[3] The shareholders could not expect divi-
dends during the first years. The 20,000 forest rangers sent in as a
vanguard were actually disguised Russian soldiers. The company
was founded by highly placed individuals who wished to interest
the Tsar's court in an enterprise whose purpose was not profit but
control of Korea. From the very outset, the objective was conquest.

Nor was the French protectorate in Tunisia established by governments taking orders from industrialists or financiers. Neither
the Mejerda railroad, nor the concession granted to Count de
Sauvy, nor the agitation of the Société Marseillaise would have
influenced the Quai d'Orsay if the latter had not seen in the estab-

[2] It should be added that Cecil Rhodes was rather the conqueror acting for
the glory of his country than the businessman eager to amass profits.
[3] E. Staley, *War and the Private Investor* (New York: Doubleday, 1935),
p. 55.

lishment of the Tunisian protectorate an appropriate complement to the conquest of Algeria.[4]

The same holds true for Morocco, in relation both to Germany and to France. The Wilhelmstrasse[5] took the Mannesmann brothers' concession under its protection not because it was under the orders of the concessionaires, but because it was glad to have a pretext for intervention. It regretted the fact that banking circles and big industry were so unconcerned with Morocco. *Die deutschen Banken streiken geradezu alle, sobald man von Marokko spricht* (All German banks simply go on strike at the first mention of Morocco). After the agreement of 1911, when negotiations were opened between the financial representatives of the two countries, it was the objections of the chancelleries and the political apprehensions that brought about their collapse.

This survey could easily be extended. The celebrated Berlin-Baghdad railway was a political project, and the German banks consented—with great reluctance—to interest themselves in it only under pressure from the Wilhelmstrasse. The Bank of Rome extended its operations in Tripoli at the instigation of the Italian Minister of Foreign Affairs. It was granted discount privileges on condition that it would invest capital in Tripoli. Once these interests had been created, the relationship was reversed and the banks campaigned in favor of an active policy. The diplomats created economic interests in the hope that the defense of these interests would result in territorial acquisitions.

The legendary interpretation can be accounted for quite readily. Colonialist statesmen, such as Jules Ferry, for instance, constantly invoked economic arguments—the prospect of acquiring naval bases, markets for products, reserves of raw materials, etc. Nothing was easier than to take such arguments literally and transform them into the real causes. It is of course possible that such long-range interests were among the motives of the statesmen. All that the documents disclose is that the initiative came from them. And it is a fact that in each epoch conquerors have found different formulas for masking the will to power, which appears to be one of the unchanging features of European communities.

[4] *Ibid.,* pp. 327–99.

[5] *Ibid.,* p. 178.

It is certain that, once a territory has been acquired, enterprising individuals and companies seek to exploit the protected areas. While this exploitation is not the primary purpose of the governments, they conceive it as one of the advantages of conquest. More than that, at a time when thinking everywhere is dominated by economic considerations, the so-called colonialists can increase the popularity of their cause by using these considerations to justify it. The public might turn away from them or rebel if they spoke of glory or national greatness.

As for the capitalists, why should it be surprising that their conduct does not conform with the pattern ascribed to it by Marxism? From the standpoint of big industry and the great banking houses of the Second Reich, there were less dangerous and more profitable enterprises than Morocco or the Berlin-Baghdad railway. The more Germany asserted her claim to a place in the world market, the more did the capitalist leaders have cause to fear a European war. In 1911, the falling stock exchange prices and the intervention of great financiers with the Kaiser contributed to the peaceful solution of the crisis. For capitalism, a war meant the risk of losing more than could be gained in Morocco.

On the other hand, it would be just as erroneous to imagine that large-scale German capitalism was devoted to the preservation of peace. The truth is that nothing in living reality conforms to this vague concept of "German capitalism," a system which did not constitute an entity aware of itself, pursuing long-range objectives and manipulating popular masses and governments to serve its ambition. In actual fact, its activities were varied, contradictory, changing with different individuals and circumstances. The membership of the naval and pan-Germanic leagues was for the most part lower middle class and nationalistic in character. In wartime, manufacturers' associations launched projects intended to ruin foreign competitors when peace came. In the event of victory, they would have clamored for the annexation of Lorraine and the African colonies; with similar motives, German banks and industrial establishments colonized the occupied territories between 1940 and 1944. Some sectors were oriented toward peaceful trade, others were largely inspired by imperialist ambition. In actual fact, capitalist circles, with their hesitations and their divergent views, reflected public opinion far more than they formed it. The central idea of Lenin's theory is this: Twentieth-century wars, though waged in Europe and precipitated by European conflicts, have as their stake and their meaning the division of the planet. The main difficulty in trying to refute this theory is that it is difficult to see how it can be proved and by the same token how it can be disproved. No one denies that the First World War broke out because of German-Slav rivalry in the Balkans. Nor does anyone deny that the victors did not return to Germany the colonies they had occupied during the hostilities, and that secret agreements had provided for the division of these colonies among the Allies. No one questions the fact that if Germany had been victorious she would have seized at least part of the French and British empires. It can therefore be taken for granted that the immediate cause of the war had nothing to do with overseas territories, and that the issue of the war inevitably implied a new division of the colonies. Beyond these facts, we are in the realm of interpretations.

The burden of proof obviously rests upon those who attribute to events a deep significance of which the protagonists were unaware. In neither of the two camps did statesmen believe that the acquisition of distant possessions justified a European war, or that the economic system had no choice but to expand. It is true that the victorious camp profited from the occasion to seize the colonies of the defeated camp; but this, of itself, does not introduce any new factor into the process of European history, and in no way proves that Frenchmen, Englishmen, or Germans—though they thought they were fighting to preserve the power or prestige of their respective nations—really fought because the capitalists, having reached the ends of the earth, had finally no other choice but to resort to arms to enlarge their respective shares in the territory of the world.

In forming national alignments, as in unleasing international hostilities, it is easy to discover the influence of traditional or emotional conflicts; but they supply no proof of the allegation that in our time capitalist rivalries exercise sovereign sway over human fate. Though the French penetration of Morocco created an additional reason for discord, France and Germany, whose economies were to a far greater extent complementary than competing, had never become reconciled after 1870. The French, while not calling for a war to recover Alsace-Lorraine, had not morally ratified the amputation of its territory. Moreover, calculations of the most classic kind regarding the balance of forces made them reject the idea of joining their powerful neighbor. If France had allied herself to her incomparably stronger neighbor she would have lost almost all of her independence, while as an ally of a naval power or of a distant land power, she essentially retained it. Such diplomatic mechanisms mark all eras.

Nor does the conflict between Russia and Austria-Hungary or Germany seem to be essentially economic in origin. To be sure, their interests may have been in conflict at one point or another. But Russia's interests—which, incidentally, were more political than economic—clashed, in Persia and in Afghanistan, with those of Great Britain more than with those of any other European nation. It was the fate of the European Slavs that definitely set apart Tsarist Russia from the other empires, despite their common conservatism, their wish to preserve the dynastic principle, and their fear of revolutionary movements.

The only way of giving some plausibility to the interpretation espoused by Marxist sympathizers is to represent the war of 1914–18 as having been determined above all by German-British rivalry, and then to represent this rivalry as an effect of trade competition. Many German publicists defended this thesis out of other motives. Desiring to clear their country of all guilt, to represent it as a victim of jealous "have" nations, they made a great deal of articles published in the English press at the end of the nineteenth century and more especially the beginning of the twentieth century—articles fulminating against the expansion of Germany, which was described as a deadly threat to Britain, and suggesting a resort to arms as the only means of saving Old Albion's prosperity.

Actually such voices were isolated, and did not in any way reflect the opinion of leading banking, industrial, or political circles. It was rather the opposite concept, as developed by Norman Angell in his well-known book, *The Great Illusion,* that underlay the predominant opinion. Angell's central thesis was that modern war does not pay, that the annexation of provinces does not increase the wealth of the inhabitants of the victorious country. National wealth is increased by a certain amount, but this must be divided by a proportionately increased denominator; in the end everyone finds himself where he was before. One may try to eliminate a rival. But in doing so one loses a customer and a supplier, and the effect of the deprivation inflicted on one's neighbor rebounds upon oneself. Modern economy creates solidarity among the nations. The idea of sharing spoils, of seizing treasures, belongs to another age. In the century of industry and trade, war would deal a fatal blow to everyone, victors and vanquished; in the damage sustained by the capitalist system, no one would be spared.

This demonstration, which is valid on the whole if Angell's implicit assumptions are granted (the existence of a world system and of respect for individual property on the part of belligerents),[6] holds true in regard to the relations between Britain and Germany, as became evident after 1918. Leading circles in the two countries were perfectly aware of the fact, even though the competition between them was very real. Germany and Britain were first-rank customers and suppliers for each other.[7] In 1913, more than 20 per cent of Germany's imports came from the British Empire, which in turn absorbed more than 18 per cent of German exports. Germany bought 1.168 million marks' worth of British products, and Britain bought 1.534 million marks' worth of German products. In her capacity as banker, carrier, and underwriter, England drew indirect profits from German exports.

It is true that from 1904 to 1913 German exports increased by 93 per cent—while British exports increased by only 74.7 per cent. But the per capita figure for volume of national exports remained far higher in Britain—233 marks as against 150. Moreover, the exports of the two countries were for the most part channeled in different directions: 66 per cent of British exports went to non-European areas, while 76 per cent of German exports went to European markets. This divergence did not bar all friction: here and there German products displaced British products. But a British

[6] It goes without saying, indeed, that if Germany confiscates Czech property in Czechoslovakia for the benefit of Germans, or if the Czech Government confiscates Sudeten property for the benefit of the Czechs, one national community is enriched thereby and another impoverished. But in 1908 the possibility of such practices was not yet imagined.

[7] A. M. Mertz, *Nationalgeist Und Politik* (Zurich: 1937), p. 261 ff.

government or capitalist class that was led by these marginal frictions to conclude that it was imperative to crush the competitor by force of arms would have been acting like the folk-tale hero who killed the goose that laid the golden egg. Before accepting an interpretation implying motives that may seem rational but are actually absurd, one should have proof. There is, however, no proof; rather, there is proof to the contrary.

It was during the phase of declining prices, from 1880 to 1895, that trade competition between the two countries was most intense, and the diplomatic relations between them at their best. After the turn of the century, the general economic upswing reduced the trade rivalry, while at the same time diplomatic relations between them deteriorated. There is no mystery in this development, for diplomatic alignments are determined not by conditions of economic rivalry or solidarity, but by considerations of power, by racial or cultural affinities, by the passions of the masses. Economically, Britain's outstanding rival since the beginning of the century has consistently been the United States. Yet the two Anglo-Saxon powers have never been on the verge of going to war against each other. Hence this admirable statement in a recent Soviet publication: "The characteristic feature of this contradiction [between Britain and the United States] lies in the fact that it unfolds within the framework of close co-operation, both economic and diplomatic." The truth is that trade rivalries between nations are one thing, and life-and-death struggles another. There is little truth in the myth that millions of men were sent to their deaths to open up markets for industries.

The essential cause of the hostility between Britain and Germany was Germany's creation of a navy. By threatening or seeming to threaten British naval supremacy, Germany, perhaps without realizing it, precipitated a break that contributed to creating the diplomatic conjuncture out of which the explosion took place. The British people know that for them control of the seas is neither a matter of prestige nor a luxury, but a question of survival. The naval policy of Wilhelm II and Von Tirpitz could be interpreted only as a challenge, and it necessarily drove Britain into joining the Franco-Russian alliance.

It might be said that Britain would under no circumstances have tolerated the annihilation of France, and that she would have intervened whether Von Tirpitz built his fleet or not. We do not have to confirm or reject this consideration, because it is irrelevant to our main thesis—that military alignments are political in origin. It was not without bitterness that Britain yielded her hegemony in the air and on the seas to the United States. She would never have yielded it, without a fight to the end, to the Germany of the Kaiser or Hitler.

Whereas the First World War followed a period of rising prices and expanding international trade, the second broke out ten years after the beginning of the greatest depression in the history of capitalism. In most countries recovery had taken place several years before the war, and production levels were generally higher than before the depression. But this recovery had a special character: it had taken place within each nation. International trade, instead of continuing to develop as in the preceding century, had not recovered its pre-1929 volume, and the dominant economy, that of the United States, had not overcome a condition of underemployment that seemed chronic. One would have to be blind or fanatic to deny that there was a relation between the slump of 1929 and the war of 1939.

One of the immediate causes of National Socialism's rise to power was indisputably the unprecedented economic crisis, with its concomitant factor of millions of unemployed. But the exceptional acuteness of the crisis, particularly in Germany, cannot be attributed to the effects of the autonomous evolution of the capitalist system. A sequence of events, accidental in relation to world economic developments (the financial policy of Great Britain, the rate of exchange for the pound, the use of the gold exchange standard, the pyramiding of credits in the United States, the high level of world prices, which were made dependent on American prices following the wartime inflation, the German inflation, the accumulation of foreign loans, etc.), had brought about the situation of 1929 and the collapse that followed. It would be possible to show that many of these accidents originated directly or indirectly in the First World War and its aftermath. Nevertheless, it is a fact that the road from Versailles to the September aggression against Poland leads through the depression of 1929. Assuming that this depression was, in a way, a consequence of the First World War, it is even more certain that it was one of the causes of the second.

Between 1930 and 1933, the Germany of the Weimar regime, stricken by unemployment, had a choice between three possible orientations. She could adapt her domestic economy to world conditions; she could undertake total planning under the leadership of the workers' party, which was inclined to co-operate with Soviet Russia, or she could undertake planning under the leadership of the "national" parties, with rearmament and diplomatic aggressiveness.[8] The second solution was ruled out by the existing balance of strength and by the popular passions. Moreover, by concentrating its attack on the "social traitors," the Communist Party was robbing the parties of the left of the small chances of success they might have had. Neither the masses nor the parties were willing to accept the sacrifices implied in the first solution. Adjustment to world economic conditions would probably have required a devaluation of the mark (which was unpopular because of memories of the inflation); failing that, a lowering of nominal wages (which was resisted by the trade unions) and a credit policy inspired by the theories of Keynes. Recovery under these conditions would have been slow and gradual. It would logically have implied a diplomatic armistice over a period of a few years. But nationalistic feeling among the people had been exacerbated by economic distress and by the propaganda against the Treaty of Versailles. Rightist circles were impatient to recover sovereignty with regard to armaments. The coalition of the Hitlerites and the nationalists, symbol of the rapprochement between the revolutionaries and the traditional conservatives, was founded on the common will to achieve certain objectives: liquidation of unemployment on a national basis, rearmament, and revision of the Treaty of Versailles.

We shall not contend that the former ruling classes unanimously desired this solution, and the share of responsibility of each group remains a matter of controversy—namely: How much individual responsibility is to be attributed to the financiers and captains of industry, who contributed money to the National Socialist movement; and to the Rhenish bankers and East Prussian landowners, who

[8]Undoubtedly a policy of full employment on a national scale, without imperialistic designs, was conceivable. But the partisans of a National Socialism wanted also to pursue a dynamic diplomacy.

brought about the coalition of January 1933? All formulas ascribing a specific attitude to any single one of the ruling classes have always been semi-mythical in character. There was no want of conservatives who were uneasy about the brown-shirted demagogues. All that can be said is that in the seizure of power by the National Socialists, the prerequisite was the consent to this adventure given by a fraction of the former ruling classes. Apprentice sorcerers, these men expected the Führer to subject the masses to discipline, to reintegrate the millions of the unemployed into the Army or to absorb them in the factories, to restore sovereignty and power to Germany; they, no more than others, wanted the thing that came to an end in the bunker of Berlin, with the crushing of their homeland.

Unemployment—that is, the economic depression—was at the root of rearmament. The formula according to which unemployment was its cause greatly oversimplifies the truth. The United States had more than 12 million unemployed, yet neither the masses nor the leaders thought of mobilizing an army or building a war industry. The resort to a war economy was natural for the Germans, faithful to their military traditions and anxious to alter, if not to supersede, the status imposed by the Treaty of Versailles. In one way or another, a little sooner or a little later, Germany would have demanded and obtained equality, demanded if not obtained a revision of the treaties of peace. On the other hand, it was not implied in the permanent elements of the German situation that a man like Hitler and a party like the National Socialist must inevitably seize power. War was implied in the style and in the ambitions of the National Socialists, not in those of the traditional nationalists.

Once rearmament had begun and the theory of full employment on a national basis was applied, was war inevitable? Did rearmament lead to aggression, just as unemployment had led to rearmament? Did the economic system of the Third Reich rule out the peace or even the truce that, on the eve of the seizure of Prague, a British trade delegation once again offered to the Berlin rulers? These questions are abstract and, in a sense, unreal. Hitler and his companions had always thought in political and not in economic terms. What they wanted for their country was power, the reward of which would be to attain the wealth of a master nation. They never asked themselves whether they could ever call a halt from an economic standpoint, for from 1939 on they had not had the slightest intention of doing so. Occasionally, at least, Hitler directly wanted war, which he thought he alone could wage victoriously, and which he regarded as indispensable for the realization of his schemes. The National Socialist system itself derived from a will to empire.

Would not Hitler have been driven at all events, by force of the economic system that he erected, to attempt conquest? This thesis is advanced by pseudo-Marxists who allege that they discover in Schachtism the same imperialist fatality they ascribe to monopoly capitalism. It is also advanced by other critics, according to whom National Socialism or Hitler himself would have been endangered by a peace, even a provisional one.

From 1938 on, after the departure of Schacht, the economic situation changed. What was feared was no longer unemployment but inflation. Not only had full employment been achieved, but there was a manpower shortage. An attempt was launched to transform the small shopkeepers, whose votes had been won by means of demagogic attacks against the Jews and the department stores, into industrial workers. At that moment, Schacht had advocated a pause. He wanted to stop issue of workers' bonds or short-term bonds because there were no longer unemployed men or machines to incorporate into the productive process. Therefore it seemed absurd to maintain that the non-resumption of private investment was threatening the economy of the Third Reich with a collapse that only war could have prevented.

In 1934, the theory of pump-priming was refuted: a limited dosage of supplementary purchasing power, created by means of public works projects, had proven insufficient to create general prosperity. Private investments had remained at a standstill. The Government had to assume the task that it had hoped to leave to the initiative of the entrepreneurs. But in 1938 and in 1939, the situation was quite different: after rearmament, after the four-year plan and the annexation of Austria and of Czechoslovakia, the Third Reich did not have to choose between military conquest and a relapse into economic stagnation.

But, it might be objected, was the threat not from another direction—namely, was it not caused by the shortage of foreign currency, needed to buy the foodstuffs that the soil of the Third Reich did not supply;[9] and the raw materials that its substratum, even after the extension of its territory, did not contain? The conquests had aggravated rather than corrected the disparity. Neither Austria nor Czechoslovakia was self-sufficient; both imported a part of their food supply, and both were bound to the world economy more than was the Reich. It is not to be disputed that in March 1939 autarchy was an ideal as remote, as inaccessible, as it had been at the outset of the adventure. In the long run, from a philosophical point of view, it might be said that the choice between integration into world economy and a supranational economy based on a *Grossraum,* an expanded national territory, continued to present itself. But the need for decision was not urgent. The Western democracies were ready to appease by concessions. Once again, Hitler was not subjected to any economic restraint.

Would Hitler's authority or his regime have been shaken by a truce? Would Hitler have lost part of the prestige he had won by his peaceful triumphs? There is nothing to justify an affirmative answer to these questions. In September 1938 the German people dreaded a general war almost as much as the British and French peoples dreaded it. They would not have found fault with their Führer for saving the peace; rather they would have taken the contrary attitude. After Munich, Germany held a hegemony over Central Europe that was more complete than that which had been refused the Kaiser's Germany before 1914. But so long as there was the Soviet Union on one side, and the Franco-British alliance on the other, the hegemony over *Mitteleuropa* fell short of assuring a European empire. The truth, concealed under the allegations of political or economic necessity, is that Hitler was not content with his hegemony. He wanted to take advantage of his temporary superiority in armament at least to liquidate Poland. And therewith he unleashed the monster.

The economy of the Third Reich gave rise to multiple incitements to imperial aggrandizement. Norman Angell's reasoning does not apply to a system such as that of National Socialist Germany. According to the English pacifist, it is immaterial whether a province containing mines and factories lies on this or that side of the frontier signs. If it is within the frontier, the populations of other

[9] The Reich imported about 15 per cent of its food supply from abroad.

provinces wishing to obtain coal or manufactured products must send goods of equal value in exchange to the national or other producer.[10] But when relations between various economic units are restricted as a result of non-convertibility of their currencies and control of foreign trade, the argument loses its force. If the coal or iron mines are situated beyond the borders of a given unit, that unit will be obliged to exploit poorer mines within its borders, and to consent to increased expenditures for equipment and labor. Otherwise coal or iron will have to be purchased by means of goods that will then be insufficient for other exchanges. In other words, in the case of National Socialism, the location of the frontier posts is of great importance: trade within economic units and trade *between* economic units become different in character.

Inevitably, a partisan of National Socialism inclines to the theory of the *Grossraum*. The authoritarian organization of an economic whole develops the more smoothly, the fewer are the obstacles encountered by the will of the planners. By definition, the planners possess no authority over the people and the raw materials situated on the other side of the customs line. They cannot foresee the free prices of the raw materials they must import, nor can they foresee the changing tastes of those who, by buying their manufactured products, supply them from the outside with foreign currency. Compulsory subjection to the foreign customer means the survival of a principle which the planners are attempting to suppress at home. Subjection changes into sovereignty on the day when sellers and buyers have been reduced by force of arms to the common law of a planned economy.

Russia, though lagging behind in her equipment, was better adjusted to the so-called Marxist experiment because she was less dependent on international trade than any other European country. Capable in an emergency of being more or less self-sufficient, she could resist the blockade and apply to the full the idea of authoritarian planning. But when applied to national economies that are traditionally bound up with world economy, the same method inevitably gives rise to imperialist temptations. The ambition for conquest and

---

[10]It goes without saying that in this reasoning the problem is simplified and schematized. Even in a free-trade period, boundary lines have their importance, although it is less.

the dream of rationalization are combined in the *Grossraum* theory.

Thus we are far from denying the imperialistic potentialities of the economic policy adopted by the National Socialists. We maintain only that the Third Reich was not driven to imperialism by residues of capitalism in its structure. If the private entrepreneurs or managers had been replaced by government-appointed managers, if the Ruhr had been nationalized, if the planning had been total, the imperialist temptation would not have been mitigated. Indeed, the opposite is true. If German heavy industry had become collective property, it would have been no less disproportionate to the needs of the domestic market for peaceful consumption. The need for outside purchase of supplies for the people and for the factories, the wish to include in the plan a territory as vast as possible, would have persisted. In short, the contradiction between the essence of modern economy and National Socialism, between political nationalism and the industrial system, would not have been overcome, and this contradiction is the ultimate cause of the suicide of Europe.

This contradiction, as we have seen, emerged only during the course of the First World War. A traditional conflict was amplified into a superwar because of the weapons that industry placed at the disposal of the combatants. In the years preceding 1939, the contradiction became more acute. The disturbances that followed the war, the depression of 1929, had thrown the states back upon the expedients of controlled trade, of planning in isolation from world economy. National Socialism marked the extreme form of this falling back on intranational resources. Such a structure is not favorable either to peaceful international trade, or to the peaceful coexistence of empires. Although the motives of the protagonists were political, although the conqueror was inspired by the will to power, Europe, before the Hitlerian adventure, was torn by an absurd situation. The European nations do not offer a rational framework for planned economy.

Modern industry and militarism have always been associated throughout the centuries of their simultaneous flowering. Although none of the fundamental discoveries that made the industrial revolution possible seems to have been occasioned by military needs, such discoveries have often accelerated progress or given rise to improvements in manufacturing methods. Assembly-line production in metallurgy and textiles was partly the effect of military requirements, and at the same time it determined the tempo of the battles.

Current expressions emphasize the analogies between the style of modern industry and that of the army. In order to create an army, thousands, hundreds of thousands, and finally millions of men must be uprooted from a communal, organic mode of life and subjected to a hierarchy organized in accordance with the sole imperative of collective action and performance. Industry gives rise to a similar process. Factory discipline is not the same as the discipline of the barracks; the worker, outside his shop, continues to have a family life. Nevertheless there is an unquestionable similarity between the two, and the labor camps of wartime Germany and of five-year plans in Russia stress this similarity to the point of horror.

The evolution of capitalism during the second half of the nineteenth century and the first years of the twentieth century had opened up a different perspective. Humanization of industrial work had seemed not impossible. Higher living standards had made it possible to restore to the worker the personal life of which he had been deprived during the stage of initial accumulation, the pioneer stage of the coal, textile, and metallurgic industries. The municipal workers' quarters in Sweden, in Germany—like those later erected in some English centers—no longer evoked the image of the "wretched of the earth." At least a part of the proletariat was gradually obtaining decent living conditions. Increasing access to middle-class comforts was mitigating the isolation of the worker and the amorphism of the masses. The industrial army was slowly returning to civilian life.

The wars did not halt the rise of the working class; in some respects, in some countries, they accelerated it. But they brought forth a danger that the bourgeoisie, during its time of glory, had never dreamed of—the subjection of all of society to the law of military organization. At the very moment when economic progress was helping to cure some of the evils chargeable to technology, war has brought about the total mobilization of collectivities. Tomorrow the rule of the bourgeoisie may seem like a precarious transition from the military order of the aristocracies to the military order of the technocracies.

*Chapter IV*

# WAR AND THE TOTAL STATE

MORALISTS through all the ages have deplored war and its ravages. Historians and sociologists, while not justifying war, have recognized an indirect benefit from it: more than once in the past it has made possible the formation of wider political units, the enlargement of pacified zones, the expansion of certain forms—described as higher forms—of civilization. No one has ever been able to arrive at an exact calculation of the price paid, in lives and in irreplaceable values, for the building of empires exalted by the grandnephews of the vanquished. In spite of uncertainties, it does not seem unreasonable to praise Demosthenes, the belated defender of the independence of Athens, without cursing Philip or Alexander. City states had outlived their historical function. Greece, united thanks to the armies of Macedon, was able to undertake the great adventures in the East. Even the phrase, *delenda est Carthago,* which our children learn at school without realizing its unspeakable cruelty, has not remained, as it should have done, a symbol of barbarity—so convinced was posterity of the benefits of *pax Romana.*

In our age the optimism of the historian, reflecting the good conscience of the victors, has rightly been challenged. It is preferable now to come to the defense of those who succumbed. What right has anyone to suppose that the civilization of Carthage was of less value than that of Rome? Did the Celts gain by Romanization? Simone Weil has carried to its extreme this reversal of perspectives: condemning violence itself, she ends by condemning every conqueror. This extreme attitude is no more satisfactory than its opposite. To ratify every historical judgment is to justify force in principle, and leads in practice to opportunism (unless, by an act of faith, one assumes knowledge of the truth about the future); but indiscriminate rejection is a denial in principle that force can ever be necessary for the emergence of a state or a social order, and carries with it a gospel of passivity.

Sociologists, neither admiring nor rejecting force, have asked themselves whether the wars of the twentieth century have still anything to set to their credit, alongside the crushing debit of millions of dead and miles of ruins.

In absolute figures, the wars of the twentieth century have probably caused more deaths than any wars of the past.[1] Even if we calculate the losses in proportion to total population, they are among the most murderous in all history. The men who fell on the battlefields between 1914 and 1918 represented 3.4 per cent of the total population of France and 3 per cent of that of Germany. If we take account of indirect losses (excess of deaths over normal mortality and deficit in births), France lost 7.7 per cent of her population and Germany 8 per cent. But from another point of view it should not be forgotten that the 20 million human lives destroyed (Russia excluded) by shot and shell, by poison gas, and by the epidemic of 1919, were nearly equivalent to the normal increase in the population of Europe in ten years. The natural plagues of famine and pestilence in the past caused incomparably greater ravages.

Different countries suffered unequally. The political and moral sequel of the hemorrhage was prolonged in France, lasting at least through the period between the wars and perhaps beyond them. Modern war produces reverse selection: it spares the old and the malingerers, and eliminates the young and courageous. The relations between the age classes were in danger of being permanently

[1]Statistics of the losses attributable to wars will be found in *A Study of War* by Quincy Wright (Chicago: Univ. of Chicago Press, 1942), and in *Social and Cultural Dynamics* by P. Sorokin (New York: American Book Co., 1937), particularly Vol. I, appendix 21.

modified.[2] Despite these reservations, the broad observations remain significant.

The first war of the twentieth century was more costly than those of the previous century (but for France probably less costly than the wars of the Revolution and the Empire); yet it did not inflict incurable wounds on the peoples of Europe. Some sociologists regard war as a method of eliminating excess population; if such a theory were adopted, it would have to be said that in this respect it is remarkably inefficient. Epidemics, civil wars, deportations all cut down human lives at a much greater rate.

Apart from Russia and Germany, the European countries were less affected by the second war than by the first. The total losses in France, about 800,000 (including the probable deficit in the birthrate) were made good in less than three years by excess births. The direct losses of the United States were demographically insignificant (some 250,000); the increase of population continued during hostilities. In the postwar years there has been observed in Europe an increase in the birthrate which had already begun during the hostilities. Contrary to all reasoning, but in accordance with an instinct deeper than reasoning, the anguish of disasters revived the will to live. The countries aided by the Marshall Plan have some 10 per cent more mouths to feed than before 1939.

These, it is true, are the countries that did not experience the horrors of total war. Britain was bombed,[3] but not invaded. She fought no battles on the Continent comparable with those in Flanders. The American armies at all times had such superiority in material resources that as a rule they were prodigal in munitions but economical in blood. The great aero-naval engagements were fought and won by a few thousand combatants. The sanguinary conquests of certain strategic positions (e.g. Okinawa) involved only some tens of thousands of men. Only Germany and Russia fought to the end of the Continental war. Only Poland suffered the extreme rigors of occupation and attempted a general popular in-

[2] Between 1914 and 1918, 20 per cent of the men between the ages of 20 and 44 were killed in France, 15 per cent in Germany, 10 per cent in Great Britain.

[3] In 1942 traffic accidents caused more deaths (6,926) than the bombings (3,221), and more casualties (147,544) than the total casualties in the armed forces during the two first years of the war (145,012).

surrection. Only Yugoslavia experienced simultaneously guerrilla warfare and a ferocious civil war. Here and there the losses, both absolute and relative, were considerable.

For the Soviet Union, the figure of 17 million has been given (7 million military and 10 million civilian losses), representing about 10 per cent of the population; for Poland, 4 to 5 millions, about 15 per cent of the population; for Yugoslavia, 15 millions, or more than 10 per cent; for Germany, 3 million soldiers and some hundreds of thousands of civilians, or about 5 per cent (but to this figure must be added the German prisoners who died in Russia or were permanently interned in the camps, as well as the falling off in births attributable to events during and after the hostilities).

The Polish losses have a special character. More than 3 million Jews were simply exterminated. In this case the deaths were due not to the war itself but to a particular policy, conceived in advance and put systematically into operation, taking advantage of the war. When in 1939 Hitler proclaimed that, if war broke out, the Jews would not survive it whatever happened, he was, for once, not lying.

Leaving aside the case of the Jews, the effects of these bloodlettings will usually not be lasting. The population increase in Poland, Yugoslavia, and Russia will scarcely be retarded, and certainly not stopped. Only the population of Germany will find it difficult to surmount the shock. Before 1933 the net rate or reproduction had fallen below par. The Hitlerite policy had obtained some results; the rate of net reproduction had risen again to slightly above par. From 1939 to 1945 it was found possible to keep down the deficit of births. In the Western zones the birthrate seems to have become more or less normal again, but what will it be among the 9 million Germans expelled from the annexed territories in the East? A population with a falling birthrate may be affected by the results of a war through several decades—as was shown by the example of France after the wars of the Empire and that of 1914–18.

For the Western countries the second war was less murderous than the first. The effectiveness of armament is not the only factor determining the number of casualties: organization and tactics contribute to reduce them—or, indeed, to increase them. The frontal attacks in Flanders and the battle to exhaustion at Verdun cost the two armies hundreds of thousands of dead and wounded. The lightning victory of the Germans in 1940,[4] and the victory of the Allies in 1944–45, were relatively less costly.

Medical progress permits the saving of a growing proportion of wounded and the combating of epidemics that in other ages carried off more victims than the fighting itself. The number of men in uniform is increasing in absolute figures and even in relation to the total population, but the proportion of casualties among the soldiers engaged tends to diminish.[5]

In any case, the statistics do not bear out the contention that the wars of the twentieth century, even if they were more murderous than those of the past, eat into the physical substance of nations. They greatly change the relative strength of states, they accelerate the demographic decadence of peoples having a low birthrate, but they scarcely diminish the rate of increase of peoples with a high birthrate.

So it is also with the scale of material destruction. It would be easy to accumulate impressive figures on the cost of war and the extent of the destruction it causes. From 1915 to 1918 the extraordinary expenditure of the French state exceeded 125 billion francs, while the normal peace budget was in the neighborhood of 5 billion. The daily cost of the war in Britain was in the neighborhood of 35 million dollars throughout the war's duration. In Germany the daily cost rose from 12 million dollars in 1914 to more than 32 million in 1918.

Similarly there would be no difficulty in collecting statistics on the destruction suffered by France in the course of the two wars, or by Germany and Russia in the second war. For example, the amount of destruction suffered by France during the second war is stated to have amounted to some 5 trillion francs—at the 1950 value of the franc—and the direct and indirect losses to 27 trillion —about three times the national income.

The real problem lies outside the controversies as to how the damage shall be reckoned (cost of reconstruction, of real estate, or of partly worn machinery, and so on). To what extent did the wars

[4] Less than 100,000 casualties, and less than a third of these fatal.

[5] According to Wright, 30 to 50 per cent of the soldiers engaged fell on the field of battle in the Middle Ages. The percentage fell to 20, 15, and 10 in the centuries that followed, and is lower still in our century.

leave the nations permanently impoverished? Does the capacity for destruction now exceed the capacity for construction?

The peoples are still, in some fashion, paying for the wars. The property destroyed must be rebuilt. The billions spent on powder and smoke are definitely lost and might have been devoted to the manufacture of useful objects. But the balance sheets of modern societies are complex, and industry succeeds in repairing quickly some kinds of damage.

Let us first recall a well-known fact, that ten years after the end of the First World War, the national income of the principal belligerents had regained or exceeded prewar levels. Agricultural production had taken seven or eight years to recover the pre-1914 level, industrial production two or three years less; and that period was not entirely governed by the limits of the material productive capacity: again and again market difficulties had slowed down the process of recovery.

The approximate return of the national income to the prewar level does not mean that all classes of the population have recovered a standard of living equal to that of the past. The distribution of income within the nation has changed. The relative situation of individuals has been entirely changed by the rapidly growing number of bankruptcies and equally unjustified fortunes. On the whole the owners of capital have been hit harder than those who depend on their earnings. Those who held government securities, whose real value was reduced by four fifths through inflation, or Russian loans whose value was destroyed by the 1917 revolution, have no opportunity of recovering their investment. But the collectivity restores its means of production within a few years. And once the land is yielding normal harvests and the factories are turning out the former quantity of manufactured products, the quantity of goods offered in the market is not noticeably reduced. The general statistics of the standard of living confirm this approximate equality of goods available.

In financial terms, governments can finance modern wars partly by taxation, partly by borrowing or by simply issuing paper money. When the circuit is closed, the monetary resources placed on the market by budget deficits return to the state in the form of subscriptions to loans. From 1914 to 1918 the principal belligerent countries financed only an extremely small fraction of their expenditure by taxation. The rules of war economy had not yet been learned. Britain, who least of all presented a bad example in this respect, attained a proportion no better than 25 per cent. Clearly the choice between taxes and loans is not equivalent to that between the bearing of burdens by existing and future generations. Year by year, populations can only consume the goods actually available. During hostilities, consumption depends entirely on the quantity of goods the population can find to buy: taxation, even high taxation, does not make any substantial reduction in that quantity, so long as the incomes distributed exceed the value of the goods in existence. The method of financing: by taxes, loans, or inflation, affects the ultimate value of the currency, the amount of purchasing power in the hands of the public at the end of hostilities, and finally the sharing of the losses suffered by the community between its various groups. The national debt in Britain grew from 650 million pounds to 7.4 billion pounds between 1914 and 1918; the French debt from 33 billion francs to 150 billion. The expansion of internal debts beyond the limits of strict necessity prepared the way for currency depreciation, of which those with fixed incomes were the victims, while those were spared whose incomes automatically increased in proportion as the currency fell. Where the currency was maintained at a steady level, as in Great Britain, the considerable amount of transfers necessary for the payment of interest exerted an influence on the working of the system which cannot be accurately measured.

There is hardly more mystery about the financing of wars in real terms. The sacrifice of investments abroad is equivalent to the dissipation of accumulated wealth. The British and French received extensive credits from abroad. As these were never repaid, Allies and neutrals alike indirectly paid a part of the costs of the war. During the hostilities and the first years of peace, the population paid a further share of war costs in the form of a reduced standard of living. The difference between the normal and the actual civilian consumption liberated resources dissipated in the purchase of guns and tanks. Finally, the failure to maintain capital—houses, lands, factories—is another method of reducing the consumption of the collectivity. It results in temporary impoverishment during the reconstruction phase, and sometimes in a lasting impoverishment if certain elements of capital (such as housing) are never restored.

This method of financing explains the conclusions arrived at by comparing national incomes before the war and ten years after its end. The collective wealth, or at least that part of it that can be expressed in figures, appears to be adversely affected only by the reduction of capital—investments abroad, and the value of certain elements of capital at home. A crisis, such as the one that raged in France from 1930 to 1938, cost the nation, in economic terms, as much as a war. If we compare what the French economic system would have produced under full employment and normal expansion with what was actually produced, the difference amounts to a figure in billions that is no less astronomical than that of the cost of war. The index number of industrial production in 1938 was 20 to 25 per cent below that of 1929: it ought to have been some 10 to 15 per cent above it.

Such is the explanation of the fact that economic systems, whose capacity for production is very extensible, can supply armies without the expenditure of the civil population being seriously cut down. This was the case in the United States. The industrial plant mass-produced war matériel, while continuing to place at the disposal of the civilian population the bulk of its manufactured products.[6] Agriculture, too, was able to increase its harvests to such an extent that, in addition to feeding part of the world, the authorities in Washington were able to dispense almost entirely with rationing. In 1945 the United States found itself richer, not poorer, than in 1939, with an industrial equipment increased by some 50 per cent. The only burden inherited from the war seemed to be the increase in the national debt. Even at that, the service of interest payments did not involve transfers of income great enough to threaten either the currency or the functioning of the system.

In many respects the case of the United States cannot be compared with that of the European countries. The fighting took place far from its territory, and its reserve of productive capacity proved to be enormous. Nevertheless in Europe, too, it would be possible to make the same comparisons of national income as on the morrow of the first war. Five years after the end of the second war in most countries, agricultural production had approximately attained the

---

[6]The manufacture of durable consumption goods—automobiles, washing machines, refrigerators, and the like—was stopped.

prewar volume, industrial production had considerably exceeded it, and real wages were higher than ten years earlier. Even in Germany, in spite of the ruined towns and the millions of emigrants, two years after the currency reform economic activity approached the index numbers of 1936.

And yet these facts do not dispose of the oft-repeated statement that Europe has destroyed itself through the two world wars. The figures we have cited thus far merely argue against a wholesale method of consideration.

Even if we confined ourselves to total figures, our conclusions would call for a series of reservations. The extermination of whole populations, genocide (to use the United Nations term), of which Hitler gave an example, carries us back to the Dark Ages. It is now the fury of the conqueror, and no longer the battle itself that endangers the physical existence of peoples. Just after the first war, at a time when the Germans were in revolt against the demands of the Allies, the German historian Delbrück exclaimed: "Let them do as they will with us; there is one thing they cannot do: kill us." He assumed the existence of civilization. Today, everything that is materially possible is morally possible. And it is materially possible to kill millions of defenseless people, in cold blood, scientifically.

The Hitlerites showed to the world the gas chamber, the Stalinists large-scale deportation. If the populations of entire Soviet autonomous republics have been destroyed or dispersed by this method, no one may exclude the possibility that during or after a third war, long-civilized peoples may be destroyed or dispersed. Finally, without accepting all the apocalyptic prophecies in which certain learned sages revel, it is a fact that a single atomic bomb can exterminate tens of thousands of people. In the course of a third war, the human losses might surpass the capacity of nations to recover.

The loss of human life has been so great in Germany that since the second war the country is probably eliminated for one or two decades from great-power politics. The bombings spread such ruin that, for the first time, modern means of destruction seem to be greater than the modern means of production. Ten to twenty years will be necessary to rebuild the dwellings leveled by bombs. During that period Europeans proud of their culture will live behind hollow façades or in hovels.

Europe represents an artificial concentration in a relatively small area of a population that draws from the soil only a fraction of its nourishment. A workshop for transformation, Western Europe created an industrial civilization, and thanks to the technological lead she had taken, she absorbed a large part of the wealth of the world.

No doubt it will be said that a vigorous civilization should be able to do without income from capital accumulated during a period of hegemony and adapt itself to new conditions. But the European nations are paying the price of a relatively high standard of living, of political democracy, and of social legislation. The economic system loses elasticity and adaptability in proportion as the masses aspire to increased security and as the authorities assume responsibility for guaranteeing the standards acquired. Sudden changes resulting from wars impose tasks of adaptation for which all the necessary qualities are no longer possessed. The rich, ruined by their follies, no longer find it easy to recover their youthful ardor and pioneering spirit.

The wars have not appreciably affected the productive capacity of Europe or the size of her populations. But the first war had impaired the subtle network of institutions, habits, and beliefs that supported the world economic system. The second war carried away the very foundations of the Old World. It is not necessary to kill so many millions of men in order to exhaust the vitality of a civilization.

Undoubtedly war confronts bourgeois societies with an almost insoluble dilemma. These societies adhere spontaneously to a materialist philosophy. Their aim is to assure to everyone the highest possible standard of living. They justify inequality by a kind of ratio between effort and reward. Financial success is accepted because it is taken as evidence of hard work or of intelligence. This logic becomes absurd on the day that shooting begins. Mobilization upsets the relative situations of citizens, without regard to equity. The family whose head—whether employee, artisan, merchant, manufacturer—is mobilized, drops down several notches in the social scale. The family whose head remains in civil employment mounts in the midst of collective hardship. The treatment received is in inverse proportion to merit. The order of values must be reversed, placing sacrifice and devotion to the public good in the front rank.

Aristocratic morality knows nothing of this contradiction. Heroism is of value for its own sake; honor, glory, inner satisfaction, are the warrior's sufficient reward. The European nations drew heavily upon the reserves of traditional beliefs. The populations—peasants, workers, bourgeois—showed that their vitality was unsapped. The development of industry and of wealth had not detracted from courage and patriotism.

On the day after the victory, the revolt in Great Britain and France against the horrors of war found expression in a fierce desire to resume what was regarded as normal life. In Italy and Germany politics were influenced by the inability of the war veterans to adapt themselves to peace conditions. Fascism and National Socialism exalted the ideology that had been popularized throughout four years of propaganda, the promise to build a new order based not on the values of capitalism or Epicureanism but on those of combat. They endeavored to meet the aspirations of the two social categories on which the strength of nations depends: the soldier and the factory worker.

The bourgeois order, like every social order, is laden with injustices. The origins of fortunes are often tarnished or accidental. The transmission of fortunes is easily justified by social considerations, but not so easily by an individualist philosophy which in theory is indifferent to groups lasting through generations. In a period of tranquillity, advancement and decline remain sufficiently closely bound to merits and deficiences not to be regarded as scandalous. All this is entirely changed in time of war. The redistribution of income as a result of inflation multiplies a hundredfold the injustices inherent in a capitalist society. Gambling pays better than hard work, and holders of securities become the victims of speculators. At the front heroic morality repulses bourgeois morality, which is turned to ridicule by the triumph on the home front of the traffickers.[7]

---

[7]During the second war, the perfecting of a directed economy in Great Britain and the United States reduced the activity of speculators. In France, on the other hand, defeat and the occupation gave them an exceptionally favorable field.

The so-called capitalist society is a synthesis of different elements, some of them contradictory. It combines a bourgeois order (respect for the law, industriousness, respectability, thrift, honesty), an industrial order (technical rationalization, labor concentration), and a financial order (abstract representation of wealth, stock exchange, manipulation of securities). Socially, the bourgeois order limited the corrupting activity which speculative finance tends of itself to develop. It offered a prospect of peaceful integration to the workers, who were half excluded from the collectivity.

The Western nations at the end of the nineteenth century, the epoch of their expansion, embraced different moral standards, as they embraced rival but not enemy classes. If the morality of material success reigned alone, it would condemn societies to rapid dissolution. The army has a soul only through the cultivation of heroic values. The administration safeguards its integrity only through its sense of public service. Skilled workers and laborers must believe in an ethic of their trade; businessmen, shopkeepers, and bourgeois must subscribe to the rule of law as an unconditional imperative. War exalts at first but subsequently distorts the worship of heroism, which in time of peace is too often transformed into a romantic worship of violence; it multiplies the taste for speculation, which, by aggravating the fluidity of conditions, renders wealth less respected because less respectable, and poverty more difficult to accept because in fact it is less acceptable; it devalues professional morality, of workers as well as of employers; it builds up individuals, upsets the ordinary relations within the hierarchy, makes claimants more impatient while reducing the means of satisfying them; it effaces traditions. It clears the way for the building of the totalitarian state.

Wars always resemble the societies that wage them. Throughout the centuries there has been a reciprocal adjustment between tools and arms, between class relations and the structure of armies. A common way of life is reflected or expressed in a certain art of fighting, as the latter by repercussion modifies the former. In the golden age of chivalry knights encased in steel dominated the battlefields. The harquebusiers, who delivered death at a distance— much to the indignation of the nobility—prepared the way for the fall of feudalism, which was completed when fortified castles could be destroyed in a few days by the artillery of regular armies. That victory heralded the birth of democracy.

In the twentieth century, the citizen is transformed into a combatant on the day the church bells sound the tocsin. No longer is the drawing of lots or the system of substitutes accepted: one man's blood is worth as much as another's. If voluntary enlistment proves inadequate, modern society resorts to conscription (even Britain has come around to establishing it in time of peace). Only collective utility justifies, in theory, some having to risk their lives while others content themselves with supplying the product of their labor or the resources of their intelligence.

Quite apart from ideological considerations, technology—according to the experts—imposed such total mobilization in 1914–18. Trench warfare devoured hundreds of thousands of men every year. Stretched across hundreds of miles in frontal combat, the enemy armies slowly used up their men, without either side being able to break through the other front. During the first war aristocracy of birth still formed a fraction of the officer cadres in the principal armies of Europe. But that fraction was no longer sufficiently numerous for the war to seem to be the private affair of the upper classes.

From 1914 to 1918 and from 1939 to 1945 martial virtues, the spirit of adventure, initiative, personal ascendancy, the acceptance of sacrifice retained their meaning and their grandeur. But teachers and budding professors, sons of the middle and lower middle classes, gave evidence of those virtues on the same prodigal scale as the descendants of great families. But technical weapons and general staffs both demanded not only those ancestral virtues but still more—the engineer's efficiency, the administrator's judgment. During the second war even more than during the first, the officering of the nation at war resembled that of the nation in peacetime.

No doubt a corps of professional officers remains indispensable. It grows gradually in wartime, as tens of thousands of specialists find tasks in the military organization adapted to their capacities. The United States went further in this direction than any other country. It gave striking proof that an industrial power possesses the human as well as the material resources needed to field great armies.

The supreme laws of the nation at war may be summed up in two words, both of importance in the industrial order: "organization" and "rationalization." Rules which in time of peace are applied only to certain enterprises, or at most to certain phases of its productive machinery, are in time of war applied to the whole country.

In wartime, administrative centralization is irresistible.[8] Four years of hostilities did much more than forty-five years of Hohenzollern rule to efface the surviving traces of German federalism. The autonomies or semi-autonomies of the towns or the states, the habit of local administration by notables rather than by officials, all these irrational but humanly valuable survivals seemed unjustified to the bureaucratic services that distributed food, raw materials, or instructions. The military leaders saw in them a cause of trouble and irritating delays. Military commanders and administrators protest against all hindrances and like to bring uniformity into local areas for the sake of the only objective that is acceptable from their point of view: the concentration of powers of decision at the center, the regular cutting up of secondary areas into units as much like each other as possible. War accelerated the final triumph of the Prussian concept of the state.

Two types of men took into their hands the conduct of Germany in war: the generals and the industrialists; Ludendorff and Rathenau, the army commander and the industrial mobilizer—a combination symbolic of modern society since it ceased to be bourgeois and pacific. The problem of production does not change, whether guns or bricks, motorcars or tanks are to be manufactured. What does change is the law of the whole. In the past, the decisions of the consumers in the market determined more or less directly the distribution of national resources. Now the demands of the military monster receive absolute priority, and only what is regarded as the absolute minimum of the demands of the population may be treated as imperative. The generals transmit the list of their requirements to the industrialists. The latter exert themselves to satisfy these demands without curtailing civil consumption drastically. But how can the resources be divided with strict economy

[8] Cf. A. Mendelssohn-Bartholdy, *The War and German Society* (New Haven: Yale Univ. Press, 1937).

and in order of urgency? The army industrializes itself, industry militarizes itself; the army absorbs the nation: the nation models itself on the army.

Under the Hindenburg plan of 1917, the trade unions, previously organs for the workers' demands, animated by internationalist idealism and revolutionary hope, were in their turn assigned a public function, indispensable to total mobilization. The state no longer treated the union secretaries as adversaries but as collaborators. They were vested with a share of delegated authority, which they placed at the service of the collectivity. The guiding idea of 1914, which had to be set against the ideas of 1789, as the German philosopher Plenge declared at the outset of the war, was the idea of organization. If socialism is defined primarily as the planning of the collective existence within the national system, then in 1917 Germany was the first to enter the era of the national socialisms. From 1939 onward, all the belligerents followed her example.

Were the democratic and industrial Western societies led by their total mobilization to fulfillment or to self-stultification? Everything depends, as a matter of fact, on what is considered characteristic of these societies. The citizen puts on a uniform just as he goes to the polling booth. Here and there the equality of individuals, who at law are interchangeable, is respected. But the citizen-soldier is integrated in an immense machine over which he loses all control. Group autonomy, freedom of judgment, the expression of opinion become luxuries which the country in peril finds it difficult to safeguard. Material wealth accumulated during the years of peace is squandered; the privileges which were accorded generously to individuals are economized. Liberal bourgeoisie abdicates; soldiers and organizers rule over the masses. Total mobilization approaches the totalitarian order.

Such is the similarity of style between the two that some historians have seen in the totalitarian regime, simply a prolongation of total mobilization, an attempt to make permanent what was necessary in wartime. The integral planning of the economic system—men and materials—was tested for the first time during hostilities. The integration of the proletarian masses in the nation, through the intermediary of the unions and with the aid of nationalist propaganda, was the guiding idea of the Hindenburg plan. The "organization of enthusiasm," to adopt the term coined by Elie Halévy, seems to be the seed from which sprang state monopoly of publicity and ideology, normal institutions of the Soviet Union and the Third Reich.

The war created a favorable opportunity for the seizure of power by the Bolshevik Party. The sequels of the war and the economic crisis of 1929 created favorable conditions for the seizure of power by the National Socialist Party. Without the war, the fanaticism and violence of those revolutionaries could not have seduced the people, and the conquest of the state would have been impossible. But the example of the Western democracies shows that mobilization implies perhaps a total state, not a totalitarian state. The parliaments continued to function in Britain and France from 1914 to 1918, and in Britain and the United States from 1939 to 1945. Planned economy does not necessarily outlive victory. The essential characteristics of the totalitarian regimes derive from a quasi-religious doctrine and a will to power.

Planning in the Soviet Union was inspired by a theory or by a Utopia, not by the German model of 1917. Private property, the mechanisms of the market and money became subjects of abuse, and there was a mystical belief in the virtues of centralized organization. The G.P.U. and the N.K.V.D. did not originate in the pursuit of traitors and suspects in wartime: it was a weapon of the civil war, the instrument of terror, the inquisition indispensable to a secular religion impatient to convert heretics and to maintain orthodoxy.

The National Socialist regime was probably more strongly marked by memories of the war or by the anticipation of another one. Ludendorff, immediately after the defeat, had drawn up a plan for the total organization of the nation, from which the Hitlerite regime may have drawn inspiration. The National Socialist ideology was intended by some of its prophets to become the equivalent of Shintoism, the "national religion" which Ludendorff admired and considered indispensable to the power of collectivities struggling for their existence.

Administrative centralization, economic planning, and ideological propaganda, necessary for mobilization or for preparation for war, were regarded by the Hitlerites as the normal state of things. The *garrison state,* the military state, belongs to the age of wars, but it results from wars not directly but through the intermediary of the totalitarian parties and doctrines.

In spite of similarities of style and institutions, there remains an inherent difference between total mobilization for war and totalitarianism. In the former case, all that is demanded is a temporary unanimity, limited to a single object; in the latter, the objective is a permanent unanimity expanded into a system of values and of thought. In the former case there is a temporary suspension of certain liberties and an organization of the integral effort of the country; in the latter, the masses are taught that the service of the collectivity is at every moment their supreme value, has sovereign rights over men and property.

This does not entirely solve the problem of interpretation. The hyperbolic wars of the twentieth century disintegrated social structures and favored the success of totalitarian parties. Will not the menace of a third world war compel even the democracies to renounce certain liberal institutions?

From now on, modern states will reserve the right to mobilize all the material and human resources of the nation. Some renounce the exercise of certain of their powers in time of peace. The freedom of the consumer to determine by his choice the uses to which the means of production shall be put becomes no more than a precarious luxury. It is limited or abolished as soon as the effort for armament attains such a scale that a "channeled" inflation becomes inevitable. The totalitarian states have a certain advantage in the fact that they have no need to modify the functioning of their system in passing from peace to war. This advantage is probably bought at the price of disadvantages: a free economy is more favorable to technical progress than a bureaucratic economy. Yet the democratic states must have the time, at the approach of danger, to mobilize their forces.

War is carried on not with steel but with guns and tanks. The country that has steel will have thousands of tanks at the end of a year or two, provided it has not first been crushed. In 1940 the United States had an annual iron and steel potential of more than 70 million tons, but not a single armored division. Only its distance from the presumed enemy had permitted it to dispense with the permanent maintenance of a great land army. The countries of Western Europe will have to live in a constant state of semi-mobilization; the United States will come under the same constraint; but is such a state compatible with its institutions?

The atomic espionage affair in Canada and the case of Dr. Fuchs have shown the most skeptical that professors, men of incontestable morality and sincerity, are capable of betraying their country because of ideological convictions. Obviously precautions must be taken against such elusive enemies. But once certain opinions and certain parties are outlawed, where does one stop? Democracies tolerate heresies, but they cannot tolerate *all* heresies, especially since in this case the heresy is cover for permanent espionage and sabotage.

There is little doubt of the direction in which the line should be drawn at present. But we are not considering what needs to be done. We are observing the consequences for the democratic regimes of the quasi war which the totalitarian states are carrying on in time of peace. These consequences are obvious: economic planning on a national scale, and the tightening up of social disciplines.

There still remains a considerable difference between such a state with increased functions and the totalitarian state, so long as the holders of power have not the will to suppress groups and parties, to stifle criticism and opposition, and to impose an orthodoxy. The victorious democracies are in danger of being contaminated by the enemy. But those who use this argument in order to refuse measures of resistance should imagine what contamination there would be if the democracies should, unluckily, succumb.

One can conceive of a society living in one way in time of peace and another way in wartime, but this depends on the war and peace being two distinctly separate states. The cold war and the risk of a surprise attack are condemning the democracies to permanent mobilization.

However freely united the free nations may be, and however fruitful—and even efficient—may be the criticism offered by informed public opinion of its governments, a third total war would set in motion such forces and would involve such stakes that the militarization of society would everywhere be enormously extended.

Demobilization does not remove the traces left on public administration and on the habits of the people by a period of total mobilization.

Let the cold war be prolonged for some years, and all countries will be transformed into fortified camps, unless they prefer the certainties of non-resistance to the uncertainties of effort and struggle. Let Stalinist totalitarianism be victorious and spread over Europe and throughout the world, and the masses will acclaim their servile triumph and the good will of their tyrants. The police will see to the stifling of dissidents reactionary enough to recall past epochs when liberty implied the right not only to protest but to be left alone. A victory of the democracies, on the other hand, would leave a chance of saving some element of political civilization.

Mankind must master the dynamism of violence. If atom bombs and guerrilla warfare precipitate the proletarianization of the masses, whence will a "new order" arise if not from the omnipotence of the organizers, sanctioned by the priests of some secular religion? In order to emerge at last from the age of wars, men will readily sacrifice personal liberties and national independence. But servitude has never guaranteed security.

## NECESSITY AND ACCIDENT

THIRTY YEARS' WAR," it was said on all sides at the end of the Second World War when the collapse of the Third Reich amidst apocalyptic disaster left Germany in a state of ruin comparable with that of the mid-seventeenth century. The Germanic empire, whether Hohenzollern or Hitlerite, still seemed the center of European and therefore of world policy. It was this empire which, because of its ambitions, had twice plunged mankind into the abyss, and against which the other nations had united. It was this empire that had started the chain reaction of wars and whose total defeat marked the end of an era.

Such a view is not entirely false. But we know today that it is, to say the least, incomplete. Before 1914 the rulers in Berlin had shown such a mixture of vanity, arrogance, and blundering that they had irritated or alarmed all the countries of Europe. *Hubris* had inspired such exaltation among the public as well as in the governing class that vague and grandiose ambitions filled Pan-German literature, which was often interpreted abroad as the expression of the secret thoughts of the responsible heads of the Government. The power of the Second Reich seemed scarcely compatible with the traditional equilibrium among the states of Europe. The course of events in the first war was, in fact, to show how disproportionate was Germany's strength to the European framework. The two wars of the twentieth century were indeed, in that sense, wars of coalition against Germany, just as those of the end of the seventeenth century or of the Revolution and the Empire had been wars of coalition against France.

But there was a great difference between the events that led up to the explosions, first in 1914, and then in 1939. In the former case they stemmed from a diplomatic failure and repeated conflicts, with the principal factor being the rivalry between Russia and Austria in the Balkans and, as an indirect result of that, the constitutional conditions in the multi-national empires. In the latter they originated in a scheme of conquest coldly worked out by a clique of adventurers who had profited by the German economic crisis to climb into power; principal factors were—in the background—the ruin of world economy, and the aspirations to a great Teuton *Raum*. It was not the same Germany that launched the two wars, and their causes were not the same. The stakes, too, were different.

If we want to think of the two wars as elements of one and the same whole, as episodes in a single struggle, we must not refer to the "eternal Germany" but to the tragic interlocking of causes and effects, to the dynamism of violence which we have been trying to analyze. All the "monist" theories, those that hold Germany responsible as well as those that inculpate capitalism, are puerile. In the historical order they are comparable to the mythologies that served in place of natural science in the ages in which men were incapable of understanding the mechanism of natural forces. If we study the effect of the first war on the internal constitution of states, on the psychology of peoples, and on the disintegration of the world economy; if in our interpretation we take account of circumstances such as the seizure of power by the Bolsheviks or the personal rivalries of the dictators, and or phenomena that are determined and yet at the same time accidental, such as the exceptional acuteness of the world crisis of 1929, then we may succeed in following the history of the thirty years, a history of wars in chain reaction.

It is history in the full sense of the term, whose broad lines one may retrospectively trace, but without making the claim that the ultimate outcome could have been foreseen or was implicit in the principal forces of the time. A local conflict was transformed by the play of balance-of-power diplomacy into a European war, and that war was magnified, as a result of industry, democracy, and the approximate equality of the forces at grips, into a hyperbolic war;

that war, in turn ended by wearing out the weakest link in the European chain. Revolution burst its way into Russia; the thrones of Central Europe and the last multi-national empire crumbled. With Bolshevik Russia on her flank, the Europe of the bourgeois democracies and independent nations tried to return to the pre-1914 world, which it still persisted in regarding as normal. The crisis of 1929 made an end of the painfully re-established order in currencies and economic systems. Unemployment opened the flood-gates, and a revolutionary movement carried the German masses toward a state of frenzy. From then on Europe, tormented by three ideologies as well as by the traditional rivalries of the powers, slid rapidly into disaster. The war, beginning in 1939 with the Russo-German alliance and the partition of Poland, this time spread throughout the world, reviving and extending the war which had been raging in China since the early thirties. When, at the end of six years, the conflagration died down, the earth had been scorched from Europe to Asia.

Across the world the two solitary survivors girded their loins for the final contest while the crash of the first atomic bomb was still reverberating.

It is so obivous a story that one is astonished afterwards at not having seen beforehand what was coming. Yet we are the more obliged to guard against any retrospective illusion of fatalism. During those thirty years there were moments when destiny was, so to speak, in suspense and quite different lines of evolution began to take form. It would have taken only a few more army corps to reverse the outcome of the Battle of the Marne. A decisive German victory in the West would probably have shortened the war, what-ever might have been the policy of Russia or Great Britain, after France had been crushed. Once more, Europe would have had no experience of the potentialites of hyperbolic war, as she had had none in 1870–71.

A compromise peace, if it had come before the Russian Revolu-tion, would have given still clearer evidence of foresight on both sides: the Germans would have recognized that with Austria-Hungary as their only ally they could not conquer the rest of Eu-rope; and the Allies would have recognized that they could not reduce Germany to unconditional surrender. Or at least the two camps would have recognized their inability to conquer without going the full length of hyperbolic war, fatal for them all. But would the passions that had been aroused have permitted the intervention of the diplomats?

The slide from the First into the Second World War was no more inevitable. To accomplish it required an almost incredible combination of stupidity and bad luck. The British evoked the century-old ghost of Napoleon because there was a Poincaré cantankerously defending the rights of France and manifesting his indifference to the economic consequences of sanctions. French diplomacy combined fussiness with clumsiness in its dealings with the Weimar Republic, at a time when generosity and teamwork in European reconstruction might have paid better. Later France was weak and resigned toward a Germany that would have understood only force and the willingness to resort to it.

After Hitler had come into power, there were still opportunities of changing the course of destiny. In March 1936, a military reply to the entry of the German troops into the Rhineland would at least have slowed down the pace of events, and might even have brought about the downfall of Hitlerism. It may be, though there can be no certainty on this point, that Anglo-French resistance in 1938 would have induced the anti-Hitler conspirators (who included some of the military commanders) to act. During the war, the British and Americans might have maintained or resumed contact with the German opposition, and tried to conquer Germany without destroying her, instead of pushing the war to the point at which the annihilation of the vanquished made a collision between the Allies inevitable. To spare the enemy when one is not sure of one's ally has always been the teaching of an honorable Machiavellian wisdom.

No less incredible was the series of mistakes through which the American victory in the Far East was mortgaged.

If, however, history finds no difficulty in discovering lost opportunities, if by noting that certain events might have happened it then avoids the mistake of declaring that the past was foreordained —when it had, in fact, been a future in the hands of the politicians —such a succession of misfortunes or mistakes no longer permits us to talk of the play of chance. The fact that opportunities were never seized becomes in turn a generalization, a dominant factor of that historical period. Events were too much for men, and the rulers were unable to master the forces unchained not so much by their actions as by the automatic consequences of their actions. They did not succeed in arresting inflation in Germany before the currency had been completely ruined, or the economic crisis before unemployment had reached a figure of several millions, or Hitler before he had accumulated arms enough to involve Germany and Europe in his adventure.

Mysterious is the evidence of history. In some epochs events forever betray the intentions of the actors. Peoples make war, but never do they aspire so passionately to peace. Statesmen try first to appease conquerors and then to resist them, first to satisfy them and then to overawe them. They discover each time that these successive methods of diplomacy have been resorted to at the wrong time: resistance when compliance would have been better, and vice versa. However immense empires may be, they never satiate the appetite of the Caesars. Hitler refused hegemony over continental Europe, which would have satisfied the aspirations of the Hohenzollerns; the Kremlin is refusing an empire reaching from the Elbe to Indo-China, which would have satisfied Hitler's aspirations—at least for a time. From war to war the stake grows, until it now involves domination over the world.

That is why at times the philosopher meditates on the end result and invokes what Hegel calls "the Ruse of Reason." Is not the unity of mankind the aim, obscurely aspired to, that magnetizes not so much the desires of individuals as the dynamism of collective forces, attracting to itself, through blood and tears, the unfortunate peoples whose sufferings will receive the subsequent compensation of a precarious welfare? The lag between the causes and the results of events, between human passions and the effects of the acts they inspire, between conflicts of ideology and power and the real issue of wars, fascinates the observer, who is tempted at one moment to denounce the absurdity of history and at another to admit its broad rationality.

The only truth accessible to positive cognition is the recognition of these contradictions. Mythologies consist of the substitution of a single factor for the plurality of causes, of lending unconditional value to a desired objective, and of a failure to realize the distance between the dreams of men and the destiny of societies.

Men of learning have discovered the secret of fire but not that of history. Lenin, who dreamed of ending the class struggle, laid the foundation of the total state, of concentration camps, and of an omnipotent police. Millions of victims curse and will curse the blindness of the revolutionary, but their curses do not permit us to anticipate with confidence the judgment of posterity.

# PART TWO

*Crossroads of History*

*Chapter V*

# THE RISE OF THE PERIPHERAL STATES

IMMEDIATELY following the First World War, Max Weber wrote that American hegemony was as inevitable as that of Rome had been after the Second Punic War. Subsequent events have brought the United States, almost involuntarily, into domination over half of the planet. The rise of the American Republic is "logical," in the sense in which Cournot used the word, i.e., predetermined by the main factors of the situation.

This American domination can be demonstrated by a few familiar statistics: In 1870 the industrial production of the United States represented 23.5 per cent of the world's total, and in 1926–29 42 per cent. Great Britain's share dropped during the same period from 31.8 to 9.4 per cent.[1] According to another calculation, the total annual production of the United States represented in 1925–29 about a quarter of the annual world production.[2] After the second war the national income of the United States in international units exceeded that of the period 1925–34 by 65 to 70 per cent. At present it represents between a quarter and a third of the world total (for about six per cent of the world's population). The United States produces more steel and consumes more gasoline than all the rest of mankind. North America's share (including Canada) of the world production of fuel and energy (coal, lignite, oil, hydro-electric energy) was 54.5 per cent in 1947, compared with 41.8 per cent in 1938.[3]

[1]T. Balogh, *Dollar Crisis* (Oxford: 1949), quoting statistics published by the League of Nations in *Industrialization and Foreign Trade*.

[2]J. Piel, *La Fortune américaine et son Destin* (Paris: 1949).

[3]*Ibid.,* p. 114.

The American economy combines natural and technical advantages. It possesses an abundance of most raw materials,[4] and it has exploited these more effectively than any other country. The capital invested per worker is at least double that of the next most advanced countries. The productivity is the highest in the world (three times that of Europe, on the average). The country has discovered the secret of combining national power and individual wealth. For the first time, an imperial nation has no need to exploit the peoples it protects or dominates. It serves its own self-interest by raising the standard of living of those whom it wishes to integrate into its system.

The transition from economic supremacy to political hegemony is normal, but it was not inevitable. The Second World War accelerated that transition and gave it a dramatic character.

Industrial potential is a necessary condition of military power, but it is not sufficient in itself. Many military critics in France and Germany doubted whether a non-military democracy would be capable of improvising a great army. From 1940 to 1945, the United States dispelled those doubts with a speed and a completeness that astonished the Germans. The managerial class quickly supplied military leaders once the country was at war. Being, moreover, less the captive of traditions and more ready to experiment than the military castes of the old countries, the American officer corps rapidly adapted itself to the requirements of scientific warfare.

Other observers doubted whether the American public would show resolution enduring enough to influence the course of history. Without the clear and present danger of a neighboring country in arms, traditionally hostile to imperialism in the European pattern, devoted by its national philosophy to peaceful industry, would the United States not remain a spectator, enjoying unequaled wealth and profiting as the result of struggles waged overseas? Here again, subsequent events gave a resounding answer. In 1917, and again in 1941, America's realization of her common destiny with Europe

[4]The United States buys abroad all the natural rubber, wool, and tin that the nation consumes; 90 per cent of the manganese, 100 per cent of the nickel, 35 per cent of the copper, 45 per cent of the lead, 15 per cent of the zinc, etc. The best deposits of iron are approaching exhaustion.

suppressed the temptation to isolationism. In both wars, it is true, the mistakes of the enemy were remarkably influential: the declaration of unrestricted submarine warfare and the attack on Pearl Harbor precipitated a decision which the President anticipated but which the Congress disliked or viewed with hesitation. Between the two wars the United States withdrew from Europe, and by this abstention thereby assumed some responsibility for the outbreak of the second war.

The development of events was nonetheless unmistakable. From 1940 onward, President Roosevelt went as far as his Constitutional powers permitted. Before December 1941, American destroyers had received instructions to fire at sight on any German submarine. The American Government was definitely more inclined to enter the Second World War than the First, and at the present time it has had no thought of withdrawing from Europe. Through the Marshall Plan and the Atlantic Pact, American presence in Europe has been assured for a long period. Not without surprise, but with a complete lack of enthusiasm, the American people have recognized their strength and their obligations. They are exercising a hegemony to which they had never aspired.

The political system of the United States was created by and for an agricultural democracy, and has been adapted in practice to the needs of an industrial society; but can it further develop and maintain a firm and continuous diplomatic policy on a world-wide scale? Foreigners have asked that question, some hopefully, others with apprehension; the future alone can supply the answer. Today it can only be said that the prospect is not discouraging.

Serious mistakes were made both during and immediately after the war. I am afraid they are beyond repair, but they were caused less by the American political system than by popular psychology. They have been attributed to a man who was at the point of death, and to his team of advisers impregnated with Left Wing ideology. But the statesmen were not the only ones to be caught by the illusory pictures painted by propaganda for the common people. A whole nation, optimistic and naïve, placed its trust in a comrade in arms.

The road to error was paved by the crusading spirit which traditionally inspires the foreign policy of the United States. Woodrow Wilson and Franklin Roosevelt envisaged their war aims not so much in any concrete form as in the terms of certain ideals—democracy, or the Four Freedoms, or the United Nations Organization. Instead of recognizing the real issue at stake, and accepting as objective the establishment of international relations in a balance that would favor world peace, they tended simply to see in the enemy the incarnation of evil. In order not to admit to themselves that, like belligerents throughout history, they had accepted the co-operation even of the worst of despotisms, the Americans white-washed their Soviet ally with all the virtues needed to allow it to fight on the side of Goodness and Truth. After the war it was decided to reconstitute the Japanese and German armies—a risk that was quite rightly accepted; but the conscience-saving delusion persists that they have been purified by democratization.

The spread of American ideas and practices was sincerely conceived as a means of promoting the conversion of the sinner. Such hopes have been bitterly disappointed. The American standard of living and the Congress were not exportable at will. Neither the Germans nor the Japanese saluted democracy as the goal either of their own aspirations or of history in general. It was not enough to expel the Europeans in order to liberate the peoples of Asia. The Americans, hostile to the age-old structure of most human societies, hated to admit that the void left by the war and the liquidation of the European empires, by the destruction of ancestral ways of living, was going to be filled by despotic instead of by free institutions.

American diplomacy tends to run, as a consequence of its very failures, from one extreme to the opposite. When there is no longer any place for the crusading spirit, the alternative seems to be force and fraud, and so as not to be duped in a world of corruption, the game of power politics is played without reserve. It is not easy to accept the strange mixture formed by human history, which never supplies irreproachable causes to defend or absolute evil to oppose; nor ever separates international or party rivalries from those of ideas. The result is that American diplomacy is alternatively threatened by cynicism and by hypocrisy.

In spite of everything, in the last decade the United States has begun to recognize its new "manifest destiny." Militant isolationism has been driven back to such an extent that the very word is presently taboo. The trade unions are the strongest supporters of the Truman Doctrine and the European aid plan. From time to time there are even captains of industry who advocate that the two great powers make a vast compromise, which might permit a world-wide armistice and fruitful commercial exchanges. It may be doubted whether these dreams or inclinations will lead to any sudden change in the course pursued by the Washington administration since 1946.

In immediate decisions the American leaders have less freedom of movement than the masters of the Kremlin. They have to convince some hundreds of congressmen and journalists and, through them, public opinion. Neither those who make the decisions nor those who form opinion have unlimited power: the governing class, in agreement on essentials but divided into competing groups, does not obey an individual word of command because it is not subject to authoritative control. Concern for election results, for individual interests, and for economic considerations is likely to obstruct the plans of the Administration. Troublesome, however, as these matters of disagreement so often are, they are not without advantages in the long run. Unity not imposed by police is often more durable in practice.

There remain the dangers which Thucydides' Pericles described to the Athenians at the outset of the Peloponnesian War. The power of the United States is great, but not unlimited. America's responsibilities in Asia and in Europe are vast. Owing to its geographical situation, it hesitates between Europe and Asia, uncertain as to the relative importance to be assigned to the two spheres. The public is inclined to attribute the nation's setbacks entirely to mistakes on the part of its leaders, as if the leaders were never faced with insurmountable obstacles. Every democracy that freely discusses the conduct of its foreign policy is likely to oscillate in the wake of public opinion and to conceive glorious plans without measuring the cost.

The American temptation to appeasement has been overcome; will expeditions to Sicily be avoided?

There is no difficulty in assembling statistics that sow the extent of the material and human resources available to the Soviet Union in the near future. The experts estimate that within twenty years the Russian population will be 250 millions.[5] Geographers and geologists are very optimistic, as a rule, in regard to its raw material resources[6]—20 per cent of the world supplies of coal, nearly half the world's oil reserves, half the iron, 10 per cent of the copper, 11 per cent of the lead, 19 per cent of the zinc, and so on. There would be no difficulty whatsoever in showing that the known reserves of most raw materials in the United States are much less extensive.

But mineral wealth buried in the earth is no exact measure of the future potentialities of the economic system. The deposits are scattered over the immense Eurasian region, sometimes in deserts. Their exploitation would require the transport of men, the building of new towns, in many cases even food transport. The famous Urals *combinat* unites a coal basin and an iron basin 1,250 miles apart. On the political scale, or even in terms of measurable human history, any comparison between the known or probable deposits in the Soviet Union and those in the United States must remain virtually meaningless for another century. Let us admit, uncertain though it is, that the Soviet Union possesses 50 per cent of the world's oil reserves. But its annual production amounted at the end of 1950 to 35 million tons, and the United States produces without difficulty ten times as much. The development of Russian agriculture faces great difficulties, for only one third of the total land surface is arable. It can hardly be said that Russia has been blessed by nature and thereby predestined to empire.

Before the Second World War, the Soviet Union had become one of the great industrial powers of the world, with an annual production of 166 million tons of coal,[7] 31 million tons of oil, 48,000 million KWH of electrical energy, and 18 million tons of steel. It was inferior only to Germany in the size of its industrial

[5]*Population of Europe and of the Soviet Union: Demographic Perspectives* (League of Nations Publications, 1944).

[6]Georges, *L'Economie de l'U.R.S.S.* (Paris: 1948), p. 89.

[7]These figures are given by Harry Schwartz in *Russia's Soviet Economy* (New York: Syracuse Univ. Press. 1950).

potential capable of being transformed into military force. (The Third Reich produced 27 million tons of steel on the eve of 1939.)

Since the war's end the five-year plans have continued to be concerned mainly with heavy industry, and at the end of the year 1950 the Soviet Union was incontestably the world's second industrial power: its annual production was 250 million tons of coal, 35 million tons of oil, more than 80,000 million KWH, 25.4 million tons of steel. These figures remain well below those of the United States, and even those of the Continent west of the Iron Curtain. But as long as Europe remains undefended, its resources in the event of war would either be of no value to anyone, or would serve the Soviet Union rather than its enemies.

The results obtained in agriculture are less impressive. The controversies over the agricultural statistics of the Soviet Union are too complicated for us to attempt even a summary of them. It appears that on the eve of the war the grain harvest was some 15 per cent above that of 1928 (which was equivalent to that of 1913), an increase mainly attributable to the increase in area.[8] Per head of the population the area under grain fell between 1913 and 1938 from 0.68 to 0.60 hectares[9]; the quantity available per head of the population similarly fell, from 4.9 to 4.5 quintals.[10]

The enormous investments in agriculture, the social upheaval, the deportations of peasants, and the suffering of millions of innocent people, have brought no noticeable increase either in the quantity of agricultural produce or in the yield per hectare. What these measures *have* done is greatly to increase the proportion of the harvest at the Government's disposal. The Government obtained less than 15 per cent of the crops in 1928 (estimated at 73 million tons); it obtained 40 per cent of a yield of 82 million tons

[8] *Ibid.*, p. 311.

[9] S. N. Prokopowicz, *Russlands Volkwirtschaft unter den Soviets* (Zurich: 1944), p. 136.

[10] On the other hand industrial crops, such as cotton, beets, flax, etc., have considerably increased, as well as have the produce of market gardens cultivated by the workers themselves, which play an important part in local food supply. Against this, the results in cattle breeding are still poor. On the eve of the war the quantities of meat, milk, and eggs available were scarcely equal to and probably less than those of 1913. It is known that the herds of cattle were reduced by more than half during collectivization.

in 1939. Collectivization, regarded as an economic measure, succeeded in its goal to free part of the farm labor for work in the
factories (the urban population was 21.4 millions in 1923 and
55.9 in 1939—a movement that has continued since the war's end),
and to compel the peasants to deliver the quantity of grain necessary
to feed the great industrial areas. It is difficult to believe that the
end secured required the terrible means that were adopted.

It is often imagined that the Revolution of 1917 transformed
primitive Russia into a modern state, an agricultural nation into
a great industrial power. This impression fails to take account of
the continuity between Soviet industrialization and the work accomplished in the course of the last years of the Tsarist regime.
Between 1890 and 1913,[11] the number of industrial workers
doubled (from 1.5 to 3 millions), and the production of the industrial enterprises quadrupled (from 1.5 to 6 billion rubles). The extraction of coal increased from 5.3 to 29 million tons, steel production from 0.7 to 4 million tons, that of petrol from 3.2 to 9 million
tons. The textile mills consumed three times as much cotton in 1913
as in 1890. During the same period, the production of sugar
quadrupled. Between 1900 and 1913, more than 8,000 miles of
railway lines were built. According to the calculations of S. N. Prokopowicz, the national income rose from 6.6 milliard rubles in
1900 to 11.8 milliards in 1913—an increase of 79.4 per cent. If
one takes account of the increase in price, the percentage is reduced
to 39.4; and if, finally, account is taken of the growth of the population, the increase in the real income per person becomes 17.1
per cent.
The average annual increase in the population was 16 per
thousand, and the growth of primary, secondary, and higher edu-
cational institutions was more rapid than that of the population.
From 1894 to 1914, the number of pupils in the secondary schools
increased from 225,000 to 820,000, and the number of students in
the universites and colleges from 15,000 to 80,000. Primary education made still more rapid strides. Among the conscripts, 21.4
per cent could read and write in 1874, 37.8 per cent in 1894,

[11]We take these figures from N. S. Timasheff, *The Great Retreat* (New
York: Dutton, 1946).

55.5 per cent in 1904, and 67.3 per cent in 1914. Among the industrial workers, in 1917, the percentage of illiterates was 22.9 among youths from 14 to 20 years of age, 35.2 among men of 30 to 35, 56.6 among those over 50. In 1880 there were 1.141 million pupils in the elementary schools; the number in 1915 was 8.147 million (21.288 million in 1938–39). The Tsarist regime was gradually "liquidating" illiteracy.[12]

From the beginning of the five-year plans, industrial construction advanced with extraordinary rapidity. Between the two wars, coal production was multiplied by about 4.5, that of cast iron by 3.5, petrol by a little less than 4, electrical energy by 20. Industries were started for the production of tractors, automobiles, trucks, machines, and machine tools. But would this development have been more or less rapid if the Revolution of 1917 had not taken place? This question has been argued in many ways, none of them conclusive. The Russians spent ten years after the First World War rebuilding the ruins resulting not only from that war itself but from the Revolution. Between 1929 and 1939, their industrial construction exceeded all previous records. Nevertheless, there are no adequate grounds on which to compare the result finally attained by the Soviets with that which would have evolved through a non-catastrophic process under a democratic regime and with the aid of foreign capital.

There is little doubt that the nature of the industrialization would have been different. Before 1913, heavy industry represented about one third of the total production, light industry two thirds. The Soviets, under the five-year plan, reversed the proportion. Their unique contribution to the economic history of the twentieth century has been to construct a vast industrial plant without having raised the living standard of the masses.[13] Under a semi-liberal economic regime or a parliamentary democracy, it would have been

[12]According to S. N. Prokopowicz, *op. cit.*, the number of pupils in the primary and middle schools grew from 7.9 millions in 1913 to 29.4 in 1937. For the universities and colleges the number grew from 112,000 in 1913 to 547,200 in 1937, 496,000 in 1945, and 574,000 under the plan for 1950.

[13]We cannot enter into discussions of the statistics of wages and prices in the Soviet Union. Most of the statisticians arrive at comparable results: the standard of living of the great bulk of the population in 1949 was hardly superior to that of the years before 1914.

impossible to ignore working-class aspirations for better living conditions. The development of the various sections of that class itself would have been better balanced. Collectivization, the deportation of millions of kulaks, the destruction of cattle, and the famine of the 1930s would not have been conceivable.

Harvard statisticians, in submitting the Russian figures to criticism and correction, arrived at the following conclusions: Out of a national income of 44.4 billion dollars in 1940, 14.1 billion had been devoted to investment and to national defense. Soviet postwar policy has not changed, and continues to favor heavy industry, iron and other metal production, and power projects. Stalin, in a speech, once spoke of 60 million tons of steel as an early objective. The security of the nation would not be assured without attaining that ambitious, but not inaccessible, total.

Whatever may be said of the future, the interpretation of past events leaves little room for doubt. The direct and sufficient cause of Russia's rise to world power is not Communism but the Second World War.

The enormous sums devoted to capital expenditure and to the Army were one of the causes of the ultimately victorious resistance to German aggression. But it must be borne in mind that a good many of the factories built at such great expense fell in 1941 into the hands of the invaders.

In fact, whatever part the Revolution played in the industrialization of Russia, and the latter in the victory of 1945, the Soviet regime contributed decisively to the political fortune of Russia not so much by its internal as by its external effects. It was Russia's good fortune (if one may regard hegemony as good fortune—though we must not judge of good fortune before the last day) that Communism found imitators among its enemies. Communism's enemies, to combat it, had to resort to the same methods of arousing their nations against Bolshevism as did the Bolshevist nations to arouse the proletariat against capitalism. They precipitated international wars in the same way that Bolshevism precipitated war between classes.

It may seem surprising that a war can develop lasting consequences. But history offers many such examples. Athens and Sparta exhausted each other in a thirty years' war, which marked the end of the age of the city states and prepared the way for the Macedonian hegemony. The outcome of a battle is capable of determining the balance of power for a long period. But in our time the validity of this general rule is questionable: as long as military force is a function of industrial potential, the vanquished will not remain enfeebled for a long time by the military defeat or the treaty terms if it can retain its industrial capacities. The war of 1914–18 is a notable example of this conception. Recent events suggest still another one.

Soviet Russia's strategic situation was radically transformed by the consequences of the last war. The German Army is eliminated in Europe as the Japanese Army is in Asia. In 1946 the world was startled to discover that there no longer existed any army that could withstand the Soviet forces. Five years earlier, the U.S.S.R. was threatened by a war on two fronts; now it is the Soviet Union that applies pressure on all sides: on Europe, on the Middle East, and on the heart of Asia; numerous divisions of the Red Army, filled with the prestige of their victories, threaten ominously because they are no more faced with an adversary of their own strength on land than the English Navy was at sea after Trafalgar.

Russia has in fact nearly achieved the "world island" which MacKinder considered the necessary and almost sufficient condition for universal empire. After 1945 the Anglo-Saxon democracies, forgetting the teachings of history and geography, suddenly accepted the fact that Stalin was achieving for himself the goal which they had forbidden Hitler: the domination of Eastern Europe and the Balkans. They even went so far as to accept the fact that by the Sovietization of one third of Germany Stalin had mortgaged the future of the entire country.

Germany partitioned, Japan disarmed, China turned Communist —surely Stalin in his most ambitious dreams could never have imagined that the capitalist states would carry on the war with such blind fury that the socialist state would become the sole beneficiary of such unhoped-for gains.

The disproportion between Russia's potential in 1945 or 1950 and her actual power explains the contradictory judgments of observers. Some dwell on the immense superiority of American industry and of the resources of the Western world, and conclude that the outcome of a third world war would be assured from the first. Others point to the immensity of the conquest within reach of the Soviet armies, and conclude that, if she escaped atomic destruction, Russia would be invincible. Both lines of argument are oversimplified.

Before 1939 there was a tendency to underestimate the direct relationship between industrial potential and military power. Today there is the opposite tendency to exaggerate that relationship. Industrial potential is the condition of military power, but military power is not the measure of industrial potential. If it had been enough to generalize from steel-production figures Germany would not have resisted for so many years a coalition which, on paper, was irresistible.

Let us leave out of account the reinforcements which the Soviet Union would acquire through the advance of its armies. The ratio of military strength between two countries is not the same as that of their coal extraction or their metal industries. Let it be admitted that at present the United States produces three times as much steel as the Soviet Union, and may eventually produce even four times as much. It remains to be determined how much of the steel produced by either country, in peace and in war, is devoted to armaments. In other words, the comparison of potentials must be completed by that of coefficients of mobilization. While the exact figures are not known (especially for the Soviet Union), it is known that the coefficient of mobilization between 1945 and 1950 in the United States was insignificant. The size of the military budget is misleading: most of the expenditure was accounted for by military pay, and after that by scientific research. Not more than 1 to 1.5 million tons of steel went into the manufacture of armaments.

In wartime especially, the coefficient of industrial mobilization is decisive. Although indisputably exact figures are not available, it is known that the coefficient was lower in the United States than in the Soviet Union. In the United States only a quarter of the steel was directly employed on war production. It may be said that if necessary the United States could considerably increase that coefficient. True, but everything depends on the privations that the nation will accept or governments can impose. Will the high standard of living of the American people allow mobilization to be carried to the lengths possible in the Soviet Union? The traditional inferiority of wealthy peoples at grips with peoples living in more primitive conditions thus reappears.

Concern for the standard of living also results in a waste of human potential. For every 20,000 men in a United States division at the front there are 60,000 in the rear, according to a statement made in 1950 by General Clark. During the last war the United States mobilized 100 divisions, the Germans 300, and the Russians 500.[14]

It is true of course that the United States had a navy and an air force far superior to those of the Soviet Union. But America's need to maintain her lines of communication across two oceans would be just as great in a future war as it was in the last one. The task will absorb an enormous quantity of material and human resources. Distance, and its insular position in comparison with the land masses of Asia and Europe, assure America a sort of protection, but that advantage is counterbalanced by the cost of transport to the field of battle.

Just as the scale of military power is not measured by that of industrial potential, so the quality of armaments is not a function solely of productivity or technique. As for quality, an element difficult to measure closely but still very important, account must be taken of the interest shown by the nation in armaments, also the number of technicians who apply their ingenuity to the perfecting of arms, and the sums of money allocated to research and laboratory experiment for purely military purposes. The United States has never in the past been a warlike nation, and the best American military critic, Hanson W. Baldwin, does not hesitate to declare that the American victories in the two world wars were due to quantity rather than quality.[15]

[14] A Russian division represents no more than 60 to 70 per cent of an American division, in men as in firepower.

[15] Mr. Baldwin gives a list of the inventions of the other countries, and of the arms in which the Americans are backward, or were at the end of the last war. In submarines and rockets the decisive inventions were German. The best fighter aircraft at the beginning of the war in the Pacific was the Japanese Zero, and at the end of the war in Europe the Messerschmidt 262. The Germans were the first to use rockets in air fighting. The American tanks were outclassed. (From an article in the *Saturday Evening Post*, represented by the *Reader's Digest*, October 1950.)

From the time when the United States applied itself seriously to the invention and perfection of military weapons, the incomparable power and quality of its industrial equipment were bound to give it superiority at least in complicated apparatus (wireless-guided projectiles, radar, and other electronic apparatus). It must also be remembered that the Russians transferred German scientists to Russia and profited by German discoveries in connection with submarines and rockets. Finally, let us not forget that an industry generally inferior to that of the United States is capable of producing tanks and anti-tank weapons equal or superior to those of the Americans because they are of relatively simple manufacture. The Russians, making use of foreign models, have a great talent for giving them maximum strength and adapting them to their particular requirements.

When the armies actually face each other, other factors besides the quantity or quality of their matériel come into play. The intelligence of the commanding officers and those of the lower ranks, the discipline of the troops, individual courage and will power—in these factors lies the secret of victory in battles and of the destiny of nations, and they are not included in statistics.

Tocqueville's famous prophecy has been so often quoted since 1945 that Russia's good fortune no longer surprises anyone. We forget that during the spring and summer of 1941 the Soviet armies suffered more terrible disasters than those which crushed the armies of the Tsar in 1914 and 1915. We also forget that at the end of 1941 German officers were able to see through their glasses the suburbs of Moscow. It required the great spaces, the cold, the horrible, and absurd policy of the Germans in the occupied territory, it required the patient heroic resistance of the Russian people, Hitler's "intuitions," lend-lease, and the air offensive in the West, to bring the final defeat of the *Wehrmacht*.

During the first half of the nineteenth century, after the collapse of the Napoleonic empire, the conviction was already spreading that the old nations were irremediably weak. That conviction anticipated the defeatism of today. Only the Russians and the Anglo-Saxons seemed to have promising futures before them. But the events of the latter half of the nineteenth century did nothing to bear out those anticipations. On the contrary, the rise of the German empire and European expansion in Africa bore witness to the unimpaired vitality of Europe and confounded the prophets.

At the outset of the twentieth century, 200 million Europeans possessed an abnormal share of the world's wealth. But the methods of industrial civilization, which European emigrants brought with them to the New World made possible an exceptional growth of material prosperity in the United States, thanks to America's vast frontiers, to its abundance of natural resources, to its lack of rigid social stratifications, and its relatively small population. In the meantime the diffusion in Asia of European liberal and nationalistic ideologies, and the introduction of firearms prepared the revolt against the West, from which Communism seems likely to benefit the most.

Neither the nature nor the rapidity of the decline of Europe had been foreseen. At the present moment Europe, or rather what remains of Europe west of the Iron Curtain, has no chance of independence. Either it will be part of a whole of which the Atlantic forms the center, just as the civilization of the ancients had the Mediterranean for its center; or else it will be incorporated in the Continental empire of which the Soviet Union is the central directing element. In that limited sense, it is not wrong to pose the alternative: Washington or Moscow? But it would be wrong to regard the situation produced by the accident of the Second World War as more durable than that created at the beginning of the century.

It is not difficult to imagine the structures that might replace the present one—the defeat of one of the two great rivals, and a resulting universal empire; or, alternatively, the restoration of autonomous forces in Europe and Asia, and a relative loss of power by the two existing giants. In any case it seems unlikely that the world will remain divided in accordance with the lines of demarcation traced by the arbitrary decisions of international conferences.

*Chapter VI*

## FROM MARXISM TO STALINISM

AS THE METROPOLIS of a religion promising temporal salvation, the Soviet Union appeals to the peasants of Asia, living on the verge of famine, as well as to an assortment of atomic scientists who, in the words of the Red master of the Kremlin, have heard the good tidings brought once more to suffering mankind.

The divisions of the Red Army would arouse less anxiety if they did not seem to be in the service of an idea. The combination of an empire, sprung up suddenly from the ruins of the old European nations, and an apparently universal message, is spreading terror throughout the non-Communist world.

Europe, hardly emerged from the age of bourgeois liberalism, is unable to understand by what ruse of reason a rationally inspired doctrine has been able to revive the superstitions of the Dark Ages.

Marxism is a Christian heresy. It is the modern form of millennialism: it places the Kingdom of God on this earth, due to arrive after an apocalyptic revolution in which the old systems will be engulfed. The contradictions within capitalist society will inevitably provoke that pregnant catastrophe, and today's sufferers will triumph tomorrow. The proletariat, the witness of man's present inhumanity to man, will achieve salvation. At a moment to be determined by the development of the means of production, in combination with the courage of the military leaders, the proletariat will form a universal class and take charge of human destiny.

Such an ideology, which we are considering not as a philosophical doctrine but as the subject of popular belief, combines three sorts of themes whose historical origins may easily be traced and whose combination has given to Marxism its explosive force.

There is, first of all, the Christian theme. All religions of salvation prophesy in one form or another the revenge of the humiliated. They offer to the humbler classes of society compensation either in this world or the next. Marxism makes possible a sort of belief in the victory of the slaves. For are not the industrial workers the true creators of wealth? Is not the elimination of the parasites and monopolists, who appropriate an exorbitant share of the collective income, irresistibly demanded by an immanent logic? Thus incorporated in a materialist dialectic, the idea of the overthrow of the hierarchy dissembles its true origin: the Christian aspirations, which atheism has not extinguished, or the more or less sublimated resentments of those who are relegated to the bottom of the social scale. The positivistic camouflage deludes the faithful without diminishing the emotional sources of their belief.

Then there is the Promethean theme. Man, having discovered the secret of fire, used it to extend more and more quickly his mastery over natural forces, as, on the distant horizon, he could see an earthly paradise which Trotsky regarded as an attainable and even relatively near objective. Ancestral poverty would be pushed further and further into the past; the curse of toil would be merely a superstition current only in societies that possessed the most meager means of production. Although the establishment of socialism called for continuing efforts and privations from the common man, scientists and technicians—the demigods of our age—would eliminate the industrial purgatory, rendering inequality useless and oppression scandalous. Leisure and wealth would no longer be reserved for a few at the expense of the many, but would become, thanks to the genius of the human race, a universal possession.

Finally, the rationalist theme. Societies develop spontaneously: they need to be reconstructed rationally. Spontaneous development itself obeyed an intrinsic logic. Human progress, because at first it depends upon man's struggle with other men as well as with nature, leads inevitably to a confused society, at odds with its own best interests. But then a new phase begins: because he knows the laws of his own history, man can anticipate the future. He still cannot eliminate those inevitable disturbances that mark periods of transition, for the passage from one social structure to another, the replacement of one social class by another, does not take place without wars and revolution. But he can know the outcome beforehand—the creation of a humane society through his own benign planning. In such a society private property and economic anarchy will give place to collective property and a planned economy.

The revolt against inequality and injustice exists in all ages. The boundless faith in science and technology nourished by the industrial achievements of Western civilization is typical of our age. It is the synthesis of that revolt and this faith that, once it is based upon a pseudo-rationalist interpretation of history, gives Marxism its popular appeal. Faith in science by itself would merely arouse a sort of messianic expectancy, a belief that in time poverty and inequality would disappear, or an acceptance of technocracy in the belief that things would be handled best by experts. Revolt by itself would only revive illusions so often proved false. (Why should new masters be any better than the old ones?) The rewards envisioned by the scientific view of man and society will come only with the victory of the proletariat.

In the last quarter of the nineteenth century, Marxism, while it had little influence in Great Britain and still less in the United States, became the official doctrine of working-class parties on the Continent. But as the proletarian parties gained strength and influence, theory and practice of social democracy drew further and further apart. Revolutionary theory was still professed, and the holding of governmental office prohibited; but reformism carried the day in practice. Ideology served to keep the militants aroused by distracting them from the prosaic, everyday demands of the movement. It convinced the members of the working class that they had a historic role to fulfill, and deterred them from fully accepting integration in the capitalist order without, however, making them permanently irreconcilable enemies of society and the state. The social legislation conceded by anti-socialist governments (that of Bismarck, for example), or wrested by trade union action, and the higher living standard made possible by economic progress had not put an end to unrest within the proletariat; but the possibility was seen that such unrest might come to an end, without either violence or revolution.

To this day nothing has proved that the autonomous development of capitalism excluded such an eventuality. The example of certain countries, like Sweden and Switzerland, spared by the two wars reveals one of the possible outcomes of the evolution which before 1914 was obscured by the ideology of the Second International. The organization of the working class into trade unions and even into socialist parties, was probably inherent in the structure of the Western democratic societies. But neither the unions nor the parties prevented the working class from acquiring a middle-class mentality under the influence of the increase in wealth and the redistribution of national income. The Communists' campaign against what they called capitalism (in which they lumped the British labor movement and the Third Reich) was not inevitable.

Stalinism continues today to avail itself of the Marxist ideology, that subtle combination of Christian aspiration and technological faith. Stalin the Terrible appeared, even in France, to millions of men of good will as the father of the poor and the redresser of wrongs, indifferent though he was to the fate of millions of human beings "condemned by history," indifferent even to the fate of the servants of the Revolution the day they ceased to be useful or violated the official discipline. One has only to penetrate the party secret or even to read the text of its doctrine or propaganda, in order to uncover radical innovations beneath the apparent continuity. The Stalinists speak the same language as the nineteenth-century Marxists, but they belong to another world.

Intellectually it is easy to explain the passage from Marxism through Leninism to Stalinism. The decisive stages were the conception of the revolutionary party and its activity, the role attributed to wars at the outset of revolutions, the doctrine of establishing socialism in a single country (or the doctrine of the "socialist bastion"), and, finally, the acceptance of the directing role of the Russian Bolshevik Party.

Originally Bolshevism was merely a single group within the social-democratic organization—a group distinguished by its extremism, its intransigence, its tendency to split up continually over controversial points of apparently secondary importance. Lenin's essential contribution today seems to us to have been neither the rather primitive materialism of his book, *Materialism and Empirio-criticism,* nor his interpretation of the general tendency of capitalism, but his theory and practice of revolutionary action. Its principal ideas are well known and may be easily summarized:

The proletarian masses, left to themselves, are in danger of satisfying themselves with trade unionism, that is to say, with the everyday, immediate struggle for improved living conditions. The intellectuals, on the other hand, seek to introduce the masses to their historic mission. They give the proletarian revolt its inspiration and its objective. The party, whose officials must include a high proportion of professional revolutionaries, is organized according to the rules of what Lenin called democratic centralism: the essentials of power are in the hands of the Central Committee, a sort of general staff to an underground army (the Bolshevik Party was generally outlawed before 1917).

At the time, this characteristic of the Bolshevik Party was insufficiently recognized by the leaders of the Second International, who considered it an aberration explainable by the conditions of the struggle against Tsarism. Democratic methods were regarded as normal, and the technique of violence and secrecy was regarded as a survival from the past. The Revolution of 1917 reversed such a view. The Bolshevik Party became the model for the other parties in the Third International.

Once they were masters of the Russian state, Lenin and his comrades sat back to wait for a European or world revolution, just as the early Christians waited for the return of Christ. When they abandoned hope for an early revolution, they adapted themselves to a situation which they had not foreseen, and which their very doctrine forbade them to anticipate: the proletariat had triumphed only in a single country; and that country—far from having arrived at the stage at which industrial development had led to the disruption of capitalism—was a country where agriculture still predominated, and whose industrial concentrations on the outskirts of the great cities were due to Western influence and capital. It was necessary, therefore, to provide a few supplementary hypotheses to realign theory with fact.

It was argued primarily that the conditions favorable to the Revolution had been created less by capitalism and crises than by wars, and that the proletariat did not necessarily win the day in the country that was industrially most advanced, but simply in the country in which the regime was the weakest and least well defended: "the weakest link in the chain." Thereafter, instead of waiting, as did the social democrats, for capitalism to ripen, revolutionaries must keep a continual watch for opportunities. Revolution thus ceased to be a quasi-mythological, almost undefinable eruption, which reversed the normal course of events. It now meant the seizure of power. All the parties in the Third International, ambitious to imitate the Bolsheviks, had but one objective, one obsession: the seizure of power. Trade union action, social legislation, economic reforms—all these things lost interest except as means for attaining that one objective.

The Russian and the other parties in the Third International work on similar principles of organization and action, and perform various co-ordinated functions within a general plan. The first task is to strengthen the bastion of socialism, that is to say, to speed up the industrialization in the only country conquered by the proletariat; for the theory of "Socialism in a single country" does not imply the abandonment of the hope of a world revolution: it implies proceeding country by country. The occupied territory is organized, and the first proletarian state is strengthened. Communist parties in other countries will be sacrificed, if necessary, to that higher priority. Expansion will take place in a later phase. What circumstances will make expansion possible? Once again the sole reply is—war. The capitalist world has entered a period of decadence, of which economic crises and especially wars are the symptoms. A first world war made possible the Revolution of 1917. A second would give the proletariat the opportunity for further conquests.

The pre-eminence of the Russian party has its doctrinal justification. The Bolsheviks do not simply claim the authority rightfully conferred on them as victors, but invoke the common destiny of world revolution and of the socialist bastion. The confusion between the revolutionary cause and the national interests of the Russian state was inevitable. Leninist centralization applied to the International soon led to similar results: the Central Committee (in this case the Russian heads of the Comintern) exercises the same rigid control, the same unconditional authority over all the sections of the International as that which the Leninist, and later the Stalinist general staff exercised over the clandestine groups before 1917 and over the various activities of the party, both before and after the seizure of power.

As long as we confine ourselves to this abstract summary, it might be imagined that the change from the Second to the Third International was limited. Communism, it might be supposed, was a version of Marxism, and the most reasonable version, since it had profited by the experience of the twentieth century. In theory, its principal originality lay in the substitution of wars for crises and the decay of capitalism as an essential factor in the proletarian revolution. In practice, its originality consisted in generalizing the method of organization and action peculiar to the Bolsheviks, and in recognizing the pre-eminence of the Russian party—both because that party controls a great state and because the fate of the world revolution seems now to be bound up with that of the Soviet Union. These innovations leave intact the traditional doctrine—dialectical materialism, the class struggle, capitalist contradictions, etc. But their scope has greatly changed. Communism has introduced a foreign body into the European societies, and in thirty years they have been unable either to assimilate it or to reject it.

The traditional doctrine had two basic elements: a conception of the world (or at least of human society), and an interpretation of capitalism and its natural development. The Marxist parties claimed to be acting on the strength of the idea they had formed of the inevitable future of capitalism. The Communist parties, however, were not interested in what we have called elsewhere "the pattern of the evolution of capitalism."[1] They were not waiting for the development of the forces of production to create the objective conditions for revolution, but were adapting themselves to circumstances, one set of circumstances in nationalist China and another in the United States. In both countries their method was identical: to form a party engaged in agitation, espionage, and insurrection. In both countries the objective was identical: to undermine the existing regime and to prepare for the seizure of power. The pattern of capitalist evolution provided the link between historical mate-

[1]Cf. R. Aron, *Le Grand Schisme* (Paris: Gallimard, 1949), chap. v.

rialism and the action of the socialist parties. The day that pattern disappeared there would remain on one hand revolutionary action, purely opportunist, and on the other hand an ideology justifying the former. Faith alone could unify action and ideology.

By what miracle, indeed, could the few thousand intellectuals or workers, registered members of the American Communist Party, represent the proletariat of the United States? Why should a party composed mainly of peasants represent the proletariat of China? In theory, it is easy to call the Communist Party the advance guard of the proletariat and to entrust it with guiding the masses toward the accomplishment of their mission; in practice, the party replaces the proletariat. Thenceforth it is the party, not the proletariat, that is invested with the historic mission. It is to the party that supreme value is attached. When a proletariat does not rally to the Communist Party, it is the former, not the latter, that is accused by doctrine.

The transfer of the proletariat's historic mission to the party has another and still more serious result. The only true road forward becomes that which is marked by the triumph of the Communist Party. The world is divided into two camps and two only: the countries where a Communist party is in power; and all the others, which are dubbed capitalist even if a labor party is in power, even if most of the enterprises are owned by the state, and even if the equalization of incomes is carried further than in the socialist homeland. This Manichean vision of the world follows necessarily from the role attributed to the Stalinist party. For if its conquest of power is the essential and sufficient condition of the revolution—whatever the material circumstances—then Rumania, tyrannized over by a few officials of the Kremlin, has had its revolution, and Great Britain, even under the Labor Party, remains capitalist. Here we have the irrefutable logic of schizophrenia.

In such a system, the revolutionary priority conceded to the countries described as underdeveloped becomes comprehensible. As capitalism spreads and the living standard is raised the revolutionary ardor of the masses cools. The famine-stricken masses of Asia will provide the professional agitators with a larger and more docile following than would the workers of General Motors. The Bolshevik technique that originated in Tsarist Russia proved to be naturally adapted to the societies of the Far East, which had been shaken by the advent of industrialism.

Within the Western societies, in Europe and the United States, the action of the Communist parties no longer has anything in common with that of the socialist parties. The latter described themselves as revolutionary, but they acted in accordance with democratic methods: they supported the claims of the workers, they tolerated more or less autonomous trade unions, they tried to improve the workers' lot, they secured social legislation and wage increases by fair means or foul. These activities have nothing in common with those of the Communist parties, even when the latter used the same language and put forward the same demands. According to circumstances, the Communists want to see the condition of the workers growing either worse or better, but they never interest themselves in securing reforms for their own sake. They aim to control the trade unions and the masses so as to increase their power of agitation and subversion, a power which they use according to directives from Moscow. It is a technique of propaganda and insurrection, placed in the service, theoretically, of the revolution but, actually, of a foreign state; such, for the past thirty years, has been essentially the action of the Communist parties in the West, an expansion to global dimensions of the militant enterprise started by the first Bolsheviks against the Tsarist regime.

It is not so easy to describe the passage from Leninism to Stalinism. There was no fundamental change in doctrine or language. The gap between the ideology supporting the action taken and the action itself widened and grew progressively wider. It would be difficult to say just when Marxism became no more than what Pareto called a "derivation."

Lenin himself began to believe that the proletarian cause was being confused with that of his own group. Several times before 1917 he preferred to provoke a split rather than bow to what he regarded as an erroneous opinion of the majority. He unscrupulously manipulated congresses, convinced that his judgment of the situation expressed the historical truth. He readily condemned as traitors to the Revolution those who did not accept his views. Never for a moment did he permit any doubt that the Bolshevik seizure of power must be regarded as the first step in the social revolution envisaged by Marxism. Kautsky, who objected that the dictatorship of the Bolshevik Party was in fact that of a small minority over the great mass of the proletariat and of the country, was immediately classed as a renegade.

The contempt of formal democracy does not begin with Stalin. He imposed the Soviet regime on the satellite nations against the will of their populations, but Lenin had dissolved the Constituent Assembly elected in January 1918 because it did not have a Bolshevik majority. Whatever the opinion of those intellectuals who vituperate Stalin and keep up a worship of Lenin, the decisive break with the West and with democratic socialism was made by the founder of the party, and not by his successor.

From the beginning the authority of the Central Committee resembled more that of a military general staff than that of representatives elected by local groups or by their delegates. Today the Central Committee has been entirely brought to heel, to obey a single man, where thirty years ago there was a continual struggle, either in secret or in the open, between conflicting ideas and views. The heads of the party and the state now maneuver the rank and file and the party officials as they choose; they have, indeed, the power of life and death over those of whom in theory they are the representatives. In short, Lenin's "democratic centralism" has become the dictatorship of the Secretary General. The Secretary's power no longer has any right to be called democratic, but had Lenin's centralism a much better right? There is still discussion within the Politburo of the advisability of one measure or another in the existing circumstances. But the discussion is purely technical and remains secret. The party line is fixed at the highest level; "self-criticism" takes place only among the executants and not among the leaders, those who carry out decisions and not those who arrive at them. "Deviationists" are ruthlessly eliminated, by physical means where the party is in power: prison, deportation, trial, execution. Where the party does not control the police, everything is done to disgrace those who do not toe the line.

Stalinism is a logical development of Leninism. For the Secretary General the temptation was great to appoint reliable men to the positions of importance, and to assure in advance a majority at the

Central Committee policy congresses. Lenin had exerted his ingenuity to keep hold of the organizational threads when the party was illegal, and he appointed as representatives of the local groups militants who were theoretically elected, but whom he knew to be docile followers of his directives. Democratic centralism, applied to the twin bureaucracy of party and state, ended by robbing the electoral ritual of all practical influence. Free discussion between the leaders became a discredited memory. The man who could "control" the all-powerful bureaucracy, just like the man who had formerly controlled the secret network, was in fact the supreme ruler.

The national parties in the Third International changed between the time of Zinoviev and that of "the struggle for peace and against imperialism." But these changes paralleled those in the Bolshevik Party. Free discussion of policies and ideas disappeared from the Communist parties as it had done from the Bolshevik Party. The Russian leaders of the Comintern increasingly tightened their hold on authority, manipulating the controls of those parties as they did the Soviet bureaucracy; they carried to its limit the Stalinist *Gleichschaltung* of German or French Communism, as they had done in the former Tsarist empire. They introduced throughout the world the same spirit of orthodoxy which they had imposed on the homeland of socialism. There was, however, a limit to that assimilation, a limit determined by the contrast between the conservative or reactionary work of the Russian party and the revolutionary work of the foreign parties prior to a seizure of power.

In the intellectual field, the party did not immediately claim to possess the whole truth, although the premises of the spiritual dictatorship may be traced back to Marxism itself. Historical materialism suggested a general interpretation of each epoch. The works of artists and thinkers are associated by many subtle bonds with industrial relations and with class struggles. The dominant class places its imprint on the whole society. After a fashion, the existing middle-class civilization will be carried away or transfigured by the proletarian revolution. All Marxists have declared more or less dogmatically that there is a relation between metaphysical postulates and political strategy. "Reformism" imperceptibly turned into Kantianism, into the dualism of fact and value; the extremists remained "monists," materialists. Most Marxists felt some inclination to regard a certain philosophical or moral orthodoxy as bound up with the revolutionary attitude.

Lenin and his comrades would have revolted against Stalinist practice. They would not have admired the official attitude toward art, they would not have agreed to the state condemnation of Mendelian theories. But they, too, had insisted on the supreme value of revolution, they had agreed to the subordination of intellectual freedom and of culture to the interest of the collectivity; they, too, had proclaimed their doctrine as absolute truth, and had regarded dialectical materialism as a rival of the transcendental religions. It only needed the coming into power of a man with no more than an elementary education for obscurantism to triumph alongside despotism.

The world as revealed by Stalinism to the faithful is peopled with some forces essentially good and others essentially bad. The Soviet Union, as such, was peaceful and democratic, even when it attacked Finland, even when it formed its alliance with Hitler, even when it reopened the concentration camps in Germany. France became imperialist from the simple fact that it accepted the Marshall Plan and received some arms from the United States. These attributes applied less to the conduct of the nations than to their essence, which was defined once and for all by the interpretation of sacred history. It matters little, in such circumstances, that the imperialist countries are or appear to be on the defensive; they are imperialist because they are capitalist, and consequently bent on expansion. Even if they were not in search of markets, they would still be imperialist because they are the incarnation of the past, as the Soviet Union is the incarnation of the future. In such an irreconcilable struggle between abstractions, such elements as current events, classes, and nations are transformed into mythical characters—capitalism, socialism, imperialism, and the like—whose ultimate end has been foreseen by the prophet.

The dialectic of purges is a simple extension of that Manichean concept. Marxists, like all men of action, have always tended to take account of acts rather than intentions, and of consequences rather than the acts themselves, and of the historical influence of ideas or procedures rather than their inspiration. Thus the non-Marxists have more than once been affected by the application of that

method: the European liberal was held responsible for colonial exploitation, and the defender of formal democracy found himself
blamed for working-class poverty. But the Communists were to act
with a complete lack of restraint against deviationists and opposi-
tionists, of whom it was asked whether they were weakening the
party and, consequently, whether they were adversaries of the
cause. The argument is commonplace: it has justified every revolutionary terror in history. But it is no longer enough to say that the
deviationist behaves like an enemy of the cause. To discredit him
and to restore the unsullied prestige of the leaders it is necessary to
denounce him not merely as the involuntary ally but the paid agent
of the enemy. Bukharin was supposed to have prepared Lenin's
assassination; Rajk was alleged to be an agent of Horthy's police or
of the British Intelligence Service for more than twenty years. By
this process of "linked identifications," anyone who ceases to obey
the leader is deprived of life and honor.

Having come this far, the interpreter of Communism is no longer
hampered by any limitation or obstacle. He can attach any meaning to anything, according to the interpretation of the world established by his sovereign decree. Since the supreme interpreter is also
the head of the state, this dialectic of the purge ends by sanctifying
success and power and by recognizing the master's word as the
criterion of good and evil. No one can be sure of following the true
path, for the paths change and the master reinterprets the past as he
chooses, just as he predicts the future. Today's orthodoxy will perhaps become tomorrow's deviation.

Clearly much has changed since Lenin, who wanted to conclude
peace with the Germans, waited for the course of events finally to
convince his colleagues on the Central Committee. Each of the historic decisions—the November *coup d'état,* Brest-Litovsk, etc.—
found the Bolshevik leaders divided. Several times Lenin found
himself in the minority, but he never dreamed of taking revenge on
his opponents when in the end they had to come round to his view.
And he was as prompt in reconciliation as he had been in breaking
with his opponent, providing that the opponent recognized his error
and gave practical evidence that he was bowing to the demands of
unanimity.

But Lenin did not extend his tolerance beyond the Bolshevik

Party. Even during his lifetime the other parties, including the Socialist Revolutionaries of the extreme left, who had taken part in the November *coup d'état,* were expelled from politics and deprived of civil rights. The principal nonconforming militants were imprisoned, deported, or forced to emigrate. What happened next? The deviationists within the party came to be treated just as the dissidents outside had been treated, whether socialists or not. Once more it must be admitted that this development was logical, if not inevitable.

It is true that nearly fifteen years passed after the Revolution before Stalin himself decided to cross the "bloody line" and put his party comrades to death. But at a time when kulaks were being killed off by the thousands such scruples were merely a survival. In the long run it was impossible for two conflicting worlds, one based on respect for your neighbor and the other on the unlimited rights of the state over the vast mass of non-party individuals, to exist side by side. There was an intermediate phase between the Leninist phase, in which everyone in the party was free to hold his own opinion so long as he respected the rule of discipline in action, and the later phase, in which the present, past, or future, actual or potential opponents confess to crimes which have not been committed. During this phase, in order to make sure of general discipline and to break any possible resistance, the public defense of any given policy was entrusted to the very men who had opposed it in the "cells" or in the Central Committee. Such men as Zinoviev and Bukharin had renounced their own views several times before taking the supreme vows and proclaiming the justice of the judgment that condemned them to death.

The successive purges trace perhaps more clearly than any theory the actual course that the Party followed. Lenin's party was decimated; three quarters or four fifths of the militants were liquidated. Many of the revolutionaries in France and Germany who had been among the first to rally to the Third International after 1917 broke with Bolshevism in the 1920s. The general staffs of the Communist parties in exile—Polish, Yugoslav, Hungarian, Spanish—were almost entirely destroyed. In Eastern Europe the Communist parties had scarcely come into power when, in 1949, national leaders, such as Gomulka, Rajk, and Kostov, who had not been trained in Moscow, or who had fought on the soil of their own countries, or who had been in touch with the West, were successively eliminated.

Most of Lenin's colleagues were intellectuals with an international culture. They followed the Bolshevik technique in action, but were uneasy in carrying the system to extremes. They rose against Tsarism mainly because they were heretics by temperament and would have nothing to do with injustice. But they were adept in revolt, and how could they make good officials? Triumphant Stalinism no longer needed the same men as militant Stalinism.

The same mechanism was at work in all the parties outside Russia. Everywhere the revolutionaries had to be replaced by technicians, intellectuals by administrators. The incompatibility of the two types was in fact greater among Communists abroad than at home. One may very well ask whether Lenin's colleagues opposed Stalin out of moral indignation, or divergence of ideas, or bitterness over defeat. But one must remember that, on the other hand, the Communists outside of Russia, who ended by breaking with the party or by being executed, had rallied to an ideal Bolshevism without being acquainted with the real thing.

Those who had been followers of Lenin thirty years earlier were extremists, irreconcilables set against social conformity; they were spiritual descendants of Rousseau, convinced that man is good and that the evils from which he suffers are the fault of society. Leninism was the ultimate form of European rationalist progressivism. On the morrow of the first war the pacifists gazed at that great Star in the East. When the economic crisis came, the country without unemployment became the model and the hope. The menace of Hitler directed the sympathy of the liberals toward the champion of anti-Fascism. After 1941, the glory of the Russian soldier was appropriated by the Soviet regime, and Hitler's conqueror was hailed as the standardbearer of peace and Europe's hope.

The pacifists of 1919 discovered that the Soviet Union did not condemn war in itself, but preferred civil to international war. The anti-capitalists of the thirties discovered that they could not approve of forced labor as a means of suppressing unemployment. The anti-Fascists discovered that Stalinism had perfected the Fascist technique. The anti-Hitlerites of the forties discovered that Stalin's European unity could be as hateful as Hitler's. The renegades or victims of Stalinism are not simply idealists disappointed by reality, or revolutionaries incapable of adapting themselves to the new order, or nationalists up in arms against the Kremlin supremacy, or Occidentals weary of propaganda or unfamiliar with "eternal Russia." In thirty years the very spirit of the revolutionary movement itself has changed.

Marxism is the exaltation of a post-capitalist future that is unknown and unknowable. Stalinism is the exaltation of a society that is disappointing to idealists and alien to the genius of the Western mind.

Yet Stalinism has not abandoned Marxism's exaltation of the future. It argues that Russia is passing through the socialist phase (to each according to his work), and has not yet reached the Communist phase (to each according to his need). More simply, the present privations are (or were) explained by the requirements of industrial construction. Consumption obviously must be reduced as long as 20 to 30 per cent of the national income is devoted to capital expenditure and armament. And capital expenditure is essential in order to reduce rural overpopulation by absorbing in the factories the men who in the countryside would be regarded as unemployed, even if they were working.

Thus the low standard of living in the Soviet Union is not the cause of disillusion, although anti-Communists cling to it as a clinching argument. More than thirty years after the Revolution of 1917, a social structure has been built up which, observers agree, presents certain specific characteristics:

No group and no individual retains any possibility of independence in relation to the state. The power of the state is total and arbitrary. Through the *kolkhozy*[2] the peasant is once more tied to the land, which does not belong to him, apart from his individual plot. Through the tractor stations the *kolkhozy* are subjected to the authority of the planners and of the authorities responsible for collectivization. Work books and internal passports limit the worker's freedom to choose his employment and his place of residence.

[2]The regrouping of the *kolkhozy* that was decided on in 1950 marks a further stage in the process of the complete subjection of the peasantry to the state.

Transfers of labor, purges, removals of populations, and forced labor camps enable the public authorities to distribute their human material as they wish, both in time of war and peace.

The Soviet society comprises social groups distinguished from each other by their occupations, their styles of living, and their incomes—*kolkhoz* workers, factory workers, skilled and unskilled workers, writers, accountants of the collective enterprises, factory managers, trust directors, *kolkhoz* managers, and trade union secretaries. But none of these groups has any power, none is able to regard itself as a historical unit with its own interests to defend. The masses are amorphous, prey to propaganda, servants of an omnipresent authority. The social and state hierarchies are identical and the considerable differences in income among the various classes are subject to official policy. The privileged hold superior offices but they are wage earners just like the non-privileged. This combination of the elements of bureaucracy and aristrocracy is not so much an innovation as a return to an age-old tradition. Similarly, the managers of agricultural or industrial enterprises, the heads of trusts, and the Secretaries of Ministries, are all officials of the Soviet state.

The party is inseparable from the regime in its ideology.[3] It regards itself as the product neither of the past nor of tradition, but of the Revolution. It finds its justification in the services it renders to socialism, but conversely it has to accept the law of orthodoxy. What socialism demands, only the chiefs, and especially the supreme chiefs, can know and proclaim. The Christian religion is not eliminated, but the supreme truth is the truth of history as it is being made. Anyone who betrays that truth is betraying the supreme value in the name of which he has exercised the right of life and death over his fellow men. The privileged class is, at one and the same time, the bureaucracy of a state that absorbs the whole community and the clergy of a militant Church.

Nothing is less Western than a society of this type. Indeed, Western societies are characterized by their rejection of unity. They distinguish between the temporal and the spiritual power, between Pope and Emperor, between national Church and Papal Church, between the nobility and the monarchy, between the bourgeoisie

---

[3]There is less association among other sections of the Soviet elite, such as the non-party technicians or the army officers.

and the *ancien régime,* between the proletariat and the bourgeoisie: life in the West is made up precisely of such tensions, which are not repressed so much as controlled—a life that requires effort, struggle, creation. The Soviet society aims at unity: it no longer allows rivalry either between the temporal and the spiritual power, or between the social forces, or between society and the state. In uniting temporal and spiritual power it harks back to Byzantium. In forcing all persons and all resources into the service of the state, it conforms essentially with all tyrannies. The transformation of the population into an amorphous mass organized by bureaucratic and military authorities is a return to a still more ancient social system.

The ideology of Stalinism is of Western origin, but no European theorist ever accepted the interpretation of Marxism given by the Bolsheviks or the technique of action they drew from it. Stalinism combines the Marxian doctrine with certain elements peculiar to Russia, which, according to the doctrine itself, was not ripe for a socialist experiment. The February Revolution was born of an intense aspiration to freedom, which the Bolshevik seizure of power destroyed after a few months by substituting for the absolutism of the Tsars a severer but probably more efficient authority. The Mensheviks and the Cadets represented the Western outlook. The Bolsheviks, using the language of Marxism, re-established the tradition of Ivan the Terrible and Peter the Great.

Stalinism owes its influence in Europe to the Western origin of its religion; it owes its conquering power in Asia to the strange combination of bureaucratic despotism with modern faith in technical progress. Paradoxically, the contradiction between myth and Soviet reality becomes a source of strength rather than weakness.

## Chapter VII

## EXPANSION OF STALINISM

**B**EFORE the First World War, the Bolsheviks represented a small part of the Russian social democratic movement, which in turn represented only one of the small revolutionary parties within the Tsarist empire. In 1917 their small sect took control of the Russian state. It soon created a new International, imposed its own techniques of organization and action upon the national groups, and established a network of espionage and subversion throughout the five continents. After the Second World War, the same Bolshevik Party, controlling one of the two great world powers, subjugated 100 million Europeans, who had been "liberated" by the Red Army. In Asia the Chinese Communist Party, repeating the exploit of the Russian party, victoriously concluded the civil war to become the master of the former Middle Empire. The Stalinist world was thereby extended from a line between Stettin and Trieste to the frontiers of Indo-China.

The extent and rapidity of those successes sowed terror everywhere. After having underestimated or despised Lenin and his companions, Europe is now inclined to admire their successors beyond all reason. Communism has even been likened to a salvationist religion and compared with Islam, whose armies overthrew the infidel and whose ideas won souls.

Bolshevism forced its way to power by violence. In Russia it began with a *coup d'état* and won the civil war that followed. In China the order of events was reversed. The Communist Party set up a civil and military organization independent of the Chinese state, and ended, after more than twenty years, by defeating the rival government of the Kuomintang. In the Eastern European countries, the Communist parties, thanks to the presence of the Red Army, set themselves up in key positions under cover of a pretended national front. After that it was child's play to seize power completely.

The technique of Sovietization in cold blood, as it was applied to the European countries of the Soviet zone, can happen anywhere. On the arrival of the Soviet troops in Rumania, the Stalinist party in that country had only a few hundred members. Polish hostility to Russia, Tsarist and Bolshevik alike, is unquestionable. Czechoslovakia had a social structure analogous to that of the Western countries. In all these countries the Stalinists succeeded in eliminating both opponents and allies and in setting up regimes parallel to that which the Communist Party had taken twenty years to build up in Russia. They had profited by experience: imitation takes less time than creation of the prototype.

It would be absurd to seek an intrinsic affinity, such as that of the peasant majority or of the Slavic race, which might predispose the countries of Eastern Europe to follow the path of the Communists. Any country liberated by the Red Army—had it been France or Britain or even Spain—would have had the same fate. Only in Russia and in China were circumstances such that a Bolshevik revolution was possible without foreign intervention.

The two great revolutions of the twentieth century, the Russian and the Chinese, which both claim to descend from Marxism, preceded rather than followed the spread of capitalism. They were produced in agricultural countries where the vast majority of the population lived off the land; and both countries suffered—although in different degrees—from rural overpopulation. In neither country would successful revolution have been possible without the allegiance, or at least the consent, of the peasant masses. In Russia, it is true, the workers of Petrograd and Moscow, reinforced by rebellious soldiers, played a decisive part in the *coup d'état*. But once the civil war had started, the Red Army would probably have achieved nothing had the peasants not hated the White armies so much. The Chinese Communist Party, after Chiang Kai-shek had broken with it and driven it from the cities, was even more closely associated than the Russian with the peasants. After the break with

Chiang the whole party, which had originally been formed in the south, trekked all the way across China to a remote province in the northwest. There it carried out agrarian reforms that were moderate at first such as reducing the rate of interest and the landlord's share of the crops, but which later became more radical in such measures, for example, as dividing up the great estates.

In neither Russia nor China was industrial civilization indigenous. Russia was Europeanized in the eighteenth century under a succession of Tsars, with the consequent formation of a bureaucracy. In the latter half of the nineteenth century, and especially at the outset of the twentieth, industry made rapid progress, but it was financed largely by foreign capital and organized with the assistance of foreign engineers. To be sure, Russia participated heavily in the Western scientific movement, as well as in continental literary and artistic enterprises throughout the nineteenth century and up to the explosion of 1917. But European influences were only superficial, limited in their effect to a small section of the upper class, a group aloof from the masses and divided between the desire for liberal institutions copied from the West and a more or less mystical aspiration to be faithful to the national soul.

China meanwhile has been in a state of crisis ever since European influences precipitated the collapse of its age-old civilization. For half a century it has sought to combine Western industrial techniques and administration with its own traditions. The Kuomintang having failed, the Communists have made a fresh attempt, based, apparently, on an extreme form of Westernization. Its rejection of the traditional organization of family and community and of the philosophical and religious ideologies of the past is more drastic even than that of earlier revolutionary movements. But Russia's example has inspired a certain amount of caution. Most of the intellectuals who formed the general staff of the Bolshevik Party thought that they were continuing the effort of the Russian Westernizers and not that of the Slavophils. Lenin, in 1917, thought that the Russian proletariat was sacrificing itself on the altar of the world revolution. Thirty years later, we find that the Bolshevik actuality has become exactly the reverse of its original conception.

The followers of Mao Tse-tung seem to be adopting the very latest Western fashions in political ideology and technique. Marxism enables the individual Chinese, who has suffered such humiliation in face of the material superiority of the West, to overcome his feelings of inferiority. When a country goes over to the "progressive" or the "socialist" camp, it feels that it has joined the advance guard of mankind, even if it is centuries behindhand in its equipment.

In Russia as in China, therefore, the revolutionary situation developed from a violent encounter between Western influences and the traditional society. In both cases Communism mobilized nationalism in its own interest in order to end the West's monopoly of power, to catch up industrially with the capitalist countries, and to outdistance them in terms of social structure. In this deeper sense it may be said that Leninism or Stalinism, once introduced not into established capitalistic countries but into countries humiliated, if not enslaved, by the West, has become a sort of National Socialism.

Leninism, a Western product turned against the West, does not triumph during those tranquil periods when only non-violent means are available to its adherents. In 1914, the Bolshevik section of the Russian social democrats had only a few thousand members. In 1937, when the Sino-Japanese war broke out, Chiang Kai-shek was unable to liquidate the Communists, but the Communists were even less capable of defeating the Kuomintang. Just as the war of 1914 had weakened the administration of the Russian state, so eight years of war in China helped the Communists to undermine the social and moral groupings of the old order, at least in the northern provinces, where they carried on guerrilla warfare as much against Chiang Kai-shek as against the invader.

The Communists count on war to create their opportunity to take possession of decadent states.

There is no country in which it is impossible to organize at least a minor Communist movement. Even in the United States some tens of thousands of people were won over to the cause, and, as it now appears, their network of espionage extended to the highest ranks of the Administration. It would be easy to explain these individual allegiances by one or another of the mechanisms of revolutionary or religious conversion. A list might be given of the types of the converted—idealists, cynics, misfits, or, at the other extreme, middle-class persons whose success has not satisfied their aspirations or who are disturbed by their privileges, those who are proud of belonging to a tiny minority looked down upon today and triumphant tomorrow; materialists with an unconscious nostalgia for the absolute, and Christians who are disappointed by the churchgoers' cult of prosperity. But individual psychology that takes no account of the historical element misses the essence of the matter, the strength or weakness of a particular religion at a particular time or in a particular country.

In organization, tactics, and ideology, Communist parties everywhere are similar if not identical. In one place they may form a clandestine group, while elsewhere they may have hundreds of thousands of adherents; here they may have sympathizers and accomplices outside their own closed circle, while there they arouse fierce hostility. But always and everywhere Stalinism succeeds in recruiting the leaders and supporters of a conspiracy. The effectiveness however of the party in its struggles, whether secret or open, depends on its possessing a considerable number of militants or sympathizers. In this respect the results obtained in the West vary considerably from region to region.

The Anglo-Saxon and Scandinavian countries have, so far, been relatively immune to the Communist virus. Not that there are no Communists in the United States or Great Britain, in Australia or Sweden, but they are few in number and are faced with the resistance not only of the middle class but of the great mass of the people, including the majority of the working class. The struggle against Communism is carried on by the trade union leaders, who have an accurate sense of the danger. For Stalinism has shown that it knows how to subordinate union action during the first phase to considerations of political strategy; after the seizure of power it knows how to subordinate the unions themselves to the state. Union leaders are too intelligent to be caught by the argument—so convincing to certain intellectuals—that there is no reason for the existence of independent trade unions after the state has become proletarian. They know, on the contrary, that union independence must be maintained at all costs; for whoever may be masters of the state, they naturally tend to misunderstand the claims of the governed. Whether bourgeois or proletarian, any state that has everything its own way slips into tyranny.

No doubt there are other causes that may explain the inability of a secular religion (or religions, for Fascism had little more success) to take root in these privileged countries. They all have a relatively high and still rising standard of living; and they had been spared all or most of the effects of the First World War. In spite of a rapid fall in the living standard, and in spite of the loss of Indonesia, Holland has hardly been touched by Communism. Great Britain, defeated by her victory and reduced to austerity, is little affected by the dream of the classless society. In addition to economic and social causes, a moral and historical cause is manifest. The rejection of a secular religion as such seems to be characteristic of the peoples of a genuinely democratic tradition, in the Anglo-Saxon sense of the term.

Individualist democracy, of Protestant origin and Christian inspiration, is thoroughly incompatible with the Stalinist ideal. The custom of settling affairs locally and the taste for initiative and for private enterprise are threatened by the all-powerful state. The sense of personal responsibility, and of a faith freely adopted, is opposed to the authoritarian orthodoxy of Stalinism and its extreme form of clericalism and obscurantism. The Christian faith has not always retained the full measure of its essential characteristics, but it has developed as a sort of moralism rather than renounce its heritage by turning into an anti-Church.

It is not possible to say as much of the French democratic tradition. In becoming Jacobin, it tended in the direction of an authoritarian, centralized state. The myth of the General Will justifies not the rights of individuals or of the opposition but the omnipotence of the majority. The disciples of Rousseau liked to dream of a civil religion. This line of non-Catholic thinkers envisaged substituting for traditional religion a cult of the Supreme Being and the Comtist religion of humanity, in short, a religion directly adapted to social needs—of which they considered themselves to be good judges.

In Western Europe there are only two great Communist parties. In France and Italy, Communism is the contemporary incarnation of anti-Catholicism, a Church to rival the Catholic Church. In these Catholic countries, unlike the Protestant countries, the intellectual and social movements of modern times have been, or have seemed to be, directed against the Roman Church, which in the past was bound up with the pre-revolutionary structure of society, or, in the modern world, the bourgeois structure. There was nothing of the kind across the Channel. Democracy, radicalism, and trade unionism remained impregnated with Christian ideas, which are universally held to justify the popular demands. Of what use is a violent revolution, or an orthodoxy, when there is neither an orthodoxy to replace nor a Bastille to be razed?

The Catholic populations find once more in the anti-Church the claims to universality, the dogma, and the discipline[1] that were or are the normal form of spiritual action. But at the same time, Communism draws remarkable strength, even when temporarily beaten, from the fact that it takes its stand as a rival Church. In France, the socialists, radicals, and rationalists who reject Stalinism prevent a direct collision between the two Churches. In Italy on the other hand the temporary weakness of the liberals left Rome and Moscow face to face in the elections of 1948. It is fair to say that transcendental religion remains the principal enemy of secular religion. But in our day transcendental religion is stronger when it is not contained within a Church and instead dedicates itself to a point of view that can be shared by both believers and non-believers.

But the spread of Communism in France and Italy is not to be explained by these generalities. Further analysis reveals other causes. Among the countries of the West, France and Italy are those in which economic progress has been abnormally retarded, and in which a pre-capitalist structure has retarded the growth of the means of production. These are the underdeveloped countries of the West.

The agricultural worker of southern Italy, without property and paid wretchedly low wages, readily becomes a rebel as soon as he stops regarding his lot as inevitable, as soon as he no longer regards his condition as ordained by God, and as soon as he perceives or is shown a glimpse of hope. Similarly the workers in the Paris suburbs in the last century, or in those of Petrograd in 1905 and

[1] This statement does not, of course, mean that the dogma and discipline of Catholicism are of the same nature as those of Communism.

1917, ill paid, recently arrived from the villages, and remote from their normal environment, were easily accessible, as isolated units in the midst of crowds, to the appeal of a faith, either transcendental or political.

On the other hand, the industrial workers in northern Italy or in the Paris region are not normally susceptible to Stalinism; rather their rallying to reformist socialism would seem to have more in common with the general political evolution of the West. It is not difficult to see the many reasons for this situation. The wage level within a given economic unity depends largely on the average productivity of labor: the maintenance of an agricultural regime under conditions of poor productivity or overpopulation brings the wages of the workers below their natural aspirations. The French skilled worker in industry often has a living standard that is in accordance neither with the quality of his work nor with his own quality as a human being. The social conditions created by urban concentration increase his dissatisfaction. In modern industry labor conditions for certain workers in certain countries create a dissatisfaction that is vented on the capitalist system, which is held responsible for them. The tradition of the French trade unions is revolutionary rather than reformist, anarchist rather than collectivist. Stalinism aims to eliminate entirely any anarchist tendency, but so long as it remains an opposition party it keeps agitation alive and urges direct action. Thus, it is mistakenly regarded as close to revolutionary trade unionism. Outside France, the trade unions of anarchist tendency—for instance, seamen's or longshoremen's unions—are the most susceptible to the influence of Soviet agents.

Finally, it must not be forgotten that the Stalinists have not so much converted the masses as colonized the trade unions in the course of the war, the Resistance, and the liberation. The operation had several stages: a party was organized, with its militants in key positions, and from those key positions they manipulated the masses. This operation reveals the essential danger: Communism is an army as well as a Church. The number of converts matters less than the strength of the organization.

In its first phase Communism is civil war in both theory and practice; in the second phase its theory and practice become totalitarian tyranny. But the inability of Stalinism to triumph by electoral means in the West does not mean its ultimate defeat. The Stalinists know that Europe cannot be converted peacefully; but it can be conquered. By converting a minority, they pave the way for conquest. The astonishing fact is not that Europe refuses to submit to an alien Church, but that there are so many Europeans who are awaiting liberation by a despotism that would destroy age-old traditions.

In the Stalinist enterprise, the secular religion fulfills a triple function:

To begin with, it dictates the mentality of the professional revolutionary; it maintains the faith and the discipline of the parties; and, during the periods of socialist struggle and preparation, it wins enough adherents for the party to be able to paralyze the functioning of liberal societies.

Secondly, it makes its adversaries doubtful of the justice of their causes and creates an attitude of sympathy toward the party.

Thirdly, once the party has gained possession of the state, it has to create the new man to accomplish the spiritual transformation that will render the ruling elite and the masses permanently loyal to the rules, conceptions, and mode of living of the Communist society.

The first function depends mainly on the actual Leninist and Stalinist elements—the party's mission, the leaders' authority, and the dialectic of the purges; the second depends on the Marxist ideologies—the class struggle, the decomposition of capitalism, the inevitable rise of the proletariat to power, and so on. The third element is probably beyond the means of both orthodox Marxism and of Stalinism.

Stalinism is obviously out to win over the masses, but, following the example of Bolshevism, it is concerned first of all with creating a party, that is to say, a reliable political organization. The unorganized masses who do not obey the directives of a general staff render hardly any service to the Communist enterprise. A party of professional revolutionaries, even if it is separated from the masses, is at least, as it has been in the United States, an espionage organization or a cover for one. Now, it has been proved a hundred times

over that the Bolshevik doctrine is highly effective when its immediate objective is to recruit a minority of militants who are ready
for anything. Why is the Leninist version superior in this respect
to the social-democratic version of Marxism? The explanation
seems simple: It is not theory that creates unstinted devotion, but
practice. The party obliges its militants to sever their relations with
the world around them and to integrate themselves in the revolutionary community. This segregation and integration bind the faithful permanently and in absolute loyalty. It is not to the profundity
or the truth of its ideology that Communism owes the fanaticism of
those who serve it: it owes it to the effectiveness of its technique of
organization and action.

For thirty years throughout Europe, those in revolt against the
injustices of the bourgeois social order have been drawn to Communism as the only genuinely revolutionary movement. Men were
not rallying to a particular interpretation of Marxism, but to the
working-class party that had not betrayed the cause of the proletariat by making an alliance with the bourgeoisie, and that had
broken with a defeatist tradition. It was by the glory of the "ten
days that shook the world" that all the revolutionaries were drawn
to Moscow, rather than by the doctrine of Lenin's *Materialism and
Empiriocriticism* or *State and Revolution* or by Stalin's *Foundations
of Leninism*. Doctrinal instruction appeared later to confirm ad-
herence and maintain the connection between the two elements of
Stalinism: on the one hand, the general philosophy of history and
the description of capitalism and, on the other, the attribution of its
historic mission to the party of Lenin and Stalin. At the outset, not
of the century, but of the 1920s, that connection was very doubtful: Why should the proletariat of a backward country assume the
leadership of the proletariat of the world? As the Soviet Union
gained strength and Stalinism spread throughout the world, the
connection became increasingly plausible. Proof that the cause of
the Soviet Union is also that of the world revolution requires,
nevertheless, the constant use of dialectics, the art of showing that
any particular political line is justified by the interest of the proletariat. For this purpose the popularized Marxism of Stalin is of
incomparable value: it offers an interpretation of history for the

semi-educated. It gives to people with no more than an elementary education the pleasant feeling of easily acquiring an understanding of the world around them. It is the typical philosophy of the age of the masses and of the popularizers.

Indoctrination of the militants enables them to accept a system of thought, or rather a collection of phrases, that offers an explanation of any event so long as the key to the system is permanently in the hands of the leaders of the movement. It is easy to call the social democrats at one moment Public Enemy No. 1, and at the next the brother party. But it is also necessary for the militant to acquire the habit of accepting the formula suited to the circumstances as dictated to him on every occasion from above. There have been occasions—for example, the Ribbentrop-Molotov pact—when an about-face has subjected discipline to a severe test.

Theoretical training, too, is combined with a sort of practical training. The reflexes of the militant are cultivated like those of the soldier; he is taught to accept orders from the responsible leader as from an officer; he is inculcated in the conviction that the authority of the hierarchy, from the Kremlin down to his immediate superior, is virtually absolute. The atmosphere of solidarity and of service becomes as indispensable to the faithful as the air he breathes. The sense of belonging to a sect, not to be soiled by the impurities of the corrupt world, a sect to which the future belongs, overcomes any repugnance that might be produced by an immorality of method. More and more it is no longer the vision of the world and of history that inspire loyalty in the militants, but the pressure of the organization. An army can survive long after the combative enthusiasm of individual soldiers declines; it is necessary to believe in the army, in honor, in the mother country in the beginning; thereafter, organization replaces a diminished fervor.

Outside the Communist Party, however, the Marxist ideology, viewed as a continuation of the rationalist and humanist tradition of the West, inspires sympathy. How could we break with the Soviet Union, one might ask, when it has created the economic basis of a classless society through the collective ownership of the means of production? How can we refuse to maintain contact or alliance with the Communists when the future of the proletariat depends on it? How can we condemn the attempt to build up socialism when, for the first time, man is shouldering the tremendous task of ordering his economic environment? Every element of the prestige of Marxism works to the profit of Stalinism, in spite of Soviet realities.

In order to tear away the veil of illusions, one needs direct experience of those realities. The Czech worker subjected to the system of socialist emulation and deprived of trade unions, the peasant fearing to be brought into a *kolkhoz,* the intellectual deprived of his freedom of thought, the priest required to take an oath of loyalty to the state, the independent workers, artisans, traders, industrialists, all turned into proletarians, become blind to the attractions of Stalinism. Hence the paradox of the historical situation: there are probably more sincere believers on this side of the Iron Curtain than on the other. The Communist faith dissolves as it spreads. It destroys itself through its victories.

In all the Sovietized countries a minority comes to the support of the regime. But it seems very probable that the religion finds its believers mainly among the privileged under the regime—Stakhanovists, officials, and managers—or among the young, who have known no other life. After twenty years of totalitarian propaganda, the Russian people felt no complete solidarity with their masters: it was the German atrocities that induced them to come wholeheartedly to the defense of their country and their chains. It is the Soviet myth that attracts the masses: Soviet reality disappoints them.

The disappointment is easily explained when we measure the distance between the militant ideology and the regime that is set up after victory. The land is promised to the peasants, and a beginning is made by giving it to them, but a few years later collectivization is imposed on them by force, indeed by terrorism. To this day the Russian peasants are neither converted nor resigned, and a second collectivization is under way, reducing the number and increasing the size of the *kolkhozy,* virtually abolishing the peasant existence, and assimilating it to working-class conditions. National feeling is roused against imperialism, and then the people's democracies are subjected to the omnipotence of Moscow. The exploitation by the homeland of socialism exceeds in brutality the worst practices of capitalism. By what miracle could the new man be reconciled to his destiny?

Yet to what extent do these Stalinists take their doctrine as a total belief? Such, indeed, may be their ambition—to make Leninist Marxism the substitute for the religions of salvation. Yet the stake in the struggle, for instance, against the Catholic Church in Poland, Hungary, or Czechoslovakia, seems to be even more limited. The Russian tradition implies the subordination of Church to state, and an oath of loyalty from the priests to the temporal ruler. The patriarch of Moscow rails against the Pope, and has fallen into line with the "partisans of peace." The first thing demanded of the Czech or Polish priests is that they recognize the proletarian state. The independence of the Church, characteristic of Western Christendom, seems to the Stalinists a relic of European civilization, which they want to eliminate, at least during the first phase of their enterprise.

Will the second phase, aimed at the elimination of the Christian faith itself, follow next? It may, but in the light of past history it seems doubtful whether Stalinism has much chance of winning that battle. It may carry Christians back to the time of the persecutions, but it will not take the place of their religion because it is not itself a genuine religion, but a miserable caricature of religion.

Intellectually, its poverty is unexampled. Even if we admitted a historical progression of society from capitalism to socialism, the confusion of the proletarian cause with the cause of the Russian Communist Party is puerile. Even if we assume, against every historical precedent, that collective ownership and economic planning were to promote the emergence of a higher civilization and free institutions, the object of that faith dissolves in the very process of its realization. There is a certain nobility in being devoted to an unknown future. For the secular religion to survive its triumph, it would have to teach the crowds to worship their masters. The Stalin cult is the first example of this return to a deification of Caesar. Does an attempt of that sort do more than mark an episode in a troubled age?

In Russia itself Christendom has resisted, and the regime is presently inclined to compromise rather than resume its war of extermination. The present compromise is inspired by tactical considerations: the Orthodox Church is rendering services to Soviet imperialism. But beyond these alternating episodes of atheist propaganda and toleration, I cannot help but anticipate the complete inability of Communism to create a new man.

Western opinion is afraid of the seductive influence that the collectivist system has upon youth; it is afraid that there will soon appear generations adapted to their lot and unable to comprehend freedom, generations that will bow to party discipline and to directed labor as a normal order of human existence. Quite certainly the Stalinists, by exterminating whole classes, will make it difficult to restore societies of the Western type. But from the proletarianized mass there should nevertheless re-emerge, through a slow ripening, social differentiations. The process will take time and to the political observer, who reckons in years, the destruction of the old order may seem final. But I am still not prepared to believe that a few decades will obliterate many centuries of Christianity. It is enough to grasp the basis of religious feeling to recognize the essential difference between Stalinist fanaticism and a genuine religion. Communism points out to its adherents enemies to hate and a future to build. It arouses passionate devotion. But it offers nothing to love.

While there is a tendency to exaggerate the moral strength of Communism, we tend too often to fail to recognize its political and military strength. There is no need to convert the masses; it is enough to have an active minority and to keep a semi-passive majority in a state of uncertainty in order to conquer or paralyze a state or even a continent.

In Asia, where the imperial powers of Europe are being forced into an inglorious retreat, and where millions of illiterate men are being roused to revolt against hunger and the white race, a party with a small but well-organized membership, under the direction of semi-intellectuals who have become professionals in political action —a party that places itself at the head of these blind crowds—has a chance of seizing power as it did in Russia and in China. In Europe, divided by the Iron Curtain, and living still in the ruins of war, the Communist parties have an efficient machine in both France and Italy. They have won the confidence of a large section of the masses, who are tempted by the Soviet myth or simply drawn to those who seem to be the only sympathetic interpreters of their indignation and their hopes. The Communists have little chance of peacefully gaining control of the French or Italian governments, but they need only prolong the impotence of Europe in order to prevent the re-establishment of world equilibrium. And they need only set in motion a few thousand tanks to destroy an age-old civilization.

## Chapter VIII

## THE ATOMIC AGE

**M**EN ARE EVER READY to accuse statesmen of backing into the future. Determined to prevent yesterday's disaster, they bring on tomorrow's. Neville Chamberlain constantly made declarations which historians had blamed Sir Edward Grey for not having made in 1914. President Roosevelt and Prime Minister Churchill waged the war of 1939–45 as if there were nothing of which they were so afraid as the birth of a new "stab in the back" legend. Soldiers and statesmen, in avoiding the mistakes imputed to their predecessors, fall, in their turn, into the pitfalls of history.

A striking exception to that generalization may be observed today. Imagination—which was lacking to Thiers to anticipate the benefits of railways, to the French general staff in 1914 to estimate correctly the effects of firepower, and to the general staff of 1939 to foresee the potentialities of armored divisions and of mass attacks by bombers—seems now to have been conferred on everyone, from the physicist to the man in the street. The question is only who will conjure up the most frightful visions of the coming apocalypse.

For the first time, the contemporaries of an invention believe themselves to be endowed with foreknowledge. They make 1945 —the year of the explosion of the atomic bombs over Hiroshima and Nagasaki—the Year 1 of the atomic age. The so-called bold spirits do not hesitate to label as anachronisms the traditional kind of dispute between states over a frontier line or over regions that for centuries have been regarded as strategic. Actually the course of international diplomacy has not yet been radically changed by the miraculous new weapon.

Soviet Russia is even more suspicious of foreign countries than was the Russia of Nicholas I, and it continues to attribute sinister designs to them. There are many evidences of these quasi-pathological suspicions. At the time, for example, when the Soviet Union was receiving supplies valued at 10 billion dollars under lend-lease, at the time of the alliance between the bourgeois democracies and the Soviet democracy, the Soviet Ministry of Foreign Affairs insisted on having a list of the names of all the American airmen who, after a bombing raid over Germany, were to land on a Russian airdrome. Whatever importance we may attach to these feelings, the fact remains that the direction of Soviet diplomacy since 1945 cannot be attributed to the fear of any early capitalist aggression, much less to the specific fear of the atom bomb.

The Lublin Committee was formed well before the explosions over Hiroshima and Nagasaki. The destruction of Polish resistance had been merciless: insurgent Warsaw was abandoned to a horrible fate; the leaders of the secret army and government were arrested and deported. In accepting representatives from the London Government on the Liberation Committee, Stalin made only an apparent concession. There, as in all the buffer countries, the Communists held the key positions. Vishinsky's intervention at Bucharest—when with the threat of tanks he forced King Michael to dismiss the Radescu Government and to send for Groza, the instrument of the Communists—dated from before what has been called the atomic fear. Those who recognized the right of the Soviet Union to demand "friendly" governments in its neighbor countries may not have realized the exact meaning given by the Communists to the word "friendly." As for the Politburo, it did not attach a different meaning to the friendship of Poland or Rumania after Hiroshima than it did before.

For thirty years Stalin had incessantly declared imperialist aggression to be imminent. (The threat from abroad, under the unchanging laws of tyrannies, justifies and multiplies internal terror.) But he really feared aggression only once, when Hitler had established himself in power in Germany. In a perfectly reasonable reaction, he sought security in two directions: first in agreement with the bourgeois democracies, and then in an understanding with Hitler. Experience suggests that fear did not inspire in Stalin and his colleagues the hyper-aggressiveness characteristic of the psychology of neurotics, but rather prudent moves aimed at reducing the danger—such as rapprochement with one section or another of the camp considered to be hostile.

After 1945 Stalin was careful to avoid an explosion, but he was convinced that as long as he did not go beyond certain limits he ran no risk—and he was quite right. It may be that he did not at once recognize the military efficacy of the atom bomb. However this may be, in 1946 and 1947 the United States apparently had scarcely more than a few atom bombs; it has been said that their industrial production did not begin before 1947. The bombs then in existence could not have determined the issue of a conflict between the mighty powers of this world.

It would seem therefore that the opinion of many anti-Communists—that the atom bomb had saved Europe from Sovietization between 1945 and 1949—is just as difficult to defend, just as open to question, as the opinion of the "sympathizers" or the "impartial," who hold it responsible for the cold war and the Stalinist invective. The atom bomb gave to Washington diplomacy of 1946 and 1947, when American opinion discovered Soviet ambitions and the weakness of the democracies in conventional armaments, a confidence that was of the utmost value. But if we ask whether the fate of Europe would have been different without the atom bomb, two obvious questions arise: Even if it had not had the bomb, would the United States have tolerated the expansion of the Soviet empire as far as the Atlantic? And would Stalin have been ready to face the risk of general war?

Great Britain and the United States, who had not stinted on sacrifices in order to prevent Germany from gaining control of the whole of the Continent, could not, without committing a really inconceivable folly, have stood by to see that same unification, fatal to the metropolis of the British Commonwealth, carried out by another Continental power, and one in every respect even more formidable than the Third Reich. What Great Britain had refused, at the price of a struggle to the death, to France and to Germany—to Napoleon and to Hitler—she would not have conceded to Stalin's Russia.

Stalin, who could not have been unaware of the reactions that would have been produced by the inclusion of Germany and France within his sphere of influence, would have done everything to put off a third world war for some years, even if the United States had had no atom bombs. Probably he regarded a third war as inevitable, but meant to set the date of its outbreak himself. An immediate drive to the Atlantic would have been contrary to his constant strategy.

Until 1949, which probably marked the end of the American monopoly, the atom bomb bore only one grave diplomatic responsibility: it was the cause of endless debates in the United Nations commission charged with organizing the control of that terrifying weapon. As is well known, the negotiations came to a deadlock, which convinced the American leaders that the leaders of the Soviet Union were systematically refusing to join in any measure of international collaboration.

We have no intention of entering into any lengthy discussion of the reasons for the deadlock. A full study of them would call for an analysis of the original proposals and the various replies from the Soviet Union. While the proposals, good or bad, contained in the Baruch plan were precise, the replies from the Soviet delegation varied. One gains the impression that the Soviet Union never wanted to accept the principles of the American plan, but that, being unwilling to assume public responsibility for a rupture, it dragged out the deliberations, agreeing to concessions on one point or another but returning to its fundamental objections as soon as the opposing points of view seemed to be drawing closer.

The guiding idea of the Baruch plan was the creation of an international agency for atomic energy, which was to exercise the rights of ownership, management, control, and supervision over the uranium mines and the industrial installations. Such an agency would have enjoyed a kind of extraterritoriality; it would have claimed the privilege of freedom of movement for its officials, of freedom of flight for its airplanes assigned to make aerial photographs, and so on. What chance was there, from the very outset, that the Soviet Union would accept such a concept?

The first stage of that international experiment would have been a census of uranium deposits and installations processing the fissionable material. Such a census would have enabled the outer world to penetrate the mystery with which the Soviet authorities surround the distribution of their industrial plant. How could a regime that regards every foreigner as suspect, and treats as state secrets most statistics which are published in other countries, be expected suddenly to throw open its territory to international officials—superspies in Stalin's view?

Let us even suppose the first obstacle actually overcome. The international agency would thereafter have sole responsibility for atomic science and industry. It would partition the installations considered to be dangerous (that is to say, carrying out the operations or processing the materials that might be associated with the manufacture of bombs) according to quotas established with a view to maintaining a sort of strategic equilibrium. It would grant licenses for non-dangerous installations, using "denatured" fissionable materials, in accordance with the economic needs of the various countries. Once more, we ask: By what miracle would the leaders of a state bearing a revolutionary message have agreed that the development of a perhaps decisive industry be submitted to the authority of an international agency on which "capitalist" states would always have a majority?

Whether one likes it or not, the Baruch plan infringed on two cardinal principles of the Soviet regime: industrial secrecy, and absolute sovereignty. The Stalinists find it somewhat irritating to have to put up with the presence of foreign diplomats on the soil of Holy Russia. They had no intention of putting up with the presence of "atomic scientists," whose privileges would have exceeded considerably those enjoyed by diplomats.

Once the inevitable incompatibility between the essential nature of the Soviet state and that of an international agency for atomic energy is recognized, the continual setbacks in the negotiations and the responsibility for breaking them off remain of purely historical interest.

When one surveys the entire period since the Hiroshima explosion, it is difficult to resist the impression that the United States has lost rather than gained by its famous atomic monopoly. It has been of no use in the cold war. The potential and actual forces of the United States and the Soviet Union have not only not been engaged, but until 1950 had hardly figured as a means of pressure or extortion. Neither in China nor in Greece has the outcome of the civil war been influenced by the relative strength of world forces. It has been said that the stock pile of bombs was equivalent to 175 Russian divisions. But the same equivalence could have been obtained by the maintenance of aerial and naval fleets armed with conventional weapons. Furthermore, it can now be seen that the United States has been led, by its atomic superiority, to adopt military and diplomatic conceptions whose dangers are now apparent.

Confident that the stock pile of bombs would suffice to prevent the Soviet Union from employing regular armies in any part of the world, the United States reduced to a minimum its own aerial, naval, and—above all—land forces capable of immediate action. It thus allowed itself to be driven into a position where, in the event of any local aggression, it would have to choose between passivity or world war—a formidable choice for a nation aiming to avoid a world war.

The strategy of intercontinental atomic war, which the Joint Chiefs of Staff in the Pentagon seemed to have adopted, is partly responsible for European defeatism. How could the nations of the Continent have failed to be discouraged in advance when their transatlantic ally and protector relied on a weapon against which they themselves would be defenseless? On the day when the potential enemy in his turn came into possession of the miraculous weapon (and that day probably came in 1949), reprisals for the destruction of Russian cities by American bombs were likely to be aimed at the cities of Europe. Every European would be a hostage in a total war—until and unless there are enough divisions to ward off Soviet invasion at the frontier.

Paradoxically, the American stock pile became really useful when it was no longer a monopoly. In 1951 America probably had a double superiority, in the number of bombs and in the means of delivering them. But by this time its aim was to overcome Western inferiority in conventional weapons and it relied upon its atomic stock pile simply to check direct Soviet oppression. For in 1950, the atom bomb had become if not a crucial factor in any potential war, at least an indispensable factor in the balance of world forces. And it is therefore easy to understand why Russian propaganda has made the bomb the target of its attacks.

But even apart from these considerations and from the propaganda that they generate, the question remains: Even in a just cause, is the use of certain weapons in itself legitimate?

The men who took the decision to employ the first two atom bombs acted in good faith; the Americans had made their choice on the basis that a landing on the Japanese islands would cost hundreds of thousands of lives. But now, after the event, it is difficult not to conclude that the decision to use the bomb was mistaken. By renouncing the formula of unconditional surrender, or simply by replying more quickly to the repeated approaches which the Emperor had been making for several months, the war could have been ended without the atom bomb and without the Soviet intervention that mortgaged the victory.

The use of the atom bomb against urban agglomerations did not constitute a radical innovation. After all, what was euphemistically called "zone bombing" struck residential districts, historical monuments, and the ancient parts of cities much harder than it did factories. The capacity of modern weapons to distinguish between civilians and combatants is limited, and zone bombing was, in principle, an acceptance of that fact. The atom bomb completes the evolution. It consecrates the use of *any* means against the *entire* population, civil as well as military, of the enemy country. By a logic that is paradoxical only in appearance, the country least warlike in its tastes and philosophy has thus played a decisive part in the advent of unlimited war.

Those who question the wisdom and the moral legitimacy of the strategy based on the atom bomb are not few in the United States. By the very fact of its concentration, the industrial equipment of the United States will one day, according to certain experts, be more vulnerable to atomic attack than that of any other country. It is contrary to the spirit of our civilization, certain other philosophers declare, to look upon whole cities as targets to be struck by the weapons of mass destruction. The citizens of an enemy nation should continue to be regarded as fellow creatures to whom we owe certain obligations.

One would have to be fanatic or blind to disregard the weight of such objections. But what can we do once the diabolical secret is out? Should the United States proclaim its intention not to be the first to use the atom bomb? The military staffs would reply by pointing out the danger of leaving the advantage of the initiative to a predatory power. Since it would have to be prepared to take reprisals, the United States could not stint preparations for an atomic war. The cost of these preparations increases the temptation to use the bomb once the moment has come. Would not renunciation of scientific weapons ultimately work out in favor of the Soviet Union? It has greater human resources, and a population accustomed to a more primitive living standard, and therefore less sensitive to the rigors of conventional war. Can the United States afford to renounce the scientific weapons, to which it owes its superiority, and give battle on a field where the enemy has the advantage?

For that matter, is the atomic weapon really unique? Has not research found other means of destruction equally inhuman, equally terrifying: poisons, radioactive clouds, bacteriological weapons? In the absence of an international agreement, which seems unattainable, the only hope lies in the wisdom born of fear.

None of the belligerents in the last war had recourse to poison gas, but all kept it in reserve in case the enemy took the initiative. Whatever may have been said, the general abstention was due much more to dread of reprisals than to any relative lack of efficiency in chemical weapons. These had, in fact, made considerable progress since 1918, but the Germans never decided to use them because the superiority of the Allied air force more than compensated for the possible superiority of their own gases. On both sides, the defenseless civil population would have been the victim of a decision from which everyone ultimately recoiled. We may thus assume that when some sort of equality in atomic weapons is established, the fear of reprisals might persuade the combatants to preserve moderation.

That hope is faint at the moment, but for another reason: the magnitude of the stake. When the chain of wars began, the stakes were not unlimited. France fought in 1914 to preserve her independence, but after two years of indecisive combat she had barely escaped the risk of being crushed. The original warlike passions had calmed down. It was not so much from a will to attain objectives indispensable to survival and unobtainable except through the surrender of the enemy that the war was pursued to the end, as from a desire to justify the immensity of the sacrifices by the brilliant reward of triumph.

In the second war this relation tended to be reversed. Hitlerite ambitions and methods aroused passions in the rest of the world more violent even than the fanaticism of the Nazis themselves. The dropping of phosphorus bombs on residential quarters by the Allies was horrible (and, after all, did more to compromise the victory than to hasten it). But how could public opinion revolt against such horrors when the Third Reich was organizing the cold-blooded extermination of millions of innocent people? The same sequence of modern weapons, political technique, and popular fury is already visible in the period of the so-called cold war.

Soviet propaganda tries to inculcate in the millions a hatred of those whom it styles capitalists or imperialists. They never suggest that the enemy may be honorably defending his homeland or his values: he is held up to the execration of the mob. The counter-propaganda of the West is of necessity occupied in spreading a hatred of the Communists which is liable to extend unfairly to the whole Russian people. The Nuremberg trials have shown the civil and military heads of states the fate that awaits them in the event of defeat. The populations of the West, with the exception of the minority won over to Stalinism, have no illusions about the consequences of a victory that would be at the same time a victory of the Russian Army and of the so-called national Communist parties. The Communist elite in the Soviet Union, once it starts the final struggle, will recoil from nothing. It will be indispensable, but singularly difficult, to convince the masses in the Soviet Union that the West bears no ill will except toward their tyrants, if atom bombs unite in death Stalinists and their opponents: women, children, and the secret police.[1]

Since the Second World War, the amplification of violence has proceeded on two levels: that of scientific weapons of mass destruc-

[1]On the level of realistic politics, this is the strongest argument against the use of weapons of mass destruction.

tion, and that of individual combat, carried on not by soldiers in uniform but by partisans. In Asia, guerrilla warfare is so changing the course of the world that the atomic age will perhaps also be called the guerrilla age. Even in Europe, partisan warfare inevitably begins when the conquering armies become sufficiently oppressive. Nothing will prevent the outbreak of clandestine fighting if the occupying power persecutes important minorities, if it tries to mobilize the workers of the conquered countries, or if by its mere presence it arouses bitter hatred.

Imagine the Soviet zone extended over the whole of Europe. How many millions of men would be doomed to death or deportation? In the end police brutality might stifle revolt. But there would be no revival of civilized values, only the inhuman triumph of enslavement.

The logic of total war runs the risk, in a third war, of dragging all mankind into an orgy of violence. The individual and the mass, actors or victims, snipers and bomber pilots, all will be committed. Atom bombs and hysterical propaganda, tanks and sub-machine guns, bombing offensives and peace offensives—every means will be employed.

At present the dread of hyperbolic war acts in favor of the cold war. If the cold war should unfortunately develop into open and general war, let us hope that this time statesmen will not let themselves be carried away by the blind fury of combat, but will remember that the object is not to crush the enemy but to attain certain political ends after the war. There are ways of conquering that quickly transform victory into defeat.

# LOGIC AND CHANCE

THE PRESENT WORLD is situated, so to speak, at the meeting point of three processes of development. The first of these processes led to a planetary unity and a bi-polar diplomatic structure; the second to the diffusion in Asia and Europe of a secular religion of which one of the two giant powers claims to be the metropolis; and the third to the perfection of weapons of mass destruction, to a total war animated both by modern science and primitive fury, with the atom bomb and the guerrilla as the extreme manifestations of unlimited violence.

Each of these processes includes—to employ Cournot's expression—one part logic and one part chance. Diplomatic unification was not achieved until this century, but it was prepared in the previous one. Thanks to their superior military techniques, the nations of Europe had conquered Africa and part of Asia, and exercised their influence even over the still independent Asian countries. The United States, which possessed a potential force equal to that of Europe, limited itself to banning the extension of colonial empires in the direction of the two Americas. The balance of power between the European countries left Great Britain the command of the seas. Since no army of the Western type existed either in the Near or Far East, Britain's possession of bases from which she could mount naval attacks was enough to guarantee the *pax Britannica*.

Since then, the influence of military power has increased considerably. In 1945 the United States maintained tens of divisions and thousands of aircraft abroad, from the Philippines to the Elbe

—that is, thousands of miles from their home bases. Similarly the Soviet Union gloried in two war industries, one in Siberia and the other in European Russia, and in two armies, one in Berlin and the other at Dairen and Mukden. In an era when heavy bombers have a combat radius of several thousand miles, when the continent-states that are the master players can mobilize populations of more than 150 million, and count on an industrial potential measured by hundreds of millions of tons of coal and by tens of millions of tons of steel, it is not surprising that the two protagonists find themselves face to face in every quarter of the globe. The amplification of the instruments of warfare and the enlargement of political units have burst the partitions between the zones of civilization. Aerial squadrons, continent-states, world-wide diplomatic unity—these three phenomena comprise a closed system; they imply one another, and no one can say which is cause and which is effect: simultaneously, they characterize the present state of affairs.

But none of these phenomena, or even their simultaneous occurrence, implied the bi-polar structure. At the beginning of the century, history seemed to be headed in a quite different direction. The rise of Japan in the Far East and of Germany in Europe led in each case to a complex configuration involving changing relations between several sovereign states, none of which was strong enough to impose its will by itself—Russia, Japan, Great Britain, the United States, and China in the Far East, and Russia, Germany, France, Great Britain, Italy, and (as was twice seen) the United States in Europe. The Japanese and German attempts at expansion, the defeat of the "co-prosperity sphere" and of the Third Reich, at one stroke transformed Europe and Asia into regions of ruins, into cemeteries for empires. In the middle of the twentieth century, Russia had not yet the industrial resources of a superpower; the United States did—but, far from desiring hegemony, would have preferred to know neither the power nor the responsibilities that these resources conferred. It was the Second World War, and especially the blind fury with which it was waged, that brought the collapse of the intermediate zones and left the two giants standing alone, face to face.

It is often wondered why the United States and the Soviet Union seem to be engaged in a mortal struggle when the two peoples do not know one another, when neither lacks wealth of its own to exploit or lands to develop, and when both have plunged headlong into the adventure of technical civilization. One fair reply is to cite the ambitions, essentially limitless, of a secular religion that claims universal value; but two other causes also exist. "Glory is indivisible," and wise men dream in vain of a partition of the globe. The no man's lands in Europe and Asia are, in themselves, a cause of instability. Two nations need not hate each other in order to come into collision in the four quarters of the globe. But the fact that they do collide in the four quarters of the globe is enough to make them end by hating each other.

Nor was Soviet expansion written beforehand in the book of history. Certain specific reasons for its spectacular victories can be identified easily. It is understandable that the proletariat in Western communities should have adhered to a gospel that gave promise of raising them out of their low estate and giving them dignity and hope. It is equally understandable that the semi-Westernized intellectuals of Asia, their nationalism offended by white domination, should have subscribed to a doctrine that promised them both independence and power, wrested at last from their European conquerors. In both cases the rise of the secular religion is less the cause than the effect of the decay of traditional beliefs. In both cases machines inspire, in those who handle them without understanding them, a sort of faith that they will bring an end to traditional poverty. In both cases there is a dream of equality, even though the doctrine itself tends simply to impose a new hierarchy, technocratic, bureaucratic, military, and in part religious, in place of the ancient hierarchy, on a population reduced to an inorganic mass.

Nor is it surprising that Marxism should have been better adapted to the needs of the revolution in Asia after its passage through the Russian Revolution. The Bolshevik Party captured power through a rising of the masses against a ruling class marked by a foreign culture. It used its power not to give the people the liberties in the name of which it had preached revolt, but to accelerate technical Westernization. It borrowed from "aggressive" civilizations the tools of their material superiority. An ideology of European origin was still proclaimed, but it no longer inspired the work of construction, having been suppressed or distorted by earlier traditions. In the same way, the revolutionary intelligentsia in the Far East has borrowed its ideas—nationalism and socialism—from the civilization whose local domination it is opposing. It is seduced by a confused picture of the Soviet regime, the prospect of erecting an entirely new social order and accelerated industrialization. From this it hopes for attenuation of an age-old poverty, aggravated by the rapid increase of population. It combines an extravagant dream with effective action; it sees itself surpassing the West by rejecting it, and imagines itself lifting its people into the front rank of a history common to all peoples, while avenging the humiliations inflicted by the white man. Even in Europe, Marxism, transfigured by the Soviet experiment, continues to appeal to certain numbers of the working classes in countries weakened by war and impatient with their own decline, as well as to certain intellectuals, disappointed in democratic methods and envious of an imagined state in which the educated would take first place and power would belong not to money but to knowledge.

While the causes of these successes are apparent in retrospect, it would be wrong to forget the events that favored them—events not necessarily a part of the social structure. Only the First World War enabled the Bolshevik Party to conquer Russia. It was the determination of the bourgeois and socialist parties to continue the war, the weakness of the liberals, and the hesitations of the Mensheviks and the Social Revolutionaries that enabled the October Revolution to follow that of February 1917. Before 1914, the great majority in every socialist party rejected Lenin's political methods. But then, for four years the military leaders of the bourgeois states treated their citizens as "human material," and the Bolshevik technique of propaganda and party organization ceased to arouse indignation. Since it was a time of horrors, at least let violence have peace as its objective, and as its enemy the civilization that had made the sterile carnage possible.

And yet, neither in Europe nor in Asia was the expansion of Stalinism impressive before 1939. It was the second war that made possible the Red Army's conquests in Europe and the Communist Party's conquests in Asia. Once again, the decisive cause of Stalin's victories was the wars that created the circumstances in which a militant sect could succeed in seizing power.

The process leading to total war is highly logical, a process which, seen in retrospect, leaves little to individual initiative and unforeseeable chance. With the advent of conscription and modern industry, war automatically became hyperbolic, unless—unlikely event—statesmen had had the wisdom to renounce certain potentialities of the system. Or, perhaps, unless the victors in the first battles had shown such moderation that the losers were able to accept defeat instead of mobilizing the entire world in order to reverse it.

The experience of 1914–18 had shown the mortal peril. Philosophically inclined historians were quite aware that a new war would mark the end not only of nationalism but of Europe itself. National Socialism, which combined obscure and remote Germanic aspirations with the social and moral disintegration of the country after its military defeat and the subsequent economic crisis and with a sharp reaction against Communism, precipitated the catastrophe. The scientific barbarity of the Nazis and the aerial superiority of the Allies led ultimately to the present situation: peoples dread the ravages of the weapons of mass destruction, but they dread even more the technique of extermination which invaders are capable of employing.

It goes without saying that in spite of this logic of violence, nothing foreshadowed the gas chambers and the extermination of millions of defenseless human beings. Similarly, it could not have been foreseen that the atom bomb would be made during the second war and tried on the Japanese. In the long run, the utilization of nuclear energy for military purposes perhaps marks a revolution comparable to the invention of gunpowder. In the present crisis it merely augments factors already visible: the ubiquity of the super powers, the relative weakening of the second-class nations, especially of the overpopulated and vulnerable ones of Western Europe; the dread of war felt by the masses in all countries, victors and vanquished alike; the obvious necessity of stopping the chain reaction of violence; and the growing difficulty of establishing a stable peace, either through the traditional device of the balance of power or through a return to the more ancient tradition of imperial domination.

The meeting of these processes itself indicates a combination of logic and of chance. To some extent each begins in a common situation: the development of science, the application of science to industry, and the expansion of industrial civilization. It was industrial technique, even more than political democracy, that rendered unlimited and inexorable a war which Europe, unaware, had undertaken as a war just like any other. It is industrial technique that weakens beliefs that have justified and upheld the age-long order of human societies; that uproots the urban masses and makes them dissatisfied with their humble lot; that makes poverty, long accepted as a decree of God or nature, a sort of scandal. It is this that precipitates the anti-white revolution in Asia and the insurrection of masses ever more numerous and wretched; and this that spurs the impatience of the peoples of Europe whose standard of living rises more slowly than their aspirations. This is what has made the political structure of the Continent an anachronism, has promoted the advent of continent-states, has favored the diffusion of a secular religion—a substitute faith for souls deprived of the Gospel, and has made of Stalinism—the religion of the proletariat and the machine—a fetish for the worship of the semi-educated.

There is no justification, even after the event, for saying that things had to happen as they have in fact happened. The decisive events of this period—the 1914 explosion, the Russian Revolution, Hitler's rise to power, the coming of the second war, and the ineptitude of Anglo-American statesmanship can be explained reasonably. One can see the causes, however remote, which favored them but one cannot ignore the interval between the cause and the effect; it is man, or rather it is men, who by their action or inaction, produced this history which they did not want, and we cannot even console ourselves with the thought that in the long run the consequences of their courage or cowardice, their blindness or foresight, will be effaced, for as far as the eye can see, there loom the consequences of Russia's industrialization in the Bolshevik and not in the Western manner.

To keep to the broadest phenomena, the present crisis is not the direct and inevitable result of industrial civilization, but of its collision with certain long-standing facts of history. If the European communities have destroyed themselves, it is not because they have proved incapable of integrating their productive forces into a structure founded on private property. The eternal rivalry of nations has continued into the age of infernal machines; and nations, in their pursuit of power, have not found a way to agree either to a common law or to moderation and compromise. The techniques of modern war have made the survival of Europe incompatible with the continuance of conflicts that long antedate capitalism and that were due only in slight measure to competition between economic or social systems.

The revolt of Russia and of Asia is directed less against capitalism than against the civilization that came from the West. In Russia it began against a Westernized ruling class, in Asia against the dominance of Europeans. As a result of wars it has become an insurrection not of workers against the owners of the means of production, but of peoples of ancient civilization humiliated by the mysterious power of the creators of machines, and of wretched mobs with a vague sense of the incapacity of their traditional rulers to build a modern nation.

The recession of national states, the rise of the continent-states, the decline of Europe, the revolt against the West—all these were to a great extent foreseeable because they were implicit in industrial civilization and its material and moral repercussions. What was unforeseeable was the pace and manner of these changes. The two wars greatly hastened them and at the same time gave them a cataclysmic character. That Russia, the metropolis of a secular religion of universal dimensions, should stand at the borders of an exhausted Europe and an Asia in revolt, and should be checked in her ambition only by the far-off force of the United States, itself anxious about the future and accumulating a stock of atom bombs—such an encounter clearly was not predetermined by any historical necessity. The wars of the first half of the twentieth century have ripened a catastrophe that would be to the catastrophes of the past what the atom bomb is to Big Bertha.

# PART THREE

*Limited War*

## Chapter IX

# THE CONVENTIONS OF THE COLD WAR

IN 1946 it was already obvious that the destruction of Germany and Japan had ushered in a new age of troubles. The bi-polar structure of world politics is in itself unfavorable to stability. Equilibrium is difficult when power is concentrated at one extremity in a continental nation and at the other in a maritime nation. The former tends normally to expand to the limits of its terrestrial mass and is stopped only by the latter's threat of defending the maritime frontiers by every means, even a general war—an inevitable method in such circumstances, but one involving permanent danger.

No one knows exactly where the *casus belli* may occur, and there is always the danger that the continental nation may go too far, not from any intention to provoke an open conflict, but from miscalculation. The continental countries that voluntarily join the maritime empire are intensely aware of their tragic situation. Protected in time of peace by the guarantee of the United States, they are certain that in time of war they will be doomed to occupation and Sovietization, which ultimately means fighting on the other side.

Had the present crisis any other cause than the collapse of the intermediate zones, it might have been hoped that the balance of two powers could gradually give place to that of three or four. The objective should certainly be to fill the European or Asian gap.

But whether it is a matter of assuring the peaceful coexistence of the two great powers, or of easing their relations by separating the two by autonomous centers of force, the obstacle is the same: the continental empire is at the same time the metropolis of a religion of temporal salvation, with universal pretensions. It does not create the revolutionary movements out of nothing: even without Stalin in the Kremlin, the Second World War would have been followed here and there by social disorders. But men fanatically devoted to Moscow have secured control of the revolutionary parties in most countries. And the very people who incessantly proclaim their desire for peace discountenance the only form of peace that is possible at present—the division of the world into spheres of influence.

Wherever the Stalinist party has won power, its opponents have been eliminated without pity. Every dissident voice is stifled. The masses are subjected to a monotonous clamor of propaganda, and required to obey and acclaim their masters. West of the Iron Curtain, on the other hand, the Communist parties are present and active, availing themselves of the freedom that bourgeois democracy allows to its enemies. What partition of the world could resist the ubiquity of the Stalinist conspiracy? Stalinism would have to be excluded from the Western zone, as Westerns are excluded from the Stalinist zone.

Even if a balance of three or four powers replaced that of two, even if the European nations and the improvised states of Asia became invulnerable to political infiltration and military aggression, mankind would remain exposed to an unprecedented peril. The weapons of mass destruction inspire universal fear. What the new weapons call for is not the return to a system of great powers, comparable on the planetary scale to the European system of last century, but a system itself radically new.

What should that system be? Ideally, there is the image of world government, but is that ideal realizable? International politics have for centuries involved struggles among sovereign states. By what miracle would that sovereignty be renounced? And what supreme authority would impose submission? In any case, even if the ideal were not contrary to the nature of men and nations, it would remain inaccessible as long as the great schism lasted.

The only road to human unity, in the present state of the world, passes through a third world war, which would eliminate one of the candidates for hegemony. That is the road which the majority of cultures (in Spengler's term) have followed in the past. It may be that history will take that road once more. But no one today would advise it, or even contemplate it without horror. Those who affect to make light of the blood spilled ought to know from past experience that the victory of a nation through the total destruction of its rival inflicts an incurable wound on civilization itself.

If war is horrible and peace impossible, what is the way out? It was hoped in 1946 that the cold war might be the way out, a way discovered not by the genius of any individual, but by the gropings of humanity itself. From the moment when the great powers resort to arms, violence is amplified enormously—two examples in our century have shown it—and most of the belligerents are victims of the monster that they themselves unchained. The destitution of Europe and Asia and the limitless ambitions of Stalinism do not permit agreement in depth, or even the stabilization of frontiers between the zones of influence. The cold war, an intermediate solution, is subject to unwritten laws, which the protagonists have recognized by degrees, applying them spontaneously and almost unconsciously.

The cold war is a limited war—limited, however, not as to the stakes, but as to the means employed by the belligerents. Seen from the West, it is the result, direct and inevitable, of the course of action followed by the Kremlin and the parties that obey it throughout the world: propaganda, espionage and sabotage, agitation and mass movements, and civil war are its four typical forms, usually combined. We might say further that the cold war results from the Soviet program of world conquest, for as long as the Kremlin does not resort to open war.

This classical definition, however, is valid but inadequate. After all, since 1917 the Bolshevik state has considered as enemies all the countries labeled capitalist, and has done its best to weaken them. The revolutionary action of the Cominform started what is called the cold war in the strange situation—resulting from the second war of the twentieth century, which the Stalinists consider to be the last before the triumph of socialism—which is characterized by the formation of two camps engaged in an irreconcilable struggle. (Before 1939, Stalin acted mainly by intervening in conflicts between capitalist states.)

Since 1946 the men of the Kremlin have taken great care not to create a *casus belli,* but their military superiority has remained one of their weapons in the cold war. It helped them to maintain an atmosphere of fear in all the neighboring countries, which would be occupied in case of war. Nobody knows whether the Kremlin will ever decide to set its legions on the march, and what date it has in mind for the irrevocable choice; but that possibility cannot be definitely excluded.

Uncertainty casts its shadow over statesmen's decisions. It compels them to examine, in connection with every event, actual or possible, the consequences that it would entail first within the limited war and then in the event of total war. These two kinds of considerations correspond roughly, though not exactly, to the distinction between policy and strategy.

Take the case of Berlin. If the limited war were regarded as the initial phase of total war, the Berlin position would not have been of any value to the West. The former capital of the Reich is surrounded on all sides by the Soviet zone. Administrators and soldiers, British, French, and American would be quickly liquidated at zero hour on D day. But when the conflict retained for several years an essentially political character, that very fact became a value of primary importance. The Western presence in Berlin constitutes a symbol. Recalling the past to the peoples of Eastern Europe, it offers them a promise and assures the survival of a hope. Had they voluntarily left Berlin, the Westerners would have shut the prison doors on 100 million Europeans. Had they been driven out by the blockade, they would have lost face and a further argument would have been supplied to those who insist that the limitless expansion of Stalinism is inevitable. In spite of the defeatists (who did not believe in the possibility of resistance), and in spite of the false realists (who deplored the choice of the battlefield being left to the other camp), the defense of the Berlin "hedgehog" brought a much bigger return than the hundreds of millions of dollars it cost.

The distinction between positions of no military value, held for political reasons, and positions properly military, is by no means as clear as it might seem. There are extreme cases, where it stands out distinctly. The Pacific islands, the Marianas, and Okinawa are little else than aero-naval bases. On the other hand, South Korea, which the American troops had evacuated in 1949, was not considered to be in any respect a bridgehead. Moral and political reasons were decisive for the help given to Syngman Rhee's government. A world power does not abandon those who have placed their trust in it. Every additional conquest strengthens Stalinism, morally even more than materially, for nothing succeeds like success. The intermediate cases are the most numerous. In Greece, Norway, the Philippines, or Indo-China, the positions have both military and political significance. Western strategy strives to hold them, whether the final map of the world is drawn progressively by the chances of the peace that is quasi war, or emerges sooner or later from the unforeseeable development of total war.

What are the objectives aimed at by each side during the period of the limited war? Each side tends to secure useful bases from which it could attack or counterattack. It strives to increase the number and the resources of its potential allies, and to reduce the number and the resources of its potential enemies. It attempts to retain control of the sources of the raw materials indispensable to the upkeep of modern engines of war. Finally, it endeavors (or should endeavor) to shake the morale of the hostile world, to spread the prestige of its own ideas and strength, and also to spread the conviction that it brings with it progress or freedom or socialism, and that the goddess of history has already decided on its ultimate triumph. In short, the cold war appears, in military perspective, as a race for bases, allies, raw materials, and prestige. It might broadly be said that American strategy has looked particularly in the Pacific for bases, in Europe for allies, in the Near East for raw materials, and more or less everywhere for the success that reassures the faithful and rallies the uncertain.

Must the Atlantic Pact be regarded as essentially one aspect of the race for allies? It is certain that Western Europe, although since 1945 it has been open to invasion and without defense, constituted, in spite of everything else, a military prize of the first order. It continues to be the only group of countries, except the two great powers, that commands human, scientific, and industrial resources sufficient to mobilize, equip, and maintain a great army. This capacity is for the moment theoretical rather than actual. Perhaps it will remain untapped. The passage from the potential to the actual meets with obstacles that have so far proved insurmountable. The United States is not yet strengthened by the "Marshallization" of the European nations, but it is beyond doubt that the Soviet Union would be strengthened by the Sovietization of the same nations.

However, the political interest has, it seems to me, weighed as heavily in the balance as the strategic interest. As the focus of modern civilization, Western Europe retains, in the eyes of the Americans and perhaps of the Stalinists, a symbolic value and a prestige that are not proportional to the millions of tons of steel and the hundreds of millions of tons of coal produced annually by the mines or the blast furnaces west of the Stettin-Trieste line. Whether we like it or not, and even if, a century from now, our descendants scoff at our blindness, the installation of Maurice Thorez in the Elysée Palace in 1949 would have had in the Western world quite a different effect from the installation of Mao Tse-tung in the once "forbidden" city of Peiping.

This double burden of the cold war that may last ten or twenty years, and of a total war that is always possible, make Western diplomacy strangely complex, and, almost at any moment, open to contradictory interpretations. There is no territory anywhere in the world which Western diplomacy does not see some reason for defending. At once two objections arise—that of the protégés, who wonder whether to fear or desire American protection, and that of the protector, who wonders whether it is not madness to thus disperse his forces for the benefit of weak countries or corrupt governments.

Sweden has maintained military neutrality, while Norway has joined the Atlantic Pact; the former is strongly armed, the latter almost unarmed. Which country has taken the decision most favorable to peace, to its own security in case of total war?

The United States, it is said, is provoking the Soviet Union at her very frontiers, while the latter has neither bases nor buffer states in the Western Hemisphere (intervening there only through the Communist parties). But this argument is logically false. Would the United States have been showing aggressiveness toward Hitlerist Germany if the integrity of Czechoslovakia or Poland had been guaranteed? What matters is not so much the geographic distance between the great and the small powers as the attitude adopted by the former toward the latter; neither Mexico nor Canada feels threatened. During the war the right of establishing friendly govern-ments in Eastern Europe was practically conceded to the Soviet Union. We now know that the Kremlin recognizes only one proof of friendliness—submission, pure and simple. To concede it a right to the friendship of its neighbors would be to agree that it had the right to Sovietize them. Bit by bit, this pretension would extend to the whole of the Continent, and beyond.[1]

For that matter, the Soviet Government is too realistic to take seriously what some Western commentators call provocation. It is hostile, as Hitler's government was, to collective security agree-ments, especially when these include nations near the U.S.S.R. But in the case of Norway Stalin confined himself to a diplomatic warn-ing. Stalinist propaganda against the Marshall Plan was at least as violent as that against the Atlantic Pact. During the limited war, the masters of the Kremlin have but little means of action against Nor-way and Denmark, where the Communist Party is relatively weak. In the event of total war, Russian armies could easily neutralize Western bases in Norway. The Atlantic Pact, as seen from Moscow, in no way alters the fact of the situation: it merely sanctions the *casus belli,* which already existed implicitly. Seen from Copenhagen and Oslo, it has the merit of permitting cheaper rearmament.

Why has Sweden not adopted the same attitude? Sweden, no less than Norway, fears the possible victory of the Soviet Union in a third world war. But the small countries willingly (and perhaps legitimately) leave it to the big ones to fight for them. When they believe abstention to be possible, they justify it by the services they render to both camps or to humanity—an argument which is some-times true, but not always, for Belgian neutrality in 1939 benefited Hitler's Germany.

The situation of each country on the operational map makes its neutrality improbable or probable in advance. Sweden, fortified by two experiences, has not lost hope that the lines of force of world strategy may skirt her territory. Norway, bearing the traces of a recent past, has lost that hope. She calculates that the Atlantic Pact strengthens her position in the time of limited war and brings her, through NATO, a better chance of defending herself against military

---

[1] The maritime power, whose strategy is defensive, is inevitably led to intervene in the periphery of the aggressive continental empire.

aggression, which her adhesion to the pact makes neither more nor less probable.

Would it not have been better, certain commentators object, to supply arms to Norway and Denmark, without requiring their adhesion to the Atlantic Pact? The truth is that nothing essential would have been changed. Armed by the United States, these countries would count as enemies in the eyes of the men of the Kremlin, even if they had formally safeguarded diplomatic neutrality. The Kremlin, for its part, would probably have preferred this latter formula: the courageous choice made by small countries so near to the monster has a value as a demonstration that the Soviet rulers do not yet reign by terror, outside their frontiers. For these reasons, as much as for the advantages of military co-operation, Washington diplomacy preferred an unequivocal formula.

Can the small countries reasonably protest that they are being dragged into a conflict which does not concern them? Even if that complaint were justified, it would be in vain. The world must be taken as it is. The spatial amplification of modern war is a fact easier to vituperate than to ignore. In this case, however, the complaint would not be morally justified. The American Republic is not provoking with the Soviet Union the world-wide conflict into which other countries would gradually be drawn. It is the Soviet Union that is in permanent conflict with all countries rebelling against the Stalinist message. It is convenient to speak, by way of simplification, of the conflict between the United States and the Soviet Union, but if, for the sake of argument, we eliminate the United States and its alleged imperialism and imagine America taking no interest in the continent of Europe, the Europeans will not suddenly become secure; on the contrary, they will be doomed to Sovietization, perhaps without a general war, but quite certainly not without pain.

It may be that the Soviet Union would trouble less about one country or another if the resistance of the United States did not lead it to anticipate a general war. The strategy of the American-Russian conflict lends a military importance to certain territories which the political conflict between the Stalinists and the rest of the world would more or less have spared. In this limited sense, some countries are victims of the quarrel between the great powers: the most striking instance is that of Korea.

The case of Sweden and Norway, which we have just examined, has no universal significance, but some results of our analysis apply generally. A small country will preserve the hope of neutrality in a total war whenever it has sufficient forces to make the potential aggressor decide that the cost of invasion would exceed the profits to be expected from occupation—as with Sweden and Switzerland. In the cold war, refusal to enter either camp will be easier where the Communist Party in a country is weaker, where the country has less need of American aid, and where it is situated further from the probable theater of operations. This explains why Western Europe has less chance of neutrality than any other part of the world.

France and Italy have been so undermined by the action of Communist parties that they slip almost inevitably from anti-Communism in domestic politics to anti-Sovietism in the diplomatic field. They have needed American aid to maintain the living standard, to rebuild their ruins, and to reopen the factories.

From a military point of view, the prospects are no more favorable. Because of its material and human resources, Western Europe is the most tempting of prizes. It is situated on the main lines of world strategy. To strike at Great Britain, the permanent ally of the United States, it is necessary to occupy the Channel and North Sea coasts. As a stake in the conflict, and a battlefield designated by geography and history, Europe could not lay claim to neutrality until she possessed a military force of the first order. But one of the principal causes of war would then have disappeared.

For the moment, the countries of Southeastern Asia, only recently emerged from colonial empires—India, Pakistan, Indonesia —are striving to conduct an independent foreign policy. The Soviet Union is far from them, and memories of the "European imperialists" are still very recent. The rulers, although anti-Communist, have a vague feeling of solidarity with the Chinese revolution, a feeling that is nurtured by a common hostility to the whites and by a strong desire for social reforms. In proportion, as the Chinese enterprise develops in Indo-China, Tibet, Burma perhaps, and on the frontiers of India, and in proportion as mass poverty excites disturbances and revolts, the rulers of the created or resuscitated states will probably incline toward the West, unless—a possibility which cannot be excluded—they pursue the phantom of yesterday's conquerors to the point of opening the way for tomorrow's.

Some Europeans complain of being drawn into an American-Russian conflict. Meanwhile there are politicians and journalists in the United States who are disturbed at the commitments undertaken by the State Department, are afraid of the country's resources being dissipated to no purpose among a growing number of beneficiaries, and are indignant at the apparent solidarity between reactionary governments and a nation proud of its liberal tradition. The doctrine of world-wide containment, to defend *all* the countries threatened by the imperialism of Moscow, arouses some uneasiness. General objections are not lacking, such as that it is impossible to stop a conquering empire at every sensitive spot; that the United States, a naval and land power, could not risk intervention on the continent of Asia and that the United States will end by ruining itself through undertaking a task beyond its strength, great as that may be. But none of these deals adequately with the complex reality. It would be absurd to defend by *military* force territories surrounding the Stalinist empire and not to defend them politically so long as total war has not been launched.

Consider the situation in Europe. What country ought to have been sacrificed? The Greek Government has triumphed over the insurgents. Turkey has not yielded to pressure and threats. Norway and Denmark could only have been conquered by an invasion by Soviet troops. In Europe west of the Iron Curtain the anti-Communists regularly win against the Communists as long as the latter are not directly supported by the Red Army. It was natural to keep that army at bay by the threat of atomic reprisals, and to isolate the different fields of battle.

Bulgarians and Yugoslavs, before Tito's dissidence, furnished supplies to the Greek insurgents, but their armies did not openly cross the frontiers. Locally, the Soviet Union had obvious military superiority, but it was not used. The conventions of the cold war did not forbid camouflaged intervention or assistance in men and arms from the people's democracies to the revolutionaries, but they did not authorize invasion by the armies even of a satellite.

The Berlin crisis of 1948–49 offered an exceptional illustration of what is legitimate and what is not during the cold war, at least in Europe. In practice the Soviet authorities could have ended in a few hours the presence of the British, French, and Americans in the heart of the former capital of the Reich. But they had not the right to use every possible means to attain that end. The interruption of transport by railway, road, or canal between the Western zones and Berlin was defended on technical grounds, and was a part of the larger policy, just as were propaganda and invective. The Allies replied in kind; they refrained from forcing a passage by armed convoy, and confined themselves to bringing in every day by air several thousand tons of supplies for the 2 million Berliners in rebellion against proletarian "liberation." The Russians respected the Allied aircraft, and the Westerners respected the road and railway barriers. The trial of strength went on without the employment of armed force.

In Asia the situation is more complex. Since 1945, and perhaps for longer, civil war has been the typical form of Communist action. In Korea the Chinese intervention was not confined to the dispatch of arms or supplies to the North Korean armies; "volunteers," actually divisions of the regular army, entered the lists and fought against the army of the United Nations.

The origin, significance, and methods of Communism are different in Asia from those in Europe. But it is possible, without forcing the comparison, to detect a common element. Stalinist strategy everywhere abstained from steps of a nature to provoke general war. It was possible, however, to go very much farther in Asia than in Europe without doing that. It is true that the "legal *coup d'état* in Prague made more noise than the military victories of Mao Tsetung in 1948–49. The only really decisive prize on the Continent is Germany. The employment there of regular armies, even of satellites, would probably bring war. An attack on Yugoslavia by the Hungarian, Bulgarian, or Rumanian armies would start unforeseeable chain reactions.

The men of the Kremlin had probably considered the crossing of the 38th parallel by the armies of Kim Il Sung as a scarcely original modality of civil war. After the victory of Mao Tse-tung, did not the whole of Korea belong to the Soviet sphere of influence?

It may be that the speculations of the Muscovite strategists were of that nature. The result went contrary to their expectations. An unwritten convention of the cold war excluded the crossing of frontiers or lines of demarcation by regular armies. The violation of this rule produced the military intervention of the United States, the rearmament of the Western world, and the undeclared war between China and the United States. North Korea's aggression expanded into a war, limited but no longer cold.

*Chapter  X*

## REVERSAL  OF  ALLIANCES

THE HISTORY of Europe is fertile in reversals of alliances. After defeating the common enemy, coalitions dissolve; the victors compete, each for himself and in his own way, for the favor of the vanquished. After the Hundred Days, Talleyrand succeeded in insinuating himself into the counsels of the Allies. Reduced to her traditional dimensions, France became once more an element indispensable to the continental balance of power.

It would be absurd, therefore, to be surprised or indignant that the future of Germany or Japan has become one of the principal stakes in the cold war. Both countries were weakened but not destroyed, and remain potentially in the front rank of regional great powers. Although outclassed by the United States and the Soviet Union, they could, however, support either of those powers and, therefore, under certain circumstances turn the scales in any conflict. Western Europe knows from of old, or should know, that it is disastrous to have as enemies both Germany *and* Russia.

The battle for Germany has developed quite differently from that for Japan. The United States did not anticipate the need in the Far East for a restored Japan. American policy was supposed to be based on a democratic China, which the United Nations had been induced to recognize as one of the five great powers. It was the conquest of China by the Communists that again raised the question of Japanese disarmament. If Japan were unable to defend herself, would she not be irresistibly drawn to the Sovietized continent?

In Europe it was the division of Germany into zones of occupation that started the conflict. There, as elsewhere, the Soviet authorities ignored sometimes the letter and always the spirit of the four-power agreements. They exploited their zone without any regard for the Potsdam principle of the economic unity of Germany. They eliminated Social Democrats by forcing them to amalgamate with the Communist Party. They proceeded with the Sovietization of their zone and provoked the West to reply by setting up the Bonn Government, the monetary reform, and other measures.

After 1918, the basis of German power remained intact, including the industrial potential, political unity (strengthened by the Weimar centralization), and a still growing population (although the birthrate rapidly declined between the two wars, and the Hitlerite policy merely brought it back to a level sufficient to renew the generations). The loss of 3 million young men, coming at a time when the population had reached the end of its phase of increase, should in itself have blunted the martial ardor of the people. The rise of Russia and the presence of the United States in Europe should have discouraged in advance any inclination to simultaneous aggression against East and West; in other words Germany would have been deprived of any ambition to play a leading role. Stripped of grandiose illusions, she might have been satisfied with an honorable retirement to pre-Bismarckian traditions. Her defeat in 1945 might have been for her the equivalent of France's defeat in 1815— the end of the imperialist period.

The decisions taken at Yalta and Potsdam, and still more the *faits accomplis* which the Russians, Poles, and Czechs presented to Europe, revived the so-called "German problem" in all its acuteness, although it had assumed a new character.

Everyone knows the facts. Stalin began by securing Allied recognition of the Curzon line as the boundary between Russia and Poland. In compensation, he offered to Poland the portion of Germany east of the Oder-Neisse line. Since the right of peoples to self-determination stands in the way of their annexation, the inhabitants of the newly recovered regions were to be dispossessed and moved to the West. As all the countries of Eastern Europe did the same with their minorities (the Czechs, in particular, expelling at a few hours' notice 2 or 3 million Sudeten Germans who had been established for centuries on the edge of the Bohemian quadrilateral), dismembered Germany was enriched by some 8 or 9 million in-habitants. At a stroke the density of population in West Germany rose to exceed two hundred to the square kilometer, or three times that of France.

Thanks to these initial decisions, the Soviet Union held apparently incomparable cards. Russia, and Russia alone, was in a position to satisfy without war the German desire to recover the territories lost in the East or, at least, some part of them. Russia, and Russia alone, retained the power to decide between Poles and Germans, and to change the frontier. There was even a chance that the West Germans, in spite of their violent antagonism toward Russia as a pitiless conqueror and occupying power, might be converted to Stalinism by despair or revolutionary fury. Could democracy take root in a country ruined, overpopulated, and without outlets of any kind? The Germans remembered with longing the markets which their products had in the Balkans and in the Soviet Union, and they dreamt of those which (not without stretching their imagination) would open to them in a Sovietized China.

The horizon is so clouded that many observers, especially the French, conclude that the partition of Germany is the least objectionable solution. While the partition lasts, with occupying troops on both sides of the demarcation line, the risks of a nationalist revival and of a German-Russian accord are eliminated. There would be no Reich or, at least, neither the People's Republic of Berlin nor the Federal Republic at Bonn would be able to play any part in high policy.

The division of Germany may well last for years, as long as the cold war continues—an eventuality in fact, that is now the least improbable and which must be accepted if it cannot be altered. But it would be a mistake to conceal from ourselves that such acceptance guarantees the success of Soviet strategy, which thereby attains its minimum objective; for non-Sovietized Germany hesitates between resistance and submission to Stalinism, paralyzed by the existence of a Germany integrated into the Soviet world. Europe is reduced to its narrowest dimensions, at the mercy of any Continental attack, and scarcely able to defend itself even with the aid of the naval powers.

In the Kremlin's strategy, the Sovietization of the Eastern zone has a double purpose, both defensive and offensive. With a peasant-like greed, Stalin regarded all the territories occupied by his armies as definitely acquired. He intended to retain the eastern third of the former Reich, or at least not to withdraw his troops until a solid instrument of power—party, police, army—in the hands of the Communists of the Unity Party had been constructed. The consolidation of a People's Republic of Germany is the minimum objective of Moscow's diplomacy. The partition of Germany constitutes, in fact, the best protection against what the Kremlin probably regards as the most serious danger. Will the West dare to rearm one Germany, which would find itself faced, in the front line, by another Germany?

Starting from the People's Republic as a base, the conquest of the Federal Republic would be undertaken. A beginning is made with propaganda calling for unity. A country, this time truly pressed for space, is given a glimpse of infinite future perspectives if only it will side with the East and not the West, and accept its real mission—the industrialization of the Eurasian plains. The West Germans are not required at once to bow to Communist discipline or proclaim loyalty to the inspired Father of the Peoples. National fronts and movements in favor of neutrality offer conceptions that the hesitant adopt more readily than the Stalinist creed and that are stages on the road to conversion.

The question is continually asked: What is the aim of Soviet policy in Germany? A strong or a weak Germany, divided or closely united? Does Moscow want to see a Germany governed by nationalists or national Communists, or to set up a satellite People's Republic? Russia's first and foremost aim is to prevent the West from re-establishing a German force of supreme quality. The *Wehrmacht* unaided very nearly won the last war, even with American industry working against it. The Sovietization of Eastern Germany almost gives her the guarantee she wants; the remainder, since it cannot yet be Sovietized, will at least be neutralized. The Communist agents there will have the task of sowing dissension, working on men's minds, and organizing a network of sabotage. One wonders whether the masters of the Kremlin will one day sacrifice their official representatives in order to conclude an agreement with German nationalists who favor eastward orientation. It is clearly impossible to reply with confidence concerning a distant future; but for the moment the Kremlin policy is unmistakable. The Germans are not trusted to the point of leaving them room for initiative. The former Nazis are rallied to a party formed for them, on condition that they accept the authority of the Soviet agents of the Socialist Unity Party. Promises, if any, to the Ulbrichts, to the Piecks, and to the Grotewohls have reference to the West. To imagine the men of the Kremlin dealing with a national Germany on a basis of equality would be to reveal an ignorance of their immense ambitions. Times have changed since Rapallo and the Ribbentrop-Molotov pact. The Soviet Union intends to integrate Germany into the socialist camp, but it will be a satellite Germany, not a powerful, autonomous Reich.

Is it true that French policy on this point agrees with that of Russia and opposes the Anglo-Saxons? Is the partition of Germany the lesser evil? I do not believe it. England was interested in 1815 in weakening France, not crushing her. Similarly, France was interested after 1945 in weakening Germany, not crushing her; she should therefore have worked for the recovery of her "hereditary enemy"—a contention that no one would object to except those who refuse to recognize the laws of international mechanics. The elimination of Germany immediately opens the West to the Russian menace. Europe could not live with such a disproportionate force as that of the Third Reich concentrated in its midst; but neither could it live with a void in place of the Third Reich—a void extending from the Rhine to the Vistula, through which the tentacles of the Russian empire would quickly spread.

Then, the pessimists will say, Europe cannot live either with or without Germany. Once more, I do not believe it. There is a possible intermediate stage between the limitless imperialism of Hitler and the limitless disaster of 1945.

There are those who fear that a German government (although anti-Communist) would ally itself with a Russian government (although Communist) primarily in order to recover lost territories, and then to find markets for industrial expansion in the vast spaces of Eurasia. I think these anxieties are greatly exaggerated, at least as far as the early future is concerned.

The reciprocal fear and hatred between Germans and Slavs is

deeply rooted, much more so than that between Germans and Latins. Sentiments have never prevented temporary agreements over joint adventures, but the restitution to Germany of even part of her Eastern territories as a condition of a Russo-German alliance under present conditions would require the actual incorporation of Poland into the Soviet Union. Moscow would only take that step if it saw no other means of preventing the alliance of the German Army with American industry, which haunts the men of the Kremlin. In other words, a Soviet swing toward Germany, though always possible, would only become probable in a radically different situation, where the Soviet Union would be on the defensive and a non-Communist Germany would be once more a great power with an independent foreign policy. By then, however, other problems will have arisen which we may leave to posterity.

Even if we imagine a Germany unified with Moscow's consent, recovering part of Silesia and Brandenburg, and allied with the Kremlin but not sovietized, is it conceivable that such a Germany would attack France, Italy, or Great Britain, and so invite the United States to atom-bomb the Ruhr? For Germany it would be a greater folly than that which drew Hitler's armies to the Volga and the Caucasus. A reconstituted Germany would tend, in accordance with old traditions, to oscillate between East and West, and to extract as much as possible from one side or the other in return for always uncertain co-operation. A precarious situation, it may be said. True, but how much better than that of today! The prospects of peace will be improved with the increase in the number of centers of force.

It will hardly be denied that a unified Germany is desirable; but is it still possible? Has not the Sovietization of the Eastern zone now reached such a point that the recovery of freedom is out of the question, short of some unforeseeable convulsion? And how can a "people's democracy" and a Federal Republic that is democratic in the Western sense be integrated into a single state? It looks, indeed, as if the time for reunion had already passed in 1950. The elections in Eastern Germany in that year took place in the Soviet style, and gave to the Communist Party full power or, at least, such power as the Russians delegate to the German rulers. The other parties were mere hostages; those of their leaders, opportunists or nihilists, who survived various purges agreed to play the Soviet game and are no longer distinguishable from the leaders of the Socialist Unity Party. What is essentially a collectivist economic system has been installed; the important industrial enterprises are owned by the state, the *Länder,* the municipalities, or the Russian authorities. Agrarian collectivization has not yet gone far, but in Eastern Germany the land does not lend itself well to the small-farm ownership that has been instituted by the occupying power to destroy the economic basis of the Prussian aristocracy and to prepare for the final *kolkhozy* phase, collective farms.

Even if it were possible to undo the social changes made in Eastern Germany, unification would require the establishment of a common government. How could such a government be secured? We can imagine three methods: (1) free elections throughout the Reich, (2) negotiations between the great powers, and (3) negotiation between the two governments that claim to speak in the name of Germany.

From the point of view of Western propaganda, the formula of free elections is irreproachable. We must not cease to expose the double Communist mystification. A proletarian party, which boasts of resting on the will of the masses, will not risk, after thirty years of power, giving the people an opportunity of expressing its will without restraint. That power, which claims to be a liberator, imposes regimes to which the nations submit against their own will. But for the very reason that free elections would reveal the chink in the Soviet armor, the Kremlin is not likely to permit them to take place. The Russians talk as if their elections were free, but they know that in the absence of police pressure the masses would vote quite differently. They therefore refuse elections "in the American style" and insist on the validity of their own method.

Again, there can be no question that the Big Four would have any better chance of agreeing on the terms of a general German settlement. Can there be any illusions as to the result of a new conference? Indeed, how could the Westerners induce the Bonn politicians even to sit at the same table with the Communist leaders? It is yet more difficult to see how a pluralist democracy could function with a Communist party installed in the Eastern bastion and infiltrating with its men and its propaganda into the Western

*Länder.* To embark on any such adventure would indeed be inviting a *coup d'état* like that of Prague.

It is very likely that the Soviet Union would agree to the "desovietization" of the Eastern zone in exchange for advantages in the West. In any case, the Kremlin would demand, in such an exchange, participation in the control of the Ruhr—which the West, unless suicidally inclined, could hardly concede. A promise to keep Germany neutral and disarmed would not be enough to induce the Soviet Union to abandon the Socialist Unity Party to its fate. If the Kremlin had none but pacific intentions and if it feared aggression, the fifty-year quadripartite pact proposed some years ago by Mr. Byrnes might perhaps be a practicable solution. An international treaty might fulfill the same defensive function as the People's Republic. But the Kremlin's ultimate objective is world empire, not peace.

Only one method of reuniting Germany seems possible—the evacuation of Germany by the troops of both sides and a struggle between the two republics, ending either in an agreed or an imposed settlement. The Soviet authorities are not sure of the reliability of the "people's" police that they have organized, and they have no illusion as to the feeling of the majority of Germans, even those who collaborate with them. Only a small number are attracted by the grandiose prospect of a Eurasian adventure or seduced by the advantages offered to the members of the privileged caste. Nowhere east of the Iron Curtain is the pressure of Western prosperity and liberty so strong. But nowhere are the new masters so well aware that their fate is intimately bound up with that of the Soviet enterprise. The German Communists—the leaders, in any case—have no possibility of escape in the direction of Titoism, because they have no popular support. They rule by virtue of the machinery of power. The day that machinery collapses the irresistible pressure of the masses will sweep away the institutions of the victor and his agents.

Western strategy in Germany shows the same weakness as elsewhere. Being strictly defensive, it can only act after the Kremlin takes the initiative; we were exclusively concerned with economic prosperity at the time when Soviet agents were recruiting security police (*Bereitschaften*).

Apart from bureaucratic paralysis and from still smoldering memories and passions, how can we explain the incapacity of Western diplomats to put into immediate practice a policy theoretically adopted long ago—the integration of democratic Germany into the Western community? Germany's situation, we are told, is such that we shall never be able to trust her, and consequently there is still hesitation between her neutralization and her integration with the West.

It is said that as long as the Eastern zone remains under the Soviet yoke, every German statesman will look eastward in the hope of achieving national reunion—an argument, so often repeated, that is both true and false. No German will resign himself to the perpetuation of the present division of the Reich; but no Minister or member of Parliament at Bonn has any faith in the possibility of restoring unity by negotiation with the leaders of the People's Republic. The German socialists, liberals, and democrats remember their parties' fate in the Eastern zone. They know what would happen to them under a Government of the National Front, the first step along the road towards a people's democracy. In other words, the simple instinct of self-preservation protects us against the "treason"[1] so feared by Western diplomats, who are obsessed by misinterpreted historical memories.

But, it will be objected, do not the businessmen—who after all are as important as the statesmen—dream of markets in Asia, markets hungry for modern machines and equipment, for all the goods for which German industry has acquired a well-deserved reputation? There is no question that the Eurasian markets are insatiable in terms of need. But whether the demand is solvent may at least be doubted. No one knows what fraction of the imports desired by the "people's" China could be paid for with exports. Before the war the whole of the Soviet zone in Europe absorbed less than 20 per cent of the Third Reich's foreign trade. If, from an economic point of view, the choice lay between East and West, Germany's decision would have to be in favor of the West.

[1]There will be no reason to fear such "treason" unless and until Europe seems definitely lost, on the eve of a Soviet invasion.

Not that her choice would be made without anxieties and regrets. German exports to the free countries overseas compete with similar exports from Belgium, France, and Great Britain. Even the contractors and technicians of the Ruhr, who hope to survive Sovietization because of the need their new masters would have for managers, want to see a renewal of trade with the East. They do not go so far as to want to change sides (as long as Soviet tanks have not arrived); and trade with the East, as such, is not necessarily contrary to the interests of the Atlantic coalition.

The integration of Germany into Western Europe is artificial and precarious if it entails the suppression of trade with the East. But there is no reasonable solution for Germany as long as Germany (like Europe and the world at large) remains divided, or at least for as long as she does not belong simultaneously to two worlds.

That indisputable fact is the origin of the theory still maintained by many people in Europe and the United States—the theory of neutrality. Whether she is a Soviet Republic or part of Western Europe, Germany will not resign herself to separation from either of the two worlds. She will strongly endeavor to maintain trade with both. Why refuse to admit that natural and legitimate desire? Instead of seeking to integrate former enemies into the community of the Western victors, why not seek Germany's independence and neutrality, now that she has fallen from her high imperial estate? As long as we cling to generalities and talk of encircling buffer states, we shall be led astray by a solution that seems to avoid the two major risks—the conquest of Germany by the Communist Party (and therefore by the Soviet Union), or the provocation of the Soviet Union by an alliance which the Kremlin will regard as aggressive. It remains to be seen whether such an objective is accessible and whether the conception represents one of the actual possibilities of the present European situation.

Neutrality may be of three kinds—political, diplomatic, and military. A unified Germany, politically neutral, would need to appear neither a satellite of the Soviet Union nor bound to the Atlantic community. She should not be a People's Republic, but neither should she profess Western democracy. It follows from merely stating these qualifications that they cannot be obtained under present world conditions. Not that there are not countries which have nothing in common with either the U.S.S.R. or the U.S.A. But any country not under Communist rule is regarded by the Kremlin as an enemy, to be vituperated as "capitalist," "Marshallized," and so on. For a German government to be considered neutral would require the Kremlin in its propaganda to recognize the existence of a third alternative. There is no sign at present of any such revolution. Thus, either a unified Germany would be ruled by Communists, and would not be neutral; or else it would be ruled by non-Communists who would be subject to attacks from the Stalinists. A government made up of both would have no better chance of survival than the Czech Government of 1945.

Diplomatically, neutrality is always possible, because no one attaches any importance to it. It matters little whether a particular country adheres or not to the Atlantic Pact. For purposes of propaganda or international discussion, it would be permissible to announce that a unified Germany would remain neutral, and would not be integrated into either coalition. The Russians will not be likely to see in such formal declarations an equivalent to the desovietization of the Eastern Republic. They rely more on the machinery of the People's Republic than on the promises of the State Department or the Foreign Office.

Would they pay more attention to them if the promise of disarmament were added to political neutrality? The Big Four might undertake by treaty to maintain indefinitely the disarmament of the Reich. I doubt whether the masters of the Kremlin would agree to dismantle their bastion, even with such a guarantee—which, in any case, is impracticable. A disarmed Germany would not form a buffer state between East and West, but would create in the center of the Continent a void which would inevitably bring intervention from both sides. The Germans would rightly consider that in case of war they would be doomed to immediate occupation by Russian troops. It would be so absurd for the West to accept the long-term disarmament of Germany that the Kremlin would not believe the agreement to be sincere.

Neutrality as a diplomatic formula might help in attempting to reunify Germany. It might represent a distant objective, since a restored Germany, united and partially armed, could be more useful if autonomous than if integrated into the Atlantic coalition. Among long-term policies, this one, which would promote the flexibility of the fronts, seems reasonable.

But it would be necessary once more not to confuse a vague and uncertain possibility with a precise objective. As a result of carefully considering every possible risk, Western diplomacy has lost momentum. The Federal Republic is entirely disarmed, while the rearmament of the People's Republic has begun. The plan for a coal and steel pool is at least evidence of good will, treating West Germany as a partner and no longer an enemy, and offering her equality of rights and an honorable place within the Western community.

In many respects Japan's situation in the Far East is comparable with that of Germany in Europe. But economically, the problem is more difficult. The population is not stable, as in Germany, but rapidly increasing (already over 80 million). Industrial expansion is indispensable if the Japanese are ever to pay for essential purchases of food abroad with exports. Their foreign possessions—Korea, Manchuria, the Sakhalin Islands, Formosa—have been lost. Most of their raw materials must come from abroad. Japan remains virtually the industrial arsenal of Asia. Cut off from China and the other people's republics, she will not easily find outlets; and in their absence she would not be able to exist at all without the support of the United States.

From a military point of view, in the age of the atom bomb or even of mass bombing, Japan is extraordinarily vulnerable. In a total war the supplying of food to the overpopulated Japanese islands would impose a heavy drain on American transport. Should not the United States look upon Japan as a source of weakness rather than an asset? Would it not be in their interests to neutralize her instead of making her an ally? That view explains General MacArthur's statements before the Korean campaign comparing the Japan of tomorrow to Switzerland.

But considerations of this sort are as seductive as they are misleading. Why should the Soviet Union agree to a policy of neutralization if it is just what the Americans would prefer? The argument is still the same: everything depends on Soviet strategy. Either the Kremlin plans to enlarge its zone of influence as much as possible, without envisaging limitless expansion—in which case the neutralization of a Japan "democratized" in the Eastern manner is conceivable—or else it plans to complete the conquest of Asia; in which case the neutralization of Japan is a wild idea, because neutralization presupposes agreement between the two sides. The Korean campaign dissipated the last illusion; the second hypothesis is correct.

But many uncertainties remain. The consent of the Japanese to their own rearmament has not been obtained any more than has that of ther Germans. Where are the officers of a "democratic" army to be found? Will the former ones be ready to serve? Will they be faithful to the new order? American policy in the empire of the Rising Sun has yielded relatively good results—agrarian reform without social upheaval, and democratization without the emperor's being either hanged or exiled. Unable to carry revolution to its completion, it safeguarded the conditions of recovery.

The objections raised against the only possible policy have so far been, *mutatis mutandis,* comparable to those raised against the reversal of alliances in Europe. Australia and New Zealand have not lost their past fear of Japan, just as France and the other European countries have not forgotten the fear with which they regarded the Kaiser's and Hitler's Germany. The Commonwealth countries still fear the competition of Japanese bicycles or cotton goods (just as the others fear German machinery or optical instruments). Let us add that American diplomacy in 1945 was based on the idea of a friendly and democratic China, and had only eighteen months before the Korean aggression in which to revise conceptions contradicted by events.

American diplomacy in Asia is now confronted with a series of unpleasant but incontestable facts. Asians are no longer, as in the last century, militarily powerless. They have an inexhaustible human potential, and arms received from the Soviet Union or taken from former protégés of the United States. The belt of air and naval bases from the Aleutian Islands to the Philippines and Okinawa constitutes the first line of defense of the United States in the Pacific. The Japanese Islands belong to that belt; from a military as well as a political point of view, the evacuation of what was the Nipponese Empire is unthinkable.

Given this situation, two policies are possible. One would be to maintain bases in a demilitarized Japan for an indefinite period; the other would be to undertake immediately Japan's partial remilitarization. This latter alternative, though not without risks, remains preferable, and American diplomacy is swinging over to it.

In the Far East as in Europe, American diplomacy has at last realized that the enemies of yesterday must be brought into the Western camp; otherwise they will surely and fatally be drawn into the Soviet camp. But it has not drawn all the conclusions from that major fact. The Westerners are too intelligent to see simple things simply. The reversal of alliances is a crude and even immoral formula. How attractive it was to speculate on the neutrality of Germany and Japan, on armed neutrality and disarmed neutrality, on political neutrality and military neutrality! But all those speculations collapsed like a house of cards when the first shot was fired in Korea.

The observer in another planet would have been tempted more than once in our century to denounce the folly of mankind. The goal that Western strategy has set itself in Japan as well as in Germany is not different from the situation that would have arisen of its own accord if peace had been concluded before the entry of Soviet troops into the Reich and Manchuria, and before the complete destruction of both armies and countries. We are trying to efface the consequence of a too complete victory, and to get back to a victory compatible with the resurrection of the vanquished.

What must be done is unquestionable: in both cases the only thing is to close the gap created by the collapse of our former enemies. We can no longer afford to spend time debating whether to include Germany in the Atlantic community or to unify her, or wondering whether a unified Germany will be, as we should wish, a conservative power. Those are serious long-term issues. But the Kremlin has left us no choice. As the democracies, from their very nature, are incapable of "manufacturing" satellites, they must make sure of allies.

*Chapter XI*

# INTERCONTINENTAL EQUILIBRIUM

THERE WERE TIMES when only part of a nation's resources were marshaled on the field of battle. That is no longer the case in the twentieth century. A third world war would be even more voracious than its predecessors. The only remaining unknown factor is the coefficient of mobilization in peacetime.

Before 1914 the coefficient in France was calculated on the basis of the estimated requirements for the first operations, which were expected to be decisive. In Great Britain the naval forces were maintained constantly at greater strength than those of the most powerful rival; and the Army was prepared to intervene immediately and reinforce the Continental ally.

In 1918 responsible British leaders anticipated no serious risk for at least ten years. The adopted program consisted of organizing cadres for future mobilization, taking the necessary precautions for the defense of the Empire nerve centers and, in the interim, pursuing scientific and technical studies. After Hitler's rise to power the rearmament pace was quickened in order to make available, at a few days' notice, air and naval squadrons requisite to the safety of the British Isles and, within a few weeks, sufficient land forces to help the French Army repel German attacks.

In France, obligatory military service was accepted as the obvious and indispensable principle of recruitment. The overseas territories needed relatively strong permanent forces. The military machine was expensive even in the period 1920–33, when France was in no way endangered. When the threat appeared, the additional effort was insufficient and the arsenals were full of outmoded arms dating from 1918.

In 1946, after premature demobilization, the United States was led for the first time to organize a military system in preparedness against an external menace. A simple theoretical conception was adopted: for a certain period (five or six years, it was said), the strategic air force and the atom bomb should prevent Stalin from contemplating any direct aggression. It was decided to maintain a navy and an air force—each considerable, but reduced from what they had been in 1945—and an army of some ten divisions, with a twofold function—to occupy certain strategic points in order to deter the Soviet from any military undertaking, and to form the nucleus of a large army which would be recruited in the event of general war. Finally, considerable sums were devoted to scientific research, but actual manufacture was slowed down as much as possible, in order not to accumulate war material that might be obsolete when required for use.

This was probably the only possible procedure for a democracy, but the United States carried it to absurd lengths. The controversy over whether there should be forty-eight or seventy air groups was settled in favor of the former,[1] giving the Soviet Union actual superiority in the air, in quantity if not in quality. The Air Force, thus amputated, was badly equipped with fighter-type planes. The Air Force would probably have been unable to maintain an effective tactical air action up to the time when the production lines, starting on D Day, would be delivering planes in quantity. The Army was imperfectly trained, and the Marines were low in men and matériel. Industrial mobilization had been more or less planned on paper. Certain defense plants were held in readiness, and the big companies knew to some extent what they would have to make. But in 1950 the American forces were negligible on land and inferior in the air to those of the Soviet Union.

Was the combination of a strategic air force, the atom bomb, and industrial potential strong enough to wage the cold war?

The events of 1950 revealed one of the defects in the American

[1]When the Korean campaign started the Air Force did not even have forty-eight complete groups.

policy. The initial idea was that there would be either a warlike peace, without intervention by the regular armies, or a total war, with air attacks on the principal Russian cities. A third possibility was discovered, which had not been foreseen—limited hot wars.

The events in Korea, however accidental their origin, contained a valuable lesson, applicable elsewhere. Between the Soviet methods of aggression employed from 1946 to 1950 and the acts likely to produce general war would fall a certain interval. The intervention of a Soviet satellite with its regular army against a country set up under American protection would seem to have occurred somewhere in the center of the interval. But no one knows exactly how long it will be before the present form of aggression is abandoned for a form that would constitute a *casus belli* for the Americans.

The fear which the potential strength of the United States was thought to inspire in the men of the Kremlin was overestimated. It was imagined that they would abstain from acts which, without starting a general war, would aggravate the tension. In actual fact, they did not hesitate to defy the United States directly.

The State Department's advisers calculated that the intermediate phase, opened by the Korean campaign, would not begin before 1952. That anticipation was founded, it seems, on the belief that the atomic monopoly of the United States would last until that date. The usual inference is that the development of the atomic weapon by the Soviet Union in 1949 gave the Politburo the confidence to risk aggressive action.

This interpretation may be right, but it is not certain, and is in any case incomplete. If the first test explosion took place in 1949, it is not likely that the Soviet Union had an important stock of bombs by 1950. The atomic superiority of the United States, both in number of bombs and in quality and quantity of strategic bombers, is undoubted. In these conditions, the production of the bomb in the Soviet Union two years sooner than was expected is not adequate to explain the Korean adventure in 1950, which stimulated the United States to rearm and allowed the West to reduce the disproportion in conventional weapons, in a period when, according to the calculations of the strategists, the atomic weapon had not yet been counterbalanced.

It will be objected that the Kremlin did not expect so sharp a reaction from Washington. Once again, it is possible and even probable that Stalin believed the official declarations from the Pentagon, that American diplomats would confine themselves to vain formal protests. But that very calculation by the men of the Kremlin shows up one of the weaknesses of the American military strategy. It is impossible to protect all the exposed territories on the periphery of the Soviet empire by a threat of general war, which the enemy hardly takes seriously. Who believes that Mr. Truman would have given an order to drop atom bombs on Moscow because North Korean tanks had crossed the 38th parallel?

The approach being taken by the United States in order to counter the new problems arising from Soviet production of atomic weapons and the existence of limited hot wars, seems to be as follows:

In the first place, the United States, which must now maintain not only the arsenal but the army of the coalition, must be secured against a sudden attack. If we assume that the Kremlin calculates rationally, one consideration should be decisive for it: the possibility or impossibility of paralyzing, or substantially weakening American power in a first attack. As long as the United States itself is invulnerable, the most spectacular initial successes would not guarantee ultimate victory. The organization of the Communist empire in the midst of war would meet with even greater difficulties than those encountered by Hitler's attempt at a European empire.

Next, in waging the cold war the West needs conventional armaments greatly superior to those it had in 1950. The reasons are obvious: The United States had not even the necessary resources for a local hot war like that of Korea. In the absence of rearmament, every Soviet aggression, direct or through a satellite, would drive them to a choice between capitulation (or retreat) and total war. The aim of the West is not to win a war, but to avoid it. Knowing this, Russia rightly expects the West to capitulate or retreat.

It may be urged that it is difficult to conceive the multiplication of local wars of the Korean type. In the Middle East, in Iran, the threatened countries do not possess the minimum of military forces without which resistance is out of the question. In Southeastern Asia civil wars are raging. Chinese intervention there would no longer mean local strife, but war against China herself.

Admitting that other local wars are improbable, the West is nevertheless obliged to make an effort at rearmament. The West did not succeed between 1943 and 1945 in using its actual superiority to influence negotiations with the U.S.S.R. But since 1950 the U.S.S.R. has used its superior armament to spread terror. The industrial potential of the United States remains a supreme argument which prevents irreparable initiatives, but it is not enough to reassure the populations doomed to occupation in the event of war, or perhaps to convince the Kremlin that its adversaries are determined to resist.

In other words, this simple proposition has finally been accepted: Regular armies have no substitutes as an instrument of cold war. Whatever the technique of the next war, divisions, tanks, soldiers, are still regarded by the statesman and the man in the street as an essential element of power. To restore confidence in the masses of Europe, of the Middle East, and of Asia and to instill fear or respect in the masters of the Kremlin, atom bombs and production figures are not enough.

Armed as it is at present, the West would probably have still more trouble in conquering the Russians than it had in dealing with the Nazis. The *Wehrmacht* wore itself out in the immensity of Russian space; but where is the land army capable of wearing out the Soviet Army? For centuries past the naval powers have in the end won the great wars, but they always had at least one great Continental power as an ally. The Germans gained control of the Channel and the North Sea coast and of the Atlantic, but hundreds of Russian divisions remained intact in the East, and the Anglo-Saxons kept control of the Mediterranean. This time the Red Army, in collaboration with satellite armies, would reign from Brest to Saigon, and could extend its divisions as far as the oil fields of Iran, Iraq, and Arabia.

The strategy implicit in American policy until 1950 accepted in advance an intercontinental war, an inevitable combination of strategic bombing, local or marginal operations, and political, psychological, or clandestine action. Such a war would leave survivors rather than victors; for even if, as a result of air attacks or popular revolts, the Communist empire were ultimately crushed or fell to pieces, the war would be ruinous for everyone. The Communist regime organized by the conquerors would destroy the structure of the old nations of Europe. The ruling classes would run the risk of extermination. The masses themselves would be exposed to deportations. The Russians would perhaps, like Hitler, be prisoners of their conquests, but it is certain that 200 millions of Europeans would be the prisoners of the M.V.D.

There remains a last argument. Atomic equality may soon result in the neutralization of the terrifying weapon. When it does, the superiority of strategic position, of land forces, and of human potential will come into full play in favor of the Soviet Union.

Then the permanent armies of the West will not merely have to threaten reprisals in order to stifle any fancy for aggression, but will have to be capable of stopping the Russian armies on the two critical battlefields of Western Europe and the Middle East.

If the above argument is acceptable, it will be immediately seen that the rearmament of the United States, however indispensable, has ceased to respond to all the needs of the situation. The Soviet Union is not content to protect its satellites by threatening to intervene in their defense; it is arming them, and reinforcing its own armies with those of the people's democracies. Still more must the Western camp, committed to a strategy of defense, complement the enormous but distant force of the United States by restoring the military machines of the countries most immediately threatened which are situated on the periphery of the Soviet empire.

Leaving aside the defense of Southeastern Asia and the Middle East (which especially concern the Commonwealth and the United States), the essential problem is the defense of Europe, or rather that part of Europe west of the Iron Curtain. There are still observers who declare that the rearmament of Europe is both impossible and useless—impossible because of the changes that have taken place in the scale of power and the measure of space. Technical weapons, tanks, aircraft, atom bombs have widened the distinction between small and great countries. As has been said since the beginning of the century, the small are becoming steadily smaller, the great steadily greater. Probably neither the atom bomb nor the hydrogen bomb is an absolute weapon. They would not be enough to bring about the capitulation of a first-class power. But could a nation of 40 millions, whose industry and administration are highly concentrated, resist the destruction of some of its principal cities? Neither the United States nor the Soviet Union could protect all their cities against atomic attack, but their cities would not all be exposed, without defense, to enemy raids. In 1940 the German Stukas destroyed methodically, house by house, an entire section of Rotterdam. If, tomorrow, France or Italy saw three or four of their cities ravaged by atom bombs, would even twenty armored divisions prevent capitulation?

The cost of defense, active or passive, against air attack is enormous. The most that is claimed is an increase in the percentage of planes shot down before they reach their objective—that is to say, a reduction in the frequency of hits on the target. But will not a few hits, if each one destroys a whole quarter, be enough to break the will to resist?

If this argument is true, then intercontinental equilibrium should be a lasting situation. Western Europe must be joined by the United States to balance the force of the Soviet zone. Isolated from the New World, the Wesern fringe of the Continent would inevitably be incorporated one day into the Russian empire. In a total war it would not escape occupation, because it is too near the enemy center of force and too far from the friendly center. It occupies a strategic position comparable to that of Belgium in 1914 and 1939, between the Continental empire and the coalition of maritime powers. The former had the initiative, maneuvering internally, and began with superiority on land. The countries bordering on the Reich were submerged after the first battles, as the countries of Western Europe would inevitably be in a third world war, the enlargement of the zone swallowed by the wave being proportional to the amplification of violence. On the scale of present-day technical science, Western Europe is hardly larger than the Belgium of 1914 was on the scale of the military science of that epoch.

It is not inconceivable, however, that Europe, although open to invasion, may continue to be spared. This possibility depends on whether the Kremlin fears the threat of a general war and is able to keep local conflicts within tolerable limits.

None of these arguments against European rearmament which we have recapitulated can be effectively refuted. It is true that

Europe must think of herself in the context of an intercontinental equilibrium. It is also true that the date when a powerless Europe would be absorbed by the Soviet empire cannot be fixed. But action must depend on the balance of disadvantages. In theory, Western Europe has the choice between three policies: to join the Soviet zone; or to resist Communist infiltration and the external pressure from the Soviet Union as long as the guns remain silent, and capitulate on D Day; or, finally, to accept support from the New World and acquire the means of self-defense. The first policy would be suicidal: we know the fate of national front governments who have allowed the Stalinists to participate. Even for the mass of the population concerned, the anticipated capitulation would not offer any promise of salvation. The Baltic countries, "peacefully" occupied, suffered the extermination of the ruling class and the deportation of peasants, as much as or more than did the German enemy. Perhaps the countries of the West are not fated to become integral parts of the Union as rapidly as the Baltic countries, and would not be treated with the same harshness. The Kremlin's action will depend more on the policy it adopts than on resistance or non-resistance. Lastly, it must not be forgotten that joining the Soviet camp from fear of attack from that quarter would increase the risk of being treated as an enemy by the maritime powers. The hostility of the latter, once war came, might well be actively unpleasant.

The second policy—peaceful resistance, in anticipation of capitulation if the worst happened—is subconsciously favored by many Europeans. But in the long run it is unthinkable: it weakens the morale of nations and induces them to surrender to a sterilizing defeatism. It fosters a spirit of passivity and evasion, and there is hesitation to do anything constructive lest in a conflict the enemy should benefit. Modern weapons, however terrifying, do not modify certain rules that are as old as nations. The diplomatic attitude implies a military alignment. One cannot choose sides only up to the outbreak of war. Such a game can be played even less today than in the age of empires; for history has confirmed the mobilization of the conquered and the arming of satellites. The less a country fights against a conqueror, the more it will have to fight for him.

The small countries have no choice but to range themselves on one side or the other, without any illusion as to their fate in a war.

But that attitude is fatal when it is a question of 200 millions of human beings who enjoy a high standard of living in comparison with that of four fifths of mankind, who control the greater part of Africa, and who show no eagerness to renounce their overseas possessions. Those who give up the attempt to decide for themselves must accept their fate. The destiny of those who resign themselves to being the playthings of history is seldom enviable.

The old center of Western civilization cannot remain empty in the field of power politics. If the European void is not filled by the Atlantic powers, it will be filled sooner or later by Soviet expansion. As long as the Continent is a territory protected only by the distant force of the United States and not a group of allied states whose contribution strengthens their coalition with America, anxiety will persist on both sides of the Atlantic, and the Soviet Union will try to disintegrate the Western community by local aggressions, by extortion based on the threat of war, and by propaganda.

The hydrogen bomb creates an additional peril for the western fringe of the Continent, but it cannot be said that it makes resistance hopeless. In any case, the Soviet Union will refrain as far as possible from using the bomb against countries which it intends to integrate definitely into its empire. When the stock of bombs has increased on both sides, it may be that, for fear of reprisals, neither side will employ the appalling weapon. It is also possible that Europe may meanwhile have acquired some means of defense against strategic bombing. In any case, if we assume that the atomic weapon has deprived Western Europe of all chance of military resistance to the Soviet Union, we will block every means of escape from the third world war; for European capitulation would make that war inevitable.

Admitting that the defense of Europe is desirable, is it possible? The troops of the Soviet Union and its satellites already occupy the heart of the Continent. It is proposed to defend the Elbe line, although the frontier between the two Germanys passes considerably to the west of the Elbe for some dozens of miles. What divisions will hold the river lines, an even more illusory defense than the Maginot line?

The reply to such questions seems to be dictated by the circumstances. Either the maritime powers will achieve in time of peace what they would be obliged to do in time of war—that is, install large land forces—or else the formerly great Continental powers, Germany and France, will reconstitute their military machine. If we are thinking of the next few years, there is no alternative. Both maritime and Continental powers will have to rearm; and the temporary contribution of the former is indispensable for promoting and completing that of the latter.

The military potential of the United States and Great Britain, even on land, is enormous. The British Isles, the American Republic, and the white Dominions of the Commonwealth together number some 230 million men. This privileged minority owns at least two thirds of the industrial capacity of the world, it enjoys the highest standard of living, and it is in the front rank in science and technology. Unfortunately it does not follow from these facts, which are repeated too complacently, that on the outbreak of war Europe would at once be protected by an Anglo-American army. Everything depends on the strategy adopted by the United States and on the decision taken by Great Britain.

Of the European countries west of the Iron Curtain, only one has a certain military power. Great Britain spent in 1950 some 800 million pounds (or 7.5 per cent of her national income) on her military budget, a higher percentage, up to Korea, than that of any other nation of the Atlantic Pact. But the cost of weapons has increased. British expenditures are high, but lower than in 1939, when compared as percentages of the national income. There is still the nucleus of an army and an air force, at present small but high in quality, and a navy faithful to its traditions. National unity has not been seriously damaged by Communist propaganda. Compared with any of the Continental countries, Great Britain is a model of health and vigor.

On the present scale, a nation of 50 millions of inhabitants, whatever its qualities, falls to the second rank. When Great Britain held the command of the sea, she freely chose peace and war. Today she could not make war except in alliance with, or at least with the consent of, the power that rules the oceans and the air. This dependence is resented with some bitterness. But the annoyance directed at the colony of yesterday and protector of today is a psychological fact rather than a political factor. After all, the British fought to exhaustion in order that the scepter, if it had to be given up, should pass to the Americans and not to the Germans or Russians.

Great Britain owed her good fortune largely to her geographical situation, to the Channel that sheltered her from invasions without preventing her from intervening on the Continent. In 1940, the Channel still proved an effective anti-tank barrage; but it was not enough, in 1944, to stop the V-1s and V-2s. If we suppose the number of V-1s falling on London multiplied by ten and the explosive power of each one multiplied by the same coefficient, in all probability the peril would attain an intensity insupportable to civilians, left to themselves, who, unlike combatants, are not held in check by discipline and the hope of returning the blows they receive. In the age of rockets and atom bombs, Great Britain, too close to the Continent, with a population too greatly concentrated in the large cities, is terribly vulnerable.

If the Red Army established itself on the Channel and North Sea coast, Great Britain would at best suffer the fate of the Continental countries, conquered in spite of victory. Each of the twentieth-century wars has cost the United Kingdom more than it has acquired. Rational strategists blame the principle of "unconditional surrender" and the strategic bombing. They are not wrong, but twentieth-century wars are not rational, and neither are the men who carry them on. There is less chance than ever that the third war, if it ceases to remain cold, will remain within the limits of reason. When the consequences of defeat are limitless, how can leaders renounce the employment of any resource? So a Soviet victory, still more than Hitler's, would involve total disaster for the West.

Great Britain ought this time to take seriously the formula "Our frontier is on the Rhine," or "On the Elbe." The British staffs are by no means unaware of the disasters that would follow the occupation of Western Europe by the Russian Army. In spite of everything, however, they retain the memory of the recent ordeal and cannot forget that they survived the Continental defeats of 1940 and the isolation of 1941. Expert and man in the street still hope that if worst comes to worst, the miracle of the inviolable isle will be repeated.

There are those who are not so optimistic, but what other strategy would they propose? The erection of a barrier to contain the Soviet wave does not depend on Great Britain. Still, the United Kingdom has decided to maintain important naval and air forces. The few hundreds of thousands of pounds devoted to the land army allow for the instruction of recruits and dispatch of some units to the nerve centers of the empire—the Middle East, Malaya, Hong Kong. Short of a huge increase in military expenditure and the return to a war economy, there will be only a few divisions available for Europe. In order to produce a great land army in time of peace, Great Britain would have both to live in a state of mobilization and to delegate to the United States, to a much greater extent than at present, the task which she understood in the last century—the protection of overseas lines of communication. Even if this division of labor were in itself reasonable in the common interest of the Atlantic community, it is not to be expected that either public opinion or the leaders in Great Britain would consent to it: an age-old tradition is not reversed in a few years.

However, recent British military budgets give evidence of an evolution in that direction. Attention is devoted first to aircraft production (protection of the British Isles), and then to the Army. An increasing part of the expenditure involved in patrolling the seas is transferred to the United States. But Great Britain would only decide to risk a large part of her resources in the land defense of Europe if (contrary to precedent) she saw a serious chance of winning the *first* battle.

In 1930 no one would have imagined that the joint forces of Germany and France could be outclassed by those of Russia alone. Now everyone is wondering whether the two enemies of last century, even united, are capable of marshaling within a few years an army of some ten divisions. The causes of this uncertainty are well known in France: Communist Party strength, war obligations in Indo-China, skepticism about the possibility of successful resistance, fear of provoking the monster by spectacular preparations; in Germany, revolt against war and an almost hopeless geopolitical situation. Will French and Germans overcome these motives for passivity? History alone will reply.

If they are to do so, one condition appears to be indispensable: the presence on the Continent, in the time of warlike peace, of an

American army that is not merely a token. In 1951 the Administration, Congress, and public opinion in the United States recognized the part that must be played by the leader of the Western coalition, even in the matter of land forces. Some additional divisions arrived in the course of the year. Americans accepted for the present the responsibility of filling the void created in Europe by the consequences of the Second World War. It is a historic decision without precedent, symbolizing the diplomatic and military unity of continents separated by thousands of miles of oceans, but also symbolizing the dangers to which Europe will be exposed for many years.

The West has the resources necessary for winning a total war if it should come; still more, therefore, has it the resources for re-establishing the balance of armed forces in time of warlike peace, and at the same time for diminishing the risks of an upheaval. The whole question is whether the democratic countries will have the courage to endure the sacrifices and efforts of semi-mobilization before the enemy legions move.

The world is living in a limited war. A semi-war requires semi-mobilization.[2] Intercontinental equilibrium dictates additional duties. We must resign ourselves either to losing valuable territories in the early weeks of fighting, or to keeping up a sufficient number of divisions in time of peace.

To the maritime powers, Great Britain, and the United States, these are new obligations; but not to the Continental powers, which have traditionally had to keep enough soldiers under arms, and enough arms and munitions in their arsenals, to resist a possible invasion. The European and Asiatic voids compel the Anglo-Saxon peoples to assume temporarily a part of the obligations which they like to leave to their land allies.

Semi-mobilization will not make it certain that aggression will be repelled. It is always to be feared that the Continental empire may accumulate, in a given sector, forces superior to those on the defensive side. The difficulty of resistance becomes for defeatist writers a motive for passivism—an attitude that is literally absurd.

---

[2] Really "quarter-mobilization." As a percentage of the national income the 1951 effort in Great Britain represented a quarter of the effort of total war, and perhaps a third in 1951–52 in the United States.

208 LIMITED WAR

An army of fifty divisions would not assure absolute safety in Europe. Indeed, it may be asked if anything of the sort ever exists in military affairs. But it would change the general strategic situation, reduce the probability of Soviet aggression, and contribute to the restoration of confidence in Europe.

The United States is learning that great powers must maintain their army, navy, and air force, and not disband them immediately following victory. For the present, American divisions must remain in Western Europe in order to fill the void created by the Second World War. But intervention would be of no use if the European countries remain definitely out of play and resign themselves to accept a precarious security from American protection and to suffer the invader's tyranny when the release of limitless violence bursts through the dams. In the long run, it is the work of Europeans to fill the European void. If they do not decide to do it, one day or another the United States will resign itself to a strategy of intercontinental war—in reply to European defeatism.

*Chapter XII*

# STALINISM AND THE SHADE OF THE PAST

THE LEADERS of the Soviet Union consider the universal diffusion of Communism to be the logical and inevitable result of the present crisis. The leaders of the West think only of live and let live, and are hoping desperately for the coexistence of the so-called socialist and the so-called capitalist countries. The U.S.S.R. carries out an offensive strategy, the West a defensive one. Face to face with the men of the Kremlin, as with Hitler, the democracies, instead of asking themselves "What shall I do?" ask every day "What will the Red Tsars do?"

Of the ultimate aim of the Soviet enterprise, there is no doubt except for those who are determined to shut their eyes. Lenin's celebrated saying continues to be accepted as a fundamental truth by the men of the Kremlin: "The permanent coexistence of the Soviet Republic and the imperialist states is unthinkable. One or the other must triumph in the end. And before that end arrives, a series of terrible collisions between the Soviet Republic and the bourgeois nations is inevitable."

It is true that from time to time the inspired Father of the Peoples accorded an interview to some foreign journalist or statesman, and declared that there was no obstacle to "peaceful coexistence." It would require a good deal of simplicity or ignorance to take such statements literally; they are for export only, and are not even always reproduced in the Soviet press. Such talk is of a tactical order, intended to disseminate illusions to which peaceful people readily incline, and to encourage the "partisans of peace"—

the ingenuous, the idealists, or the fellow travelers. For that matter, there is no need to consider such statements as lies. The only lie is one of omission. It is merely necessary to qualify the coexistence of the two worlds as temporary for the thesis to become strictly orthodox. In 1922 Lenin passionately desired coexistence in order to consolidate the regime that had proceeded from the Revolution. In the same way, in 1945, Stalin himself wanted it, for some years at least. For both men it was only a matter of different phases in a struggle to the death, the outcome of which must be the victory of one system or the other.

That the historical concept of the Stalinists is catastrophic, that the men of the Kremlin look forward to a series of monstrous wars, civil and foreign, until the final triumph of what they call Communism, does not, it seems to me, admit of argument. Such a doctrine implies *preparation* for the expected cataclysm, but not necessarily *provocation* in cold blood. It does not even imply a military interpretation of the inevitable struggle between the two systems.

In this respect, Western commentators have oscillated between two extreme theories. According to some, the Kremlin is afraid of a general war, which would slow down the building of socialism and prevent the Soviet economy from proving its intrinsic superiority. According to others, the struggle between the socialist and the imperialist camps is destined to assume a definitely military character. It is in war and through war alone that the country of the proletariat will prove that the future belongs to it. The second theory seems to me to be nearer the truth.

A century ago Marx was, or seemed to be, convinced that capitalism was doomed to self-destruction through its internal contradictions. It would today require a strange obstinacy to uphold his economic determinism. The so-called proletarian revolution was the outcome of wars, not of crises, and becomes the more probable the less well developed are the forces of production. To count on a *spontaneous* collapse of American capitalism would require a blind fanaticism which has never in fact dictated the conduct of the Stalinists.

Will it be said that Soviet progress in Asia and Europe ought, according to the doctrine, to aggravate the capitalist contradictions? There is no doubt that the loss of markets or of sources of the supply of raw materials creates some extra difficulties for the American economy. But, short of admitting Rosa Luxemburg's theory of the irreducible surplus that must be placed abroad (a theory never adopted by Lenin or Stalin), an insoluble crisis does not logically result. There has been much talk in the West for several years about an American depression being the opportunity for which the Soviet Union was waiting to accomplish its designs. The "confession" of Varga, who was guilty of having maintained that capitalism was capable of modifying if not suppressing the oscillations of the market, seemed to confirm the idea that the rulers of Moscow were speculating on a transatlantic collapse of a catastrophic character.

Such speculations may have existed. It may be that the Kremlin strategists imagined that Europe would be left to herself when millions of unemployed caused American public opinion and, consequently, the United States Government to withdraw its interest in the outside world. But those hypotheses, so often put forward by commentators, are not convincing; and for a simple reason: according to the doctrine, rearmament—an ideal form of large public works—would be an effective reply to insufficiency of purchasing power in the masses. And rearmament, in turn, would certainly inspire an aggressive diplomacy rather than a return to isolationism.

No matter what part the Kremlin may have assigned to the eventuality of an American crisis, socialism, according to the theory, could not conquer by peaceful means. Let us admit that the thinkers of the Soviet Union themselves believe their constantly repeated arguments about the superiority of the Soviet economy, with no crisis and no unemployment. They know very well, however, that any economic system can create a shortage of labor by starting grandiose public works, and can radically eliminate unemployment by filling the barracks and concentration camps. By such proceedings the living standard of the masses is not raised and that of the Russian masses has for many years been even lower than that of the Western masses. If the masters of the Kremlin counted on the spread of ideas through the value of the Soviet experiment, they would not keep 150 divisions on a war footing, and in their five-year plans they would not put the accent on heavy industry, which is the foundation of economic and military power, but not favorable to the well-being of the present generation. In the rivalry of the two systems, as the facts sufficiently show, the socialist (Bolshevik type) aim is not the satisfaction of the citizen, but the strengthening of the state.

Leninism, and then Stalinism, substituted wars for crises in the dialectic of history.[1] The employment of the Red Army to diffuse the system built up in the U.S.S.R. is not contrary to the doctrine. From the moment when the advent to power of a Communist party is held to be the essential characteristic of revolution, the rising of the masses, their spontaneity, and their feelings cease to be indispensable elements. The return of Anna Pauker in Red army trucks marked the outbreak of a revolution. (According to this system of thought, we must call the return of Louis XVIII in the ammunition wagons of the Allies a monarchical revolution.)

If we agree that the Kremlin's goal is world conquest or universal diffusion of the Stalinist system, then the immediate postwar phase could not have been other than it has been, namely, the Sovietization of the countries "liberated" by the Red Army, agitation within the European countries west of the line of demarcation, and sabotage and civil war in Asia. The Communist expansion, carried by the revolutionary wave, conformed precisely with doctrinal logic: it was bound to break up the coalition of the victors. A period of temporary relaxation of tension, for the sake of reconstruction, was perhaps not irreconcilable with permanent mobilization, an essential feature of totalitarian regimes. Molotov's rejection of the Marshall Plan doubtlessly facilitated the congressional vote in Washington, but even in order to torpedo the enterprise, the Kremlin could not have subscribed for a moment to the American thesis and admit that European unity was in the interest of all European countries, or that American generosity was anything but camouflaged imperialism. Always marching towards an infinitely remote fulfillment, Stalinism—like all religious sects, all conquering empires, all tyrannies—needs enemies. Fascism and reaction having been crushed, the United States must take the vacant place.

There was no hesitation between revolutionary expansion and an entente with the free world, and there was virtually none over the

---

[1]The doctrinal revision is dissimulated, on the one hand, by maintaining as an ideology the Marxist conception of crises and, on the other, by the verbal assimilation of wars and crises (war is supposed to be a crisis of capitalism).

choice between Europe and Asia. People enjoy exhuming old speeches of Lenin or some phrase of Zinoviev, more or less prophetic, about the part reserved for Asia in the revolutionary enterprise, for instance, "The road to Paris passes through Peking and Calcutta." It is true that the Bolsheviks learned from their Russian experiment. They grasped the fact that they had better chances of conquering the West indirectly than by a frontal attack. To incite the colonial peoples to revolt against their European masters, and to stir up the masses of Asia against imperialistic exploitation seemed the most effective method to the Moscow staff. Once victorious in China and India, the ultimate triumph of the revolutionary cause would be assured because its forces would be numerically superior. The Kremlin strategists also had to distinguish between those theaters of operations where an advance was still possible without risk of general war and those in which the advance would encounter resistance as yet too strong to be overcome by sabotage and guerrilla warfare. It would be wrong to interpret as essentially significant the priority given to such a tactical maneuver.

In total war, each belligerent is obliged to split up his necessarily limited forces between many theaters of operations. In cold war this difficulty of rational distribution does not arise, at least for the side which, instead of supporting is satellites, exploits them. The victory of Mao Tse-tung cost Moscow next to nothing in men or money. The Soviet authorities dismantled factories in Manchuria as they did in Eastern Germany. In 1947, when the Marshall Plan was launched, Stalin probably saw with joy how American diplomacy was forsaking Chiang Kai-shek, who was already weakened; but he was anything but delighted to see dollars hastening the reconstruction of the Continent, because the Continent continues to figure in the Kremlin's plans. Perhaps it follows Asia in the chronological order of conquests, but not in order of importance.

Some assert that Stalin had too much contempt for democratic Europe, with its weak governments and popular demands, to want it in his empire. Corruption is contagious when accompanied by a relatively high standard of living. In the Soviet Union the standard of living, low as it is, does not rouse indignation, because it tends to improve, and the people expect further improvement. Already, in certain countries of the perimeter, particularly Czechoslovakia, the "liberation" of the proletariat has so depressed the conditions of existence that the Government is even more unpopular than had been expected. What would happen in Western Europe, where the masses are used to relative abundance (at least in comparison with the Soviet workers), to incessant demands, to a relaxed discipline, and to timorous rulers?

There is no doubt that Stalin despised Europeans, their systems of government, and their ideologies. But Europe continues to possess the elements of strength: millions of skilled workmen, industrial installations, and technicians and trained military personnel equal or superior to those of the Soviet Union. If the Soviet could swallow the whole of Europe as well as continental Asia, it would equal or surpass the United States in power.

Apart from these realistic motives, we must not overlook the moral and historical significance of the oceanic fringe of Europe. Like Rome at the beginning of the fifth century, London, Paris, and Frankfurt are the symbolic capitals of Western civilization, which is on the way to becoming, on the material level, world civilization.

It was in Europe that science, industry, and modern armies first developed. The nations which, at the start of the century, dominated the world scene have managed to exhaust themselves simultaneously by hyperbolic wars. Tired, morally or politically even more than physically, they still seem great in spite of their decay.

Even the contradiction between the Iron Curtain policy and the conquest of the rich countries may be overcome more easily than people think. There is truth in the celebrated saying that Stalin was wrong to show Europe to the Russians and Russia to the Europeans. The occupying troops have had to be frequently changed, soldiers who have been in contact with capitalist corruption have had to be re-educated and told that European culture is a fraud. Relations between troops stationed abroad and even the "converted" populations have had to be restricted as much as possible. Russia's isolation is one of the fundamental necessities of the regime: a monopoly of propaganda, and the prohibition of any comparison of life in the socialist state with the life of the masses exploited by capitalism. It is essential to prevent the free circulation of men and ideas. But the extension of the empire does not suppress the Iron Curtain, it shifts it westward. Europe would no longer be able to spread the maladies from which she suffers—a high standard of living, freedom, criticism, culture—once she had been brought to heel.

Freedom would soon disappear from Paris, as it has disappeared from Budapest, Bucharest, Prague, and Warsaw. The enthusiasm of the enslaved masses would drown the claims of trade unions and of the groups of interests which today fill the air. The refinement of culture—a luxury dangerous to despots—would be abolished by the "Marxist vigilance" of the new masters. The new elite, the Communist Party and the technicians, would enjoy with a good conscience the privileges which they had denounced as odious when others enjoyed them. Liberated by the Red armies or by satellite armies, and ruled by Communist parties, Europe would sink into silence and poverty, and would no longer be a menace to the stability of the tyrannical power in Russia itself.

For that matter, even if the efficacy of this technique appeared slow or uncertain, why renounce the goal of conquest? The multiplication of Iron Curtains between the different parts of the empire would suffice. This exists already. It is as difficult to cross the frontier between Red Poland and Red Russia as to pass that between Red Poland and the West. The task of Sovietization could be delegated to satellites, so as to reduce to a minimum the number of Russians called upon to live in the West.

Whatever the policy finally adopted, it seems certain that the Kremlin is too sure of the limitless resources of power, and too contemptuous of the passive resistance of majorities without a faith and without organization, for the wealth of the corrupt West to seem either an obstacle or a peril. Socialism will not win the game, and the Third Rome will not accomplish her mission of reconciling the Continental nations until the day the hammer-and-sickle flies in Paris and Rome over the ancient stones, witnesses of a past greatness and symbols of a historic fortune of which the victors will believe themselves the heirs, but of which they will be only the gravediggers.

The Russians are faced (and they know it) with only one enemy of their stature: the United States. If it collapsed, they would be the masters of the world. But, so far as one can judge, the Soviet Union has no means of striking immediately and by surprise a mortal blow at the United States, or even of repeating Pearl Harbor on the atomic scale. No one can foresee the duration of a total war between the two giants. Each country thinks that it would have a good chance of not losing (that is, of not being forced to capitulate), but neither (apart from the hypothesis of a rapid victory due to a strategic bombing) has any chance of winning decisively in a limited time. Between Athens, whose fleet ruled the seas, and Sparta, invincible on land, the war lasted thirty years. Risk and the uncertainty of the future have rarely stopped men, but such factors make them hesitate. The war between Athens and Sparta was preceded by a truce of fourteen years and marginal conflicts in which the satellite cities were at stake.

For the Kremlin the satellites, both in Europe and in Asia, fulfill an important function which is primarily defensive. At present the Soviet Union is protected by an immense *glacis*. China shields it from intervention based on the continent of Asia, and the countries of Eastern Europe shield it from intervention from the West. Only airplanes are capable of forcing the barrier. The protection is not only physical—that is, spatial—but military and political.

The Soviet authorities have re-established the armies of these countries—whether former enemy or ally—while the Western diplomats believed themselves bound either by the terms of treaties or by the respect due to public opinion. In 1950, Bulgaria, Poland, Hungary, Czechoslovakia, and Rumania, probably had more divisions than all of the nations west of the Iron Curtain. In case of general war they would enable the Soviet to economize its own forces, and the would implement a vivid rejoinder to Western propaganda. While London and Washington tirelessly broadcast the crusade for the liberation of the peoples, the liberators would struggle on the fields of battle with the enslaved nations, apparently devoted to the defense of their chains.

The same method would be applied to the conquered. A year or two after the Russian invasion and the proletarian revolution, France and Italy would, in their turn, be largely if not exclusively "occupied" and policed by French and Italian armies. The Soviet loud-speakers would denounce the Americans and the British, at war with Europe and the world, and alone opposing the happiness of the masses and the freedom of the workers.

It is even possible that the offensive function assumed by the North Koreans is envisaged for certain European satellites. Everyone knows the two main possibilities: the aggression of Rumania, Hungary, and Bulgaria against Yugoslavia, and that of the People's Republic of Eastern Germany against the Federal Republic. The second could take several forms: the blockade of Berlin by the army of the "people's democracy," sabotage and revolt in the Western zone, supported by raids, or an invasion organized by the "people's" army.

I will even risk an extra hypothesis. Why should not Germany, in compensation for her losses in the East, receive a mission of the first order in the Soviet plan of conquest? Why should not the prospect be opened to her, after the Sovietization of Western Germany, of annexations at the expense of France? Behind the Iron Curtain, the Kremlin has carefully forbidden any federation of satellites. Each of them is enclosed within its frontiers. The historic rivalries between the Danubian and Balkan peoples have left memories and resentments which the Kremlin suppresses or stirs up to suit its own interests. The Soviet empire is not a great homogenous area with a single occupier, and does not accord equal status to all satellite countries; it introduces between them a subtle hierarchy, according to their complacence and their temporary utility.

It is objected that Russia cannot be sure of her satellites, especially East Germany. It is true that the Sovietized peoples are not yet either converted or resigned. But Westerners underestimate considerably the efficacy of the Soviet technique.

Whether it is Germany or China, the Soviets have taken an essential precaution: they have taken over direct control of the industrial districts from which the satellite country draws its strength: Manchuria on one side, Silesia on the other. Polish (or Soviet) armies are installed at the gates of Berlin in such a way that the geopolitical situation of Germany, should it desire independence from Russia, would become desperate. Germany is obliged to turn against the West, China to advance into Southeastern Asia.[2]

A second guarantee is the suppression or reduction of the na-

[2]East Prussia is incorporated into Russian territory, as is Rumanian Bukovina. The direct presence of Russian armies is the first guarantee of the fidelity of the satellite states.

tional war industries. The bulk of the German, Polish, and Rumanian weapons—the heavy ones at least—are Russian. Standardization, which the West talks about continually, is carried out by the Soviet Union in the simplest way. Tanks, aircraft, and submarines are to be Russian. The best German technicians have been transferred to the Soviet Union; trained men are today the most valuable prizes of war.

If these two arguments are not convincing, the masters of the Kremlin have a third. The Communist leaders who betray from conviction, who abandon the sect the day they no longer believe in the truth of the doctrine, are few and will remain few. The important thing to prevent is the dissidence of the semi-opportunists, of the half-faithful, of those who justify themselves by "historic necessity," by the irresistibility of Slav-Communist imperialism, the dissidence of those who prefer the privileges of power to the austere virtues of renunciation. The bond between the Politburo and the national Communist parties is all the stronger the fewer the temptations to which the national parties are exposed. When party leaders commit acts which any anti-Communist regime would find unpardonable, they have become reliable. Solidarity in crime (in the acts so regarded by heretics) strengthens the bonds of a common faith. Tito had enough popular support, and was sufficiently master of his own party, to maintain himself against the Kremlin. No other Communist party in Europe is yet strong enough to risk schism.

Finally, let us not forget a fact that is not well known but is of critical importance: the activities of the Russian secret police extend throughout the *glacis*. Not only are the key positions (foreign policy, commercial policy, and so on) everywhere held by Communists whose fidelity to Moscow is regarded as above suspicion, but the Minister of Internal Security of each satellite is in direct contact with the corresponding Ministers of the other satellites, and all are subject to the Soviet Minister of Internal Security in Moscow. The M.V.D., through its network, can transmit the orders of the Politburo to any point of the Soviet empire, and is in a position to supervise the administrative machinery of the people's democracies, whose independence has become as illusory as the right of secession granted by the Constitution of the U.S.S.R. to all the Federated Republics.

As soon as the loyalty of the satellite elite has been assured, it would seem that it remained only to win over the people. But to say that would be misleading. The first thing is to win over a minority —the members of the Communist Party, the administrative personnel, the police and army. The method of doing so is fundamentally the same everywhere: they are granted tangible or intangible advantages; they become priviliged persons, hated or envied, and every means of escape from their situation is closed to them. There is added, for the young and the nostalgic, a special education, a sort of systematic training. Experience shows that men are not difficult in the choice either of ideas or of leaders. For that matter, when the moment of battle comes, organization, discipline, and the quality of the officers count more than the sentiments of the soldiers (at least in the first phase of the conflict). As for the masses, some end by being half convinced by obsessive propaganda, others are at least troubled and bewildered. The risks involved in dissidence or revolt are immense; a sense of helplessness overcomes people and paralyzes them. (The intellectuals of the West have only to admire the force of the idea, and the tragedy ends as a farce.)

The enterprise that we have sketched does not proceed without encountering obstacles. The many purges and trials throughout the satellite states reveal the resistance of those who have not lost their patriotic feeling, of those who have known the outside world, and of those who do not recognize in Muscovite tyranny the achievement of their heart's desire. Even when the "Stalinization" of the national parties is complete, unspoken opposition remains deep in some consciences: the system is inhuman, the Communists are insane in their desire for power, and the absolute power of the Kremlin makes nonsense of delegated responsibilities. People do not forget their lost freedom; and they remain faithful to their religion, to the God of their fathers. The fanaticized masses will be disappointed in their turn. But let there be no illusion: the edifice may be built on sand, but it is imposing. The hidden defects will not be revealed until the foundation—that is to say, the socialist bastion—gives way.

Hitler's state resisted for years, and yet it was torn by internal quarrels. The old ruling classes, regimented but not converted, multiplied their intrigues. Compared with Soviet totalitarianism, Hitler's was amateurish.

Between the two wars, Stalin had developed a theory of the flow and ebb of the Revolution which completes that of Lenin. According to this theory, imperialism pits the capitalist states against each other, all prisoners and victims of a dialectic. Their wars offer an opportunity of revolt to the exploited classes. The First World War was followed by a revolutionary flow that was repulsed only by Polish resistance and by the "treason" of the social democrats in Germany and of Chiang Kai-shek in China. Then came the ebb, as capitalism recovered from the shock and temporarily stabilized itself. The second war was followed by a revolutionary tide that submerged Eastern Europe and China and is beating against the last outposts of imperialism in Southeastern Asia and Western Europe.

Will there be an ebb of the revolutionary tide that has followed the Second World War, and a consolidation of capitalism? Our reply is not dogmatic because the conduct of the men of the Kremlin also depends on what the West does. For the moment it is apparent that, far from abating, the conflict is growing worse. In Asia the Sovietization of China puts the whole of Southeastern Asia in the front line of the cold war. The so-called civil wars of Malaya and Indo-China may last for years or end in a few months with a Communist victory, according to the form taken by Chinese intervention. Sabotage is intensifying in India; in Indonesia, it should find good soil. Why, we ask, should the Kremlin stop a campaign that costs the West so much and the Soviet Union so little?

In Europe it is possible that a temporary stabilization may be achieved. The Communist parties of France and Italy might try to return to the tactics of the popular front or the national front, and to dissociate the Atlantic coalition from the interior of the Continent. It is not even certain that the other parties would refuse the proffered hand.

In 1939 the Communist line was adapted to quite a different situation, characterized by mortal conflicts between the capitalist nations, and between moderates and Fascists within the nations. Neither type of conflict is likely to recur, at least in the near future. The tactics of 1945–47 were a consequence of the alliance of the

Big Three. The subsequent splitting of the world into two camps—the camp of peace and socialism, and the imperialist camp—broke that alliance. If the Kremlin was thinking of re-establishing it, the intent would be even clearer than in the preceding periods: to disrupt the Atlantic alliance, conquer the key positions in European countries, and prepare for Sovietization in a legal manner. It is to be hoped that, in spite of everything, the non-Communists will not again fall into the trap.

In 1945 it was possible, in theory, to envisage two conceivable methods of lessening tension: either the positions of the West would be so reinforced in Asia and Europe as to make Soviet aggression less dangerous if it came; or else the Soviet regime might change its character and lose its urge to conquer. Today there remains only the second hope.

Let us recall a few propositions, ordinary enough but consistently misunderstood. Why should Stalin have halted of his own accord if there was no obstacle in front of him? Why was Napoleon not content with his first victories? Why did not Hitler enjoy in peace the hegemony over Central Europe which the Munich agreement had handed to him? History explains the desire to advance with arguments that, in each case, are more or less credible. But it is not certain that sociology and politics are adequate to cover the phenomenon. It would be necessary to examine the human heart, and to understand why nothing satisfies the ambition to power (and to love), except total possession which, after all, is inaccessible.

In the present case, the reasons for what seems an insatiable will to power are not lacking. The Stalinists have constructed for themselves a certain vision of the world. For them, the proletariat, socialism, and peace are at issue with the bourgeoisie, capitalism, and imperialism. Between good and evil, the future and the past, no peace is possible. Good must conquer evil, the future the past. To consent to a peaceful coexistence of the two worlds would, according to the Stalinist doctrine, be sinful.

Hitler acted logically, in accord with his guiding ideas until 1941. Without war he could not achieve the conquests which he considered indispensable to the future of Germany, and he intended himself to wage that war, which was to be "decisive for a thousand years." The men in the Kremlin are convinced that ultimately Communism will either be universal or disappear. They believe, perhaps sincerely, that the capitalists are planning the destruction of the socialist bastion; and the capitalists ought certainly to so plan if they are to resemble their portraits in the Marxist primers. The Stalinists would be denying their doctrine, and would cease to lend it the value of a universal message if they did not preach the death of capitalism, and, consequently, the inevitability of an irreconcilable struggle between the two worlds. In asking the Kremlin to stop making war on the West, we are asking them, in effect, to abjure the religion that justifies their power.

A ruling class whose promotion is recent normally remains attached to the ideology in whose name it fought it predecessors and seized power. There is no reason to doubt the genuineness of that faith. The leaders of the Western world cannot bring themselves to believe that the Soviet elite really want to convert or conquer the world. The politicians of the democracies incline to believe that they are more intelligent than the leaders of totalitarian regimes. Their vision of reality is, indeed, less deformed by passion; but, failing to bear in mind that the difficulties of ruling a democracy and a despotic state are not the same, they end by acting foolishly. Through lack of imagination they fail to understand fanaticism.

This very fanaticism, it will be said, constitutes the problem. What are its origins—psychological, historical, social? To what extent is it sincere? Who are the real believers in a classless society? The masses, if we are to trust the evidence, have easily discovered what Western sociology took a long time to grasp clearly, namely, the reconstitution of a hierarchy, the spontaneous distinction beween "Us" and "Them"—the governed and the privileged. Without doubt, the Soviet elite is still, broadly speaking, open for opportunity. As the socialist organization grows, the number of places for engineers, officials, and administrators increases, and the youth, molded by the regime, adheres more or less enthusiastically to the system that provides them with rapid promotion. But up to what point do the non-party specialists, and the technicians watched by the secret police, take the ideology seriously? Stalinism, the religion of the masses in so far as it is militant, tends to become the automatic justification of the new masters when it is triumphant. To what extent is that justification genuine? To what extent does cynicism corrode the faith of those who are apparently faithful. Is it a matter of building a human society, or a powerful one? To convert mankind, or to conquer the world? Does not the sense of an imperial adventure, for the glory of Holy Russia or of the Third Rome, get the better of the socialist convictions with which Lenin and his companions were imbued?

In one sense it would be easy to return to an interpretation of Marxism that would not exclude peace, at least temporarily, between the Soviet states and the rest of the world. It would be sufficient to admit that the Russian road to socialism is not the only one, that the working class is capable of taking control within parliamentary democracies (for example, the Labor Party in Great Britain), that capitalism succeeds in avoiding or reducing crises by economic planning, and that there is no need for imperialism so long as full employment is maintained in the home country. Varga suggested a similar interpretation toward the end of the last war against Germany. He was preparing, it seems, to lay the ideological foundations of a prolonged collaboration between Russia and the Anglo-Saxon democracies.

Why were these inclinations to a sort of Communist "reformism" quickly stifled? Why was there a return to the orthodoxy of non-collaboration with the West, of the single path to socialism, and of revolution attained solely through parties obedient to the Kremlin? Two principal reasons stand out: Anglo-American diplomacy between 1943 and 1946 was so senseless that it created a situation which would have tempted imperialists even less thirsty for power. There followed—let us once more recall it—the bond between Russian and world Communist Messianism, the rupture of the bonds with the Western world, internal terrorism, and the ambition to conquer. The regime will not and cannot tolerate the happy citizens of socialism comparing their lot with the citizens of countries "exploited" by capitalism. It will not and cannot admit that collectivist institutions can be set up by any other party or by any other method than that of the Bolsheviks. It will not and cannot relax the authority it exercises over the so-called "national" Communist parties, which simultaneously prepare the way for Soviet expansion and confirm the universal value of the Russian experiment. It will not and cannot tolerate a world settlement that would deprive poverty, work camps, forced industrialization, and terrorism of their highest justification.

What could bring about a change in the regime? Those who attribute Communist Messianism to the survival of revolutionary enthusiasm base their hope of more peaceful relations on the arrival in power of a new generation. This generation will not have known Russia before 1917, will have no knowledge of the West, and will care more about maintaining its dominance at home than pursuing the phantom of a universal empire. Those who attribute Messianism to the internal needs of the regime (it is pointed out that an elite which attained power by violence, in spite of the preference of a popular majority, needs an ideology to convince itself and its subjects of its own legitimacy) base their hope of peace on the progress of socialist internal expansion; as the living standard rises and socialism seems to become more a part of the natural order of things, its leaders supposedly will cease to cherish immoderate dreams—an attitude that always expresses apprehension rather than strength and confidence. Lastly, those who compare the universality claimed by Stalinism with that which so many Russian thinkers of the last century claimed for the Orthodox Church base their hope of peace on the revival of the Christian faith. Secular Messianism will, supposedly, be enfeebled in sensitive souls by the call of the transcendental.

None of these hopes is in itself absurd. One day or another, the Soviet elite, like those of the past, will be content to enjoy life instead of pursuing endless conquests. One day or another the Kremlin will try to appease the masses by improving their lot instead of urging them to redouble their efforts on the pretext of warding off imaginary enemies. One day or another the Communist doctrine will shed its religious potential and will be reduced to an ordinary political ideology applicable to a particular social organization.

But for the present these hopes, philosophically well founded (for philosophy thinks in terms of decades or centuries), are only political illusions. The Communist elite has lost nothing of its dynamism. On the contrary, the victories of 1945 and subsequently have inspired it with fresh ardor. It is inspired by its successes to ever vaster ambitions.

It may happen that the Bolsheviks of the second generation will be more Russian and less internationalist, less believing and more cynical. But they will maintain the dogma as long as possible, even if they see in it only an excuse for power; for the dogma is the cement of the empire, the basis of the Bolshevik Party's claim— and therefore that of the Russian state—to the exercise of its authority in relation to other parties or other states.

More than once the historical analogies made fashionable by Spengler and Toynbee have been invoked: Islam and Christianity, it is pointed out, fought one another for centuries. Today Moslems and Christians have given up converting or exterminating one another. They live peaceably side by side. The same will happen one day, it is suggested, with Communists and anti-Communists. To my mind, the comparison would suggest a contrary conclusion. There is very little room for Christians in a genuinely Moslem state, where religion pervades customs and politics. The coexistence of Communists and non-Communists within a nation will involve permanent civil war, open or masked, as long as the Communists insist, as articles of faith, upon their right to total power and upon the duty of obedience to the Kremlin.

## THE COLD WAR—PREPARATION OR SUBSTITUTE FOR TOTAL WAR?

Is the cold war a preparation or a substitute for total war? If the former, the two camps are simply maneuvering for position until the day of final settlement. If the latter, the propaganda battles, the struggles among national parties, the fighting localized in Greece or Korea, constitute the war itself—inevitable because of the incompatibility of the two worlds, but limited so as to reduce the ravages of violence.

These distinctions have never been drawn by statesmen. The current alternative is: war or peace. But what magic wand would produce peace throughout Asia and Europe, the former in revolution, the latter divided, impoverished, disarmed? Why should Stalinism stop exploiting subversive movements in the four corners of the earth. How could the two great powers agree to partition the world as long as the Stalinist gospel claims to be universal? How would they agree to "control" atomic weapons as long as each is convinced of the other's bad faith and as long as the Soviet empire prevents the free exchange of ideas and persons?

Surely, no peace was or is conceivable unless the Kremlin abandons the fight against heretics. Pending such a conversion, which is improbable for years to come, cold war is the normal state of the world, and this limited war must continue till Stalinism acquires a new soul, either of its own accord or under external pressure.

Is it an illusion, this hope that the cold war may be a substitute for total war? History may indeed render such a verdict, but the verdict is not to be foreseen. The Stalinists, in accordance with their

doctrine, anticipate terrible struggles between capitalists and socialists before the final victory of the latter; but there is still reason to
believe that for some time they will not deliberately provoke the
upheaval. Accordingly, a new map of the world can take shape,
and a new order emerge from the chaos in Asia and Europe. Political aggression should prove less and less profitable, military aggression will be seen to be more and more dangerous. The peace
that resulted from the third world war would be all the more solid
because that war had not been waged, or at least had been limited.

I. In Asia the Soviet Union has scored sensational successes, but
certain of the means employed amount to a violation of the unwritten conventions of the cold war. With Communist expansion the
recourse to regular armies tends to wear down the brakes that still
keep the violence from increasing.

Western victories would have increased the chances of warlike
peace. The Soviet victories have reduced those chances. The West
is not animated by any crusade or desire to conquer. If it had
succeeded in checking the advance of Stalinism, it would not have
taken advantage of its success to press on and attack the vital
interests of the Soviet Union. On the contrary, having become more
self-confident and less apprehensive about the future, it would have
agreed more readily to discussion.

On the other hand, the ambitions of Stalinism are excited, not
appeased, by partial satisfactions. The more the Soviet empire
extends, the more the men of the Kremlin become convinced of
their superiority and inclined to use their power as a means of
extortion. Under the bi-polar structure of world politics, the danger
is not that the Soviet Union might be driven by weakness to desperate acts. The danger is that every chance of equilibrium will
disappear when regimes faithful to Moscow fill the European or the
Asian void. Thanks to the Sovietization of China, Stalinism is able
to push toward Southeastern Asia and India under conditions such
that the chances of halting it without a general war have diminished.

The crossing of the 38th parallel by the North Koreans was an
event whose symbolic import even surpassed its real import: for
the first time a line of demarcation traced by agreement between
the Soviet Union and the United States of America had been

crossed, for the first time the camp claiming to be that of peace had embarked on military aggression pure and simple.

II. The hope of prolonging the cold war and of arriving little by little at some sort of stabilization depends on reinforcing the West, on restoring a balance between the two worlds, on consolidating the political and social structure of the free countries, and on establishing armed forces. We are still far from that goal.

Eight years after the end of the war, the partition of Europe has not been effaced but reinforced. Eastern Germany has become a People's Republic, consolidated to such a degree that it would be very difficult to undo its Sovietization. Western Germany has regained economic prosperity, but its political regime is weak. The Communist parties act freely west of the Iron Curtain, and maintain secret armies whose function would be to act as a fifth column when the time comes.

The cold war has not been lost in Europe, for Soviet expansion has not exceeded the limits fixed by the agreements between the victors. But neither has it been won, for the Red Army has not been pushed back, Germany is not unified, and the nations west of the Iron Curtain remain politically and, even more, militarily weak.

III. It is true that the West has at last awakened to a sense of danger. The United States has undertaken rearmament on a large scale, and the countries of Europe themselves are beginning to shake off their lethargy. Two or three years hence the disproportion between ground forces will be less, and Western Europe and the Middle East will be sheltered, if not from invasion, at least from a surprise attack, with a chance of repelling local aggression. In the past Russia did not consider that the presence of Japan in the Far East and of Germany in Europe was an infringement of her security, but the temporary effacement of these two powers is sufficiently in her interest for her to try to make it permanent.

General and total war would be an unforeseeable venture for the Soviet Union: the atomic and industrial superiority of the United States is hardly in doubt. War would become inevitable on the day when one of the two great powers had come actually to want it, or to look upon it as inevitable. That is not the case today. Rulers and peoples alike see the abyss toward which mankind is slipping. The United States is preparing for an eventuality which it judges probable. This foresight, in its turn, forms an element in its deliberations, but does not suggest resignation to the worst.

Rearmament, if pushed beyond a certain point, spreads or risks spreading a war psychosis; but primarily it comforts and encourages those who were previously inferior and without defense. An armament race has often preceded an explosion, but without being its principal cause: the race itself was the effect of conflicts which ultimately led to war. It did, however, create a supplementary cause of a psychological order. This time, rearmament is to be considered neither as the anticipation of an approaching apocalypse, nor as the promise of certain peace, but as the price of security, payable not in one installment but annually for a generation or more. The effort embarked on by the United States can be continued indefinitely without the collapse or dislocation of its economic life. The maintenance of armed forces, even on a considerable scale, in time of peace, would not absorb more than about twenty per cent of the gross national income. Moreover, at the end of a few years this proportion would decrease. Economic considerations will no more make total war necessary for the Soviet Union or for the United States than they did for Hitler.

It must not be imagined that there exist tactics, infallible but unknown, that will change the world situation at a stroke. All that can be done is to improve a line of action which can hardly be changed in essentials, because it results from the very structure of the two opposing camps.

Today as yesterday it remains true that, in every sector of the periphery, the Soviet empire has forces that are locally superior. Today as yesterday the West can prevent the *military* expansion of Communism only by threatening, in certain events, to reply with general war.

What can be done to improve this strategy? The first task, as everyone agrees, is to reduce the inequality of the present forces in the two camps. Pushed beyond a certain point, this inequality eventually inclines the aggressor to doubt the resolution of his adversaries. Already he knows that the capitalists, the bourgeoisie, and the democrats have a mortal dread of total war. (And why should they not dread it, after two experiences of it?) He tends to minimize a threat which the Westerners use simply in order not to have to carry it out. This skepticism is in danger of provoking the explosion through misunderstanding.

The West must not only possess actual forces sufficient to impress the men of the Kremlin; but instead of being concentrated beyond the seas, their forces must be spread over the theaters of operations which, in case of unlimited war, would suffer the first attack. The Stalinists know that the United States will find difficulty in committing itself unconditionally as long as Europe is defenseless. One does not abandon to the enemy one of the essential stakes of the struggle, a stake that is lost whatever the final result if it serves as a hostage for some years to Stalinist imperialism.

At the same time, the West ought to review rigorously the decisions that it would take in certain eventualities. It is not necessary to proclaim publicly that the crossing of the Yugoslav frontier by Bulgarian and Rumanian armies would constitute a *casus belli;* but if, as seems probable, such an aggression would unleash general war, it would be best to intimate this probability, discreetly but firmly, to the masters of the Kremlin.

Once this general principle is laid down, there remain some uncertainties. The most serious of these concerns the attitude to be adopted toward Communist China: must she be considered henceforward as an enemy, bound body and soul to the Soviet enterprise, or as a great power, allied to the U.S.S.R. but perhaps capable of an autonomous diplomacy?

India and Great Britain have assumed the second alternative, and acted accordingly. By recognizing the Peiping regime they aimed at encouraging a development which they held to be possible. The Soviet Union, while claiming the admission of Communist China into the United Nations, seems nonetheless to have exerted itself to prevent contact being made between the new regime and the West. These maneuvers gave some weight to the British argument in spite of the invectives hurled against the West by Peiping propaganda. Some American diplomats themselves were inclined to the same opinion. The Chinese intervention in Korea brought that position to an abrupt end. Regardless of mistakes, history is irreversible. It is unlikely that Communist China would retrace her steps to the point where Washington would consent to renew the effort at reconciliation.

Supposing that Mao Tse-tung ended by accepting the original compromise—the re-establishment of the two Koreas—the State Department would hesitate for a long time before sacrificing Formosa. Not only a strategic position is at stake, but also the fate of Chiang Kai-shek and the remains of the Nationalist Army and administration. Was it really a mistake to have supported the former generalissimo? Probably—even though experience of Communism may have lessened the unpopularity which the Kuomintang ultimately suffered because of its inefficiency.

Does the Washington administration contemplate waging total war against Communist China? It is certainly not wished, but it is considered possible. Above all, Washington will give up nothing that will be militarily useful in the hope of appeasing Mao Tse-tung. Impressed by the outbreak of Chinese nationalism, and by the hate campaign against America, the leaders of the United States see no chance of coming to terms with the present Chinese leaders; Washington does not believe that a regime tied to Moscow will be satisfied with partial concessions.

The United States is in a position to impose an economic blockade on China, to interrupt sea traffic, to supply the partisans, to arm the troops in Formosa. China is in a position to invade Indo-China, Burma, Siam, and perhaps Malaya. None of these steps would imply world war; the Soviet Union would not be responsible for Chinese aggression in Indo-China, and would not be obliged to intervene in the event of American bombing of Manchuria. But should such steps be taken, no one can foresee exactly their ultimate consequences.

In the Far East, the Soviet Union has succeeded in conferring on the conflict the character that suits its preferences. Europeans are fighting directly against Asians, and thus contribute to the strengthening of the anti-white feelings which Moscow promotes for its own purposes. The Chinese can keep the troops of Ho Chi Minh supplied indefinitely with arms and ammunition. Although there is no *casus belli,* certain local conflicts, as in Indo-China, hardly portend a happy outcome for the West.

To determine clearly the cases in which the threat of general war is applicable, to implement that threat by rearmament, to fill gradually the European gap, to abandon the Asiatic outposts whose local defense is too expensive, to maintain a line of resistance while leaving open the possibility of negotiations with Peiping—these are the lines of action in the immediate future which are indicated by good sense.

After basing excessive hopes on economic aid, it is now unduly depreciated. Although in Europe it has greatly speeded recovery, clearly it has neither eliminated Communism nor given the political systems an artificial robustness. Nevertheless, it has created conditions such that a military effort appears possible without serious troubles, even for the parliamentary democracies. Has economic assistance been ineffective in Asia? It has been in places where feeble rulers have failed to prevent either inflation, or the squandering of dollars, or distress among the masses. Distributed without guarantee and without precaution, money or supplies could no more weaken Communist strength than lessen American unpopularity in the Far East.

The distribution of American aid between Asia and Europe has been in inverse proportion to the poverty of the recipients. Europe has received the most by far, while Asia had stronger claims, if claims are equated to needs. When one thinks of how the millions of Indian, Chinese, or Persian peasants live, one is tempted to say that Europeans have been given luxuries while elsewhere necessities are lacking. That statement is materially correct, but is open to criticism on many counts. Needs are measured with reference to habits and not to physiological data. Complex economic systems resist certain privations with more difficulty than more primitive systems. The European populations do not resign themselves to disaster; they blame the evil works of men and not the cruelty of fate. The immensity of the needs in China and India tends to discourage good will. It can be maintained that, in return for aid, the economic, political, even human, yield from some 20 billion dollars has been higher in Europe than it would have been in Asia.

And yet, if certain guarantees about its administrative management had been demanded and obtained, substantial aid to China would perhaps have stopped the decay of the Nationalist regime.

Substantial assistance to India and Pakistan would help to revive the energy of the rulers, and to overcome the alternative of apathy and revolt among the masses. The haughty nationalism of the rulers in countries recently given over to self-government will resist everything that looks like a *quid pro quo* or a political condition for aid. Money will be refused rather than privileges granted to foreigners. If these latter are sufficiently clear-sighted not to desire discrimination in their favor, they will perhaps obtain indirectly the reforms without which the dollars would be spent in vain.

I shall be careful not to present the "Marshall Plan for Asia" or Point Four as a miraculous cure. Perhaps Chinese expansion will assume such a military character that resistance by force of arms will supersede resistance by economic aid. Yet the dominant idea remains no less valid. The intellectuals of the West are at liberty to vituperate technology and its monstrous development; but for four fifths of mankind, technology means the application of scientific knowledge to the struggle for existence, the promise not of abundance but of a decent life or of less fearful poverty. The West, far more than the Soviet Union, has the means of translating this promise into reality.

The Soviet Union employs even during the pretended peace all the devices of propaganda, sabotage, and infiltration, often described by sociologists but rarely recognized by the victims. We must wage this war, imposed on us by Stalinist aggression; and military means are only one of the arms of this Protean combat. The Western military experts are not sufficiently freed from traditional conceptions, and keep wondering whether war will come, when it is raging all the time. The battle against propaganda and infiltration must be waged indefatigably; the elimination by trade unions of Stalinist ringleaders often signalizes a victory comparable with the formation of an additional army division.

James Burnham's central idea in *The Coming Defeat of Communism* seems therefore correct. But one question must be asked: What results could the West secure from a psychological offensive in countries already subject to the Communist regime, and in threatened countries? Burnham is certainly right when he refuses to accept the current view that tyranny and terror make the "popular democracies" invulnerable. That the West retains allies on the other side of the Iron Curtain is shown by the flood of refugees. In 1941, in the Ukraine, there were elements of the civil population who put hatred of their masters above hatred of the invader. It would be playing the enemy's game to accept the myth of unanimous populations. Modern technique permits the production of Communist militants, of resigned crowds, of fanaticized youths, but it is not infallible. It is possible to shake the conviction of the militants, restore hope to the crowds, and penetrate the armor of juvenile fanaticism. What remains doubtful is the degree of possible success.

Consider Eastern Europe, apart from Albania—the feeblest of the satellites, and the only one (except North Korea) with which the Soviet Union has not concluded a treaty of mutual assistance. Is it conceivable that psychological warfare, even aided by clandestine infiltration, could imperil the Communist state in Poland or Czechoslovakia? We may recall the partisans who continued the war in the Ukraine. But the mass of the Czechs and Poles have no thought of liberation, except conceivably through a general war. The militants, the party officials, the leaders of the people's democracies, or at least some of them, probably have doubts about the merits of the regime. The longing for national independence is found in the elites as well as in the masses. Personal quarrels and rivalries, even more than differences of ideas, rage within the new ruling classes. But as long as the Russian forces are actually present, and the remote Western forces only potentially so, no imitation of Stalinist methods will suffice to batter down the walls of the Communist fortress.

The Stalinists know well that political warfare is efficacious, that it levels obstacles and wears down resistance, but that it is no substitute for civil war or invasion by the Red Army. Surely the inadequacy of these means is still more evident when they are employed by the West, which in this respect is obviously in a position of inferiority.

The strength of the psycho-political activity carried on by the Stalinists does not lie in their exceptional skill, but in another sort of advantage. Once in power, they monopolize the dissemination of news and propaganda. It is easier to persuade or stupefy men when they are submitted exclusively to one propaganda line. An obsession cannot be fully created unless all those who would hinder unanimity are reduced to silence. A system of interpretation, however stupid and absurd, ends by leaving its mark on men's minds when it is applied every day, every hour, every minute, to the innumerable events that occur in the four corners of the earth; so that the public learns of those events only after they have been refracted through the official doctrine. The democracies renounce on principle the creation of such a monopoly which would be fatal to the very values for which they are fighting.

In the long run, it may be that the beliefs slowly acquired and founded on traditions are more solid than the attitudes imposed by techniques of violence and dehumanization. But in the ordeal of limited war the democracies clearly reveal all their weaknesses, while the totalitarian regimes hide and partly suppress theirs up to the end when disaster strikes for all the world to see.

In clandestine action, as was seen in the course of the second war, the Communist Party is an incomparable instrument. Organized for secrecy and disciplined more and more tightly through the years, it obtains from the militants unreserved devotion, nourished by faith and obedience comparable to that of a soldier. Even when the insurgents against Stalinism are animated by an equal devotion, they have to learn the rules necessary to underground activity, and to find leaders. But as they are never in agreement about long-term objectives, their united efforts are deprived by conflicting views of the monolithic unity characteristic of the Stalinist movement.

Nowhere is the United States supported by an American party. In liberated countries Fascists and collaborators were removed, and then the democrats were told: "And now go and argue." What wonder that the Stalinists exploit the disputes of political parties and labor difficulties when the politicians and the public alike seem more concerned about rivalries and ambitions than about the unity needed to combat the Stalinist menace.

In Asia the American influence is, at bottom, more revolutionary than any other. Consider the policy followed during the first years of occupation in Japan. The worship of the Emperor was shaken, women's suffrage and trade union organization were encouraged, entire freedom of party propaganda and activity was recognized, and private persons were invited to take part in public affairs. The process of secularization and rationalization that required centuries to evolve in Europe was carried through in a few years. But the essential fact was forgotten: the democratic institutions thus transferred—parties, trade unions, freedom of persons and ideas—tend to develop social divisions rather than social unity. Formal liberties sometimes destroy nations, they never create them.

Group demands and social conflicts are softened by expression. The working classes adhere to a government that gives them the right to make themselves heard and allows them a better chance to improve their condition. Trade unions and political parties, as long as their disputes are kept within certain limits, contribute to the protection of the governed. There is no incompatibility between liberal institutions and industrial civilization.

But neither is there a pre-established harmony. Liberal institutions have accompanied the development of industrial civilization only in countries where political democracy was a continuation of national traditions. Respect for others and their rights, when felt by every citizen as an obvious duty, contributes more to the survival of parliaments than the words of a constitution or even economic progress. Liberal institutions are no exceptions to the rule: they are founded on unprovable convictions, "transrational" if not irrational, and transmissible only with difficulty.

Rebels against the colonial domination of the Europeans, rebels also against any secular hierarchy, the Americans create an emptiness which Communism tries to fill. They upset ideas which for ages have governed people's attitude toward parents or rulers. Freed from the old conditions, everyone tends to push egalitarian claims to the limit. Communism adopts and exaggerates these claims in theory, while preparing to deny them in practice. At least it offers a kind of society to those whom the factory, the dissolution of the family, or the beginning of religious disbelief has left in a soulless solitude. Stalinism completes the revolution created by that Western influence, and brings it temporarily to an end through a new regimentation of the masses adapted to the exigencies of the industrial age.

What is required to avoid such a development and strengthen conservative governments? Obviously, it is necessary to satisfy the peasants by giving them the land, or by exacting a smaller part of their crops, finding efficient administrators, augmenting the common resources by economic progress, checking the rise in population, and slowing down the revolution in ideas and beliefs. But such a program is difficult to carry out and would not give immediate or sensational results.

The American influence, in itself revolutionary, does not immediately replace the abolished regime with a new order, whereas the Communist action revolting against the past is exercised through a sect capable of administering the new regime and organizing the masses.

This difference explains why, even where the transfer of authority from the former colonial power to an independent state took place without disturbance, military impotence results from the liberation. British India was able to contribute 2 or 3 million men to the defense of the Middle East and of its own frontiers. In the Kashmir dispute India and Pakistan now employ their few divisions (whose officer corps is still partly British). But in a general war it is to be feared that India, too, would be helpless. No such result seems to have been produced by the Communist victory in China.

It is often said that the weakness of the West in the political war is due to the absence of a leading doctrine. It is easier to rally the crowd to a false idea, so long as it seems attractive, than to a whole number of ideas that are true but prosaic. Freedom and a higher standard of living are genuine aspirations of the European peoples, and perhaps of the Asiatics. But Communism itself makes capital out of the hope of better conditions of existence, and transfigures that hope through a sort of religion of the machine and the proletariat. In Europe the reality of Stalinism is sufficiently understood or suspected for more people to see through its fictions. But in countries where poverty and overpopulation are rampant, where inequality is spectacular and offensive, and where independence was acquired quite recently, while poverty was left undiminished, the traditional disciplined resignation is upset, so that any sect, even a small one, has a chance of instigating popular revolts and, under cover of the disorder, establishing itself in power.

Are the ideas themselves at fault? Yes, when we think of the Western intellectuals, or even of the simple folk who, lacking a transcendental faith, have a vague longing for some revelation. But the West is not as destitute of ideas as that. When the battle is waged in Europe with equal weapons, the West wins consistently. The things it lacks are the weapons of violence, the monopoly of propaganda, and the support of parties on either side of the Iron Curtain.

There is no doubt that Communist Russia, allied with Communist China and protected by the European satellites, is in a position to maintain for years the pressure of the cold war, without starting a total war or accepting a general settlement. Europe west of the Iron Curtain will never completely recover as long as the Soviet Army occupies Eastern Germany. The limited wars in Indo-China and in Malaya will never be won as long as Russia and Red China agree to support them. The economic system of the free world will always be threatened by the disproportion of resources between the United States and its European allies, by the contraction of the zone open to normal trade and the expansion of the Soviet zone.

Only unpredictable events such as the retreat of Russian troops into the frontiers of Russia or a peaceful solution to the Asiatic conflicts could bring a decisive improvement.

# PART FOUR

## *A Helpless Europe?*

## Chapter XIII

## DIALECTIC OF THE EXTREMES

THE PARLIAMENTARY DEMOCRACIES were restored throughout Europe after Fascism and National Socialism were crushed, just as the monarchy had been restored in France after the defeat of Napoleon. In both cases the object was the same: to arrest the revolutionary movement by returning to the institutions of the past. In both cases there was a similar anxiety: would the forces that had provoked the collapse of the old order bring about the ruin of the restored regimes?

Against the Third Reich the coalition proudly inscribed "democratic" watchwords on its banners, without examining too closely the precise meaning of "democracy." It was casually assumed that Communism and the Western democracies would eventually collaborate within nations as well as in international councils. Election was recognized as the only legitimate method of choosing rulers. The Second World War must result in the restoration of parliamentary Europe, that is to say, of the Europe that had emerged from the first war and had already been conquered before the armored divisions of the *Wehrmacht* crossed the Polish frontier.

We know what became of those comfortable illusions. In Eastern Europe the so-called national Communists and the Russian occupation authorities gave a demonstration of the "legal" capture of power, which became classic. We shall soon find taught, from the elementary schools onward, a technique whose modes vary but whose guiding principles are constant. In the West, the rules of electoral competition have largely been respected; the non-Communist parties have won, as they would have won everywhere in

Europe if the consultation of the will of the people had been carried out honestly. But this victory of Western democracy seems precarious, to say the least.

The monarchies restored in 1815 continued the fight against the temporarily defeated enemy. They anathematized the revolutionary spirit and banded together in a Holy Alliance to support the tottering thrones and to furnish irresistible armies to defeat any popular rising. Futile or not, this resistance to the "movement of ideas and events" made sense, in the long view. The revolution had issued from the old order, but had rejected the principles of that order. The kings fought without being untrue to themselves.

Fascism and Communism reject Western-style democracy, but are they not its heirs? Can it fight them without being false to itself, or, at least, without reforming itself?

On the institutional plane, democracy is defined as the rivalry of parties for the exercise of power. Thus defined, it arouses two oppositions, which for simplicity's sake we may call that of the Right and that of the Left.

According to the doctrine of the Right opposition, democracy aims, or should aim, at raising all the members of the community to the level of citizens, not at degrading politics by reducing it to deals between bourgeois.[1] The citizen considers participation in the councils and armies of the "city" to be a privilege and an honor, and does not think of using his rights for personal advantage. But in modern democracies the voters behave like bourgeois and not like citizens: they organize themselves into associations to defend their incomes, wages, or profits, and into parties in order to seize the government or to exert a controlling influence upon it. In the strife between pressure groups, concern for the general good vanishes. Coalitions between parties and compromises between social groups produce governmental weakness. The Right opposition untiringly reasserts the need for a party against the parties, of a rally above parties, or of a monarch aloof from parties, in order

[1]The opposition of *citizen* (member of the "city") and *bourgeois* (private person, thinking of his own interests) is taken from B. Groethuysen, *Die Dialektik der Demokratie.*

that the unity of the nation and the idea of the state may be incarnated in a man or a team or an organized mass.

While the opposition of the Right deplores the lack of an interpreter of the common good, the opposition of the Left denounces the electoral or parliamentary game as pure illusion. As long as society is divided into hostile classes, there will remain masters and slaves, privileged persons and victims. The parties and the politicians hold but a shadow of power; the real power always belongs to the owners of the means of production. The ideal of democracy does not consist in seeking an agreement—always unstable—between private and collective interests, but in extirpating the roots of discord between the classes.

Neither opposition takes a hand in the party system willingly. The first accuses the system of causing the decomposition of the state or even of society itself, and the second asserts that it camouflages social injustice and inhibits or slows down the measures that might correct it.

The opposition of the Right does not claim to efface the divisions between individuals and groups. It is normal that there should be peasants and workmen, employers and employed, officials and those who remain independent. But it does not follow that the rulers should be supported by these very differences, that the state should be governed by the delegates of these social categories, delegates whose main concern will be to favor those who have elected them. The leaders, as the opposition of the Right imagines them, would be consciously and resolutely in the service of the general will, inspired by the greatness of their country—however desirous they may be, secondarily, to do justice to all private and collective interests.

The opposition of the Left, on the other hand, holds that the very notion of general interest is meaningless as long as private property, and as a consequence, hostile classes, exist. National unity could only become real after a revolution. Capitalism implies the exploitation of the proletariat, which, as the result of the injustice of which it is the victim, finds itself excluded from the community. Those who speak in the name of the proletariat refuse legitimately to recognize the authority of the laws. They consider solely the interest of the proletariat, which is identical with the interest of the revolution. In the extreme case, the opposition of the Left claims to ignore the party game. It is of little consequence whether power is in the hands of one party or another, and exercised by democratic or authoritarian methods. These are but shadings or modes which do not touch the essence of the system.

There is an immediate temptation to identify the Right opposition with Fascism and the Left with Communism. These are, in fact, the extreme forms assumed in our epoch by the two oppositions. But not every Rightist opposition is Fascist, and not every Leftist opposition Communist. Within every democracy the aspiration to the unity of the state which animates the one, and the aspiration to the unity of society which animates the other, are normal. A party system contains, in fact, a double risk: that the general interest may be sacrificed in parliamentary contests, and that formal democracy may cloak and crystallize the class structure.

In origin, the Rightist opposition may claim to be derived from Rousseau and the *Social Contract,* for, according to the current formula, the general interest is not the sum of particular interests. Each party looks at the situation from a special angle, and each recommends measures suited to the ideas or the claims of its clients. Ought not calm voices be raised amid the tumult of propaganda, and unregimented men uphold the principle of a non-partisan truth? As a protest voiced by citizens against the parties, the Rightist opposition represents an indispensable reaction to the ills which we know from experience to be inherent in modern democracy.

But citizens are seldom content to protest. They seek in turn to reach the forum in order to defend the general interest. At once the Rightist opposition becomes a political formation, and, although in principle directed against the parties, it inevitably transforms itself into a party.

How are we to define the general interest, how determine the general will? There is no party that limits itself to defending the selfish interests of certain groups and does not invoke some conception of the common good. How are we to arbitrate the conflicts that affect ideologies and not interests alone? The sovereign—that is to say, the people—will pronounce the verdict at the elections. But that verdict will be equivocal; it will not give a clear majority to any party or to any "rally" above or against the parties. From the moment it enters into the democratic game and submits to the majority rule, the Rightist opposition returns to the compromises and the coalitions which it had undertaken to denounce.

Henceforward it is forced into a choice between two courses. The first is to accept universal suffrage on a provisional basis and with the reservation of "manipulations." Once master of the state, it will fabricate its majority and impose its own interpretation of the general interest. The Jacobins and later Bonaparte claimed to incarnate the national will: their power, though actually authoritarian, remained democratic in idea since it ascribed its original conception to the popular decision. Even more clearly, Fascism (a party declaring itself to be the incarnation of national unity and imposing on everyone its doctrine of collective life, and sometimes its doctrine of the whole world) is one of the results, not inevitable but logical, of the Rightist opposition. In our time, the general interest is an equivocal thing—to such a degree that it seems to be safeguarded only when it is defined by those very persons who rule the state.

The second choice of the Right opposition is to submit to the majority rule, to refuse to follow the path that leads to the single party and the authoritarian state, and to assign itself simply the aim of introducing sufficient institutions free of partisan rivalries to consolidate democracy. The presidential system represents one of the possibilities. The parties tend to "colonize" the administration, Parliament, the intermediate bodies, and the government. The Rightist opposition would lead a permanent struggle against this "colonization," which is ultimately fatal to the regime: impartial administration, trade unions, members of Parliament elected by the citizens (and not by the parties), Ministers supported by Parliament and not delegated by the parties—these would be the watchwords of the resistance to party imperialism. Even traditional institutions such as monarchy would justify themselves today by the needs of that resistance, never definitively victorious but always necessary, a resistance that some will term reactionary, and that nevertheless alone gives pluralist democracy a chance to escape from the corruption that now is destroying it.

The claim which motivates the Leftist opposition arises spontaneously out of formal democracy. Equal as citizens, the members of the community are unequal in concrete terms: they do not profit to the same degree from the prosperity of the common civilization. They are divided into groups arranged in a hierarchy. It is not true that in the Western communities the proletariat has nothing to lose but its chains. But it is true that in the last century, and to some extent in this one, it was deprived of full participation in the "city." The political equality proclaimed seems logically to imply at least an effort to reduce economic inequalities.

Such an effort does not break down the party system. The Leftist opposition does not necessarily result in Communism, that is to say, in the Messianism of the Revolution and in permanent war against the capitalist world. The transition from the claim to equality to permanent war occurs when the disinherited or their ringleaders begin to feel a radical skepticism about any prospect of reform. If the economic system, as such, excludes the peaceful integration of the proletariat into the community, then one becomes accessible to the Communist argument: war, open or secret, against society and the class state and against the camouflaged forms (e.g., social democracy) of capitalist domination, as well as against its extreme forms (e.g., Fascism).

The ideal of the pluralist democracies, disturbed by contradictory claims, is equilibrium. This cannot be static, and does not exclude incessant modifications in the relations between the various groups: it even implies to some extent an irreversible evolution. In the long run, majority rule must operate to the advantage of the greater number. The various sections of the ruling classes vie with one another in making vote-catching promises. Overbidding, difficult to distinguish from democratic competition for the exercise of power, gradually brings about a reduction of inequalities. The pluralist democracies experience periods of good fortune when an apparent disorder masks a genuine order. The two oppositions do not separate into autonomous formations because the government voluntarily satisfies their claims. The parties in power display an equal anxiety to be just to private and collective interests, to safeguard the independence and greatness of the country, and to improve the lot of the poorer classes. The "national revolutionaries" do not consider that the "city" is the victim of the parties, and the "social revolutionaries" do not think that democratic methods arrest or limit the movement toward justice. Both sides recognize the legitimacy of the electoral and parliamentary procedure.

More than any other system of government, democracy is menaced by corruption. If one party breaks with the community and proclaims that compromises between parties in power are sacrificing unprotected groups or even the general interest, if another party breaks with the community and proclaims that no reform will put an end to the permanent inequality of which one class is the victim, then the regime, attacked on both flanks, is no longer justified except as a lesser evil. It maintains the majority rule, but the parties that support the system no longer have at their command a real majority against the revolutionaries of the two wings, irreconcilable but in coalition. Freedom is temporarily safeguarded, but it is freedom to conspire against the constitution rather than to serve the state.

Within stabilized democracies, the function of voting is to designate those who are to govern and the ideas or programs preferred by the electorate—the framework and the procedures being imposed on all. From the moment when the two oppositions isolate themselves, a decisive change occurs. The votes are now for or against the regime itself: the party system rejected by the Rightist opposition, and the system of private property rejected by the Leftist opposition. Democracy then acquires a quite different meaning: in a fight which does not admit of a legal ending, there is agreement that any and every means shall not be immediately employed. Democracy, now a camouflage of civil war, confines itself to fixing the conventions of the warlike peace.

In what circumstances do the Rightist and Leftist oppositions isolate themselves into autonomous formations and launch the dialectic of the extremes?

The first example of a triangular fight between Rightist authoritarianism, a parliamentary republic, and a revolutionary threat was seen in France from 1848 to 1851. There was a kind of historical anticipation of the modern conflicts of democracy, Fascism, and Communism. The June risings in Paris did not represent the equivalent of a Leftist opposition, but they had aroused in the conservative classes—the middle class and the peasantry—the same fear of total subversion that Communism arouses in our time. The hazards of French history and the revolutions that had successively overthrown the Bourbons and the House of Orléans had divided the ruling classes into factions savagely opposed to one another. Legitimists, Orléanists, Bonapartists, and Republicans detested each other and were unwilling to submit their differences to the judgment of the electorate. Thanks to the Napoleonic myth the enthusiasm of the masses could be aroused, and at the same time the Prince-President secured the adhesion of the monarchists who saw in a Bonaparte a substitute for a king. The National Assembly had adopted such reactionary measures that the President aroused the people against its members and promised the restoration of universal suffrage. Thus there came about an association of conservative forces with an ideology that was partly of the Left.

The situation from which Bonapartism arose, exceptional for the epoch, did not appear in any other of the great countries of Europe during the nineteenth century. Nowhere did the ruling class feel the need to capitalize on the prestige of an acclaimed leader. The monarchies were still firmly rooted. The parliaments, recruited from the aristocracy and the bourgeoisie, were elected under a property qualification, and the masses had little part in the political struggles. Even in France universal suffrage still proved conservative. The rural masses did not object to the hierarchy, and sent notables, mainly monarchists, to the Assembly of 1848. The Left opposition did not seriously threaten the governments of the bourgeois democracy. Except in France, the conflicts within the ruling class did not come to such a pitch that the various factions, forgetting their common interests, would have appealed to the people against the established power. The revolutions against the thrones failed, but these setbacks did not prevent the progress of liberal institutions and ideas.

In the twentieth century the social stage on which the dialectic of the extremes unfolds is quite different. The parliaments include a growing number of representatives who, if they do not themselves belong to the popular masses, are at least members of the parties that profess to speak in their name. The traditional hierarchy is shaken, and the prestige of the notables, of the aristocracy, or of money is affected. The various social categories are organized in professional groups. The parties keep the voters in play by presenting or instigating claims from the poorer classes, and by diffusing ideologies of a vague and passionate character. The workers adhere to a socialism that is sometimes pragmatic (trade unionism), sometimes doctrinaire and reformist (social democracy), sometimes systematic and violent (Communism). Since the last century the names, and in some cases the constitutions, have not changed, but the realities have become quite different. Aristocratic democracies have been succeeded by popular democracies, and parliaments of bourgeois and notables by assemblies of parties.

Party democracy by its very nature offers good soil for the dialectic of the extremes. The Leftist opposition, the interpreter of popular claims, has had a normal existence for the last few decades within the European nations. On the other hand, the Rightist opposition does not disengage and isolate itself except in reply to a threat, real or imaginary. The fear of revolutionary movements, genuine or artificially aroused, is most often the origin of the authoritarian reaction of the Right. Certain supplementary conditions are also needed for its success. There must be millions of men in revolt against the party system, and hostile to the proletarian message. A movement, an ideology, a man must succeed in mobilizing the rootless masses. The people themselves must be inclined to political religiosity, that is to say, must carry their religious feelings into the political domain.

The Rightist opposition recruits its adherents among the victims of a crisis, but also, more generally, in the social categories which have a feeling that they are not being defended by the democratic parties and accuse those parties of making compromises at their expense. The workman who has a job and whose nominal wages are maintained remains attached to the social democracy; the unemployed man has no reason for fidelity to it. But an industrial community such as the German comprises—in addition to the masses who are in the true sense the working class and the majority of whom continue to the end to vote for the Marxist parties—nonproletarian masses, approximately equal in numbers to the working-class voters: clerks, artisans, businessmen, members of the liberal professions (more or less officialized), engineers, civil servants, and so on in the cities, and agricultural workers, farmers, or small landholders in the country. The members of these very different social categories have one feature in common: they do not recognize any of the proletarian parties as expressing their desires or their interests. The non-proletarian masses, which the development of capitalism automatically creates, form the potential troops of the Right opposition.

The economic crisis had caused the non-proletarian masses to be unattached. Hitler, and not the Marxist parties, succeeded in mobilizing them. Insofar as the struggle developed between the Rightist and the Leftist oppositions, between Hitlerism and Stalinism, the issue appears to us to be historically still logical. The mythology of the Third Reich and of German greatness had a more powerful appeal than that of the classless society. The Leftist opposition promised a millennial kingdom, but only after an unforeseeable upheaval. It was bound to a foreign country that was feared, and to a class with which union was refused. Those who accused fate and the republic of having reduced them to a proletarian state were not going to submit to a party that gloried in its proletarian vocation.

The men who start a mass movement aiming at revolution and denounce the existing system employ a technique that never varies in its essential features: they inflame hatred and concentrate it on those held to be responsible for existing evils, and they arouse unlimited expectation. The Communist Manichaeism is made up of abstractions: capitalism, proletariat, and bourgeoisie play the principal parts in the drama. The Hitlerian Manichaeism designated beings of flesh and blood—plutocrats, liberals, socialists, and especially Jews; these last embraced and incarnated all that Nazi propaganda held up to the execration of the mob. All essentially totalitarian regimes and movements need, even more than enemies to fight, inferior beings to despise and ultimately to exterminate. The humiliation of these inferior beings gives, by comparison, a feeling of pride to the most mediocre members of the chosen race or class. The Jews were the lepers of the Third Reich. As a principle of evil, an image of subhumanity, an object on which to fix resentment, they fulfilled in Hitlerite religion and practice a negative but essential function. Primitive religions teach people to fear and fight demons or the devil rather than to love the divinity.

At the beginning of the thirties, everything in Germany conspired in favor of the dialectic of the extremes and the victory of the Rightist opposition: an economic crisis of exceptional gravity affected the whole nation, and struck especially at the interstitial groups—the victims of the party system, or those who thought of themselves as such. Memories of defeat and bitterness against the victors maintained nationalist ardor; the threat, more mythical than real, of Communist revolution inclined a section of the masses and a larger one of the ruling classes to join hands with the revolution of the demagogues; and finally, the parties defending the Weimar Republic from the attacks of the extremes did not succeed in co-operating to form a stable government. The parliamentary confusion reflected and amplified the divisions in the country. This situation may be called the typical and ideal breeding ground of Fascism in the twentieth century.

We rarely find elsewhere the combination of all these elements. None of the authoritarian governments between the two wars achieved the essence of modern Fascism so fully as National Socialism. France's Fascism, for instance, is more characteristic of Spain than of the industrial communities of the twentieth century. It is certain that National Socialism would not have risen to power without the complicity of a segment of the old ruling classes, but the Hitlerite movement was not of a conservative nature. By degrees, as the adventure proceeded, the blind fury that animated the revolution of nihilism became apparent even to those of the traditionalists who for a time had subscribed to the Brownshirt demagogy. In July 1944, the opposition included the greatest names of the German aristocracy. Franco's regime (if we omit the military aid given by the Axis) was carried to power by the joint action of the Falangists (a Fascist movement in the twentieth-century style), the Carlists (a conservative movement of ancient origin), and the ruling class (Army, Church, great landowners, industrialists). The result is a military dictatorship, profoundly conservative; it maintains the social hierarchy, the power of the Church, and the privileges of the Army.

Between the conservatism of Franco and Hitler's revolution, Italian Fascism occupies an intermediate position, less reactionary than the one, less revolutionary than the other. The non-proletarian masses which Fascism strove to mobilize emerged from a social structure that was largely pre-capitalist. The crisis that helped Mussolini's enterprise was not of the same gravity as that of 1929 in Germany. It was mainly due to the consequences of the war, and abated by itself. The occupation of factories had ceased several months before the march on Rome. Fascism had never obtained sufficient votes at the polls to endanger the party system. Parliamentary confusion rather than the dialectic of the extremes, and the support of the leaders of industry rather than the enthusiasm of the masses finally assured its success.

At the beginning of certain authoritarian regimes—as in Yugoslavia and Poland—we find neither non-party masses stirred to revolt by a crisis, nor national resentment, nor political religions, nor the dialectic of the extremes. The suppression or anesthetization of the parties was achieved by a simple police measure. The dictatorship of the colonels in Poland was anti-parliamentary but not totalitarian, and assumed a large measure of passivity on the part of the people, mainly peasants.

The sole common cause which can be attributed to all the authoritarian regimes of the Right between the two wars is the difficulty which parliamentary governments found in functioning in a disturbed period. But these difficulties in turn had various causes. In the new countries, just liberated from foreign domination, they were due to the absence of political personnel capable of respecting the subtle rules of peaceful rivalry. Elsewhere, they were due to the violence of the struggles between national groups, as in Yugoslavia, or between social groups, as in Germany. There are many explanations for the reverses of parliamentarianism, tormented by party conflicts and abandoned by the frustrated masses.

Today there is no risk of failure to recognize these reasons for the weakness of the pluralist democracies, but rather some risk of exaggerating them. There is an inclination to ascribe inevitability to the temporary victory of the Fascist movements; nothing is further from the truth. Even in Germany, where the situation was ideally favorable to it, National Socialism did not win its victory unaided. It, too, was finally successful because of treachery in the fortress.

In spite of legends, the real lesson taught by the period between the two wars is not that revolutionary enthusiasm—of the Right or of the Left—can easily carry away the fragile barrier of democratic legality. The lesson is quite different. A party that resolutely employs all the resources of police technique holds power indefinitely, once it has won it. But it will experience great difficulty in winning it as long as those in charge of the state are resolute in its defense. Even in the twentieth century there is no instance of universal suffrage ever having given an absolute majority to a revolutionary party where the freedom of the vote has been respected. Though the electorate is less conservative than in the last century, it has not yet become revolutionary.

In Italy, no parliamentary arithmetic obliged the King to choose Mussolini as head of the Government. A few companies of soldiers would have sufficed to disperse the Fascists marching on Rome. It was by direct action rather than by any electoral success, by plundering the premises of the co-operatives or the trade unions rather than at the polls, that the Fascist Party demonstrated its will to power. But direct action, in Western Europe, implies the complicity of the police. It is a symbol of violence rather than actual violence. And a party system can easily find, in the arsenal of the modern state, means to defend itself against "symbols."

As to the conquest of power by the electoral vote, the German experience has shown how extremely difficult it is. The traditional parties, moderate or reformist, retain a considerable body of supporters in time of crisis. The non-party masses, although adrift in desperation and rebellion, never represent a majority of the country. In order for the democratic parties to be relegated to a minority, there is usually required a union of the revolutionaries of the Right with those of the Left, and sometimes in addition the nationalist conservatives. The Hitlerites alone never received as much as 40 per cent of the votes before they seized power. In coalition with the German nationalists they assured themselves of an absolute majority only after the expulsion of the Communists. It may be said that, sooner or later, this alliance was bound to come. The reduction in the Hitlerite votes in October 1932 persuaded the protectors of the Nazis and the old-style conservatives to galvanize the movement into action and to organize a national coalition with the object of liquidating the Weimar Republic. But this does not impair the contention that we wish to establish. The victories of the revolutions of the Right in Italy and Germany were the result not of an irresistible mass rising, not even of an insurmountable weakness in the democratic states, but of an agreement between revolutionaries of the Right and moderate parties, themselves the interpreters of a section of the old ruling classes.

The trumpets of propaganda are not sufficient to bring down walls. There are traitors to be found who will hand the keys of the city to the besiegers. The revolution comes after the seizure of power, and the violence most frequently comes from the state itself.

Will democracy restored be the victim of the same divergences of interest? The danger, at least in the form in which it appeared between the two wars, seems to me to be slight.

The nations which rejected the secular religions in the past— Britain, Belgium, Holland, the Scandinavian countries—stand even more firmly against them today, after the collapse of the Fascist movements and the confusion of the "social religion" with Russian imperialism. As for the three principal Continental nations—Germany, France, and Italy—they do not seem destined to offer in the course of the coming years either ideological or social conditions favorable to the dialectic of the extremes. Neither in Italy, nor in France, nor in Germany do there exist bewildered non-proletarian masses who consider themselves victims of the party system, and whom a demagogue might be able to mobilize or fanaticize.

Without doubt, the refugees in Germany constitute a potential body of supporters for a Rightist opposition, and in Italy, particularly in the south, there is a risk of the surplus population, partly or wholly unemployed, rising against the dilatoriness of parliamentarianism. But, short of an economic crisis, one cannot see millions of men anywhere who are sufficiently unfortunate and sufficiently enthusiastic about an ideology to follow blindly the call of a man or a party. If a crisis should occur, unemployment would be met by inflation.

It is probable that in Germany and Italy, in the next few years, the Christian Democratic Party will lose votes from its Right to formations of which some will resemble the conservative parties and others the Fascists. Depending on circumstances, the Christian Democratic Party will be led to come to an understanding with the socialist troops or with the old "reaction." Possibly social democracy will come into power at Bonn. In neither case does it seem that a Rightist opposition need isolate itself as a great revolutionary party, standing simultaneously against the party system and against Communism.

The ideological climate has changed even more than the social situation. No opposition at present risks professing explicitly the theses of Fascism, the suppression of democratic liberties, or the system of the single party. National exaltation has disappeared, as have the bewildered masses. Neither the Germans nor the Italians will be dreaming tomorrow, for the second time, of the Germanic or the neo-Roman Empire. The Italians were hardly taken in by the imperial myth, and it cost the Germans too dearly. Propaganda has succeeded in discrediting the very name of Fascism, and certain of its ideologies.

There remains the case of France, where, it seems, one may observe the triangular fight—Third Force, Communism, and Gaullism —incarnating the three protagonists of the drama of the modern democracies.

Gaullism is a species of what we have called the "Rightist opposition." It belongs to the Bonapartist tradition, which is specifically French. It combines the appeal to the soldier and the appeal to the people; it combines radical, republican, cockade-wearing followers, as well as conservatives, from the west, north, and east of France. It does not rely on the rootless masses, revolutionary out of resentment, as German Fascism did, but on heterogeneous masses, more conservative than revolutionary; some faithful to the democratic slogans but with a taste for authority, others traditionalists. But the Gaullist group has neither the strength nor the vices of the Fascist parties. The brakes on authority in France are strangely powerful. For lack of an ideology, of popular fanaticism, of an organized party, a Gaullist government, should there ever be one, does not seem likely to break away from the traditions of a more or less clearly presidential republic.

For that matter, if the sole objective, or at least the supreme objective, is the safety of pluralist democracy, experience teaches the best means of defense. In Italy and even more so in Germany, proportional representation was one of the causes of parliamentary confusion, which in turn was one of the causes of the Hitlerite triumph. It is doubtful whether a new party would have gained 107 seats in the Reichstag at one stroke in 1930 if the vote had been on a majority basis. Such a basis could not have guaranteed the formation of a stable government, but it would at least have prevented the crystallization of the old parties, the rapid rise of new formations, and at the same time the succession of general elections. A subtle electoral procedure in France has permitted the parties known as the Third Force to obtain a majority in Parliament without having a majority in the country. But has the problem of the regime been solved at the same time?

When we look in detail at the succession of events that brought Mussolini and Hitler to power, we have an impression not of an inevitable process but of a conspiracy of stupidity and luck. Nothing would have been easier than to disperse the bands of Blackshirts. Hitler was not a predestined victor. His path could have been barred if the Weimar parties had been capable of governing together until the abatement of the economic crisis and waiting, without general elections, for the ebb of the Hitlerite tide. It will be said that in Italy the King, and in Germany Hindenberg and his advisers, decided otherwise. That is partly true.

The decisions can, nevertheless, be explained by the impotence of the parliamentary system and of the political personnel of the traditional parties. Germany under the Weimar Republic had ceased in 1931 and 1932 to be a nation. Rival parties organized the passive or fanaticized masses, and carried on a sort of veiled civil war. The recognition of the rulers by the ruled and national unity had disappeared (the situation is, to some extent, analogous in the France of today). It would have been better for Germany and the world to prolong for several years the impotence of the state and the disintegration of the country. Both would have diminished progressively, and the catastrophe that completed the ruin of European civilization would at least have been deferred. But governments incapable of fulfilling the functions indispensable to the survival of the community end, in one way or another, by being swept away.

We wonder whether the restored democracies will succumb to the same forces which, between the two wars, brought about the triumph of the Fascist movements. It should also, and above all, be asked whether the restored democracies are fit to perform the task which history imposes on continental Europe. Only yesterday the liberal parliamentarianisms failed to surmount the economic crisis. Will they succeed today in repelling Stalinist aggression? Only yesterday the Fascist movements justified their enterprise by a Communist peril that was still far off. Today the peril is near. And there are no defenders on the ramparts.

In our epoch, for permanent reasons, the Western or pluralist democracies are weak regimes. The strong regimes are those which escape discussion, or arouse enthusiasm, or impose themselves by their efficiency. The authority won by a state through the passage of time, the hope it inspires of a radiant future, and the quality of its administration give it solidity and its leaders security. After their restoration the pluralist democracies had neither the prestige of the past, nor that of promise, nor that of justice: they were simply there, in being. A soon as the technique of universal suffrage is applied, on the principle of popular sovereignty, as soon as individuals are authorized to group themselves, the community dissolves into rival factions and the state is delivered over to the party system.

Before 1914 parliamentarianism was regarded as the normal product of European evolution, as the highest form of political organization. The most ardent defenders of the restored democracies will no longer accept so naïve a view. Neither the advent of industrial communities nor the effacement of the traditional hierarchies has brought the political liberties that were supposed to be implicit in a parliamentary regime. At the same time, this regime has been deprived of the support which the "eternal ideas" brought to it—self-government, the reign of law, and individual liberty. A kind of rupture has taken place between the theory and the practice of democracy.

Will the sovereignty of the people be invoked? The principle was impressive only to the extent to which the two words "sovereignty" and "people" designated two superior and mysteriously respect-commanding realities. But how can the sovereign people win respect when it is not conscious of itself, when it is scattered into groups according to interests, prejudices, and passions? Party organization interposes a screen between the voters and the state, and canalizes popular opinion in the directions fixed by the oligarchies of the press, of business, or of Parliament. After the performance of the electoral rite—except in a few countries like Switzerland, where certain elements of direct democracy remain— the sovereign is, so to speak, excluded from the game.

It was once believed that democracy was a system based on discussion, and that the truth emerged from an honest comparison of opinions. Honest comparison has become the exception, and the clash of propaganda the rule. Each party has its truth, which it is less concerned to correct than to propagate. Sure of its doctrine, it expects obedience from its devotees. It savagely defends the interests of its supporters, and is ready to conclude agreements with the representatives of other groups. Instead of dialogue, we find nothing but the unending repetition of "slogan systems," which take the place of thought. A plurality of lies is better than one solitary lie decreed by the state. The lies limit one another, and objective information and the search for the truth insinuate themselves into the chinks. But, once more, this is merely a justification by the reasoning of the lesser evil. Men are more ready to die for an illusory good than for a real lesser evil.

Democracy tends to produce anonymity of power. Functions, rather than men, are known and recognized. The men emerge from the shadows and return to them according to the chance of popular or parliamentary votes. The functions remain, the individuals pass on. This anonymity is the end result of a long evolution that reverses the initial relationship. In the beginning, it is beings of flesh and blood who secure obedience. In democracy, authority belongs to the officials or to the laws, never to individuals as such.

The system of anonymous powers may be morally of a high order, but it corresponds neither to all the aspirations nor to all the needs of communities. The crowds follow a man on the path of sacrifice more willingly than an abstraction. In war and in troubled times the democracies enlist a dictator (in the Roman sense) not only in order to concentrate responsibilities in the hands of a single person, but also in order to give the invisible state an incarnation.

No doubt the parties seek to mitigate this weakness. They throw the spotlight of their propaganda on the chiefs, whose prestige must gradually be merged with that of the movements they direct. But in proportion as the party leaders take the form of phantasmal chiefs, democracy loses on one hand what it gains on the other. When the demagogue, exalting and exalted, exercises a function of state, he communicates some of his prestige to that function. But if the head of the opposition enjoys equal ascendancy, there results a dispersal of loyalty of which the state itself is the victim.

The democratic power is not only anonymous but also secular. The churches, Catholic or Protestant, remain conservative forces, but they seldom defend a particular constitution, economic system, or party, provided the principles of the faith are safeguarded. The democratic state is not founded on any system of beliefs and does not seek consecration by any faith. It sets the rules under which the various parties carry on a peaceful contest for the exercise of governmental power. As long as the parties are also lay (in other words, represent simply a combination of opinions and interests), their laity does not imperil the state, because all politics presents the same character. But as soon as certain parties come forth equipped with a world philosophy and arouse ardors of a quasi-religious nature, democracy suffers from a fundamental contradiction—the dissociation of the spiritual and temporal powers. The state, itself without religion, has nothing left but the police with which to fight the secular religions.

Theoretically it might be objected that democracy or liberalism also represents a conception of man and society as a whole, just as Communism and Fascism do. Why, others will ask, should democracy arouse less enthusiasm than the totalitarian doctrines? These objections have no bearing on present realities. Democracy or liberalism, as philosophies, are worth more than National Socialism or Stalinism, but the technique of multiple parties or of parliaments is not an object of faith in Europe today. The state of multiple parties has not and cannot have the support of a religion without becoming a partisan state, that is to say, without the state's becoming confused with a party and its doctrine.

The regimes of the countries west of the Iron Curtain all belong to one type. Establishing as a principle the freedom of professional and political groups, these regimes each experience the same tumult of propaganda, the same conflicts or claims, and the same weakness of authority, an authority subject to the control of the governed and forced into making compromises. The organization of the masses and the decline of the aristocracies of birth and of money have modified the origin of the members of the assemblies.

The differences are nevertheless as evident, and probably more profound, than the resemblances. In Britain, constitutional usages retain the prestige of long duration and of tradition, and they are not separated from those subtle values which a nation regards as characteristic of its genius. The British are not addicted to political mythology, either because their Protestant upbringing gives them protection against the secular religions and the party churches, or because they remain attached to a morality, Christian in origin and individualist in essence, which inspires in them both a sense of responsibility and loyalty to the state. Democracy there does not mean simply an electoral technique for the selection of rulers, but a certain concept of collective existence.

Starting from this example, it would be easy to identify the circumstances favorable to the pluralist democracies. In Britain and in the small countries of Northwestern Europe (Belgium, Holland, Denmark, Norway, Sweden) the oppositions that reject the methods of parliamentarianism on principle consist only of more or less feeble minorities. France and Italy, on the other hand, are torn by the action of the Communist Party, which is in a state of permanent dissidence—indeed of open war against society. The Germany of Bonn belongs neither to the former nor the latter category. Its Communist Party is not numerous, but electoral and parliamentary institutions inspire less respect there than anywhere else in Western Europe.

To take full account of these differences, it would be necessary to recall the history of each country in addition to its present structure. The institutions of the pluralist democracies are more deeply rooted in the countries with a maritime civilization, where Parliament has continued a tradition, aristocratic or bourgeois, and prolonged the customs of local autonomy. One of the foundations of democracy was lacking in countries where individuals regarded the centralized administration as an enemy.

In certain cities and regions of Germany, representative institutions developed spontaneously, but the modern Reich owed more to the spirit of the Junkers, the officials, and the Prussian officers than to that of the Hanseatic towns or of the Rhineland. The imitation of British parliamentarianism in the military states of the Continent has never resulted in solid and self-confident regimes. All the more reason why the restoration of the democracy of parties following the catastrophe makes for doubt and anxiety.

Strong peoples do not exhaust themselves in internal disputes. In addition, the stakes in their disputes must remain limited, and the disputants must voluntarily adopt moderation in the means they use. Unfortunately the Continental parties have never set limits to their ambitions, and they do not subscribe sincerely to the rule of non-violence. They are not expert in the arts of collaboration, of compromise, of restraint. They amplify their propaganda, they strive to enroll militants, they teach them to think of the world in terms of a pseudo doctrine, that is to say, usually, to stop thinking altogether. All the Continental democracies suffer from the same contradiction: they spread the totalitarian spirit, while weakening the structure of the community and of the state.

These restored democracies have been given the task, not of maintaining the community and state, but of remaking the unity of nations, of reconstructing the machinery of the state. Perhaps, in spite of everything, they will succeed if they have twenty years at their disposal. But how much time do they have?

## Chapter XIV

## THE NATIONAL SOCIALISMS

AFTER THE First World War the leading countries, Great Britain and the United States, were convinced that it was possible to turn back the clock. It was thought necessary to re-establish the international monetary and commercial system that had favored the extraordinary expansion of wealth and trade during the preceding century. But then, only a few years after the stabilization of the European currencies, the great depression brought about the collapse of an edifice of which the façade rather than the foundations had been restored.

In 1945, opinion was far from unanimous concerning the economic objectives of the Western world. The United States continued to dream of monetary convertibility and free trade, while Great Britain, without rejecting those principles in theory, considered them inapplicable during the so-called intermediate phase, which seemed likely to last many years.

Actually American preferences exercised only a slight influence on events. Reconstruction proceeded within each country according to the preferences of the public, the parties, and the government.

It seems possible to group the changes of economic systems, in the last half century into three categories. All the countries of Western Europe tend towards what the Germans call *Wohlfahrtsstaat,* the British "welfare state," and the French *Etat-providence* or *Etat de services sociaux.* All substitute, though in different degrees, collective for private ownership, and all (again in different degrees) resort to economic planning, that is to say, the attempts to replace automatic mechanisms by deliberate action of the public authorities. When partial planning is used to isolate the internal from the international economic situation, to guarantee full employment, whatever the world situation, we arrive at what may be called National Socialism. At present trade unionism represents the extreme form of this movement, but it is the fundamental aim of the policy followed by most European states.

Without making an exhaustive analysis, it can easily be seen that the two first movements, towards the welfare state and collective ownership, have essentially psychological and social origins. On the other hand, partial economic direction is mainly the sign of reaction to circumstances of an essentially economic order.

It was Germany that originated the movement of ideas and institutions of which the present welfare state appears to be the culmination. The first European state that deserved the title was Bismarck's. It led all others in the development of social legislation (accident insurance, provision for sickness and old age), which was worked out by conservatives as a reply to both socialism and liberalism, and as a weapon against the Marxists. These last, after some hesitation, were not slow in claiming the credit for the laws originally intended to win the working class from their influence. Sociological writers, especially in Germany, were fond of contrasting the Bismarck state, the ideal of which was the integration of all individuals into the collectivity, with the British state, with an ideal that called for the free play of initiative and rivalry. On one side the ideal was that of the civil servant and on the other that of the *entrepreneur,* the gentleman, and the parliamentarian.

There would be no difficulty in tracing the German influence exercised on the originators of trade unionism. The Fabians, especially the Webbs, were basically hostile to the liberal philosophy, and they felt some sympathy with the Bismarckian theory of the state as protector and integrator. But it would be absurd to attribute the diffusion of social legislation to German influences alone. This form of state interference has spread because it answers real needs and expresses aspirations which opinion in the Western communities has ended by supporting almost unanimously.

It should also he said in fairness that the issue has rarely been the subject of open conflict. In the United States some recent strikes have sought to force employers to pay the whole or part of the levies for pensions.[1] In this case, the desire for security comes from the working masses themselves. Neither in France nor in Great Britain has the progress of social legislation been preceded by violent popular manifestations.

Social insurance was introduced in France by moderate governments between the two wars. It was greatly expanded after the second war at the instigation of some high officials, who believed in the advantages of the system and were at the same time animated by a sort of bureaucratic imperialism. Certain of the principles actually applied, such as family allowances, had long been rejected by the unions with socialist tendencies. It was the Christian Socialists or the heads of paternalistic companies who endeavored to make wages proportionate to needs by means of family allowances, even though this meant rejecting the old trade union formula of equal pay for equal work. The problem of stopping demographic regression, with which the leftist unions and parties did not concern themselves, was at the root of many of the provisions of the *Code de la Famille* reproduced today in the *Sécurité Sociale*.

The extension of social services proposed by the Beveridge Plan, and carried out by the Labour Party was not the subject of serious party differences, at any rate before the cost of reform was revealed. The plan received general approval, its purpose being to suppress extreme forms of poverty and to safeguard all the beneficiaries against misfortunes due to the hazards of existence. It will be said that this agreement gives better evidence of a collective will than do noisy claims or strikes. To put security first is indeed the sign of a certain attitude towards existence. Societies are characterized by the priority they establish between different goals. But the obsession about security has been found above all in officials, intellectuals, and politicians. Its exaggerations are not due to excessive demands from the masses, but to the doctrinal, systematizing, or demagogic mentality of a few leaders.

British workers would not have demanded the health service

---

[1]It is known in France that the workman himself ultimately pays the cost of pensions in the form of reduction of direct wages, even though pensions are financed by employers' contributions.

free for all any more than French workers would have demanded the progressive application of social security to all classes of society (a development of which they are victims rather than beneficiaries). After a certain point, the growth of social security has been due to claims advanced by the excluded categories. It is nevertheless true that in general, it was the leaders with their theories, and not the impatience of the masses, who pushed social legislation to a point where it has brought about a vast redistribution of incomes.

Unlike the welfare state, nationalization traditionally appears in the program of the trade unions and the socialist parties. Some nationalizations—the railways in France, and coal mining in England —were justified on economic grounds. But the great waves of nationalization in France and Great Britain followed political movements: the liberation in France, the victory of the Labour Party in Great Britain.

The transition from private to public enterprise has not generally been the result of necessity or of economic dialectics. The state has not been obliged to take over the giant enterprises or the trusts which paralyzed the operation of the markets. Neither the electric and coal-mining companies nor their customers asked for government aid. The intermediary between private and public concentration of economic control was political democracy.

Is it inevitable that universal suffrage shall bring into power advocates of collective ownership? The word "inevitable" is equivocal. The fact is that in the United States the workers—or at least those who speak for them—are generally hostile to nationalization. The majority of union leaders hold that it is better to bargain with private employers than with the state. Socialist mysticism has beguiled only a small part of public opinion. Even in Europe there are socialist parties, in Belgium or the Scandinavian countries, which, without renouncing collective ownership, have recognized that it settles nothing in itself. They recommend nationalization in a particular case and for a particular purpose, but not mass nationalization out of loyalty to an almost outmoded doctrine.

In spite of everything, it is not surprising that political democracy has usually instigated measures of socialization. In order to gain the votes and the confidence of the masses, the politicians profess to reduce inequalities and to put an end to certain privileges. The idea that by transferring the means of production to the community the lot of the workers is improved is mistaken—although attractive at first sight. It is too much bound up with the socialist ideology, which has had too much influence on the intellectuals and workers of the West to be easily renounced. Only experience refutes it. If returned to power, the anti-socialists in France and Great Britain would not interfere with most of the nationalization; they would have neither the power nor the desire to do so.

The capitalism[2] of the great corporations is probably as different from the capitalism of the British textile industry in the middle of the nineteenth century as that, in its turn, was from factories before the days of the steam engine and the automatic loom. But the transition from private to public ownership, as in French or British nationalization, has nothing to do with historic necessity (in the Marxian sense), or with any stage in the development of the forces of production.

Alone among the three principal aspects of Western socialism, a partially planned economy may pass as a result of the functioning of the economic system; it must be added that such a result appears only if the victims of the market mechanisms have the right to form associations and to protest—that is to say, if political democracy exists.

Partial economic planning is not derived from a theory. It has assumed quite different forms and different scope in different countries. It is not to be confused with other forms of state intervention (otherwise there would be no point in making the distinction). We apply this term only to interventions that attempt to modify the results which the market mechanism would have brought about by itself, that is to say, either the replacement of the mechanism by administrative action, or the reduction of market fluctuations, or the controlled expansion of the economy toward such particular objectives as are considered desirable.

To the first category belong the various measures intended to keep prices up when the producers think they are too low, or to prevent them from rising when the consumers think they are too high. In certain markets, especially those for agricultural produce in which the demand is not elastic, prices would so fluctuate at

[2] In its structure, if not in its operation.

times that an excess of supply might not only ruin certain producers but, by affecting the incomes of one social level or another, precipitate a crisis. In the United States, in Great Britain, and in France government is at work in different degrees and by different methods in the same direction—to maintain the prices of agricultural produce at a certain level or in a certain relationship to industrial prices, so that, in obedience to considerations of net cost or of equitable relationship of prices, the ups and downs of the market may be avoided. The objections of theorists will not prevent any group under a democratic government from refusing to accept passively a drastic cut in its income. The revolt against the vacillations of the market is a part of the general desire for security.

When official price-fixing or assessments do not suffice to produce a healthy market, the public authorities take a further step and endeavor to modify the factors that decide the state of the market. Thus "Malthusian" practices arise. Giving up hope of reestablishing equilibrium by lowering prices and increasing the demand, public authorities and trade associations try to reduce supply, to stop competition, to dig up vineyards or forbid the opening of new shops. In a way, they try to secure the equivalent of what the mechanism ought to have secured. Too often they do something else: they protect vested interests, they do not trouble to eliminate marginal producers to promote selection according to efficiency, they crystallize the existing structure and paralyze the effort to lower costs. This tendency, more or less marked according to the country, was particularly prevalent in France before the war. But it is not a necessary result of economic planning, which may just as well aim at expansion.

More important are the interventions aimed at the economy as a whole, where the mechanism has failed to act. In our epoch devaluations are a substitute for the deflation that is impossible today because of the rigidity of the factors and, in particular, because of the resistance to the lowering of nominal wages. During the thirties, after the devaluation of the pound sterling, every country had to modify the value of its currency in order to re-establish equilibrium not only between internal prices and world prices but between the different internal prices. Since the great crisis of 1929, governments have become responsible for what is called full employment, in other words, for the level of activity. This responsibility was the origin of partial economic planning. No government could look on passively at growing unemployment and declining production. When deflation reaches a certain degree, the leaders cannot avoid the task of reversing the tendency. The dislocation of world economy resulting from the 1929 crisis drove even democratic states to seek prosperity within the national framework.

National Socialism, as practiced by the Third Reich, was not the necessary or general consequence of the remedies which the different governments applied. The repayments of foreign loans, in 1930–31 had made Germany's trade balance largely a credit one, but had also precipitated an unprecedented deflation. From the moment when the new government set out to reintegrate all workers into the productive system, it was obliged to isolate the internal market from the world economy. The policy of full employment necessitated a budgetary deficit or the expansion of credit; hence the control of wages and prices and the limitation of distributed incomes. Gradually economic planning was extended throughout the whole system without eliminating either private ownership of the means of production or the operation of markets at a microscopic level.

Keynesianism was the theoretical justification for the search for prosperity within the national framework, but it was not its cause. The policy of expansion (implemented by a budgetary deficit, a low rate of interest, and large-scale public works) as a remedy in time of crisis has not always required control of exchange and of foreign trade and the isolation of the internal market; but in certain circumstances (Germany in 1933 and Great Britain in 1945) partial economic planning inevitably results in a sort of National Socialism, or—if one prefers to avoid the ambiguity of the term Socialism—in a planned national economy with a view to full employment, prosperity, or military power; monetary convertibility is sacrificed and the control of exchanges and imports with the outside world is established by administrative action.

The countries of Western Europe have not all gone so far along the road that leads to the welfare state, to nationalization of the means of production, and to National Socialism. At present Great Britain is in the lead. Free health services and food subsidies (450 million pounds in 1949–50); nationalization of coal mines, gas and electric utilities, transportation, civil aviation, and steel production; the policy of full employment; monetary inconvertibility or convertibility only within the sterling zone; the tendency to internal inflation channeled or repelled by "controls"—with all this the birthplace of liberalism is trying to create a model of national economic planning.

The differences between the theories and the practices of the governments of Western Europe cannot be ignored, but it is no less important to clarify their exact scope. In the matter of social services, there is controversy concerning the extent but not the principle of the reforms. In certain respects, the philosophy of each community dictates its preferences. Universal insurance against accidents, illness, and old age considerably reduces the number of cases of undeserved suffering. Within certain limits, social legislation is an unquestionable step forward. The protection of *all* the population against *all* the hazards of existence may seem a mistaken ideal, inaccessible because self-stultifying. The obsession with individual security is a reaction, comprehensible but absurd, to the collective insecurity created by the threat of wars. The more completely individual security is secured by administrative perfection, the more another sort of insecurity will be produced—that of the individual in relation to a state that will exact payment in obedience, even in respect and adoration, for the benefits it distributes. Some persons fear inequality more than state interference, others prefer to see people be responsible and assume risks rather than be perpetually assisted.

In the concrete it is not impossible to eliminate these abstract metaphysical conflicts and confine controversy to technical data. Insofar as indirect wages (insurance, family allowances, pensions) are deductions from direct wages, there is a point where the claims of social legislation increase to compromise the operation of the economic system. A certain proportion between effort and reward must be maintained. When social subsidies are mainly financed through the general budget, the limit is fixed by the possibilities of taxation. Certain redistributions now practiced in Great Britain are hardly justifiable from any point of view. The British health service and food subsidies have the disadvantage of treating all social classes alike. There is no sense in reducing the price of tea or bacon for the wealthy. In any case, there is a point that must not be overlooked: taxation must not paralyze the spirit of initiative, and individuals who are protected against risks must not at the same time be deprived of ambition and enterprise.

The controversies over the question of nationalization are partly metaphysical. For a century and a half so many hopes have been attached to the collective ownership of the instruments of production that the socialists have difficulty in dropping this propaganda theme. They ask: Would not the *total* nationalization of industry yield what scattered nationalizations have not yielded? Does the failure of nationalizations prove the vanity of socialization? (But there has never been a clear definition of what would be the status of the great enterprises taken from private ownership without being transferred to the state.)

The type of ownership does not itself modify the lot of the workers; it determines neither the standard of living nor the conditions of work. It is of course possible, by distributing the profits of a particular company, to increase the remuneration of certain workers. But in the great industrial concentrations the profits distributed have no common measure with the total wages. Whatever the ownership, part of the profits must be reinvested, whether the enterprise plows them back into its own plant or they are returned to the capital market through individual saving. For the working class as a whole, the standard of living depends more on productivity than on the owners of the means of production.

In the end, there are only two important arguments, one belonging to politics pure and simple, the other to economic policy. There is less feeling against trusts (after all, the national companies of the coal mines or railways are simply enormous trusts) than against the men of the trusts. Nationalization aims at modifying the relations of authority within the community, at eliminating the excessive influence ascribed to the heads of industrial concentrations, at replacing private directors by directors appointed by the state, the "two hundred families" by two hundred officials. When nationalization extends to the whole of industry, there comes a renewal of directing personnel which may well be called a revolution. In the case of partial nationalizations, the renewal of staff is less drastic; it is necessary of course to find competent men. Only violent revolutions can afford the luxury of neglecting competence: the people pay the price of apprenticeship; enthusiasm and the police compensate for the losses.

Apart from this will to power, the desire to occupy certain key positions may logically inspire nationalizations. It may be easier to correct the oscillations of the market when part of heavy industry is removed from private ownership and responds obediently to the directives of the planners. The capital expenditure of the nationalized sector enlarges the field of large-scale works dependent on public authorities. In this respect one may ask whether the nationalizations are essential. This question will be discussed.

Although the controversy has not lost all meaning, it seems to have quietened down. Disillusionment in France and Great Britain is calming passions. There is less impatience to expand nationalization than to improve management. Neither the social services, which no one rejects, nor the nationalizations, which no longer arouse fervor, constitute the essential issue in the ideological conflicts. What is essential is the mode of operation: liberalism or economic planning say the French (*dirigisme*); liberalism or trade unionism, others prefer to say.

The opposition has developed out of the different choices made in Belgium and Great Britain for the period of reconstruction. The principle of Belgian policy was to create as soon as possible the conditions indispensable to the operation of a competitive economy. Taking advantage of foreign currency reserves, the Belgians first imported goods for current consumption rather than means of production, and strove to re-establish equilibrium between the level of prices and the quantity of available money. Restrictions of credit and high rates of interest prevented the development of internal inflation, of which monetary non-convertibility and the administrative control of foreign trade are the inevitable results. The "hardness" of the Belgian franc, and the freedom of trade internally and with foreign countries showed the success of the method.

In Great Britain, the Labour Government followed the other path. Deciding to start a grand plan of capital expenditure, it ac-

cepted the disparity between the quantity of money available and
the level of prices, between available consumer goods and the incomes which private persons wished to spend. It checked inflation
by controls, and kept the cost of living artificially low through food
subsidies and considerable taxation. The deficit in the trade balance
in the early years was allowed to grow beyond the inevitable level.
Since then, inflation has been not only checked but mainly reab-
sorbed, thanks to increased prices, a large budgetary surplus, and a
certain prudence in credit policy.

The issue between liberalism and austerity is of mainly retrospective significance. But there is risk of a renewed discussion in a form
only slightly modified. Must the goal of full employment be given
priority, with a permanent tendency to inflation channelized by controls—in short, by national economic planning? Or, once conditions
of approximate equilibrium have returned, must the national economy be freed to compete on world markets, consumers be allowed
to choose foreign goods (without distinction between the necessary
and the unnecessary), physical controls and price-fixing be renounced, and government influence on markets be limited to action
through taxation and credit?

It is not a question of planning in one case and integral liberalism
in the other. The policy followed by the Labour Government was
far from conforming in all its aspects to the ideal type of national
economic planning. Food subsidies, a legacy from the war, were in
no way inseparable from the system. The essential object was to
protect the internal economy from the repercussions that would result from a depression in any part of the world, and never to resort
to deflation to restore the equilibrium of the trade balance. Labour's
defenders replied to the admirers of the Belgian technique by quoting the unemployment figures in Belgium.

Between the country that holds the record for the redistribution
of the national income by social services, the nationalization of certain means of production, and partial economic planning, and the
one that restricts those reforms as much as possible—between Great
Britain and Belgium (or the Western Germany of Dr. Ehrhardt),
the distance is great: those responsible for the two policies come
from different circles and profess opposite philosophies. The latter
want to restore the mechanism of the market, and so, they think,

the conditions of a liberal and individualist community; the former dream of a state with an organized if not a planned economy, which would ensure security and work for all without trespassing on personal rights.

Economically, it would be easier still to show an opposition of principle. Such measures as redistribution of the national income and nationalization of certain enterprises are not forbidden either to liberals or to socialists. The line of division between doctrines and practices is traced by the attitude adopted toward the price mechanism: Shall enterprises, national or not, be subject to the laws of the market? Is the relative lot of wage earners to be improved by fiscal measures, or by subsidies which falsify price relations? In one case, the goal is a *social liberalism,* the principle of which is the utilization of the liberal mechanisms so as to obtain certain results conformable to socialist conceptions, while in the other there is a plunge into a system of planning that will have a tendency to grow.

In spite of these divergences and in spite of polemics between labor and liberals, the different regimes of the European countries seem to be, sociologically, species of the same genus rather than representatives of different genera. They all practice the redistribution of national income through and for the social services, they all admit that the state is responsible for prosperity, and therefore obliged, morally and politically, to intervene in order to attenuate, if not eliminate, the oscillations of the market. All, in case of a crisis, would be led to resort to the Keynesian remedies.

It is true that the divergence between labor and liberals exists. The former, in order to combine full employment with an ambitious program of capital expenditure, consent to a certain internal inflation resulting in controls, the limitation of monetary convertibility, and an administrative management of foreign trade; the latter allow the liberal mechanisms to function within the national unit and in their relations with foreign countries, limiting themselves to the control of currency and credit policy. It is indeed an opposition of techniques inspired by contradictory philosophies. Before admitting its fundamental character, let us apply two hypothetical tests.

If Great Britain could no longer count on credit or aid from abroad, would she not be forced to give priority again to the balance of foreign payments to an extent which would render unattainable the present objective of full employment once foreign currencies necessary for the purchase of certain raw materials were lacking? On the other hand, would Belgian liberalism resist a serious depression in the United States or elsewhere in the world? Rather than put up with the consequences of a deflation, the Belgians would isolate the national economy from the world economy in order to try to restore prosperity within the national framework.

As long as there is no international system, as long as it is the duty of governments to maintain a high level of production, and as long as the monetary automatisms of the last century do not function, the different countries of Europe will hesitate between diverse methods; they will rely mainly on universal or partial controls, monetary or physical, and in a period of tranquillity they will establish a different priority between the exigences of the balance of payments and those of full employment. Considered historically, these composite systems belong to the same genus and the same epoch, just as, in spite of their individual features, the pluralist democracies seem to be variations on one and the same theme. "Composite systems" and "pluralist democracies" form, moreover, a unity: both are derived from the same fundamental characteristics of European society.

Just as we are considering the capacity of survival of the pluralist democracies, so we are considering the future of these composite systems. Are they self-contradictory formations, historical freaks, doomed either to degenerate into integral economic planning and totalitarianism, or to return to liberalism? I fear that the question formulated in these terms can have but one answer: if these "freaks" are incapable of living, totalitarian degeneration is more probable than liberal "involution." But I do not agree that these composite formations are incapable of living, at least for a certain time. Pure systems of government do not exist except in the books or plans of theorists.

It is feared that political democracy is not compatible with economic planning, even partial. In part, this fear is well founded. Parliaments find more and more difficulty in carrying out their work, if only because of the tasks imposed on them by the excessive functions of the state. The consequence is the growing part played by the bureaucracy, and the decline of elected assemblies in prestige and effective action. Nowhere is the contrast so accentuated as in France, where the bureaucrats rule, the Ministers making not the most important decisions but those of a more clearly political character (that is to say, those likely to call forth protests from economic blocs or from parties). As for the National Assembly, it overthrows Ministries from time to time, and passes hundreds of laws every year, but it does not determine or even discuss the guiding ideas of internal or external policy. A regime of administration, tempered by parliamentary anarchy and the contradictory claims of groups of interests—such, approximately, is the Fourth Republic. In other countries of Europe the crisis is less acute. A common evolution can nevertheless be discerned. Wherever economic planning gains ground, Parliament loses, and the administration receives or arrogates to itself a delegated right to make laws. The direct conduct of economic affairs by the state ends in the triumph of the bureaucrats. At best, parties and parliamentarians limit and control the new masters.

The movement toward National Socialism weakens or corrupts parliamentary regimes, but the latter seem almost inevitably to involve the former. Pluralist democracy is defined on the institutional plane by competition between parties; economic liberalism, by competition in the markets between individuals and groups. National Socialism appears as the component of these two forces. Workers, farmers, merchants, craftsmen are the voters. They may be expected to demand from their representatives protection against the blows of fate, whether arising from atmospheric conditions or from the oscillations of markets. Classes or social categories try to influence the state to better their position, and expect it to ensure permanent prosperity. From then on, it is in the lobbies of the Ministries that the delegates of the workers too often agitate over wages and the delegates of the industrialists over customs duties or quotas. It is in the shadow of power, as much as in the place of work, that success is secured.

In the last century, state intervention did not reach the same dimensions. The masses, even where they voted, were seldom represented except by men belonging to the ruling class. The Western communities had not suffered disturbances comparable to those which the wars and crises of the twentieth century have inflicted on them. Today, instead of asking whether political democracy is compatible with economic planning we ought to declare that political democracy excludes a properly liberal economy. Partial planning—redistribution of the national income, security for producers threatened by the instability of markets, governmental responsibility for full employment—belongs to the economic system which is normally combined with pluralist democracy.[3]

These mixed formations require a great deal of wisdom on the part of those—leaders, officials, and representatives of employers and employed—who participate in management. Every government must concern itself simultaneously with private and collective interests and with the interest of the whole. This last cannot be defined without ambiguity, but it sometimes appears clearly. If an advantage accorded to a group reduces the expansion of production, it is contrary to the collective interest (for instance, the forty-hour-a-week law in 1936 in France). Modern communities are of such complexity that the social balance sheet can be drawn up by only a few specialists (and even then, as a rule, not without uncertainties). The Ministries, besieged with contradictory demands, are in danger at any moment of favoring particular groups at the expense not so much of other groups as of the community itself.

An economy half free and half planned, in a system of political democracy, involves permanent rivalry for the division of the national income. No group is conscious of the mechanisms by which the social product is divided between the different categories of the nation. The workers who extort a raise in wages, the farmers who obtain higher customs duties, the merchants who, by direct arrangement or by administrative intervention, eliminate competitors and keep prices artificially high do not foresee the ultimate repercussions of the advantages in which they rejoice. This inevitable struggle results in consequences the more equitable and the more favorable to the general prosperity, the better the leaders of the government and those of the private coalitions are able to realize the ultimate effects

[3]Even in the United States. Opinion is hostile to nationalizations and more tolerant of mobility. On the other hand, the problems are those of abundance. The postwar prosperity has enabled the mechanisms of the market to be allowed full play. The movement toward the "welfare state," the redistribution of incomes, the control of markets, is none the less evident.

of the claims of either side. Objective information is as necessary as the competence of the private or public persons responsible for the functioning of the systems supposed to be dependent on public opinion. Actually, free discussion often degenerates into a clash of lies.

Conflicts of doctrine are added to conflicts of interest, and become confused with them. To some extent the former are only a rationalization of the latter. People support a union technique or a certain tax because they see in it a means of modifying the distribution of the national income in favor of wage earners or, more generally, of the non-privileged. There is no standard of equitable distribution. No single year could be taken as a valid criterion for reference. The popular parties set themselves more or less clearly the objective of reducing inequalities. No taxation of large incomes seems to them excessive. The political democracies tend to confiscate legally and to destroy progressively private accumulations of fortune. These eternal conflicts—Aristotle explained the origin of tyrannies as the reaction of the rich to the threat of despoiling laws —maintain tension within free countries. As long as the demands of the non-privileged can be satisfied by making drafts on the surplus offered by the increase of production or of productivity, these social tensions may animate the efforts of the community toward greater well-being. When wars or crises substitute a reduction of the collective resources for the expansion now regarded as normal, the repartition of poverty is a severe trial for a system that already finds difficulty in distributing wealth.

The composite regimes that combine partial planning with political democracy are the most difficult to manage. If the state either abandons the community to itself or assumes complete direction, a simple structure appears. In one case, the groups wielding authority (owners, entrepreneurs, etc.) rule, and the laws of the state seem to have no other purpose than to protect their rule. Such was the situation that Marx thought he observed and on which he founded a general theory, which was not even entirely true in his time, and which is not at all true for history as a whole. In the other case, the autonomy of the community is entirely alienated in favor of the state, which becomes the sole master of the collective existence. When no social class possesses an indisputable authority, when the state neither blends with the community nor separates itself entirely from it, there results a constant instability: the social forces collide and oppose the state.

Does the preceding mean that on the economic plane these composite formations are condemned in advance? Experience has not yet proved that they are perceptibly more inefficient than others. Five years after the end of hostilities, industrial production in Europe averaged 25 per cent above the level of 1938, agricultural production had nearly reached the prewar level, and real wages were generally 10 to 20 per cent higher than ten years earlier. (Germany was an exception, for obvious reasons, and France, for more complex reasons.) Even productivity, to judge from the statistics, has made satisfactory progress in recent years.

The fact that production made a more rapid recovery than after the previous war does not prove that this partial economic planning is more effective than a liberal economy. Western Europe has been powerfully aided by American gifts, and technical science has advanced in twenty years. In spite of everything, these systems, whether they take the form of Belgian liberalism or of British laborism, are probably more efficient[4] than total economic planning, and are probably hardly less so than the liberalism of the preceding century.

It is complained that the Western European systems of partial economic planning tend to conservatism, to an excessive desire to safeguard the positions acquired. The charge is justified. In one degree or another (in this respect again the French case is an extreme one), in all the European countries, competition is feared less on account of the waste it is supposed it would bring than because of the changes it would necessitate. The elimination of marginal enterprises and the regrouping of units according to rational requirements—these painful but indispensable conditions of economic progress—are avoided by the socialists in their anxiety to spare the workers the sufferings of transfer, and by the leaders of industry,

---

[4] We are thinking exclusively of the increase of individual productivity and of the standard of living of the masses. If it is a question of the development of heavy industry and of power, authoritarian economic planning permits more rapid progress.

who share the same feeling and would rather divide a market between them than expand it by lowering prices. This mentality, which is denounced almost everywhere, is less the effect than the cause of the composite system.

It is difficult to measure exactly what the excess of conservatism costs the community. It would be too easy to contrast results obtained with those theoretically possible. Economic progress actually achieved always remains a good way behind that technically obtainable. On the other hand, the mistakes made in France between 1931 and 1939 would suffice, if repeated, to condemn a country to death. But these defects are attributable not to the composite system as such, nor even to the particular kind that exists in France, but to the shortcomings of the community and still more of the ruling class.

Comparable errors are hardly to be feared any longer. The memory and the dread of stagnation have remained. The slogan of expansion will tend rather to produce a permanent inflation than deflation. Most countries have themselves assumed responsibility for much of the national capital expenditure, so that they run a greater risk of multiplying mistaken enterprises than of permitting mass unemployment and allowing the production index to fall.

Such systems have gradually become incapable of enduring even slight deflation. Nominal wages must only move upwards. The taxation would become almost unbearable if a serious fall in prices and activity were to take place. If a crisis came in the United States, almost all the countries of Europe would apply a Keynesian therapeutic. This might not suffice to protect countries that had not the foreign currency needed to buy raw materials abroad. It would hasten the drift toward National Socialism, but would not precipitate a catastrophe analagous to that of 1929–33.

If the method by which the community annually withdraws from consumption the resources necessary to the maintenance and development of capital is characteristic of every system, it should be said that Great Britain and France have now adopted a collectivist system. In France, the confusion of public credit with the credit of the nationalized enterprises makes it improbable that the national companies will be able to secure from public issues the billions of francs indispensable to the development of plant facilities. In Great

Britain, the immensity of taxation has reduced the function of individual savings almost to vanishing point. Budgetary self-financing and surplus have become the rule. At the same time, the selection of capital expenditures has ceased to function through the capital market, and has become to a large extent an administrative decision of the state—a political decision. How is the state's distribution of the collective resources to be reconciled with the sense of individual income which individuals retain? In the long run, will not an economy still based partly on private ownership and individual responsibility be paralyzed and sterilized under a system of taxation dictated by the desire for a social redistribution of income and by the magnitude of the public capital expenditure?

Finally, partial economic planning intensifies economic nationalism. It would be absurd to consider countries with populations of 5, 8 or 15 millions as limits to the size of production units. By its political division Europe is perpetually threatened with falling into a condition, ultimately fatal, that would present neither the advantages of free trade nor those of authoritarian planning. The composite systems do not prevent a more or less rational division of labor between nations, but they do nothing to facilitate it.

Collaboration between economic systems based partly on planning according to democratic methods subjects the ingenuity of experts and the courage of statesmen to a severe test. The chaos of the thirties or of the recent postwar years threatens to arise again as soon as rearmament stirs the fear of penury or depression the fear of unemployment. Export prohibition and import quotas symbolize in turn the spontaneous blind egoism of National Socialism in the various European countries.

We have treated the economic systems of the different countries of Europe as of a like order, but it would be just as reasonable to insist on their different situations. The differences between the nations are considerable, whether we consider the size of the national income, the productivity of labor, or the distribution of the workers over the three sectors. On the road of economic progress, Sweden and Switzerland, spared by the war, are at the head, Italy is in the rear, and France in an intermediate position. The measures to be taken to encourage the increase of productivity—in other words, long-term economic policies—are not the same in London, Paris, Rome, and Stockholm.

The short-term economic policies are no less varied, so much does the legacy of the war differ from country to country. Great Britain was obsessed by the necessity of re-establishing her trade balance, Italy by her labor surplus; France ought to have been equally obsessed by the burdens resulting from the crisis of 1930–39 and the war, that is to say, by the joint imperatives of housing and industrial modernization. As for Western Germany, she is almost a monstrosity, with a density of population three times that of France and with her cities in ruins. How trivial seem differences due to a greater or less degree of liberalism or economic planning compared with the contrast between a Sweden intact and a Germany cut into two, covered with ruins, and severed from Eastern Europe!

A favorite subject of popular passion and of controversy between the theorists and the politicians is the part to be assigned to the mechanisms of the market or to administrative control. The scope of the controversy is narrow, and it should be settled by reference not to ideologies but to the tasks to be accomplished.

*Chapter XV*

## CAN EUROPE LIVE?

THE POSTWAR SITUATION made it immediately necessary to re-build the ruins, restart the factories, re-establish the means of communication, and restore agriculture. The need for these things was too urgent and too evident for controversy.

The appeal of the Old World to the resources of the New was nothing out of the ordinary. As a result of the war, the United States had increased its productive capacity in industry by more than 50 per cent, and in agriculture by 40 per cent; the country itself had been spared attack and manpower was not crippled by casualties. The United States was in a position to place at the disposal of the populations who had been victims of the historic catastrophe its agricultural surplus and a certain quantity of raw materials and manufactured goods—a quantity small in relation to the American market, but important to Europe.

In this light the Marshall Plan might be regarded as a more subtle form of aid to devastated countries, and better adapted to the exigences of the American Congress, than that which U.N.R.R.A. was the first to offer. No explanation was needed to understand that Europe thankfully accepted gifts whose cost to the donor was less than the relief they brought to the recipients. Stalinist propaganda, echoed more or less by the anti-capitalists, united with the complexity of the industrial system to raise questions relating not only to the reconstruction period but to the future.

Would Europe, in her inability to be self-sufficient, be doomed to mendicity? Would the United States, unable to sell its own production on a domestic market, be doomed to generosity? Would the only international system that could emerge from the disaster be founded on philanthropy?

Three sorts of causes might explain why the European nations appealed for outside help in the summer of 1947. In the first place, the direct and physical consequences of the war were pointed out. In the whole of continental Europe, agricultural and industrial production had fallen considerably below prewar figures. A bad harvest aggravated the penury. Countries like Germany and Austria found themselves in an artificial situation. Great Britain had been less affected: the land and the industrial plant were intact; but the complex economic structure was dislocated, investments abroad had largely disappeared, and in eighteen months the American loan had been spent.

In the second place, the policy adopted by the Western European nations tended to increase the scarcity of foreign currency. The effort to carry out vast plans for expanding industrial facilities during the phase of reconstruction inevitably produced inflation, owing to the disproportion between available goods and purchasing power currently distributed or inherited from the war. Finally, in the new situation created by the war, even an increase of production and ultimate equilibrium in the global trade balance of the European nations might leave a deficit between European requirements of goods to be imported from the Western Hemisphere and the foreseeable receipts of dollars.

In the abstract, these three causes can be dissociated: the first would require substantial but temporary aid; the second a reform of the internal administration, and above all, a fight against inflation; while the third aroused long-term anxieties and controversies, in which theoretical and historical considerations were mingled. But in practice each qualified the other: according as accent was laid on one or another, one type of remedy or another seemed called for.

The objective observers—experts of the Marshall Plan, of the O.E.E.C. or of the Economic Commission for Europe, and high officials charged with drawing up reports to the American administration and Congress—analyzed in numerous documents the changes that had taken place since the Second World War, giving an account of the difficulty experienced by the Continent (or rather, its Western part) in living on its own resources.

In 1938 the European countries (that is, the beneficiaries of the Marshall Plan) covered 20 per cent of their imports from abroad by the income from their foreign investments (13 billion dollars at 1938 prices). Three quarters of that income had been lost, and the investments in the Western Hemisphere in particular had been almost entirely liquidated. In the years preceding the war, Europe was able to finance its imports only by transferring to the United States all newly extracted gold (about 500 million dollars in 1938). The purchasing power of gold has fallen by half, because the price of goods has approximately doubled, while that of gold has been stabilized by the American Treasury at thirty-five dollars an ounce. The gold of the Transvaal, the extraction of which had diminished up to the devaluation of September 1949, was no longer entirely at the disposal of Europe, South Africa not having adhered to the dollar pool of the sterling zone. This loss, added to that of the external investments, amounted to about a third of the European imports from abroad.

About two thirds of this loss appears to be definitive. Such is not the case with the losses suffered immediately after the war by "invisible" exports (e.g., freight, insurance), which before 1939 covered 10 per cent of European imports. (Invisible exports totaled 700 million dollars in 1938.) Since 1948, however, shipping has again been remunerative. Norway, Great Britain, and France have reconstituted their merchant fleets, and tourist receipts have reached record levels.

Europe has been divided by the Iron Curtain, but this has not radically arrested trade, though it has modified its composition and reduced its amount. The exports from Eastern Europe (Bulgaria, Czechoslovakia, Finland, Hungary, Poland, Rumania, Yugoslavia) to Western Europe (Austria, Belgium, and Luxemburg, Denmark, France, Germany, Holland, Iceland, Ireland, Italy, Norway, Portugal, Sweden, Switzerland, Great Britain) amounted in 1938 to 747 million dollars, and the exports of the latter to the former to 539 millions. In 1947, the figures dropped to 229 and 226 millions, or 31 and 42 per cent of the prewar figures. Account must also be taken of the trade between the East and West of Germany, internal trade before 1939 (1 billion dollars at 1938 prices), now reduced to practically nothing and become trade between the two worlds.

Before 1939, Germany received from Eastern Europe foodstuffs worth 150 million dollars (at 1938 prices), and raw materials worth about 100 million; she sent there goods, and especially manufactured products, worth 275 millions. In 1948, the reduction of the East-West trade was attributable above all to the virtual disappearance of Germany, to the profit, both as supplier and customer, of the Soviet Union. The substitution of Russia for the Reich seals the defeat of the Germans and the victory of the Slavs. Is it possible to reverse this historic verdict without war?

These figures of the deficit in East-West trade are not large enough to justify ascribing the main responsibility for present difficulties to the partition of the Continent; but the comparison between present and past is an imperfect measure of the economic consequences of the Russian conquest. It would be more to the point to estimate, not the reduction of trade between 1938 and 1948, but the increase possible if the Iron Curtain had not been lowered, or if, by a miracle, it was raised. The political structure established in the East since 1945 hardly allows us to count any longer on substantial surpluses of foodstuffs. Agrarian reform, at least in the short run, does not bring an increase of crops. The plans for industrialization entail a growth of the urban population, and hence larger deliveries from the countryside to the cities and a reduced export surplus.

Considered as a whole, the composition of European trade with the outside world is of a simple, classical type. Western Europe mainly exports manufactured articles (to about 70 per cent in 1938), and mainly imports from overseas food and raw materials (more than 90 per cent of the total). The rest is made up of production goods, in which the United States have a monopoly or an incontestable lead, or finished products of unique quality (these last, in 1938, accounted for 400 million dollars out of a total of 5.6 billions).[1]

[1] We take this figure from the Report on Europe of 1948, p. 69, prepared by the Economic Commission for Europe. This last figure is different from that given by the first preparatory report for the Marshall Plan, which calculated European imports at 6.5 billions. All these statistics are only indications; they fix an order of magnitude.

It follows that the balance of European trade depends not only on the volume of purchases and sales abroad, but on the relation between the prices of the one and the other, in other words, essentially on the relation between the prices of primary and secondary products. Europe does not seem to have been particularly at a disadvantage in this respect between 1937 and 1947.[2] In general the American prices of raw materials and foodstuffs had risen more than the prices of manufactured articles. But one could hardly speak of world prices in the first postwar years, since so large a part was played by deals under bilateral agreements, and by prices arbitrarily fixed by the sellers of scarce products.

So long as inflation was raging in the world, the long-term agreements negotiated by Great Britain, whose external trade represents an important fraction of the total foreign trade of Europe, enabled the rise in prices of imported products to be slowed down and limited. The European countries have been able to sell their manufactures at more than the current price of similar American products, either because of the "seller's market," or in protected markets.

The position of each European country has been modified in consequence of changes in the world around it. The non-convertibility of the pound creates additional difficulties for the Continent. The position of Europe, as a whole, suffers from the repercussions of the troubles in Southeastern Asia and South America resulting from the war. In the days of multilateral trade global equilibrium resulted from numerous surpluses or deficits in balance which ultimately compensated for one another. It is only necessary that one great economic unit or one of the principal zones of world trade shall be affected for the need for readaptation to spread gradually.

Great Britain already had an adverse balance of trade with the United States and Canada (about 600 million dollars) before the war, and a general adverse trade balance not much smaller (440

[2] If we take the year 1937 as a basis, the terms of trade were more favorable to Europe in 1946 and 1947, and about the same in 1948. If we took 1938 as a basis, the terms of trade would have been the same in 1946, but worse in 1947–48. Moreover, the evolution is different according to the country. The terms of trade for Great Britain were from 10 to 20 per cent less favorable in 1947 and 1948 than in 1938; they are slightly more favorable for some European countries. From 1948 to the third quarter of 1949, the terms again improved for Europe.

millions). She covered these deficits with the newly extracted gold that was indirectly at her disposal through her trade surplus with the Dominions, and also, in good years with the sales of raw materials of the sterling zone to the American continent.

On the other hand, when the territories of Southeastern Asia attached to the sterling zone had no surplus with the dollar zone—in 1938, for instance—Western Europe (Great Britain and the Continent) did not cover expenses in the Western Hemisphere with current receipts. A part of the Continent's gold reserves crossed the Atlantic to bury itself in the cellars of Fort Knox.

Finally, to the direct impoverishment of Europe were added the consequences of an evolution produced or hastened by the war. The Asiatic suppliers of raw materials wanted to industrialize themselves as quickly as possible; Europe's customers had learned to do without European goods, either manufacturing them themselves or buying them elsewhere. This situation inevitably raised the questions of whether Europe was capable of conquering or recovering enough markets to pay with exports for her irreducible purchases of food and raw materials.

These questions caused passionate controversies, especially in 1948–49, when the level of prewar production had been regained without the dollar deficit's being made good and thus produced a clash between two extreme conceptions.

According to certain orthodox liberals, it would have sufficed to return to the mechanisms of the market within economic units for an international system to re-establish itself automatically. According to others, the international system of the nineteenth century was due to a factual situation, within the nations and in the trade between them, which was exceptionally favorable to the operation of automatic mechanisms. That situation no longer existed and could not be restored. In an age when the United States was the dominant economy, in which the action of the leaders was limited by the claims of the masses, and in which the so-called underdeveloped countries were ambitious to set up industries of their own, the dream of an automatic equilibrium was an anachronism. Administrations replaced the mechanisms of the market as governmental gifts or loans replaced private investments or bank loans.

Let us follow these two lines of thought, not in order to add anything to the expert discussions, which will be found in specialized literature, but to make clear the historic significance of the European crisis, of which the dollar gap ranks as the typical expression.

Just as men in good health do not take their blood pressure or their temperature, healthy economic systems need not trouble about their trade balance. In the last century none of the great nations of the Old or the New World considered the balance of external payments as a problem to be solved, or balance as such an objective to be reached. Impersonal forces sufficed to maintain or re-establish balance. Economists analyzed with astonishment the anonymous action, willed by none and accomplished by all, thanks to which slight oscillations of prices ensured the harmonious development of international trade. The miracle was not that there was equilibrium, which, by definition, always occurred. It is impossible to buy abroad to a greater value than that of the foreign currency in hand. The miracle was that the equilibrium favored the continued expansion of world trade, the regular supply of raw materials to the industrial countries and of manufactured products to the agricultural countries. The "Republic of Trade," people were fond of saying (not without a tinge of mythology), extends its benefits to all, and injures none.

After the defeat of 1870, France had to pay an indemnity of 5 billion francs to Germany. The French trade balance, formerly adverse, became for several years favorable. Once the indemnity had been paid, the deficit reappeared. The unilateral payments, through the mechanisms so often described, had themselves created the necessary surpluses. Even in 1929–31, when foreign creditors withdrew their capital from Germany, the same mechanism operated. A considerable favorable trade balance succeeded the deficit which had accompanied the previous inflow of capital.

But this last example also indicates the ultimate cost of this miracle. The deflation caused by the withdrawal of external credits did in fact produce additional foreign currency. But it was accompanied by the unemployment of several million workers. The essential uncertainty turns on that point. The dollar gap can always be bridged, and the deficit abolished, by stopping aid and credit. The mechanisms of the market will re-establish balance, without any doubt or exception. But at what level will it settle? What troubles will it entail? These questions the liberals have never answered clearly.

There is hardly any doubt that the policy followed within economic units by the majority of governments between 1945 and 1948 has aggravated the shortage of dollars. The open inflation in France, the easygoing policy of the Dalton period in Great Britain, the rapid liquidation in extravagant and partly unnecessary purchases of the foreign currency accumulated during hostilities by the neutrals (such as the South American countries, and even Sweden), the plans for capital expenditure added to the burdens of reconstruction obviously augmented the need for foreign currencies, and especially for hard currencies. If the object was to dispense with American aid as soon as possible, these inflationary practices are to be condemned with the utmost severity. Most governments employed a technique designed to offset depression in a period when the dangers and the needs were of the opposite character.

In spite of official assertions to the contrary, the object was never to dispense with American aid as soon as possible. The object was to hasten the restoration and modernization of the production plant. Most of the countries accepted inflation, open or repressed, in order to construct buildings, dams, factories, machinery. As long as they obtained the dollars required to bridge the gap in their balance of trade, they cannot be said to have been wrong in preferring internal expansion to external balance. In saying this, we do not mean to justify the policy of inflation, French or British, which had other defects than the widening of the dollar gap. We merely want to emphasize a simple proposition; no more than in the nineteenth century was the objective of the different governments to make international loans unnecessary; nor, immediately after the war, was it the objective of each government, or of those statesmen who were capable of considering the common interest of the free world, to put an end as rapidly as possible to the unilateral transfers of dollars from the United States to Europe. It would be excessively cynical to say that the Europeans' aim in widening their own gap was to obtain an increase in American aid. Let us say only that up to 1948 reduction of their dependence on the Western Hemisphere was not their main concern.

From 1948, when Great Britain approximately balanced her

global trade account, the liberals again blamed economic planning for the continuing dollar shortage. And, once more, it will be seen that the policy followed by the European countries was not that which most favored the increase of receipts and the reduction of dollar expenditures. The sterling zone formed a sort of protected market in which British exporters found selling more attractive and more certain. The internal market and traditional customers absorbed all that the manufacturers could produce: why should they make great efforts to open up, in the United States, uncertain outlets, vulnerable to any change in the economic climate? And further, before September 1949 the rates of exchange tended to lower the prices of imports coming from the dollar zone, to raise those of European exports, and to restrain the competition which European goods might have offered in other markets to goods made in the United States—in other words, to go in a direction contrary to the object theoretically aimed at.

These arguments were scarcely to be refuted when considered abstractly. But they were not sufficient to demonstrate the general thesis that the lack of dollars is artificially created by economic planning, or again, that the re-establishment of a competitive economy, within units and in the relations between units, would automatically restore a balance.

The uncertainty in 1948–49 in regard to balance with the dollar zone as in 1945–47 in regard to the global balance, related not to possibility but to cost. What troubles would have been brought about by an attempt to restore free play to the mechanisms of the market? At what level would the rate of exchange have been established so that receipts and expenditure in dollars by Europe or Great Britain would have compensated for one another spontaneously, without administrative control of foreign trade?

It was legitimate to ask in 1948–49 for the correction of measures that aggravated the dollar shortage. It was legitimate to insist on a struggle against inflation and on the necessity of correcting the exchange rates,[3] of enabling European goods to compete

[3]The devaluation of the pound, to which the British Government resigned itself at the last moment, followed by that of most of the European currencies, started a spectacular improvement in the balance of trade. From the year preceding the devaluation to the following one, we find an improvement of 3.4 billion dollars in Europe's dollar account, a third of which was due to

with American goods in neutral markets, and of urging manufacturers to export to the dollar zone. It was a question of improvement, not reversal, and that policy was dictated, in essentials, by the facts.

Europe's crisis has not been due to governmental policies, however large the part assigned to National Socialisms and internal inflation. The deficit in the trade balance from 1945 to 1948, and the shortage of dollars in 1948–49, were ascribable above all to the changes that had taken place in the European situation and in the structure of world economy. British economic policy enabled imports to be reduced by some 20 per cent in quantity in 1949 and exports to be increased by some 50 per cent. Could the automatism of the market, of money, of prices, and of credit have improved on that record?

Must we attribute to this crisis a profound and lasting significance? Are we to think of Rome waiting for the corn ships, without which the populate could not be fed and calmed? Is not Europe suffering from the loss of her Asiatic empire, which was one of the sources of her wealth? Has the middle class not become incapable of maintaining its ascendancy, since it is no longer in a position to grant the European peoples the advantages formerly derived from the exploitation of colonial peoples?

Observers rightly trace Europe's present difficulties to an evolution that began well before the start of the Second World War. In 1870–80, a third of the world's manufacturers were producing for international trade; in 1913, a fifth; in 1933, a tenth. At the end of the nineteenth century, when the European population represented only a tenth of that of the globe, nearly nine tenths of manufactured goods sent to non-industrialized regions came from Europe. She has now lost her quasi monopoly. For a large number of manufactured articles, she has even lost her position of superiority.

It has been suggested that there is a secular movement of prices,

---

changes taking place in the trade balance. Great Britain's holding of dollars had diminished by 437 millions in 1948–49; it increased by 1.416 billions in 1949–50. Even if other causes were at work, it is clear that devaluation was not entirely ineffective.

unfavorable to the exporter of manufactured goods. Technical progress being more rapid in the manufacturing industries, an increasing number of manufactured articles is needed to pay for a constant quantity of food or raw materials.

Neglecting the oscillations in the terms of trade, ascribable to the alternate rise and fall of prices, and admitting that, full employment being assured throughout the world, there will not be a temporary collapse of raw material prices, we must sell more and more bicycles to buy a ton of corn or rubber. But if we calculate in terms of work hours, the relationship does not necesarily become more favorable to the exporters of raw materials. The drop in the unitary price of the bicycle translates the drop in the number of work hours incorporated into each machine.

As industrial development proceeds, new manufactured articles of growing complexity are perfected. Europe will not be able to finance her purchases of food and raw materials by selling, in quantities increased in proportion to technical progress, the same things she sold a half century ago. But why should she not finance them by the sale of production goods or manufactured articles of growing complexity and price? There seems no reason why Europe should not continue for many years to possess some superiority over countries industrially less experienced, in dealing with goods that need accumulated capital and exceptional knowledge.

The comparison with Rome, waiting for the corn ships or living on the exploitation of the provinces, is only partially valid. It is true that weak bourgeois governments tremble before the masses as soon as they can no longer guarantee the accustomed standard of living. But the standard is not mainly due to colonial exploitation, as some would have us believe.

In the two last centuries Holland drew considerable advantages from Indonesia, and Great Britain from India and Southeastern Asia. The sale of the raw materials from these regions left Dutch and British companies with foreign currency and profits, partly invested in the homeland and not in the colonies (equipping the former at the expense of the latter). Often the industrialization of the colonies was prevented or hindered in order to guarantee markets to the home industries. Certain European enterprises took advantage of the low wage levels in the colonies to set up factories there and accumulate additional profits; these, too, were spent on luxuries or repatriated rather than invested on the spot.

It would be absurd to deny that in the two last centuries Europe sometimes "exploited" the rest of the world. But, without entering upon doubtful calculations, or enumerating the benefits conferred in exchange, voluntarily or involuntarily, we must refuse, on the economic plane, to admit that capitalism raises the condition of certain workers only by worsening that of others. The example of the United States is conclusive: a market economy has no more intrinsic need to exploit some to favor others than a planned economy has, and each system offers opportunities of so doing. If capital accumulates and the productivity of labor progresses, all the proletarians profit, or can profit, from the economic gain.

The liberation of Southeastern Asia deprives Europe of protected markets, and of the currencies she automatically drew from the sale of raw materials. But let her supply manufactured articles to her former colonies, while they sell their raw materials to the dollar zone, and Europe will obtain from triangular trade the currencies she wants. Industrialization or improved methods of agriculture in Southeastern Asia would ultimately be more useful to Europe than the ancient and primitive forms of exploitation. Modern economy, in the long view, invites mutual enrichment by sharing economic progress.

There remain two obvious objections. Whence will come the capital for the industrialization of the so-called underdeveloped countries? And why should they spend in Europe the foreign currencies acquired by the sale of their raw materials? Indeed, nothing proves that things automatically arrange themselves in the best way. The automatisms guarantee balance, but not a balance with an expanding volume of trade. The corrections of exchange rate, necessary in order that European products shall be cheaper than American products in neutral markets, may conceivably prove painful. The colonial territories and the liberated countries are asking for European capital now that non-Europeans no longer resign themselves to poverty.

The crisis is therefore attributable to the historic process and not to a particular method of regulation. Europe lacks capital, both for herself and for the territories for which she is directly or indirectly responsible. The old mechanisms of individual saving no longer work, in consequence of social reforms, of the tendency to equalization of incomes, and of financial disasters. Houses must be built, factories modernized, and, at the same time, the agricultural appliances of the Dominions and colonies must be improved, so that the millions of extra mouths to be fed in India or in North Africa do not aggravate an ancestral poverty. Individuals save less because they do not believe in the future and because taxation eats seriously into large incomes. The state must now impose collective saving.

It would be wrong to believe this crisis insoluble. Since the end of the war, the sums put at the disposal of Europe by the United States have enabled her to lend and to repay wartime debts to overseas territories and to invest capital there. Between January 1, 1947, and July 1, 1949, Great Britain invested abroad 468 million pounds and repaid 467 million in sterling balances. Up to July 1, 1949, she received 335 million pounds under the Marshall Plan.[4] What has been done semi-consciously could be done deliberately.

We may distinguish at present within the non-Soviet world three zones: the rich countries (the United States and Canada); the countries of Europe, impoverished by the war; and the countries whose methods of cultivation are primitive and whose living standard is deteriorating.

There is no need for a complex theory to make it clear that Europe will more easily find the hard currencies she needs by helping to build up the underdeveloped territories than by direct export to countries with a first-class industry. It would be absurd to insist that Europe cannot live without a certain quantity of dollars, or that the world could not do without American credits or material aid. But by putting at the disposal of Europe, Asia, or Africa 1 to 3 billion dollars, in addition to the sums spent in the purchase of goods or services, the United States will facilitate an expansion of international trade, the restoration of European economies, and the equipment of overseas territories.[5]

[4]During the same period the reserves of gold diminished by 206 million pounds.

[5]This figure is trifling when we compare it with that of the military budgets (more than 50 billion dollars in 1951–52), or with that of a possible total war.

An economic system is always the result, not of scientific theories, but of facts and especially facts outside the economic sphere. The market economy, a longing for which persists, was neither the creation of the experts who analyzed its mechanisms, nor of the leaders who respected its subtle workings.

In the last century, the gold standard created a solidarity between the different national units. Currency and credit were tied to the movements of stocks of the metal. Usually—at least for the principal countries—limited oscillations of the rate of interest, of the quantities of money, or of global activity sufficed to re-establish the balance. It was the violence of the fluctuations caused by the wars and the great depression that provoked administrative regulation. It was the resistance of the workers and of the trade unions to the movements of deflation, and the social disturbances resulting from those movements, that gave rise to the technique of National Socialism. From that time, experts and public have tended to blame a country that balances its trade account at the cost of some unemployment, rather than one that allows a limited inflation with a view to full employment. The crime now is deflation and not the appeal for foreign help. The economists' report to the United Nations on national and international full employment recommends that the United States shall never reduce the amount of dollars placed at the disposal of the rest of the world below the quantity corresponding to the amount of visible and invisible imports regarded as normal.[6]

The international system results not only from the method followed within units, but from the relations between them. A century ago, circumstances were much more favorable than now to the operation of an international economy. The dominant unit was Great Britain, which presented three characteristics favorable to her assumption of this role: acceptance of free trade, the need to buy abroad an important part of her food and raw materials, and a liking for foreign investments. If the United States were ready to abolish all their customs duties and to place abroad an annual

[6]Hence, if, as a result of depression, the United States, in a certain year, substantially reduced their purchases from abroad, they would have to provide, in the form of loans, the difference between their reduced and their usual disbursements.

sum similar to the annual loans of Europe before 1914, this would probably be sufficient to make the dollar deficit disappear of its own accord, without the employment of administrative measures and without serious troubles.

Great Britain never occupied a position in the world similar to that of the United States today. In 1870, she possessed 31.8 per cent of the industrial capacity of the world, but the United States possessed 23.5 per cent, Germany 13.2 per cent, France 10.3 per cent. In 1926–29, the United States possessed 42.2 per cent, Great Britain 9.4 per cent, Germany 11.6 per cent. In 1936, the United States possessed 32.2 per cent, against 18.5 per cent belonging to Russia. In 1948, the value of industrial products in billions of dollars, at 1938 prices, rose to 36.551 in the United States, against 26.317 for *the whole of Europe,* the U.S.S.R. excepted.

The American economy, as has been said a hundred times, is less well adapted than England's to function as a dominant economy because of its double character: it continues to export raw materials, such as cotton, cereals, and hydrocarbons, although it possesses the leading industry in the world. The value of American imports, as a percentage of the national income, has steadily fallen from 4.5 per cent in 1929 to 2.4 per cent in 1946–47. A fraction of these imports is marginal and extremely sensitive to variations in market prices, so that a fall in activity is reflected in a more than proportional drop in imports.

It will be objected that the discrepancy between the desired purchases and those which can be paid for is constant, and that in the nineteenth century too the world would have liked to buy more in Great Britain than it was able to. Strictly speaking, this discrepancy always exists, but it takes various concrete forms. When millions of people in India are dying of starvation, and certain stocks of food products are being destroyed in the United States, the formula of insufficient dollars at the disposal of underdeveloped countries assumes incontestable human significance.

But, it will be asked, does not that very example suggest that the United States has as much need to give as the rest of the world has to receive? Is not the dollar shortage essentially the counterpart of an American surplus? The moment the Marshall Plan was launched, the Communists, and even some independent economists, set out to show or to suggest that the American economy had as much need of an excess of exports as the European or world economy had of an excess of imports.

This theory of the inevitable surplus, like that of certain doctrinaire Marxists in connection with imperialism, involves an immediate and obvious difficulty. How is this surplus placed? If it is exchanged it does not diminish the surplus of production to demand. Nor, if it is given abroad, but financed by taxation, does it reduce an ultimate global excess of supply. If the material aid is not financed by taxation, but by a budgetary deficit, we have an inflationary procedure which does not imply the transfer of the goods to another economic unit.[7] On the other hand, partial surpluses in certain markets are an easily identifiable fact. For instance, the American administration has maintained the prices of certain agricultural products at the level dictated by the principle of parity of prices.[8] To the extent to which the American leaders try to minimize the displacements and regroupings of the means of production that would be involved in the free play of the market, the purchase by the administration and the gift to the Allies of certain agricultural surpluses are, in fact, one of the most attractive solutions, combining political expediency (support of the European countries) with economic utility (use of stocks which would in any case have been accumulated by the policy of price maintenance). In 1949–50, certain stocks of agricultural products could no longer be sold: the countries that needed them most lacked the currency, and the funds voted by Congress for the various aid programs were exhausted.

When the American Government launched the Marshall Plan, there was no global surplus of supply over demand and there were hardly any partial surpluses in particular markets. With a few rare exceptions, the goods which the European countries obtained under the Marshall Plan were selected by those countries according to their own needs, and not by the donor according to his surpluses.

[7]For example, if the state buys the agricultural surpluses, without giving itself corresponding receipts, it can destroy the cereals or the potatoes instead of giving them. Economically, the result is the same.

[8]By so doing it has increased the deficits of the European countries through making them buy cereals or cotton at artificially high prices.

In any case, from the moment the American taxpayer settles the bill for the purchase of a portion of the American production, the Government has the choice of those to whom it will send the goods bought with the taxpayer's money. If we suppose that the United States have as much need to give as the other countries to receive, the position of the latter is less easy than that of the former. The donor fixes the amount and the destination of his aid, while the beneficiaries must cultivate the good will of Santa Claus.

Taking as the basis of its estimates the volume of European imports from the dollar zone regarded as indispensable and the volume of American imports from Europe regarded as probable, the second interim report of O.E.E.C. came to the conclusion (in 1950) that there would be a deficit at the end of the four years of the Marshall Plan (in the middle of 1952).

These forecasts seemed in the second six months of 1950 and the first of 1951 likely to prove inaccurate, but the exceptional events that followed the opening of the Korean campaign finally confirmed the experts' conclusions. For some months Great Britain was able to forgo Marshall aid and the sterling zone was able to double its reserves of gold and foreign exchange, because the American economy, under the impact of rearmament, had a movement of inflation, strategic purchases sending up the price of raw materials to an abnormal level, especially the three materials to which the sterling zone owes a large part of its dollar receipts (i.e., tin, rubber, wool). When the American purchases slowed down and prices fell back in the world markets, and when rearmament got into its stride in the European countries, the deficits reappeared. Not only deficits, but the dizzy spiral of international prices at the end of 1950 started inflationary troubles in the sterling zone, and these troubles in turn disrupted the balance of accounts. The euphoria of 1950 was paid for by the sterling crisis of 1951–52.

These changed fortunes, which everything indicates may continue for years to come, illustrate the fundamental data we have been analyzing in the previous pages. In view of its importance in the world economy, the American economy exercises an even greater influence over the fate of the other economic systems than the British exercised in the last century. Even a slight depression in the

United States, if it entailed a reduction of imports by a quarter or a third, would impose rigorous and painful adaptations on the other nations, particularly in Europe. Even in a period of full employment the American economy, in the absence of a liberal customs policy and because of its very structure, does not furnish by its purchases of goods or services, apart from governmental loans or gifts, enough dollars to enable the world to buy at the same time the fraction of certain crops, such as tobacco, cereals, and cotton, which the United States would like to sell, and certain raw materials and machines that Europe and Asia would find it difficult to procure elsewhere.

On the other hand, the policy of full employment as applied by the European governments makes for a continual inflationary tendency and consequently for a deficit in the balance of accounts, at a time when the loss of foreign investments and the extension of the Soviet zone, which is half closed against free exchange, add to the difficulty of re-establishing a balance. Even if, by its size, wealth, and productivity, the United States did not dominate the European countries, they would find it difficult to meet popular needs and also to sell enough abroad to finance their necessary imports. Obviously the demands of rearmament aggravate the crisis.

These fundamental facts seem permanent. They will produce within the Atlantic community more or less violent tensions in proportion to economic fluctuations. They will prevent the reconstitution of a liberal system of currency and trade, except in the unlikely event of the United States' embarking on sensational new moves, such as decisive modifications of their tariff practices, or long-term projects of loans to the underdeveloped countries or of orders for European industry. But while we must expect crises and mutual recriminations, it would be a mistake to live in constant apprehension of disaster. Now that the European machinery of production has been restored, the amounts of dollars which the United States will have to place at the disposal of Europe to avert upheavals will not be beyond the generosity of Congress or the ingenuity of statesmen. And there are all sorts of ways of making this assistance available—through private loans, governmental loans, orders for European industry, and triangular trade with the underdeveloped countries in receipt of dollars under Point Four.

The Atlantic community will remain precarious economically, owing to the disproportion between the resources of the Old and the New World. This precariousness could be surmounted only by exceptional measures, either in Europe or in the United States. This precariousness will endanger the Atlantic community only under two sets of circumstances—either such an extension of the Soviet zone as would deprive the West of indispensable suppliers and customers, or a profound and lasting American depression.

The hopes of the liberals of seeing a new world system of convertible currencies and of free trade do not seem any nearer realization than the hopes of the Stalinists of a sudden collapse of the American and the world economic system.

## Chapter XVI

# CAN EUROPE UNITE?

SURELY, we have no alternative but to support European unity. Consider the nations, surrounded by tariff barriers, prisoners of their recent quarrels, inconsolable because of their vanished greatness, brooding bitterly over their losses, boasting of their culture and their past, finding a morose pride in their decadence. Why should they not unite to marshal their energies and their talents against the future?

Three principal arguments—military, economic, and moral—support the thesis of European unity, which authors and journalists have been defending and illustrating ever since the war.

The techniques of combat determine at every period in history the dimensions of the political units. The cost of combat material has now increased so greatly that a country of 40 millions can no longer afford to pay for a complete panoply. Fifty years ago the armed forces of a small country reproduced on a microscopic scale those of a large country. Belgium had, or could have had, a little of everything that France had. Today, nothing of the sort is possible. France cannot provide herself with military equipment comparable to America's, even on a smaller scale; she must build up something qualitatively different. A coalition now results in the integration, not the juxtaposition, of national armies.

From an economic point of view, the argument seems equally convincing; the size of the market conditions, the volume of production, and the latter partly decides the net cost. A market of 40 million people forms an insufficient basis for a great industry; it hampers the growth of productivity and, therefore, of the popular standard of living. Free trade would lessen the inconveniences of national boundaries. But experience of half a century has abundantly proved that political frontiers inevitably acquire economic significance. The ultimate return of free trade is more improbable than the creation of great political aggregations.

Six years ago, the European idea was regarded as discredited as the result of Hitler's misuse of it. Today everyone subscribes to it from the non-Communist extreme left to the right. Through the ages the Europeans have dreamed dimly of union, less from love of "Europe" (which is only an abstraction) than from the memory of the Roman Empire, from consciousness of a common Christianity, or from a vague sense of a common civilization. In spite of the incessant fighting, which never prevented intellectual intercourse, a civilization was produced that made Europeans for a time the teachers and rulers of the world. Impoverished and impotent, they look to the future for promise of a higher community. Their weakness and the ruins around them are not the sole cause, perhaps not even the principal one, of European defeatism. The outlook seems gloomy on all sides. Conflicts, once fruitful, have reached such a pitch that immobility or rupture sometimes seems the only issue. To the rivalry of values, classes, elites, the West has owed the good things of which it is justly proud: freedom to create, personal freedom, freedom of thought, and civil liberties. This dialectic threatens to end in paralysis.

Would not unity be a means of surmounting these conflicts by transferring them to a higher plane? Within a wider field, would not liberals and advocates of economic planning, conservatives and socialists, defenders of Parliament and reformers of semi-authoritarian inspiration be able to join their efforts, instead of mutually inhibiting each other's desire to act?

Modern arms, because of their costliness, are inaccessible to small and medium-sized states. American strategic bombers, such as the B-36, cost between 1 and 2 billion francs apiece.[1] The whole of the French military budget for 1949 would have been absorbed by 300 of these machines. A tank of medium tonnage costs from 30 to 50 millions, a radar set for an airfield 15 millions, and one set

[1] At the value of the 1950 franc: 350 francs to the dollar.

for anti-aircraft defense 25 millions. The complexity of equipment has so increased that the same weapon costs five to ten times as many work hours as it did at the end of the former war. A fighter plane required 10,000 work hours in 1940; it needed 50,000 in 1950. Its hourly consumption of petrol has risen from 20 to 1,000 liters. It is reckoned that the equipment of an armored division amounts to 300 million dollars, and that of a motorized division to 150 millions.

Such figures prove that certain weapons—strategic aircraft, atomic bombs—are beyond the industrial and financial resources of a second-class nation. The cost not only of manufacture but of research has become such that the choice must be made from the scientific stage. The multiplication of prototypes, following the Liberation, necessary to enable France to provide herself with an air force including everything from training machines to heavy bombers, was ruinous. From 1944 to 1949 dispersion vitiated not only aeronautical studies and production but the whole armament program. Could united Europe possess a complete panoply, provide radio-guided projectiles, strategic bombers, and atomic bombs? Theoretically, it was possible. But this possibility, in order to become reality, would have quickly led to political, moral, and economic upheavals. Is it conceivable that France, Germany, and Italy should succeed in a few years in unifying their laboratories, their military staffs, and their armies? Apart from the unlikelihood of total fusion, the French will naturally be more likely to ask, in scientific and technical matters, for co-operation with the British, and especially the Americans, than with their recent enemies. As long as the latter are disarmed, the other European nations west of the Iron Curtain, far from adding up to a great power, represent a sum total of weakness.

The difficulty that the European countries find at present in organizing and equipping armies worthy of the name is not due solely to the small dimensions of the political units. Both France and Germany had to start from scratch. In 1939 France had armed, but imperfectly, about a hundred divisions. If we assume that the cost of weapons has, on the average, been multiplied by three or four, then some thirty divisions would represent an equivalent effort at the present time. Spread over a number of years, that effort would not be beyond reach. Concentrated into two or three years when the arsenals are empty, it obviously requires outside help.

Every country's military capacity is a composite of several factors: the elasticity and output of the industrial equipment, the public's consent to the reduction of their living standard, the cost of production of weapons in hours of work and in cash, and so on. From all these points of view, the European countries are in a bad position, France particularly so. Russian weapons are in general less costly, not because of any superior organization or productivity, but because they are less complex. The Russians do not increase the complexity and the price of a bomber or a fighter for the sole purpose of providing their men with greater safety.

The Russians certainly have no equivalent to the B-36 or the B-52, but it is not necessary to construct these flying laboratories in order to carry on (or even win) wars. The French, influenced by the Anglo-Saxons, want equipment in no way inferior to that of any other nation. But their industrial development is not comparable with that of the United States, whose superior output meets the demands of its users. Since the first war France's industrial potential has increased less rapidly than the French desire for comfort; and the margin of production capable of being mobilized in time of peace for national defense by a democratic government is narrower than in countries like Russia, whose population is accustomed to a low standard of living, or the United States, whose economic system can carry out an immense armament program without serious privations for the civil population.

Europeans are afraid of the Russians and need the Americans. They dream of uniting, partly in order to raise an insurmountable barrier against the onrush of the barbarians and partly to recover the independence they have lost in their relations with both Russia and America.

The propagandists of the European Movement demonstrate by statistics that the countries west of the Iron Curtain together possess an industrial potential superior to that of the Soviet Union. If we include Great Britain in Western Europe, the combined steel production of Germany-Benelux-France-Britain (over 45 million tons in 1950) is greater than that of the Soviet coalition. But these truths might easily become illusory. The economic structure of Western Europe would remain, in all that matters, different in nature from that of the two real giants. Europe lacks an important part of her food and raw materials, such as cereals, sugar, meat, cotton, wool, petrol, non-ferrous metals. The different countries of Europe are buyers of the same products, and cannot render each other equivalent services by pooling their resources.

The Russian and American systems owe their strength not only to their size or to the amount of coal extracted but also to the fact that both of them are only slightly tributary to the outside world. The United States, it is true, imports a growing proportion of their raw materials as their own reserves become exhausted. The Soviet Union would have difficulty in doing without the wool, rubber, tin, and certain other metals which it buys in world markets. But the dependence of the American and Russian economies is in no way comparable with that of the European economy. At the end of the nineteenth century, Western Europe was the workshop of the world. Could the present decline be arrested by eliminating the frontiers?

With or without war, Western Europe would not have escaped relative decadence. By publicizing scientific knowledge and manufacturing processes, she gave her customers the means of doing without her. The two wars of the twentieth century accelerated the movement. The United States, which took a decisive part in the hostilities without suffering from them, obtained an increased lead in output. Goods "Made in U.S.A." have replaced those "Made in Germany" or "Made in Great Britain." New industries have started up all over the world, so that there is less need for the products of European industry; or, rather, there is no longer need for the same products. Means of production are in demand, machines and plants, rather than manufactured articles of relatively simple construction. How would free trade throughout Europe help her to adapt herself to these new conditions? All the beneficiaries of the Marshall Plan are short of dollars. Adding deficits together is no way to produce a surplus.

It is repeated on all sides that the enlargement of the units would permit a rapid improvement in output. If we admit this point of view, then unification becomes desirable in itself. What the consequences would be concerning the balance of payments is less evident. The level of production alone does not settle the possibilities of export. If wages rise with production, there remains no premium on export. Taking a long view, the balance of trade between Europe and the Western Hemisphere would be better if the differences in productivity were less accentuated. Even more important than the actual level would be an increase in European productivity compared with American. In fact, if the American lead steadily increased, the Continent would be perpetually doomed to devaluations or deflations. But the unification of Europe would only help to accelerate economic progress to the extent to which the European countries accepted methods favorable to one or the other of these things. The very circumstances, however, that hinder progress raise obstacles in the path of unification.

For years, thousands of pages have been written on this subject, without materially modifying the data of the problem, which are simple in theory and extraordinarily complex in practice. Fundamentally, two types of policy are envisaged, one inspired by liberalism and the other by planning.

Before 1914, the different countries of Europe did not form a unit, but they were largely integrated. Customs duties were moderate, and a certain amount of industrial specialization had come about of its own accord. In proportion as they became industrialized, the countries of Europe became better customers for each other, not worse. The increase of wealth opened new outlets.

The First World War, and still more the crisis of the thirties, forced the European countries into the system of controlled trade. Nearly all of them jealously protected their economy, and, with the twofold object of providing work for their unemployed and reducing imports, favored the development of the industries they had lacked. When the Second World War ended, National Socialisms and inflation further accentuated the disintegration of the European system.

Inspired by a simple idea and by its own example, the United States, not unreasonably, pressed for freedom of trade. The reestablishment of inter-European trade, regarded as normal (whatever risk there is in confusing normality with a situation irrevocably past), required in the first place a healthy state of the national economic systems, and therefore the liquidation of inflation, whether open or disguised, and the establishment of real rates of exchange (and these, in turn, were possible only when domestic prices had been more or less stabilized at a level corresponding to the incomes distributed and to the quantity of money). In 1949, open inflation was killed in France and Italy, repressed inflation further reduced in Great Britain, Holland, and Norway—in short, inter-European trade, in spite of everything, automatically recovered a volume equal to or above that of the thirties. A certain measure of European integration was thus achieved. The next stage, envisaged by those directing the Marshall Plan, required the extension of the list of freed articles, that is, of articles for which quotas had been abolished. At the same time, the agreement on inter-European payments produced a partial equivalent of monetary convertibility, and made possible multilateral compensation.

Meritorious as these results are, the question arises whether liberal integration could have been carried to the point at which it would have become an important factor in long-term economic progress. The intensification of inter-European trade, desirable in itself, was mainly considered as a means. International competition was to keep down prices, incite producers to reduce their profit margins, and compel the closing down or reorganization of undertakings with an excessive cost of production. The freeing of exchange on the lines adopted up to 1952 will hardly have those results.

Each country drew up its list of freed articles in such a way that domestic producers were not seriously threatened. Tariffs, often high, were substituted for quotas. The former were rightly regarded as less harmful than the latter, but if they reach a certain level they soften the impact of foreign competition. The freeing of trade and the unification of payments at the end of 1950 were still far from having brought Europe back to the pre-1914 integration; such a goal could not be hoped for, even in the course of several years, such was the ingenuity shown by administrators in their choice of freed articles and in manipulating customs duties or purchase taxes.

All governments vied with one another in the liberal fervor of their words, but apart from Switzerland, Belgium, and Western Germany, they did not practice what they preached. Fair competition presupposes certain conditions not yet existent. Objections are raised against the practice of having two sets of prices, the inequality of the social services, direct or indirect subsidies, the discrepancy between the prices paid by industrial consumers in the different countries for coal and steel. All, or nearly all, of these protests have some basis. It is difficult to allow free play to competition between countries when government interference influences most prices. We can no longer use competition to measure the comparative efficiency of firms or of industrial sectors when competitors cease to work under similar conditions. On the other hand, inequalities of wages and of social services are in no way abnormal. Theoretically it would seem that, on the whole, wages in a given economic unit are proportional to the mean productivity within the unit (regardless of the division of wages into direct payments and "social services"). Industrial sectors whose productivity is above the unit average ought to be favored on the international plane, and those with inferior productivity discouraged. But there is no evidence to suggest that, at least for certain fundamental sectors, individual governments are prepared to submit themselves to the verdict of a free market.

In other words, the liberalism is confronted by a double series of obstacles. The first arises from the interference of the national administration in the details of economic life, resulting in the artificial character of the relations between prices (both within each nation and between nations). The second comes from the refusal, unexpressed but deep-seated, to allow free play to competition, even if fair, to an extent that would involve important alterations in the structure of the industrial organization. Italy, with resources of neither coal nor iron, will not sacrifice the 3 million tons of steel that her works produce.

By a logical reaction, the other method, theoretically possible, came under consideration: what has been called co-ordination of investment—a method that in its ideal form would be elevated into a sort of international planning. But its failure has been still more rapid and striking. The extent of domestic planning in the different European countries is very unequal, varying between the maximum of Great Britain and Sweden and the minimum of Belgium and Switzerland. But even where the maximum has been reached, it does not go as far as to foresee the expansion, six months ahead, of the various industrial sectors. To plan the European whole, starting from incompletely planned economic systems, surpasses the intellectual and administrative resources of the most learned experts. They cannot determine, several years in advance, the outlets open to the steel trade as long as oscillations of the market and political crises cannot be exactly foreseen. For that matter, supposing that these limited forecasts for basic sectors were reliable within a sufficient degree of probability, no one would have the necessary authority to dictate the revision of domestic plans. Either the "coordination of investments" is a meaningless expression, or it must imply a supranational authority, with power of decision. That power does not exist, and none of the governments with planning tendencies whether in Scandinavia or Holland or Britain would agree to submit to it.

It is easy to see why. Domestic planning, even partial, gives those who control the state considerable powers, which are exercised in favor of some social group or some branch of industry. While political democracy exists, these powers are exercised according to the implicit rule of compromise, and no group feels that its vital interests are threatened. But if a supranational authority had to carry out similar functions, it would have to be armed with planning powers like those belonging to the national administration. The dangers are inevitably too great for governments to contemplate lightly such a transfer; for no one knows how compromises on the level of the higher power would work out.

In other words, Europe as a whole cannot carry out economic planning as long as the various units are only partially planned and every government regards the national interest as the ultimate criterion of its action. Competition cannot be given free play between the economic units as long as each government strives to protect the majority of producers from the dangers of competition. Shall we conclude that the method of European integration must be a mixed one, like the domestic regimes of each nation? Or that European integration is impossible because mixed forms of government are essentially conservative and exclude liberal mobility as well as the mobility of planning?

The former conclusion has evidently been enthusiastically adopted by the politicians and propagandists. Private and public assemblies have always agreed on one of those formulas of conciliation dear to political parties, for example, the co-ordination of key sectors and the freeing of trade for manufacturing industries—a transposition of the classical formula of a controlled sector and a free sector. Good or bad, the juxtaposition of the two sectors is possible, for such is today the structure of the British and French economies. The same juxtaposition on the European scale would be equally possible in theory. But up to now the governments have never accepted the implications of either method, even within a limited domain. They have certainly compared programs of capital investment, and the experts in each branch have been better acquainted with the plans of their competitors—an exchange of information more fruitful in some respects than might be imagined, but far from representing the single market, the free circulation of goods, capital, and persons, or the single plan for Europe dreamed of by those who hope to set Europe in the place of the old mother countries.

More interesting is the attempt to apply a mixed method within a chosen sector (as with the Schuman Plan). Might not an elastic control be adopted in order to create the conditions in which government, professional associations, and Parliament would agree to experiment with a free market? This seems to have been the idea that inspired the Schuman Plan for a European pool for coal and steel. The initial document, in fact, explicitly assigns as the purpose the free circulation of coal and steel products, and contemplates the co-ordination of capital expenditure. The High Authority would endeavor to maintain by its intervention the conditions of fair competition, and, at the same time, fulfill certain functions of a planning agency, in time of either plenty or shortage.

It remains to be seen to what extent the object can be attained. There is no need for a new international bureaucracy in order simply to abolish double prices. But much more than a bureaucracy would be needed to suppress the natural advantages enjoyed by some producers—richness of mines or proximity of coal to blast furnaces. Normally Ruhr coal will cost less than that of the Pas-de-Calais,[2] and those steel works which have to pay less for transport of iron ore and coal will produce more cheaply.

It does not follow that the free circulation of steel products is definitely impossible. The differences in net cost may be made up by the increased transportation charges which the French user would have to pay if he ordered the goods outside the country. The most favored undertakings do not have a potential so extensible that they would be able to increase their production substantially in a short time. The fact remains that the free circulation of products would not entail a uniform price for coal or steel on the spot where they are used. In the case of the planning of investments, exclusive consideration of natural advantages would endanger the political equilibrium between the national economic systems.

Under the direction of national representatives or of independent technicians, the High Authority is likely to be less conservative than the cartels of the past. In time it will perhaps permit a rational reorganization of European heavy industries, and ultimately the free circulation of the products and competition between the undertakings. It would be illusory to believe that a supranational institution is all that is needed to surmount the obstacles that impede present European efforts. The High Authority will perhaps have a certain power of decision, and we may suppose that it will close some substandard mines in France or Belgium. But in the end it too will have to take account of industrial realities as they have developed spontaneously. Between the dreams of total rationalization, fear of cartels, national rivalries, and conflict of interests, it is bound to be an organism of conciliation and compromise. Only experience can show whether semi-control leads in time to a free market or whether, on the contrary, it favors the crystallization of existing structure.

It is improbable, but not out of the question, that the European countries will suddenly agree to surrender a fraction of their sovereignty in favor of a superstate. But this institutional revolution, however spectacular, would not be sufficient to create European

---

[2]Unless wages in the Ruhr are higher than those in the Pas-de-Calais, or more precisely, unless the differences between the wages are equal to or higher than the differences between the productivities.

unity. By what miracle would a superstate be endowed with powers which all the European nations refuse to their own rulers? There are complaints that no European executive exists which is capable of imposing the reorganization of particular industrial sectors. But individual governments are not capable of carrying out such tasks within their own countries. In France the closing of a mine that is running at a loss usually causes a strike lasting a few days or weeks. Trade unions and their members hold that every workman has a right not only to a job—which is a reasonable claim—but also to a job of a certain sort and in a certain place. The claim is humanly understandable, but it limits the mobility of labor, and, consequently, the range of action open to a national or supranational power.

Revived political democracy and the mixed economic regime both have the same dominant characteristics—strength of braking power and weakness of engine power. It is hopeless to imagine that the federal superstate would be driven by a more powerful engine and be less hampered by brakes than the present national states.

Of the two ideologies—European unity and the Atlantic community—between which Western opinion hesitates, it is the latter that we must choose, if a choice must be made. Even united, Europe would be lost if the United States, because of discouragement, yielded to the temptation of isolationism. Europe, even divided, still has a chance of safety so long as the national states remain integrated in an Atlantic community, however imperfect. For that matter, a glance at the map is enough to show why one idea is true and the other false, or, if one prefers, why one idea has a meaning in present circumstances and the other has none.

Ought we to go further and abandon entirely the pursuit of European unity? The anachronism of national states and the harm done by customs barriers are undeniable; but is Europe the supranational unit into which the national states ought to merge? Let us overlook the transitory caprices of diplomacy, which make Turkey, but not Spain, a part of the Strasbourg Europe. The Scandinavian countries on the one hand and the Mediterranean countries on the other belong to distinct complexes, and it is difficult to see why they should submit to a "European power" seated in Paris, Strasbourg, or Frankfort. Through her merchant fleet, Norway is much more integrated with the world economy and with the Atlantic zone than with the countries of continental Europe. The name Europe distinguishes a continent or a civilization, not an economic or political unit.

The argument in favor of a European federation is still more doubtful when we consider the position of Great Britain. It has been repeated hundreds of times during the past few years, but these trite sayings are true: The Government and the people of the United Kingdom generally have the feeling of being Britons in the first place, and Europeans afterwards (if the word even means anything to them). The Labour Party manifesto that mentioned this precedence of loyalties was attacked by the insincere, but it stated the simple truth. An Englishman is conscious of relationship in blood, culture, and destiny with an Australian or a Canadian, and even with an American, much more than with an Italian, a German, or even a Frenchman.

Great Britain has fully shared, in turn giving and receiving, in the intellectual movements that have marked the history of Europe. Intellectually and morally England is European. Politically and economically, reservations must be made. For centuries, allied to one nation or another, she has had no other object than to prevent the hegemony of a Continental power, and *a fortiori* the unity of the Continent. She needed a prosperous Europe, but the fortune of Britain depended much more on the relations into which she had entered all over the globe with all races and all peoples. The Europe of the Marshall Plan accounts for about a third of the foreign trade of the United Kingdom. In what way, British economists persistently ask, would European unity solve our problems or diminish our difficulties? We have not succeeded in getting enough dollars to pay for what we should like to buy in the Western Hemisphere; inter-European free trade would divert to countries with a soft currency commodities that would otherwise be sold for hard currency. To ask Great Britain to make herself an integral part of an area, political or economic, called Europe, is to ask her to renounce her historic functions as an intermediary between the Continent and the rest of the world, the metropolis of a federation

ns, the center of a subtle network of relations that are
and commercial as well as moral. A symptom of this dis-
that no customs tariff would at the same time suit the countries or the Continent, which largely feed themselves, and the
United Kingdom, which imports 60 per cent of its food.

If one is to think along these lines, the very idea of a great area,
or at least the application of the idea to "little Europe," must again
be questioned. The regional organization of economic life is a reply,
from the theoretical point of view, to the collapse of the world.
Such regional organization is inspired by the philosophy of planning. The would-be planners no longer want to take a nation but
a zone as the framework of rationalization. Europe has been
chosen as the zone, without preliminary study, for political and
moral reasons. European unity is not excluded by natural factors
(nor is it imposed by them). But its realization at an early date does
not present any considerable advantages over those of the national
units. Great Britain in particular does not seem to be in a position
to derive substantial benefits from it.

European free trade (which is equivalent to a sort of reciprocal
preference between the countries of Europe) brings only a limited
contribution to the restoration of European economic life. Europe
needs to sell to the rest of the world because she is obliged to buy
raw materials and food from other countries. It is only in the long
run that European integration would bring reduced imports or
increased exports. Even apart from political obstacles, the different
countries are too unlike in structure to be able to agree within a
few years to a real fusion. As long as the European zone does not
permit a unified apparatus of production, European preference
(monetary convertibility and suppression of quotas for inter-
European trade) remains of real but secondary importance.

What is there that is essential in the European idea, as propagated in recent years? To my mind, it is a simple and almost
obvious proposition, which Mr. Churchill grasped immediately
and which propagandists and intellectuals have since obscured,
namely, that Western Europe must build up its military strength,
and that strength can only emerge from a reconciliation between
France and Germany.

At the same time, the fundamental components of European unity can be discerned. Neither the presence of the Scandinavian countries, nor that of Greece or Turkey, is indispensable. It is difficult to conceive of the presence of neutral Sweden in a Europe determined to rearm against the Soviet threat. The "little Europe" of today comprises France, Benelux, Germany, Italy, and it ought also to include Spain. The Scandinavian and the Mediterranean countries would get protection directly from the United States and Great Britain, that is, from the maritime powers, the natural protectors of coastal nations.

It may be asked whether this "little Europe," the major part of the Marshall Plan Europe, should set up a supranational state and transfer some of its sovereignty to a federal executive? The answer is, at least, doubtful. What is important above all is not to hide the genuine necessity for action behind abstract formulas. If the essential point is not kept in mind, discussions will go on for months, if not for years, before the form and the limits of the transfer of sovereignty are determined. The one place where the European idea is capable of being realized within a limited time is in the armed forces. Logically, political institutions should come first; in practice, they will emerge from the requirements of common defense. The general staff will precede the Defense Department.

The austerity of this conclusion will come as a shock. Is it possible that this should be the only immediate translation of the European idea? Unfortunately, I do not see what else can be suggested. In the economic sense, Europe of the Marshall Plan is made up of three groups: Great Britain and the Scandinavian countries; Benelux, Germany, and France; and the Mediterranean countries. These three groups cannot be subjected to a single plan or to a homogenous liberalism. We can ask—outside economic and administrative matters, which are essentially national—what function a European executive organization would have if not military. Too many questions arise between the countries, even those of the second group, for a common diplomatic service to be immediately conceivable. Since Great Britain, with her global interests, and the Scandinavian countries all prefer direct solidarity with the United States, we necessarily arrive at the unified military defense of the second group in close collaboration with Great Britain and the

United States. "Europe" is the grandiose name provisionally given to a Continental sector of the Atlantic community.

Is such an interpretation of the idea to be considered treasonable? Even if it were thought that this interpretation betrayed certain of our hopes, the objection would be without weight. The question today is whether Europe will survive, not whether she will conform to our preferences. I do not even think the objection is valid. Countries that pool their means of defense consent to a sacrifice of sovereignty which is as serious an action as can be imagined, because they forbid fighting among themselves and make mutual trust the safeguard of their interests. Once that step has been taken, the rest will follow in time. After all, that is the way empires have grown: a victorious army organizes, for its own advantage, the unification of military forces. A federation or an empire founded by mutual consent requires the spontaneous decision of the member states to unify their military resources. Without such unification there is no supranational state. With it, the supranational state has been created, even if the public is not yet conscious of the fact.

The military conception of European unity does not suffer from lack of imagination and from excessive prudence. On the contrary, it may be too revolutionary. Patriotism is not made to order. It is easy to say, and it is true in the abstract, that national states are an anachronism, because they are incapable of unaided self-defense. But popular feeling does not change with the same speed as industrial progress. National passions are supposed to be on the way to extinction (although rivalries in sport are sufficient to revive them), but they are replaced by ideological passions. For example, those Frenchmen who are indifferent to the fate of France are either Communists, who love the country of their dreams and the empire in which their religion triumphs, or the purely self-centered. The European idea is empty, it has neither the transcendence of Messianic ideologies nor the immanence of concrete patriotism. It was created by intellectuals, and that fact accounts at once for its genuine appeal to the mind and its feeble echo in the heart.

## HAS EUROPE A HISTORIC VITALITY?

EUROPE, west of the Iron Curtain, in spite of its humiliation is since the last war one of the rare and privileged places where the great majority of people escape the danger of hunger and torture. If we consider the living standard, personal rights, and the limitation of arbitrary interference, she remains almost exemplary compared with the Soviet zone, where police violence strikes at millions of innocent people and compared with immense regions in Asia or Africa, where famine every year carries off millions of helpless victims.

Of course, neither plenty nor formal liberty is the aim or the criterion of civilizations, but the values which Europe realizes less imperfectly than the greater part of mankind are the very ones of which the enemies of the West make empty boast. The Stalinists of France, the rationalists, the progressive Christians denounce economic inequality, the poverty of the masses, the abuses of power. A Soviet regime increases coal or steel production more rapidly than it improves the conditions of existence. It eliminates landowners, capitalists, industrialists, but it replaces them with a hierarchy of prosperous officials and subjects the public to the arbitrary authority of party and police. If the struggle between the two Europes took the form of an examination in morality or in economic efficiency before an impartial tribunal, the verdict would not be in doubt. Unfortunately, that is not the character of historic conflicts. Victory may fall to the more virtuous, but that virtue has nothing in common with a sense of justice or respect for humanity. It is a matter of the stern qualities needed in difficult times—discipline and devotion on the part of the people, vision and resolution in the rulers. Do Europeans still possess that sort of virtue?

Great Britain has escaped from the political and ideological broils of the twentieth century. The British Fascists were never really taken seriously. The Communists have captured some positions in the trade unions, and they enjoy more sympathy from intellectuals than is generally supposed. But the union leaders remain fiercely hostile to them. The masses of the workers are enlisted in organizations which are faithful to democracy. Reduction of inequalities and the protection of individuals against accidents and excessive poverty have been carried further than anywhere else. The Labour experiment, a sequel to the policy adopted by the National Government during the war is, on its own level, and taking a short view, a success.

One hesitates, however, to be unreservedly optimistic. In Great Britain as well, the contradiction characteristic of our communities is beginning to appear: the disproportion between the tasks which the government undertakes and the authority that it possesses. The discrepancy is not so acute in Britain as in France. The absence of Stalinist agitation moderates the violence of political pretentions, and negotiation in good faith remains the accepted rule and the regular practice. The institutions transmitted from the past—the Navy, the Treasury, the parliamentary tradition too, which entrusts immense prerogatives to the executive—have saved the machinery of authority indispensable to great powers. But already the freedom of action of the rulers is dangerously restricted. The functions of the British Government in the middle of the twentieth century are enlarged but its authority is enfeebled.

Social peace has been preserved through two wars, though taxation is no longer a method of distributing the burden of public expenditure, but an instrument of cold revolution. It is progressively destroying the wealth accumulated in families. The transformation of a country once noted for its economic inequality is in keeping with aspirations regarded as legitimate by Western societies. None the less, it raises certain questions. Will the old ruling class survive the loss of its economic foundations? Will a new ruling class arise from the trade unions or from the middle classes? Will the strife between parties retain the moderation indispensable to survival of the system? Will economic progress permit of the regular improvement of the lot of the manual workers when fiscal redistribution has reached its extreme limits?

The Britain of today is incomparably more just than that of a century ago. But in the past her greatness was due above all to the work of a few. Will the administrative organization of collective existence favor the rise and promotion of the minority which has contributed decisively in all ages to the historic advance of communities?

Already, in the past half century, British diplomacy has been strangely unfortunate. Hesitant before 1914, it did not succeed in dispelling the doubts felt in Berlin about the intentions of London. After 1918 it was greatly mistaken about the relative strength of France and Germany, and did not see that Germany alone was a future menace to peace. After 1933 it failed to realize the extent of Hitler's ambitions, and multiplied concessions until the spring of 1939. At the last moment, after the fall of Prague, it went to the other extreme and gave Poland a guarantee, thus depriving the Soviet Union of all motive for negotiating with the West.

These reasons for long-term uneasiness would matter little for the near future if the position of Great Britain had not been shaken by the consequences of the wars. Trade with the Soviet zone is paralyzed. The sterling zone continues to offer a relatively protected market, but the Dominions, old and new, which are subject to the attraction of the United States, decide freely on their economic orientation. Investments—for instance, those of the oil companies in the Near East—are threatened by nationalist passions, manipulated by big landowners and Communist agents. Nevertheless, pessimism is not justified, and nothing proves that the British Isles are doomed to overpopulation or that mass emigration is the only way out. On the contrary, emigration, taking from the community its most active elements, would probably aggravate the difficulties. But from the double pressure of the loss of capital accumulated abroad and the growing demands of the masses there results a permanent tension, which rearmament will augment in the coming years.

Still more serious are the changes brought about by military

technique. Great Britain has lost most of the advantages of in-
sularity. It may be that in future she can defend herself only on
the Continent. The establishment of conscription in time of peace
is the symbol of a revolution with unforeseeable consequences.
Will the military solidarity of the British Isles with continental
Europe be reconcilable with the grand attempt at a renewed Commonwealth, incorporating the republics of Asia and later of Africa?

The crisis, so far as that term may properly be used, is in Great
Britain the result of external events rather than of any causes within
the nation itself. The same cannot be said of France, Germany, or
Italy.

Communism is, in a way, a foreign body within French democracy. But would that democracy work more smoothly if, instead of
a Communist Party that separates itself from the community, there
were a great Labour Party to deal with, supported by 40 per cent to
45 per cent of the electorate, or even two labor parties, one extreme
and the other moderate, competing for the favor of the proletariat?
In spite of appearances, the Fourth Republic, in its present form,
owes its existence to Stalinism. It is this alone that gives the
moderates an influence which would inevitably diminish on the
day when the trade unions and the labor parties, freed from
Kremlin control, acquired an influence proportional to the number
of their adherents and the strength of their organizations.

Modern democracies carry in themselves a seed of corruption,
which is at the same time the origin of their merits: the leaders
must secure the votes of the citizenry, an obligation that has been
rare through the ages and contrary to the traditional order in which
the masters make themselves not only obeyed but respected, even
worshiped, by their subjects. The minority in power is not united
and does not form a permanent hierarchy. Appointments depend
on popularity and on competition between individuals, groups, and
parties. The angling for votes usually benefits the majority of the
people, at least in the short run and as regards the standards of
living. Democracies foment discontent, totalitarian regimes organize
enthusiasm. The latter have no need to make concessions to the
public whose happiness is proclaimed over the loud-speakers every
morning. The former try to meet the claims that they encourage.
From political equality to equality of income, from the state as

protector of the disinherited to the state responsible for the welfare of all, from the state as guarantor of the freedom of individuals and enterprise to the state as director of the economic system, the transition seems almost inevitable, though not equally rapid, in the industrial societies of the West.

This evolution is not, as such, a form of decadence. But the leaders must manage to control its pace. Even the rich democracies are tempted to distribute more purchasing power, in these days, than there are products to consume. The poor democracies, such as that of France, when they are unable to improve really the conditions of existence, are inclined to make countless concessions, the total of which amounts to a proliferation of abuses ruinous to the community.

Historically, parliamentary regimes are a peculiarity of Great Britain that has spread, with more or less success, throughout the world. They have acclimatized themselves with relative ease in countries with a maritime civilization and a bourgeois tradition. In France, with a monarchical past, a centralized administration, but also a powerful bourgeoisie, nearly a century elapsed between the overthrow of the monarchy and the stabilization of a parliamentary republic. The future of the democracies restored after 1945 is still in suspense.

For my own part, I do not feel the slightest temptation to despise formal liberties in the name of the alleged real ones. If one had to choose between the Fourth Republic on the one hand and Fascism or Communism on the other, no doubt would be possible. The acceptance of decadence would seem less intolerable than the choice of either totalitarianism, that is to say, of abjuration. No one can say definitely that Europe is still capable of finding an original path and reforming the pluralist democracies without the sacrifice of fundamental values. It can only be shown that such a reform is conceivable.

To accomplish the tasks essential to the survival of Europe, the Continental democracies must put into effect part of the program characteristic of the "Right Wing opposition": they must restore to the executive a capacity for decision above the tumult of private and collective interests, restrict the activity of pressure groups, maintain an unpolitical administration, rouse the trade unions to a realization of their duty of educating and disciplining their followers as well as making demands, and advance the promotion of a ruling minority animated by the consciousness of a national mission.

It will be objected that the fate of Europe depends less on Europeans themselves than on events over which they have little control: on the development of the conflict between the United States and the Soviet Union, on the maintenance of the present partition, or, conversely, on the unification of Germany and of the Continent. In a sense, the objection is valid. But, just as the strength of the Communist parties in France and Italy is at least as much the effect as the cause of social decomposition, the Soviet-American conflict is partly the effect, and not entirely the cause, of European impotence. Europe is in danger of being a field of battle, and therefore the victim of the conflict between the big powers. But she is also, through her weakness, one of the causes of the conflict.

Let us leave aside the European Communists and fellow travelers, who detest the United States as the enemy of their real country and a hotbed of imperialism. Let us leave aside the intellectuals who, even when they have broken with Communism, continue to abuse capitalism. Let us leave aside the critics of American life, who, mixing true and false, compare the highest successes of Europe with the general level of culture attained by the American masses. In the matter of conditions of living, of productivity, and of social justice, the economic system of the United States, in spite of the term "capitalism," is more progressive than that of the majority of European countries. When Europeans who boast of democratic values denounce the American way of life, they do so at bottom in the name of aristocratic values.

The real ground for the bitterness which so many Europeans display in their references to Americans will not be found in the blunders, the clumsiness, the indecisions of Washington diplomacy in its sudden promotion to a global role. The European nations are themselves, through their wars, responsible for the rise of their transatlantic ally. The political fortune of the United States is inseparable from the humiliation of Europe, and is its symbol. When

Europeans deplore the power of the United States, they are unconsciously thinking of their own downfall. They are all the more
severe on the shortcomings of American civilization (and shortcomings are not lacking) because they are dependent on the wealth
and strength of that distant protector. Even among nations, too
great disparity stands in the way of friendship.

When they evoke the past, Europeans vaguely resent America's
profit from the disasters of the twentieth century. When they think
of the future, they envy America's separation from the potential
enemy by thousands of miles of ocean. It is the disparity of risks
(real or supposed, for after all, the United States can become the
target of atomic attacks) that rouses bitterness. The rest of the
argument follows: Neither the people nor the Government of the
United States wanted or wants the third world war to attain total
violence. Vigorous resistance offers at least as many chances of
avoiding the explosion as concessions and signs of weakness. The
armaments of the United States are not such as to proclaim to the
masters of the Kremlin the nearness and inevitability of hyperbolic
war. Someday perhaps, American opinion may tire of limited war,
and end by calling for a "showdown" to call a halt to the ordeal
before it becomes intolerable. But for the moment there is nothing
to justify such accusations.

Certainly an astonishing tumult accompanies the development
of foreign policy in the United States. The press and other organs
of publicity amplify beyond all measure the voices of journalists,
senators, Ministers, and the President, Hollywood stars, or atomic
experts. Even when there is basic agreement, a strange cacophony
is noticeable, made worse by the alternations of triumphs or disasters casually announced in official or semi-official statements. It is
easy for the foreigner to denounce a great power, whose leaders,
disagreeing about essentials, publicly evoke possible events tragic
to others, such as scorched-earth tactics, the destruction of the
Ruhr, or the Breton redoubt. These discussions are the toll levied
by democracy: every representative of the American people pretends to form his opinion for himself.

Many Frenchmen, even anti-Communists, like to picture the
world as though the Americans had a personal quarrel with
the Russians, or the capitalists of Wall Street with the Com-

munists of the Kremlin. Arguing from that viewpoint, the
parts are exchanged: Europeans are no longer protected, but
victimized. The United States is seeking to recruit mercenaries, not
to safeguard national independence. For anyone uninterested in the
result of the world struggle, that view may acquire a measure of
truth. For those who accept with indifference the ultimate victory
of Communism, who fear nothing but war, the American determination not to tolerate the extension of the Russian empire to the
Atlantic becomes an obstacle to an integration dreamed of as
progressive if not painless.

The gravest reproach which Europeans could address to the
United States is seldom formulated: it is the policy followed from
1943 to 1945, the abandonment of Central and Eastern Europe
to the Soviet Union. There is no heavier mortgage on the future of
the Continent.

Lack of space creates for communities a danger comparable
with lack of oxygen for human beings. Western Europe, as long
as the Russian Army is established less than 120 miles from the
Rhine, will feel herself threatened with suffocation.

She can turn, of course, to the West, and find room for activity
there, in the two Americas. The Atlantic would become the center
of a civilization, as the Mediterranean formerly was. In Asia,
European influence seems to have hastened the ruin of the old
societies: perhaps, after the troubled period, it will produce some
original syntheses. In any case, whether in promoting economic
progress or intellectual exchanges, there is much to be done by
Westerners, who, as a privileged minority, dispose of means of
production and technical knowledge considerably superior to those
of the majority of mankind.

A civilization must expand in order to live, especially the civilization born in Europe, the most expansive known to history. Driven
to fall back on itself in anxious defense, it would be doomed. Thus
the Stalinists try to isolate the West by fomenting the peoples of
Asia and Africa to revolt against an alleged imperialism. The
Europeans have no need of colonial domination or spheres of influence in order to maintain their presence and pursue their historic
task. The improvement attained is, in the long run, more useful to

the colonizer himself than cruder forms of exploitation. Europe should fear less the collapse of empires than hostility to their former masters from countries that have become independent.

But though these distant perspectives justify optimism, they do not solve the short-term problems posed by the conflict between the Soviet Union and the free world. The resources of Africa or of Asia will not bring Europe the indispensable minimum of security. The evacuation of Central Europe by the Russian Army does not depend only on what Europeans will be or do. Yet their historic vitality will play a part in determining the result of a trial of strength.

We use the expression "historic vitality" without overlooking its equivocal character. Historians and sociologists have not identified all the causes of the greatness and decline of civilizations. We have shown here some of the most obvious and therefore superficial causes of European decadence—the weakness of the parliamentary regimes, the conservatism of the democratic socialisms, the difficulty of balancing possible exports against desired imports, the loss of accumulated wealth, the rupture of ties with other continents, the historical desire to form larger units, and the resistance by the interests and traditions bound up with national states. All these causes are real, but none is decisive. The essential one probably escapes objective grasp. Every social order is one of the possible solutions to a problem that is not scientific but human, the problem of community life. Every civilization is animated by beliefs that transcend reason. Are Europeans still capable of practicing the subtle art required by liberal communities? Have they retained faith in their own system of values?

We ask these questions, to which history alone will reply, merely so as not to be charged with the simplicity of economists or generals who believe blindly in their statistics of steel, divisions, or tanks. Wealth and weapons are not enough to decide the fate of nations.

# CONCLUSION

*The Stake*

*Chapter I*

## AFTER STALIN

FOR A REGIME founded on the absolute power of one individual, the tyrant's death constitutes the supreme test. As the future depends, or seems to depend, on decisions taken in Moscow, there has been in the West ceaseless speculation, both hopeful and fearful, as to the consequences of the death of the man who had been the founder and remained master of the Soviet state.

We abstained from such surmise when this book was written. It seemed more important to expose the main lines of the conjuncture than to formulate hypotheses on events which by their very essence were unforeseeable in any detail. In any case, it seemed that the diplomacy or strategy of Stalin's heirs would not differ, *in a short period,* from those of Stalin himself; not to the point of decisively modifying the factors of world politics.

Nothing which has happened during these last months gives cause to revise this judgment.

The policy of the five-year plans, applied since 1928, has gone against the natural aspirations of the masses. It has excluded the consultation of the electorate and even respect for individual rights. The speed of industrialization during the first two plans lowered the workers' standard of living; great expectations and the enthusiasm of the builders would not have sufficed to reconcile the majority of the workers to their lot if a pitiless police rule had not made up for any insufficiencies of faith. In the country peasants were forced with violence to sacrifice their individual farms and enter the *kolkhozes*. Judging by German reports on areas occupied in Russia, ten years ago the peasants had neither forgotten the old regime nor accepted the new.

The state of the Soviet economy at Stalin's death does not permit the satisfaction of the demands the workers and peasants would make had they the right to organize and express themselves like the workers of the West. The collectivization of land has permitted the levying not merely of some 15 per cent of the harvests—the approximate percentage at the end of the New Economic Policy— but between 35 and 40 per cent, and even more on crops destined for industrial uses. Voluntary deliveries of a comparable size would mean inevitably that cereals, cotton, and flax would have to be bought at high prices, in other words that the state would have to dispose of a considerable mass of consumer goods. As long as the planners want to increase production of coal each year by some 30 million tons, and steel by 3 million tons, they will have no other choice but to force the consent of the *kolkhoz* members and maintain the conditions of exchange, which is equivalent to relegating a large part of the burden of industrialization to the peasants. Although the present five-year plan, announced during its second year at the Nineteenth Party Congress, reported a substantial increase in agricultural production and light industry, it followed the same general lines as previous plans. In 1950 producers' goods represented 72.6 per cent of the total industrial production; it is forecast that in 1955 producers' goods will represent 73.8 per cent. The percentage of consumer goods would then fall from 27.4 to 26.2 per cent.

Without modifying the general direction of the plans, Stalin's successors have the same means of calming the discontent of the peasants and workers, means that Stalin knew and used in case of need—in the country, relaxation of the rigorous collective methods, leaving a little more margin for the property and possessions of the *kolkhoz* members (patches of ground, animals . . .) and in the towns, reduction of tax on turnover and certain price reductions. Certainly the raising of the living standard depends first and foremost on the goods available. However, the leaders can favor one category of revenue or another, and by arranging a certain interval between the drop in prices and forced loans, can temporarily grant an increased purchasing power.

It must be added that the closing of the frontiers and the monopoly of propaganda prevent the masses from comparing their condition with those of the Western peoples, and force them to a comparison otherwise favorable between the present and the past, the present and the promised future. During these last years, there is not a doubt that conditions have improved for the Soviet population. This improvement dominates the experience of the Soviet citizen and lends a certain weight to the wonderful future forecast by official ideology. Lastly, the differences caused by remuneration according to output, much more marked than in capitalist industries, create a minority of privileged workers. According to the esoteric doctrine of power, it is more important to encourage the rise of the most vigorous than to satisfy the passive majority.

The 50 million men and women employed in agriculture and the 40 to 45 million employed in industry are to all intents and purposes politically neutralized. Except in case of some exterior shock or discord within the elite circle, the leaders have nothing to fear from the people, whether they are adored or cursed by them.

To use Marxist language, it can be said that the development of productive forces (value of production per head of the population or per employed person) and the relations in forms of production (collective property, distribution of the gross national production) fix a limit to the transformations that Stalinism is apt to undergo after and without Stalin. Within certain limits reforms are possible in the way of a relaxation of tension, but in the main they will be granted by authority, not forced by the action of the masses.

In any despotic regime the wishes of the privileged few produce a more immediate reaction on the administration of affairs than the confused sentiments of the many. According to Malenkov, 5.5 million specialists are employed in the Soviet economy. If professors, writers, and artists are added to this figure, a total of 6 to 7 million people is arrived at, some 20 to 25 million with their families, that is 10 per cent of the population, which constitutes the Soviet bourgeoisie. The whole of this bourgeoisie is directly or indirectly employed by the state. In the companies and trusts, engineers and administrators are classed in a rigid hierarchy, each grade with its uniform and distinctive signs of rank, in the manner of the old tsarist bureaucracy. Whether baptized bourgeoisie or bureaucracy it makes little difference—the average technician earns not 5,000 to 6,000 rubles a year like the unskilled worker, but three to six times more, and the managers of companies and trusts twenty or forty times more. They tend naturally towards a life similar to that of the average middle-class Westerner. Their ambitions are to own the same things—cars, refrigerators, television sets —and they aspire to the same satisfactions. The Communist Revolution has eliminated the social categories usually connected with the old middle classes: there are almost no more peasant landowners, independent tradesmen, or industrialists, and the members of the liberal professions have become civil servants. But it is impossible to industrialize a country without forming larger and larger "cadres" (the number of technicians in the Soviet Union has increased two or three times more rapidly than the number of workers). The people whom Western sociologists consider belong to the new middle classes are present in any industrial society, whether capitalist or Communist.

In the U.S.S.R. they enjoy various privileges. Income tax ceased to be progressive beyond 12,000 rubles. In education, fees are charged during the last two years of secondary education and in the universities. The members of the bourgeoisie have the means to promote their children's careers. There is still room for new talent amongst them (the economy has a growing and continual need for trained personnel), but already almost 50 per cent of the students come from families of technicians, administrators, and functionaries.

What complaints can the privileged have to make against the regime, when most of them owe their success to the Revolution and industrialization? Logic, as well as direct evidence, suggests a simple answer—insecurity. Engineers and factory managers, in addition to an often overwhelming amount of work, pay for their position by risking forcible displacement, imprisonment, or the concentration camp. Stalin never repeated the absurd and horrible purge of 1938, which threw millions of Soviet citizens, many of them members of the ruling classes, into prison. However, without the commotion, without the phenomenal numbers, purges have remained part of the usual train of events. It is possible that the head of a Soviet company accepts political dangers more easily than his capitalist counterpart today, who in fact would not accept the economic dangers that his predecessors considered normal in the pioneer days of the United States. There can hardly be any doubt though that the technicians—in the widest meaning of the term—long for the terror to end. There is a contradiction between a stabilized bureaucracy and the precarious social positions that it seems to be the function of the purges to maintain.

If certain extreme forms of terror—the mass arrests of 1936–37 and the confessions—can be imputed to the personality of the tyrant, the purges are unquestionably closely bound up with certain fundamental characteristics of Soviet society. The successors, in the first phase, are going to soften the rigorous police rule. But could they do away with it entirely, without endangering the very existence of the whole system?

Illegal operations are indispensable to the head of a concern who wants to fulfill the plan in order to procure the labor and raw materials he cannot obtain in a legal way. Would an entirely planned economy function with any vigor if the leaders could protect themselves from the threat of arrest by respecting the letter of the rules and by throwing the responsibility from one to the other? Within the companies the relations and competition between the manager, the accountant, the workers' representative and the Party's go on in a very complex and partly clandestine way, and finally arbitrary decisions are taken in favor of one or the other. Parallel markets, an integral part of the economic system, do not of course demand constant terror, but they hardly permit a reign of law.

Politically the struggles between individuals or groups offer scarcely any issue other than a decision by superiors or, in the last analysis, by the supreme authority. The Stalinist regime did not dispose of the recognized methods, whereby the rivalries present in any state are guided and resolved. In theory, the Communist dictatorship should have been collective, and the votes in the Politburo and in the Central Committee should have expressed the will of the Party, itself mythically conceived to be the interpreter of the proletariat. But is it possible to reconcile the despotism of the Party over the rest of the population with democracy inside the Party? Could the Communists, in the long run, keep for themselves the rights they refuse to the masses? After twenty years of rule by a single person, the regime would have to evolve in the opposite direction and give back to the Party members the right to think, speak, discuss, and quarrel. History offers few examples of such a metamorphosis.

To speak in Marxist terms again, Soviet society suffers from an internal contradiction. Authority cannot renounce terror. If the bourgeoisie obtained security of employment, the regime would lose its force of expansion. The immediate future assured, the character of this bourgeoisie as a privileged class would become even more sharply defined, and as the chances of social advancement for simple workers grew less and less, an aristocracy would arise whose status would conflict with the official ideology.

However, it would be falling into the error of the Marxists themselves to push the dialectic of contradictions too far. There are middle courses between the great purges and the security of civil servants in the West. *Stalin delayed them.* Many cases of repression were explicable only by the tyrant's humor and not by an alleged historic or political necessity. There was no need to put Lenin's old companions to death after their defeat, or to extract from them a series of humiliating confessions. There was no need to persecute the Jews; there was no need, if a choice had to be made between Gottwald and Slansky, to hang the latter. Stalin's successors have a margin of retreat before they reach the essentials of the regime.

The Soviet ruling class does not recognize the distinction of groups that exists in the corresponding classes of the West. It does not allow the various professional interests to organize. Factory managers, trust administrators, and Cabinet Ministers belong to one and the same category. The managers are not the owners of the means of production, nor are the Ministers civil servants in the Western meaning of the term, where their career and income would differ from those of directors in industry and commerce. However, this unity is compensated for by a distinction between the administrations (state, Party, Army, police) and above all by a double opposition between the bureaucracy (of the state and the economy) that makes the machine go and the bureaucracy (of the Party) that holds the legitimacy, and between the latter and the bureaucracy possessing the real power (the police).

The legitimacy of the Western democracies expresses itself by constitutional procedure, ranging from the election of representatives to the election of a president. The ruling minorities of the West are divided into groups, which enter into competition in order to exercise or influence authority. Democracies always appear to be in a state of crisis, but as long as the groups respect the rules of the competition these crises resolve themselves peacefully. In the Soviet Union for the last twenty years the unconditional authority of Stalin, who was the head of the police as much as he was head of the Party, who held the reins of administration and had neutralized the Army, forestalled any visible conflict. The rivalry of the multiple bureaucracies was manipulated and controlled from above. Will this continue when the deified chief has gone and supreme authority is vested in two or three men obliged to rule together or shake the solidarity of the system?

The man who was named head of the Praesidium of the Party and of the Council of Ministers after Stalin's death had received, at the Nineteenth Congress, certain of the honors normally accorded to the chosen successor. The choice was logical as Malenkov came immediately after Stalin in the Party organizations, and the Party, as spokesman of the proletariat, incarnated the justifying idea of Soviet authority. However, from the time that Malenkov, voluntarily or not, abandoned the Party secretariat (which handles nominations) and the control of the police, he lost the instruments of power. The president of the Party Praesidium is, in theory, only *primus inter pares,* and this ideological pre-eminence would not carry much weight if the formula of divided power revealed itself to be a fiction destined to cover a struggle between pretendants.

The members of the Politburo (or Praesidium) will oppose the rise of a new tyrant because they remember the fate of many of Stalin's companions. The preceding chief consecrated his authority by putting to death his rivals after their political defeat. Perhaps the members of the Praesidium would have been willing to recognize an heir promoted to the first rank if they had been certain they would not share the fate of Zinoviev and Bukharin. A balance of power between the successors is, for each one of them, the only conceivable guarantee of survival.

This balance of power should act in the same way as the desire of the bourgeoisie for more security. There is no doubt that if the rivalry between the successors continues in secrecy the purges will continue, because each faction will seek to hold the key positions. However, as long as the successors agree, if only in order to defer a decisive struggle, by implicit agreement they will tend to respect a certain distribution of patronage between the various groups. By opportunism and necessity they will seek to conciliate the technicians and the Army, and will be inclined to relax both orthodoxy and violence.

If such is the case, the regime will evolve slowly, not towards a democracy of the Western type—the elements of the economy established by the five-year plans would not permit it—but towards the attenuated despotism of a technical bureaucracy, for which Marxist ideology would serve as a justification far more than as a faith.

Some think that the contradictions of Soviet society preclude a moderate solution. The regime demands an undisputed leader, yet Stalin's useless cruelties have put almost insurmountable obstacles in the way of the rise of another Tsar. The Soviet bourgeoisie desires the end of the revolution, yet the regime, unless paralyzed, is condemned to a kind of perpetual forward flight. Millions of Russians are being taught to read and a culture based on science is being spread and yet an ideology is maintained as official truth, which in spite of its pretensions is the scorn of the scientific mind. It is impossible to say in what upheavals these contradictions will express themselves. Stalin's companions, who are trying to save the essential by sacrificing the useless excesses, will not last long in the atmosphere of a wiser Stalinism. Either a tyrant will restore a tyranny after more or less violent upheavals, or the gradual democratization of the Party will carry with it the "embourgeoisement" of the whole society.

For the next few years, it would be better for the West not to have too many illusions. The new leaders will strive to maintain the regime, while eliminating the pathological phenomena, imputable either to the economic crises or the bloodthirsty whims of an old man.

Soviet authority does not dispose of sufficient production to satisfy the masses, and, at the same time, maintain the present rhythm of industrialization and armament. The Party chiefs must preserve their rights in the management of the state, and these rights derive from the Marxist-Leninist ideology.

Stalin's heirs have been his companions during the last twenty years, and they share his philosophy and ambitions. They know what is at stake. Their common interest is the safeguarding of the Communist venture and should prevail temporarily over the dialectic of Soviet contradictions.

The strategy adopted by Stalin in these last years, even more than the style of this strategy, has in a way facilitated the task of the Western governments. The dissension between Britain and America on the attitude towards Communist China was a small matter as long as the absurd continuation of the Korean War prevented any negotiation. The discussions on the possibility or the impossibility of a united, neutral Germany remained academic as long as diplomatic relations between the two camps were as good as broken. The tensions inside the Western world were concealed and, in a sense, repelled by the necessity for union which the Soviet menace made clear to everyone. The leaders in Moscow do not need to change their policy; it is enough for them to change their manner for the divergent opinions and old rivalries within the Western community to come to the surface again.

In Europe the major factor is the division of Europe, Germany and Berlin, and the presence of the Red Army in the center of the old continent, 125 miles from the Rhine. The situation would have appeared untenable to the diplomats of the old school, even though a Russian army would have been that of the Tsars and not the army of world revolution. When Kremlin propaganda ceases to call Americans cannibals and Russian authorities permit the entry of a few Western journalists and the departure of a few diplomats detained for the past two and a half years by the North Koreans, it is pleasant, but of no particular significance. The cold war will come to an end in Europe only on the day when the two camps agree upon a territorial statute, and this agreement could not be the status quo. The West can tolerate the status quo, but it cannot recognize it.

In other words, an agreement after negotiation would necessitate concessions from the Soviet Union, above all the dismantling of the "popular democracy" in the Soviet zone of Germany and the evacuation of Austria. What can the West offer in exchange, apart from a promise of neutrality that no one would take seriously? At Yalta, Churchill and Roosevelt contented themselves with a promise from Stalin that the independence of Poland, mutilated in the east and enlarged in the west, would be respected. The leaders in Moscow are too sincerely Machiavellian to have confidence in the words of those whom they consider their enemies.

There would be a real change only on the day when the leaders of the Soviet Union consented to the retreat of the Russian Army behind its own frontiers, to the relaxation of the dictatorship over the satellite zone, and when they ceased to seek an eventual extension of the Communist system or of Moscow's imperial power towards the coasts of the North Sea and the Atlantic. There is nothing to inspire for an instant the hope of such a revolution in Soviet strategy.

In Asia, Stalin's successors have been in favor of a cease-fire in Korea. However, the Korean War, whatever the enormous consequences have been, was only an incident in a train of events. The zone which is menaced is Southeast Asia—Indo-China first, Thailand and Burma next, India and Pakistan later. Why should the men in the Kremlin plan to stop a movement which, according to their philosophy, expresses the law of history? And could they, if the whim took them, force the Vietminh or the Peiping Government to a temporary halt? The modes of tactics may change, but without altering the major lines of the conjuncture.

What events would be likely to modify the conjuncture in its essentials? An extension of hostilities and the defeat of the Chinese armies, or the recognition by the United States of the Communist government of Peiping, followed by the resumption of commercial relations between China and the West, or, lastly, a gradual dissociation of the Soviet Union and China. The first eventuality would improve the chances of resistance in Southeast Asia, the third would bring about a change in the constellation of the world, in which the two theaters of operation, the European and the Asiatic, would no longer have the same degree of solidarity. The second eventuality would, according to Western commentators, indicate a relaxation. It is not certain that it would turn aside Communist China from pursuing the liberation of Southeast Asia, in the sense that the Peiping leaders give to the word.

Not one of these eventualities could be a direct consequence of Stalin's death. Even if in the future the optimists who ascribe intentions of appeasement to the new Politburo are proved right, the chances of stopping Communist expansion, restoring stable regimes in Southeast Asia, or breaking up the Moscow-Peiping axis will hardly be improved. Whatever the amount of authority preserved over local organizations, the center of world Communism is, in many respects, a prisoner of the Communist venture. It is true that if the members of the Praesidium *wanted* to break the ties between the different Communist parties of Europe, Africa, America, and Asia and the organizations in Moscow, they would be bringing a decisive contribution to the ending of the "Great Fear."

However, in this case it would no longer be a matter of moral conversion or political revolution. It would be a miracle: has a great power ever, of its own accord, thrown away the most redoubtable weapon fate has placed in its hands?

The regime, founded on the bureaucratic framework of an industrial society, is still governed by men of the first generation, not the generation that destroyed the previous regime, but the one that built the new order. The elite have kept intact a will for power, the expansion of the empire has awakened ambitions of conquest, the heroic but horrible phase of industrial construction has been passed, but the five-year plans still do not supply simultaneously butter, cannons, and factories in abundance. If the conflicts between individuals provoked an explosion, it would be a happy accident: one must not count upon the improbable.

The relative relaxation in the interior will not make the task of Western diplomacy any easier. The successors will strive to increase their hold on the satellite states to the extent that they fear dissent. The West will have difficulty in stemming the tide of Communism in

Asia, in repelling it in Europe, there because Communist expansion is animated by a deep-seated historic force, here because the leaders of the Soviet Union could accept a retreat, even a local one, only with great difficulty. Stalin's heirs do not believe, any more than he did, in a real agreement between the two worlds.

The variations in Soviet diplomacy lie within narrow bounds: less violence in propaganda intended for the exterior, less police frenzy, some exchange of goods, people, and ideas, a slowing down in the armaments race—such changes will not end this period of ordeal. Between Communism and the rest of the world rivalry will continue, without total war or genuine peace.

However, if the circumstances exclude real peace, and if the people justly want to avoid total war, time must be the stake. It is time that, in the long run, could wear away a conflict which at the moment can have no issue other than the outbreak of a war, which, like the first two, would inevitably be hyperbolic.

Stalin's death does not close the cold war, which stems from the conjuncture itself and not from the evil intentions of one man.

## Chapter II

# THE END OF THE SOCIALIST MYTH

THE SUCCESSES *of Bolshevism do not prove the truth of the Marxist or Lenino-Stalinist doctrine, but the efficacy of a technique of action.*

The historical process suggested by Marxist doctrine is one of capitalism destroying itself as a result of internal contradictions, and gradually giving way to the rise of the socialist regime, which rejects capitalism and succeeds it. This theory has been refuted by the facts and has been implicitly abandoned by the Stalinists, at least in their esoteric conceptions. From the first, the Leninists had thrown doubt on the classical theory of revolution. The workers, left to themselves, incline to trade unionism, thus betraying the mission which history, as interpreted by the intellectuals, confers on them. Bourgeois democracy, in the absence of war, gains strength with the development of the productive forces. The pauperization of the working class, an indispensable intermediate stage between the contradictions of capitalism and the final apocalypse, does not occur.

Leninists and Stalinists have nevertheless maintained the theory of capitalist contradictions and crises. Anyone can see equally well that free economy, in the West, has developed through alternate phases of rising and falling prices, and has involved depressions at more or less regular intervals. The Marxists assert that the crises get worse, but that has not been proved, as the exceptional severity of the great depression in 1929 is explained by certain events not connected with the essential structure of the system. For that matter, even if we admitted the aggravation of crises, there would follow a growing state control of economic life, but not the Bolshevik version of the arrival of socialism. However severe it has been, a crisis has never furnished an instance of the seizure of power by a proletarian party in any country with a highly developed capitalism.

In other words, to pass from capitalist crises to the Lenino-Stalinist process of history there must be inserted an intermediate link, the Leninist theory of wars, or, rather, the assimilation, current in Soviet propaganda, of war to a capitalist crisis. We have tried to show that the Leninist theory of wars is not in conformity with the facts. Competition for overseas markets has been a real phenomenon, but a marginal one. Colonial outlets had a considerable importance before 1914 for certain sectors of industry, but not for the European economic systems as a whole. The expansion of internal trade offered much more business than the underdeveloped countries. Commercial rivalry was only a subordinate factor in the tension between London and Berlin. The same rivalry between the United States and Great Britain has not prevented an intimate alliance. Europeans undertook distant conquests long before the time of monopoly capitalism, and they have not ceased to fight, through the centuries, more for power and glory than for wealth.

The mechanism of the catastrophe resembles neither that imagined by the classical Marxists (namely, the accentuation of class conflicts as a result of capitalist development) nor that imagined by the Leninists—irreconcilable war between the powers, once the partition of the world had been completed. It depends on the disproportion between the traditional pace of European politics and the scale of modern means of production and destruction. Europe's fortune did not suffer from the wars between nations while they were as limited as in the eighteenth and nineteenth centuries (although the danger was revealed by the wars of the French Revolution and the Empire). The continuation of traditional rivalries in the era of large-scale industry and conscript armies produced the simultaneous abasement of victors and vanquished.

There remains only one way of interpreting the origins or the present crisis in a Marxist perspective, that is, to represent the Revolution of 1917 as a proletarian revolution. In this sense, the cause, unconnected with the autonomous evolution of capitalism, is considered to be less important than the fact itself. The proletariat, it is asserted, seized power in Russia and henceforth became the standard-bearer of the new idea. Thanks to the Red Army and to the Chinese peasants, the proletariat (the argument runs) is building up socialism in Russia and spreading it throughout the world. There are, however, no grounds for calling the Revolution of 1917 proletarian, in the sense which Marx and the Marxists gave to the word.

The Bolsheviks, according to their own testimony, took no part in the February Revolution. It was brought about by the difficulties in feeding metropolitan areas, the dissatisfaction among the bourgeoisie and the aristocracy with the Tsar and his entourage, and by the prolongation of the war and the succession of defeats. The soldiers kept in their quarters, unoccupied and without weapons, together with the housewives and the workers of Petrograd, were the agents of the revolt. The imprudence with which the Government had sent the reliable divisions to the front (for until February 1917 there was no revolt in the field army) seems in retrospect its most fateful error. Stalin did not forget it in the Second World War.

The second revolution consisted of an organized insurrection of Red Guards, partly workers. It was ridiculously easy: "The October insurrection was," to use Lenin's own words, "easier than lifting a pen." The revolutionaries took possession of the public buildings and finally of the state. Once again, the Provisional Government had failed to recall to the capital the troops on which it could have relied. The events—as has been repeated a hundred times—are more reminiscent of Blanqui's idea of the *putsch* than of the Marxist theory of the revolution prepared by the maturing of a new order within the old community.

By what pseudo-philosophic jugglery can anyone see in the surprise attack carried out by a revolutionary party, and under cover of the decomposition of the state, an act of the proletariat which is supposed to have taken into its own hands its fate and that of the world? It was not an inorganic mass of millions of men (as the proletariat in fact is) who seized power, but the Bolshevik Party. That party had 8,400 members in 1905, 23,600 at the beginning of 1917, 40,000 at the time of the all-Russian conference of the party in April 1917, 200,000 in October—and of these half were intellectuals, who formed the majority among the leaders. Why should the power of this party be confused with that of the proletariat, their will with its will—if, indeed, a will can be ascribed to the proletariat? The majority of the proletariat was passive at the moment of the decisive action. Both before and after the Revolution it gave more votes to the Social Revolutionaries and the Mensheviks than to the Bolsheviks. In the elections for the first all-Russian Congress of Soviets, in July 1917, the Social Revolutionaries obtained 285 mandates, the Mensheviks 248, and the Bolsheviks 105 (or 13 per cent of the votes). In the elections for the Constituent Assembly after the *coup d'état*, the Social Revolutionaries received 58 per cent of the votes, the Bolsheviks 25 per cent, the Mensheviks 4 per cent, and the Cadets 13 per cent.

It is true that in the Second Congress of Soviets, in October, the Bolsheviks gained a slight majority, with 51 per cent of the votes. Between March and October the radicalism of the masses—to employ their jargon—had certainly increased. Lenin's party had made progress, thanks to the efficiency of his propaganda and his organization. The Mensheviks refused power: the Revolution, in their view had to be democratic: they wanted to leave its direction to the representatives of the bourgeoisie. They were victims of their hesitation, in a period that demanded simple and forthright action. In a country with no more than 3 million factory workers, the outcome of the crisis was due to a rally of the non-proletarian masses (mainly peasants, who were won over by the magic words peace and land) at least as much as to the adhesion of an advanced fraction of the proletariat.

The events of 1917 have in restrospect nothing mysterious in themselves. The historian of Russia is not surprised that the sudden collapse of the absolute power should have left a void which was ultimately filled by an extremist party. The sociologist finds in the period when the days of February slipped into the days of October, from Kerensky to Lenin, an instance of a typical evolution that has often been observed. The only theorist who finds difficulty in interpreting the Russian Revolution to fit his doctrine is the Marxist. He has to multiply supplementary hypotheses in order to maintain simultaneously his general theory of capitalist development and the credibility of the so-called socialist victory in Russia. Even Trotsky, who explains the Revolution by the dialectic of the class war, shows in the end that victory was bound to fall to the party capable of restoring discipline in the Army and the nation. This was, in fact, exactly what the Bolshevik Party achieved. But the merit for it belongs to a technique of action and to the genius of the leaders, not to some strange participation by means of which the Bolsheviks became the authentic representatives of the proletariat.

Fortune has continued to favor the adventure of Lenin and his companions and successors. After the abortive insurrection of July 1917, the Provisional Government could have aimed a mortal blow at the Bolsheviks if it had consented to employ against them the methods of violence which Lenin and Trotsky, once in power, used ruthlessly against their adversaries.[1] Kornilov's attempt obliged the Provisional Government to turn to the left and seek support from the popular organizations; the Bolsheviks profited by this to regain the ground lost in July. Lenin saw that circumstances made a *coup d'état* easy and that the possession of power would open up indefinite prospects. Nobody doubts the strategic or tactical talent of the Bolshevik staff in 1917, but this talent no more demonstrates the truth of the Marxist philosophy than Napoleon's victories proved the truth of Rousseau's *Contrat Social*—unless by Marxist philosophy is meant Bolshevik practice put into theoretical form. But then it is a question of a simple philosophy, which has nothing in common with a proletarian Messianism, and is limited to teaching the best ways in war-torn eras to stir up trouble, to sabotage established regimes, to excite conflicts between classes or nations, to conquer the state, to organize the masses, and finally, from the socialist bastion, to extend through the world the joint power of the Bolshevik Party and the Russian state.

*Class conflicts have been one of the elements of the present crisis, not the privileged cause that would reveal its essential significance. Stalinism does not mark the advent of the proletariat to the ranks of the ruling class.*

In modern communities, and particularly in those of the nineteenth century known to Marx, only one class can be seen whose determination is relatively clear: the proletariat. In this case, and in this case alone, the different criteria which the observer may use to

[1]The Provisional Government's incapacity to employ force was not accidental. It was characteristic of moderate men and parties.

identify social groups (such as origin and amount of income, kind of work, mode and style of living, spatial coherence, sense of community, and the like) apply simultaneously, although in different degrees—discriminations become evident within the proletariat in proportion as the interval increases between the workman and the foreman, who is close to the engineer. The other social categories which one is tempted to call classes do not present all the common characteristics which can be taken as typical (except perhaps the landed gentry, which is rapidly disappearing); the result is that the very enumeration of classes varies from one author to another. In his historical studies, Marx, too, enumerated the classes empirically, and he did not find the same ones in the Germany of 1848 or in the France of the eighteenth of Brumaire. The peasantry includes landowners, farmers of all sorts, and agricultural laborers, partly associated together in consequence of a similar mode of living, partly opposed to one another vertically (workmen against employers, farmers against landowners, small landowners against great ones, etc.). The upper middle class includes salaried employees, civil servants, people with independent incomes, and the owners of the means of production. Still more heterogeneous are the intermediate groups, called lower middle classes. A feeling of community seldom unites the whole of a middle class, which hardly exists except by and for those who use it as a goal for ambition.

Rivalry between social groups in complex societies is a normal and universal fact. It remains latent when discrimination or a hierarchy is hallowed by tradition or by a system of beliefs. In our times, this rivalry is particularly acute, or is at least particularly evident; the inheritance of wealth or authority is contrary to egalitarian ideas, so that transmitted inequalities seem less respectable. Modern economic life implies rapid fluctuations. The alternate rise and fall of prices prevents a merely nominal amount of money from being considered the legitimate income, and it quickly modifies the relative position of the different groups. Each member of them strives to fight against the deterioration or for the improvement of his lot, perhaps at another's expense. The only way of suppressing this sort of class war—which we should prefer to call conflicts of social groups—is to restore the old institutions of absolutism, to worship power, to teach the masses that their masters rule by divine right, and to give the state a monopoly of propaganda.

The rivalry between groups is combined with a struggle between minorities for political power or social influence, as in the case of the contest between the bourgeoisie and the aristocracy at the end of the *ancien régime* in France, when the stake was not so much the redistribution of wealth as the division of authority and prestige. These two kinds of conflict are never separate: in France in 1789, and in Russia in 1917, the insurrection of the peasants against feudal rights or the great landowners was an essential element of the revolutionary crisis; but neither are they to be confused the one with the other: the rise of the Bolsheviks was favored by the demands of the peasants and their riots, but power, after changing hands, remained outside the masses and was monopolized by a ruling clique.

Class war, in the two senses we have analyzed, does indeed run throughout history. But this fact, which is obviously important in terms of causes and effects, assumes *philosophical* significance only through the proclamation of a future state of affairs when class warfare would disappear. It is in the extent to which the proletariat would put an end to class war that such war becomes the saving violence, the indispensable instrument by means of which men achieve their humanity.

It is stated that the proletariat, on the day of revolution, will make itself the ruling class and will take into its hands the destiny of society. The "constitution of the proletariat as a ruling class" is an expression which, strictly interpreted, means nothing, for it does not describe any event that could possibly happen in this world. In every great nation the industrial proletariat comprises millions of workers and could no more become a ruling class than a circle can be a square. At the time of the French Revolution, the bourgeoisie represented a minority of privileged persons. The minority that will take the place of the bourgeoisie may issue from the working class, but it will be distinct from that class. The mass of the non-privileged will not blend with the small number of rulers of the state and of industry.

The promotion of the proletariat is an expression that has two meanings, which our experience in modern times helps us to define: either the seizure of power by a party which, by begging the question and by a mystical participation, pretends to be an emanation of the proletariat, from which it is partially recruited; or else the exercise of power according to the rules of formal democracy, by a party which mainly relies on the votes of the proletariat and is partially recruited from it. The former way is that of Communism, the latter of social democracy. Each of these methods has various modifications, but a third method has not so far been discovered.

The Revolution of 1917 and the Labor victory of 1945 mark the conclusion of the struggle carried on by minorities in the name of the masses against the old ruling class and the established order. The Revolution entailed the physical liquidation of many privileged persons and the elevation of a new *elite*,[2] partly originating in the proletariat, an elite which after thirty years consolidates its position by organizing the transmission of its advantages. The Labor victory involved a partial restoration of the ruling class, into which intellectuals or former trade union secretaries have penetrated. The political or trade organizations are one of the paths by which, in the West, the sons of the people rise into higher spheres of society. Neither Communism nor trade unionism corresponds to the Messianic idea of a revolution carried out by the immense majority for the benefit of all; they fit into the classical formula for all revolutions—the accession to power of a minority in the name of the masses who are more or less passive or compliant.

Just as they do not put a final stop to the rivalry of elites, so neither Communism nor trade unionism suppresses the conflict between social groups. Communism stifles it by centering all incomes in one source and by forbidding private interests to organize. But these groups exist potentially, and the leaders have to take account of the latent tension between city and country, between factory and *kolkhoz* workers, or between workers and the hierarchy, just as the rulers of democracies have to listen to the noisy claims of other parties. The idea of suppressing the class war by a revolution is rather silly. On the other hand, to attenuate that war by the reduction of economic inequalities, by the progressive effacement of prejudices, and by multiplying the opportunities for the non-privi-

[2] In the sense which Pareto gives to the word.

leged, is actually within the bounds of the possible in communities that favor economic progress.

The proletariat, as a universal class raising itself to the dignity of a ruling class at the end of a relentless and finally victorious war waged against the bourgeoisie, has never existed except in the imagination of philosophers or in the speeches of agitators. But minorities, at first fanatical, then more or less cynical, spread such an ideology as a means to power. Thus, to the extent to which they believe in such an ideology, or act as though they did, the reality ends by resembling the myth.

For thirty years, in no Western country have the bourgeoisie on the one hand and the workers on the other behaved as though they assigned a supreme value to class solidarity or interest. In 1914, the immense majority of the proletarians of Europe put their country before their class, and in 1917 they refused to recognize Lenin and his companions as the leaders of the universal class and Bolshevism as the advance guard of the international proletariat. In Germany, after the defeat, the bulk of the proletariat followed the Social Democratic leaders, who were patriots and parliamentarians, and not the Independents, who were Spartacists or Communists.

The bourgeoisie, even more than the proletariat, on many occasions sacrificed their class interests to their individual or national ones. The German general staff, wanting to shake off Russia in order to win the victory in the West, did not hesitate to allow Lenin to pass. Never, from 1917 to 1947, did the bourgeoisies succeed in forming a common front against the country of socialism, nor did they seriously consider it. They vied with one another in supplying the machines indispensable for the five-year plans. The *Reichswehr* did not cease, even after 1933, to maintain good relations with the Red Army. The French and British democracies strove to secure the alliance of the Soviet Union, in the first place to prevent war, and later in order to win it. To the indignant surprise of Hitler, and to the delighted surprise of Stalin, Western statesmen entirely forgot the savage war, predicted by Bolshevism, between the one and only proletarian state and the capitalist states. They could hardly have shown more confidence in a traditional Russia. "The union of the proletarians of all countries," "world revolution," "capitalist solidarity"—who took these bygone formulas literally, when democrats and Fascists were exterminating one another and so-called capitalist and bourgeois Europe was torn by the quarrels of nations and ideologies?

Since 1945, the power of the Soviet Union has become such that the Kremlin ideology tends to give form to the real world. Stalin, by proclaiming the division of humanity into two camps and acting accordingly, himself created the coalition that his mythology postulates. Not that the opposition of social systems and of ruling classes is insurmountable. Planned economies and semi-liberal economies can coexist without difficulty, just as the British and American middle classes were and are prepared to trade or negotiate with the Kremlin proletarians. It is the latter themselves who cement the union of their pretended enemies. They have not succeeded, it is true, in giving the "imperialist" alliance a coherence prohibited by the absence of a common religion, the weight of historic memories, and the democratic regime of the leading power. But in spite of everything Stalin succeeded in inspiring the countries of Europe, torn by age-long quarrels, with a certain feeling of solidarity. He cured the United States of isolationism. Perhaps the end result will be the creation of an Atlantic community, which would not be the last stage of capitalism but civilization's best defense in the face of danger.

Some will argue nonetheless that Stalinism has laid the economic foundation of a socialist society. If collective ownership and planning constitute the substructure of such a society, the proposition is unquestionable. But we have learned that *the traditional values of socialism are not implied by a collective or planned economy. What is being laboriously attempted is to prove that they are not excluded by such an economy.*

Must we attribute to collective ownership an intrinsic superiority over individual ownership, and to planning a superiority over the mechanisms of the market? Or must we not rather judge these different institutions by experience, without assigning to any one of them a particular dignity with reference to eternal values?

What do we demand from an economic and social system? The improvement of the lot of the majority? Government enterprises, as such, have not displayed superior efficiency to private enterprises.

The greatest production is reached by the great American corporations. If we are concerned with raising the workers' living conditions why should we give systematic preference to a legal form whose economic merits are at least questionable?

Integral planning of the Soviet or Hitlerist type has never been framed with a view to prosperity. The planners reply that they are sacrificing the present generations for those to come. It is difficult to understand why the people who are moved by the sufferings of the non-privileged give their sympathy to a system that begins by multiplying sufferings on pretense of lessening them. Experience shows that the masters of a planned economy use their power much more for its own sake than with a view towards the general welfare.

Is it held that it is less important to attain the highest possible living standard (for then it would not be clear why the intellectuals of the left reserve their severity for the country which in that respect surpasses all others) than to reduce inequalities? There again, we cannot see that there is necessarily a bond between collective ownership, planning, and equality. The hierarchy within great modern enterprises is not modified by the kind of ownership, but depends on a structure, technical and bureaucratic, which the substitution of one owner for another (both being more fictitious than real) leaves intact. As for the inequality of incomes, it tends, apparently, to lessen in the long run with economic progress. Taxation is probably the most effective short-term method of curbing the accumulation of individual fortunes. Integral planning of the Soviet type allows a minority in possession of all power to deduct for its own benefit a considerable fraction of the national revenue. It is always dangerous to take absolutism as a means of creating an egalitarian regime. Freedom is lost along the way, without the promised equality being attained.

Will it be said that it is not a question of productivity or of equality, but of revolt against a system of domination, the worker being dispossessed, a slave of the owner of the means of production and of the blind mechanisms of the market? One has only to pass from the abstract to the concrete to see the weakness of that argument. In the great enterprises, subordination to the hierarchy would not be modified essentially by nationalization. As to the numerous small or medium-sized concerns, where the owner is still present in

flesh and blood, why should they be contrary to the human vocation, provided that the relations between those who work at the
same task are those of collaborators? The distinction between
owner and proletarian undoubtedly creates an inequality of status
more likely to produce tension than peace. This distinction can be
effaced only by the generalization either of the status of the proletarian or of that of the owner. It would be absurd to make the whole
of society proletarian out of indignation with the proletarian condition. Social laws, trade union action, reform within the companies themselves, all lessen the isolation and helplessness of the
worker, giving him protection and community, pending a wider diffusion of property among the proletarians as a result of economic
progress.

The mechanisms of the market appear as a blind and inac-
ceptable determinism when they scatter unemployment or cause mi-
grations of farmers or workers, driven from their homes by a fall in
prices. A system of free competition, left to itself, in a vast economic
unit, sometimes involves cruelties against which indignation is easily
roused. But authoritarian planning, when it is handled by ruthless
bureaucrats, is in danger of striking still harder. Deportations and
work camps mark an extreme form of the mobility of the means of
production.

The intellectual does not contrast the real capitalist society with
another real society, but with an ideal society. When he insists on
the intrinsic superiority of public over private ownership, he is not
thinking of the superiority of Renault over Citroën, or of French or
British railways over the American, or of the Kirov over the Ford
factories—because such a judgment might be subjected to an ex-
perimental test. He is thinking of a public ownership that would not
be state ownership, would not be managed by a staff of civil servants but by a committee of workers or of delegates elected by
workers. Planning, the intrinsic superiority of which is assumed, is
not that of a planning office or of an autocratic politburo or of the
British Treasury, but a planning that would be the common work
of the masses, the experts, and the scientists.

By abolishing individual ownership of the means of production,
and family concentrations of real and personal estate, one of the
sources of the classes that rule society is eliminated. From the mo-

ment when the government owns the means of production, it is the government that will normally appoint the managers. Except in a small number of exceptional cases, management by the workers is impracticable. The election of the heads of enterprises would soon give results comparable with those which would follow were officers elected by soldiers. The function of making claims, which belongs to the trade unions, could not be combined with the function of direction. Union secretaries could perhaps exercise that function, but in so doing they would pass to the other side. Short of assuming a working-class education and a collective discipline without precedent in history, collective ownership entails the creation of a vast bureaucracy and a technical hierarchy, the keystone of which is the state.

Instead of attributing to the Soviet Union the merit of having laid the foundations of a socialist society, must we reproach it with having built a system that is inevitably despotic? Looking at the organization of the Soviet economy in its concrete details as it has developed through the five-year plans, we can hardly see how it could produce anything but a totalitarian state. Industry entirely state-managed, peasants grouped in *kolkhozy* with drastic restrictions placed on the size of the individually owned plot of land, plans for accelerated industrialization, with the development of remote regions and compulsory transfers of workers—how could such a system be carried on except by a minority wielding absolute power? How could the peasants be allowed to discuss and vote freely, when their first reaction to their rewon liberty would be (as most observers testify) to restore individual ownership? To imagine the Soviet economy, as it works at present, put under the direction of a limited government is to imagine a winged horse.

Is the extension of collective ownership and planning destined to destroy the reign of law and of personal and political liberties? From the time when it takes direct responsibility for certain enterprises and fixes by a plan the framework of collective activity, the state joins an economic power to the political power that is its very essence. Is this accumulation compatible with the balance of power that is the origin of all the freedoms? Will not the contradiction grow between the state, as origin of the laws to which everyone's activities are subject, and the business state, favoring by decree, in defiance of all universality, the supposed interests of the sectors that are its own property? The so-called socialist conditions of production (public ownership and planning) tend to increase the authority of the rulers, and to emphasize its arbitrary character. As a trend our conclusion seems confirmed by the experience of this century.

It does not follow that an economy in which a section of industry is nationalized and in which the administration has authority over such things as foreign trade, credit, capital expenditure excludes personal freedom or parliamentary institutions. Nowhere have pluralist regimes become progressively totalitarian to the extent to which public ownership or planning has spread. These regimes have been brutally eliminated on the day when a party with absolutist ambitions has seized power.

Some may fear that the incapacity of parliamentary regimes to make a partially planned economy work may end in creating a sort of chaos from which an authoritarian state will finally emerge. But that incapacity has not been proved. The socialization of the economy, it is true, even in freeedom, modifies the structure of social relations, increases the dependence of the individual on the state, and creates a new ruling class, essentially bureaucratic, and a functional hierarchy allied in spirit to the public authorities. Classical parliamentarianism, the work of aristocrats and the bourgeoisie, is no longer in harmony with such a community, although it may survive with a changed spirit and reduced prerogatives. But, after all, this is a matter of a normal process: institutions that belonged to a vanished world adapt themselves slowly to a new age.

In other words, to those who reserve their indulgence for the Soviet Union on the pretext that it has laid the foundations of socialism, we shall reply: Even if collective ownership and planning are held to be components of socialist conditions of production, yet the historical creation of such conditions must not involve the elimination of values which it is intended to integrate in the new order. But the Soviet method of total planning is inseparable from the single party and the omnipotent state. It is in the West that the progressive socialization of the conditions of production leaves the personal freedoms a chance of survival.

Those of the intellectuals who, half a century behind the thought of their time, continue to condemn the mechanisms of the market or private ownership for philosophic reasons have no cause for uneasiness. With or without Stalinism, the danger is not that of free enterprise trampling on the nationalized sectors or of the excesses of competition paralyzing planning. The danger is the reverse. And, at the same time, the task is just the opposite of what these out-of-date persons suggest. What matters is not so much the pace at which the conditions of production evolve toward the socialist type as the fate of persons and freedoms in the collectivist society.

Socialism has ceased in the West to be a myth because it has become a part of reality. It is legitimate to discuss the limits which it is best to assign to the sector of public property, the possible reconciliation between the planning of certain global quantities and the liberty of the consumer, the balance which should be established between equalization of incomes and the social necessity of encouraging initiative and offering a career to talent. Some economists of the liberal or Keynesian schools try to bring passion into the debate, some by raising the bogy of the total state in order to defeat attempts at controlling prices, others by raising the bogy of drastic deflation and mass unemployment to persuade the rulers to restrain the mechanisms of the market and especially to subordinate the balance of payments to concern for full employment at home.

I do not deny the importance of these discussions. Excessive claims by the planners would end by sapping the foundations of the liberal communities, and a precipitate return to automatism, in a period of crises, might put social peace in danger. But the result, on one side or the other, would be decisive only if an extreme solution were adopted. At present the controversy is about the best combination of the two techniques, a controversy between social engineers, the solution of which will proceed little by little from experience.

There is no miracle-working regime called socialism which would bring into activity productive forces or wealth paralyzed by capitalism. No revolution would abolish inequality of conditions, put an end to the tension between workers and management, or give power in industry to the masses. But progressive improvement is achieved by reforms derived from the results of patient research. Leftist intellectuals do not usually interest themselves in the only methods capable of reducing the evils they denounce. As for Stalinism, it still inspires faith in millions of hearts. That faith, maintained at fever heat by discipline, is pledged to a phantom. All who have lived on the other side of the Iron Curtain are filled with wonder at the illusions of the many people who dream of a regime which, once they had experience of it, they would furiously detest. This mystification reveals not so much the seductiveness of Stalinism as the decay of certain communities. People seek refuge in the Red metropolis because they hate the society in which they live.

Grave as it may be in certain cases, this phenomenon of ideological compensation is only of limited importance on the world stage. But the menace of violence grows as the force of ideas diminishes. Counter-propaganda would be able to make short work of the prophet of the good tidings, if only that prophet did not at the same time command countless legions.

## Chapter III

## FAITH WITHOUT ILLUSIONS

EUROPE, threatened by the expansion of Communism, and a stake in the conflict between the Big Two, seems to be seeking reasons for not committing herself. The intellectuals vie with one another in finding ways of depriving the peoples of faith and hope. It is not enough for the eventual war to be horrible, it must also be absurd. What better method of displaying its absurdity than that of covering the protagonists indifferently with the same reprobations? The same fate, they say, awaits humanity whoever wins.

At the level at which these controversies usually take place, they do not deserve our attention. Not a single partisan of the double refusal is known who would look to the East for freedom in the event of American occupation. Many are known who under a Russian occupation would look for it in the West. In the United States the economic system, the political institutions, the social order are loaded with injustices, as in all known communities. The principle of the equality of men of all races, and of all religions is proclaimed there, but not always followed. But in spite of everything, if we compare American capitalism and Russian Communism in their actual concrete reality, we cannot, without aberration or bad faith, dismiss them together with the same invectives. If we consider personal rights, the possibilities of opposition or of creation, or the effect of methods of production and trade on the welfare of the masses, the American system is the exact opposite of the Soviet system, not another sample of the same type.

The defenders of neutralism invoke the similarity, at bottom, of the two civilizations, American and Russian. Both tend to expand industrial technique in a vast region of unrestricted trade, to build immense factories, to organize millions of men in industrial discipline. How can efforts inspired by the same ambition fail to yield similar results? This argument, which is widely diffused in varying shades, assumes what needs to be proved: that every industrial mass society presents essentially the same characteristics.

No one will deny that the modern methods of production and the concentration of millions of human beings in cities bring in their train certain features of social structure or of psychological attitude (a tendency to uniformity, the manipulation of the masses, a permanent search for efficiency, and so on). But this dependence on technology is not total. To regard it as such would be to fall into a primary Marxism, which would make not the conditions of production but its instruments the creative force, all other historical phenomena being determined thereby. The builders of dams and blast furnaces may treat man as a material or as a person, believe in God or not, stir the individual to thought or dictate what he is to read, restore an aristocratic bureaucracy or reduce economic inequalities, concentrate political power in a party-church or divide it as much as possible between many authorities. Disputants belonging to the same historical surroundings have always had something in common. It does not follow that the stake in the rivalries between nations or parties is negligible.

The doctrinaires of the double refusal have another point: the condemnation of technology in itself. They tell us that it is bound to lead to the horrors we have just experienced, concentration camps and totalitarianism. Man himself, they contend, will have lost his soul once he has delivered it over to the cult of the machine.

Only the ignorant can doubt the considerable rise in the living standard of whole populations in Western communities during the past century. The works of Colin Clark and his French disciples, such as Fourastie,[1] have demonstrated the fact, with a prodigality of statistical evidence of which the details may be discussed but not the general trend. But it has not been shown that the same evolution

[1] Cf., for example, M. Fourastie's latest book, *Machinisme et Bienêtre* (Paris: 1951).

must take place everywhere, or that it goes on indefinitely. The reign of plenty, like a mirage, recedes as one seems to be approaching it.

In Africa and Asia the struggle against famine still goes on. The fundamental lack of food has not been surmounted. In this respect the essential is the relation between the growth of resources and that of population. In the first half of the nineteenth century the European communities rid themselves of the threat of famine that was present in former times. The threat does not seem to be on the point of disappearing in Asia, with the birthrate at its present level. The so-called Colombo Plan, which rearmament will probably prevent from maturing, envisaged the investment of 5 billion dollars, which would merely have made it possible to avoid deterioration in the conditions of existence. In the twentieth century, poor communities have still not succeeded in emerging from the initial vicious circle: to improve the methods of production they must either have reserves available or save part of the annual income; but the income is too small not to be consumed almost entirely.

It may be said that this crisis, characteristic of the primary phase of industrial progress, at most slows down a progress which ultimately is inevitable. Let us admit that, with the assistance of countries already industrialized, or through a collective saving imposed by pitiless coercion, all communities do finally escape from the original vicious circle. In the long run the dispute between pessimists and optimists, neo-Malthusians and theorists of indefinite economic progress, is still not settled. Prevision is barred by the limits of our knowledge and by the partial indetermination of reality. Argument rages about the maximum volume of foodstuffs which the earth could supply. But any figure can only be valid for a certain state of knowledge and of methods of cultivation, and there is no sufficient reason to regard that state as final. If we assume that the planet, scientifically exploited, would produce food for 3.5 billions[2] of human beings, what fraction of the inhabitants will apply the teachings of science? Will the movement to protect and recuperate the soil triumph over the tendency to devastate it by a selfish exploitation that takes no thought for the future?

[2]Cf. Kirtley F. Mather, "The Social Implications of Science," in the *Bulletin of Atomic Scientists,* July 1950. The author is a professor of geology.

The high living standard attained by some Western communities is partly due to a fortunate phenomenon: technical progress has overtaken the increasing number of mouths to be filled. But will the same phenomenon[3] repeat itself elsewhere? And in how many years' time? Meanwhile, the Western communities will suffer the repercussions of the crises brought about by the overpopulation of the other continents, and the disparity of demographic pressures may produce other perils. Even in the industrial order, counting in centuries, it is permissible to speculate on the relation between the exhaustion of the subsoil and the increase of productivity thanks to the accumulation of energy, capital, and knowledge.

With these cursory and superficial remarks we merely wish to point out that distant extrapolations, even on the plane of the theorists of economic progress, are risky. We do not know how many centuries will elapse before we arrive at a stationary society, dominated by the tertiary sector,[4] nor even whether we shall ever reach it. The period of troubles, bound up with the advance or the backwardness of different nations along the path of industrial civilization, is very far from being over. It is more likely to last for centuries than for decades.

In any case, it would be the worst of follies to seek safety by trying to arrest a movement that is now irresistible. France knows only too well the price that is paid for a slackening of economic progress. Social peace and liberal institutions in the West have difficulty enough in coping with stagnation of the collective income. Elsewhere, want or famine is the penalty for inability to make the most of existing resources. There is too much picturing of technical science in the apocalyptic form of gigantic factories served by the modern slaves. In Asia efforts are now being made especially to improve the methods of cultivation and the farming implements. In Europe, better organization would often increase productivity more than renewal of machinery or enlargement of the units or production.

[3]It has often been observed that the birthrate tends to fall with the improvement of the conditions of existence. But there is nothing to prove that the level of population will necessarily be thus automatically regulated.

[4]In the meaning which Colin Clark gives to this expression in his book, *Conditions of Economic Progress* (New York: Macmillan, 1940).

In the strictly material order, the reasons for optimism seem to me to prevail in the long run over those for pessimism. If it is a question of exploitation of natural forces or of the prolongation of human life, the conquests of the past century forbid discouragement. Do the romanticists of the anti-technical school envy the communities in which famine is endemic? Do they envy those in which the expectation of life does not exceed twenty-five years? Anyone who has helplessly witnessed the death of his child will never again be tempted by the pride of Prometheus. Man is not, and probably never will be, the master and owner of nature. Neither is he any longer her trembling slave or a resigned victim.

But serene optimism in the faith that social or spiritual progress will automatically follow scientific progress is dead. There is no need to dissect the corpse. The raising of the living standard does not suffice either to spread happiness or to satisfy the peoples. The French workman, for a shorter working day, receives real payment higher than in 1913. Yet he says, and frequently believes (and the intellectuals keep on repeating to him), that he has nothing to defend. Thirty-eight years ago, he had no doubt that he had something to defend, something that he called *la patrie* or *la France*. The reasons for this skepticism are many, and perhaps they have at bottom nothing much to do with the relation between income and prices: men go to war for a way of living, never for a standard of living, which war does everything to lower. Industrial civilization creates new desires as fast as it satisfies old ones. Sometimes, indeed, it creates them faster than it satisfies them. Part of the supplementary resources is absorbed in the service of a complex existence. Changing conditions, and the almost incessant alterations of modes of production and consumption, make everyone inclined to compare his lot with that of others. Social envy, almost inevitable as soon as the notion of the customary style of living becomes blunted, is in danger of damaging the cohesion of collectivities which mistakenly make material success the supreme aim.

Economic progress is probably a less inevitable phenomenon than is thought by the apostles of industrialization at all costs. It depends on a number of conditions in addition to the quantity of energy or capital to each worker or the quality of the machinery.

The importance of the organization of work in the factories or in the community as a whole has been recognized. There is a dawning suspicion that other institutions are also important—the rule of law in relations between individuals, a career open to initiative or talent, mutual confidence between the different elements of the community, the development of science through freedom of research, the intensity of trade between economic units, international division of labor, etc. Formerly the economic calculation made possible by market prices was held to be indispensable. The intellectual fashion has changed: the amount of capital expenditure and the building of great factories pass now for the things that matter. If power were the question, that might be so. Doubt is at least permissible if we are thinking of the productivity of labor and the welfare of the masses. Economic progress was not the object consciously aimed at by the actors in the capitalist system, but it was the effective result of their competitive efforts. If tyranny shatters the rub of law, on the pretext of aiming directly at progress, there is a risk of missing it.

Such uncertainties scarcely occupy the public mind. Industrial civilization is vituperated because it is held responsible for the disasters we have just suffered or fear in the future—savage wars, concentration camps, totalitarian bureaucracy.

Are the ravages of violence increased by the power which science and industry put at the disposal of states? Incontestably. Morally neutral, technical science can be used for good or for evil, to give millions of men honorable conditions of existence or to exterminate millions of innocent people in a few minutes. The profit and loss account is not yet closed. Even in the matter of war, it has not been proved that the debits outweigh the credits. Medicine saves more lives than explosives destroy. Sparta and Athens did not need radio-guided missiles and atomic bombs to exhaust themselves in fighting. Pestilence and famine have ruined communities which the demon of knowledge had spared. The population of Germany after the Thirty Years' War had fallen by more than half. That of Western Europe has risen by 10 per cent since 1939.

The first concentration camps of the twentieth century are said to have been set up by the British during the Boer War: a military action against popular resistance. In Russia, they developed slowly between 1920 and 1930, and at the end of N.E.P. in 1929 they held some 660,000 prisoners.[5] They seem to have been originally a means of eliminating political adversaries. No one will maintain that the persecution of opponents is a peculiarity of the age of the machine. Starting from the five-year plans and collectivization, the hunt for the enemies of the new order was combined with the recruitment of cheap labor and with the modification of the peopling of the Soviet Union. The builders of pyramids do not date from our era: technical science did not give rise to these cruelties; why should we be surprised that it has not abolished them?

How many times in the course of history have conquering armies put to the sword tens of thousands of men, women, and children in cities taken by assault? The Romans, whose heirs we boast of being, did not leave one stone on another when they had Carthage at their mercy, and they sold as slaves the survivors of a city whose strength had made them tremble and the glory of whose civilization had spread throughout the ancient world. The Chinese, in the epochs when their civilization flourished, had carried the art of torture to refinement. No one before the Nazis had established the process of mass death in gas chambers; but if chemical science had been lacking they would have exterminated millions of Jews without recourse to laboratory processes.

Technical science has set its seal on modern barbarism. To the inquisitors it presents the resources of psychophysics, and drugs that destroy personality, and to assassins it gives factories that make up for the slowness of firearms. It has not been demonstrated that these horrible ends were conceived because the means existed. Knowledge puts at the disposal of mankind a collection of instruments; it does not determine the use to be made of them.

On the plane of causes and effects, more or less close relationships would be discovered between all the aspects of any community at a particular epoch. As the origin of the collision between cultures fundamentally different and of the fall of various ancient orders, industrial civilization bears part of the responsibility for the horrors of our time. But on those lines we might condemn all the

[5]According to D. I. Dallin, *La Vraie Russie des Soviets* (Paris: 1948), quoting Kiselev, a former G.P.U. official.

new civilizations whose emergence is accompanied by civil and foreign wars.

The accusation would assume tragic gravity if the totalitarian frenzy showed itself to be the final and inevitable expression of the dynamism of technical science. The risk of that dynamism exciting such a frenzy has, indeed, been shown. But it has not been shown that that development is inevitable. Western science brings means of action at the same time as verified propositions. In this sense, according to Spengler's interpretation, it is animated by a will to power, even if, at the outset, in the psychology of the greatest men of science, it is born of curiosity about the truth. But this does not make it *ipso facto* demoniac.

The aspiration to know and master nature constitutes the unique greatness of Western man. To heal sickness, to capture energy, to multiply the strength of men's arms by that of machines—what romanticist would dare to denounce these ambitions? In a creative enthusiasm that is in danger of overshooting the mark and turning against itself, technical science gone mad would end by treating man himself as constructional material.

One of the elements of totalitarianism is assuredly the immoderacy of the engineers, but those who are ignorant of the limits of science are rarely real scientists. The acceptance of a primary Marxism by specialists in physics or biology is evidence above all of the permanence of a religious need, which is not satisfied by the accumulation of positive knowledge. Why should technicians be ignorant of that in man which surpasses matter?

Specialists in the social sciences are no less susceptible to such aberrations. They also are beginning to learn the method by which individuals and groups, bodies and souls are manipulated. They also, observing the irrationalities of the social organization and the shackles which certain beliefs place on the development of productive forces, are sometimes inclined to wish for absolute power in order to impose so-called rational solutions. Psychoanalysis and psycho-technics do not teach man not to respect his fellow, though they present him with the possibility. The danger of science treating men as objects is evident, but the contrary danger also exists of subscribing to traditions whose value does not increase with time.

Historically, industrial civilization has contributed to the decline of transcendental religions. It has disintegrated the local communities that framed the existence of individuals through the ages. It has hastened the formation of urban masses, a phenomenon common to most civilizations in the epochs preceding their collapse. But perhaps it provides a chance of surmounting the shapelessness of multitudes and of promoting a new form of integration. It does not necessarily arouse the militant atheism that recognizes no other vocation and no other hope for man than physical comfort, in a community satisfied with itself and subject to the will of its planners.

Neither idolizing technical science nor inimical to it, Europe should no more be ignorant of its potentialities of barbarity than she should ratify a condemnation without appeal. Humanity is not doomed to lose itself in the conquest of nature and in forgetfulness of itself. The habit of prophesying disaster testifies less to lucidity than to resignation. The twentieth century is not the first century of wars, and the human adventure is not yet over.

"We are defending a half-truth against a total lie," recently wrote a novelist, who is an anti-Communist and ex-Communist. True enough, but why feel the need to repeat it, with a mixture of bad conscience and frankness?

Soviet society claims, it is true, through the loud-speakers of its propagandists, to be on the march towards perfection. People are always ashamed of the real when they measure it against the ideal. Many European intellectuals are in mourning for the socialist myth. Nowhere, apart from Stalinism, have they found the hope of a revolution that would open a new era.

Socialism is an economic-social system whose advantages and disadvantages will continue to be discussed against those of free enterprise and the mechanisms of the market. It is certainly not an absolute good or the accomplishment of human destiny. We may think that the universal diffusion of Communism would, for the first time, bring about a universal empire in the full sense of the term. Such an empire is no longer a dream but a nightmare. Either it would be maintained by an iron despotism and the supranational solidarity of a theocratic bureaucracy, and the peoples would think longingly of the times when the anarchy of national sovereignties raged; or else it would break up into a rivalry of diadochi and schismatics. The wars between irreconcilable disciples of the prophet would arouse regret for those of the kings who did not invoke ideas in the service of their ambitions.

The various cultures are too far apart, the nationalisms which Europeans have spread with their machines across continents, are too ardent for a universal empire to appear to be an early possibility. We can close the age of hyperbolic wars without again falling beneath the yoke. It is enough if one country possesses a quasi monopoly of the decisive weapons, or simply a superiority such that it is able, if not to arbitrate all disputes pacifically, at least to forbid the unlimited extension of violence. In this way the influence of Great Britain was exercised in the past century, and in this way that of the United States is exercised in South America today. The hegemony of a naval and aerial power would progressively surmount the alternative between a peace of equilibrium and a peace of empires. It would protect humanity against the mortal peril created by the massive weapons of destruction and the total mobilization of peoples. As a reasonable solution, this semi-pacification, due to the domination of an industrial republic, would have nothing in common with the end of history. It would continue to disappoint souls severed from Utopia.

There is no fighting without faith, and faith transfigures the realities to which it is applied. People have fought for the right to vote, for the freedom of the press, for national greatness. A partial reform became, for those who desired it passionately, a boon which they preferred to their life. But secular religion is only one modality among others of the collective beliefs. Its peculiarity is to site the greatest good in a distant future and, from now on, to confuse that good with a particular party or country.

The Westerners are incapable of taking a social order, present or future, as the equivalent of the millennium. Parliamentary institutions or economic mechanisms matter to them mainly in so far as they are conditions or symbols of a certain style of collective organization. The right to choose one's God, the right to seek truth freely, and the right not to be at the mercy of the police, of officials, or of psycho-technicians, are, or should be, for them values as unconditioned as the triumph of the Soviet Union for the Stalinists.

Do these traditional values awake the same ardor as a false ideal?

Fidelity seems to be weakness beside a fanaticism with its eye on the future. In the long run, perhaps fidelity will win the day against the fury of a pseudo novelty. The totalitarianisms are original only in method. They borrow some weapons from the arsenals of our time, but they use instruments supplied to them by the engineers of bodies and souls, and use them with a view to a return to the past. They bring back a secular despotism, a bureaucratic hierarchy, a theocratic state. It has not been proved that the totalitarian regimes are any more than an episode in the age of wars. The survival of hope depends on the victory of the liberal communities.

The faith of the peoples was never more living than during the First World War, the stake of which was incomparably more limited than that of the second. That of the third is vaster still. If Europeans had become indifferent to the safety of their political rights, of their intellectual freedom, of their national independence, if they were not ready to defend either their altars or their hearths, then Europe would be dead and its heirs would fight over a corpse.

The moral crisis affects especially the rationalist intellectuals who teach superstition or despair, repeat that God is dead, and do not resign themselves to the loss of their idols. Politics, we are told, is destiny: rarely have the conflicts of parties, ideologies, and nations called in question so many values. But politics cannot give existence its final justification. The future of the communities was misread when a Revolution was expected to give an answer to all our questions. Once the mythology of progress is abandoned, there is no reason to regard the future and the victors as in the right. Unfinished history does not judge men.

Are the peoples deceived because we have only half-truths to defend in this imperfect world? I am not sure. The real cause of skepticism is different. The lesson of the two wars has been learned: The unleashing of violence settles nothing. Europe would be the victim of a hyperbolic war, whatever its issue. We have not concealed this antinomy of means and end. The object of the West is and must be to win the limited war in order not to have to wage the total one. But the West will not succeed unless it is animated by an inflexible resolution, unless it believes in itself and in its mission of liberty.

Can the third world war be won without becoming total? No one knows. But we know that in the limited war more even than in the total one, courage and faith count as much as material resources. The will to win will not eliminate the perils that are to be our daily lot for years, but it can give us a better chance of overcoming them.

# INDEX